ADOPTING
— IN —
AMERICA
How To Adopt Within One Year

4th Revised Edition
—2004—

RANDALL B. HICKS
Attorney at Law

———◇———

WORDSLINGER PRESS
Sun City, California

Dedicated to my wife and children,
who make home the best place to be.

Copyright 2004 by Randall B. Hicks

Thanks to my personal assistant, Tammy Rendon, for her invaluable assistance, to editor William Rockey, and to Jeff Parker for his help and encouragement, sandwiched between sets, with the book still on the computer.

Excerpts used with permission:
A Letter to Adoptive Parents on Open Adoption, by Randolph Severson Ph.D. (Copyright 1992, House of Tomorrow); *Towards New Ethical Guidelines for Pregnancy Counseling,* by Michael Spry (Copyright Michael Spry 1991).

Library of Congress Cataloging-in-Publication Data

Hicks, Randall, 1956-
Adopting in America: how to adopt within one year / Randall B. Hicks — 4th ed, New rev. ed.
p. cm.
Includes bibliographical references and index.
ISBN 0-9631638-4-1
1. Adoption—United States. 2. Adoption—Law and legislation—United States. I. Title.

HV875.55.H53 200
362.734'0973—dc22

2003063158

Printed and manufactured in the USA.   **4th Revised Edition**

Table of Contents

Agency Adoption • Private Agency Adoption
• Public Agency Adoption • The Foster Parent
Shortcut • Independent Adoption • Nonresident
Independent Adoption • Identified Adoption
• International Adoption • Facilitators

The Role of the Adoption Attorney • Selecting an
Adoption Attorney • Networking with a Photo-
Resume Letter • Preparing a Photo-Resume Letter
• General Mail-Out Networking • Personal
Networking • The Cover Letter • Starting Your
Networking Campaign • Advertising • Facilitators

Working with a Birth Mother • Handling a Birth
Mother's Initial Call • Meeting a Birth Mother
in Person • Key Issues to Explore • Post-Birth
Contact with Your Birth Mother

Introduction

When people think of the parties to an adoption—adoptive parents, birth parents, and the child—it is usually the adoptive parents who are perceived as the *lucky* ones. After all, it is reasoned, it is the adoptive parents who get to bring home a beautiful, newborn baby and start their family. And it is true . . . the adoptive parents are lucky, and will owe immeasurable gratitude to the birth mother who made it possible through her own sacrifice and unselfishness.

However, many people fail to realize the pain faced, and overcome, by every couple who has been unable to conceive their own child. Often years of frustration dealing with the unfairness of infertility must be overcome before even being emotionally ready to start considering adoption. So if anyone intimates that compassion in the adoption process should be reserved for only the birth mother and the child, excuse them for their ignorance, but recognize it for what it is—ignorance.

Adoption is a triad, with the adoptive parents, birth parents and the child having equal roles in its success. Adoptive parents should never let anyone tell them they have a secondary role in the adoption, or deserve any less respect. Adoption counselor

Randolph Severson Ph.D., writes in his insightful booklet, *A Letter to Adoptive Parents on Open Adoption*, about his recognition of the trauma of infertility:

My lesson came from an older man who didn't know enough to use the word *infertility*. He hadn't been *educated* as we say. After seeing each other in therapy for a few months, he ended a session by asking me if we could skip a week since the next week he had something to do. When I asked him what, he explained in a matter of fact voice, that next week's session fell on a day 20 years ago that he and his wife had lost their baby. It was a boy and he had been stillborn. And they had never been able to have any other children.

'So every year on that day I go fishing,' he said, 'so that up there, in the stillness, with the water lapping quietly up aside my boat, I think of all the things that me and Bob—we named him Bob—could have done together.

You know it has been so long it's got down to three things I think on. I wanted to show him how to ride a bicycle. I wanted to run along behind him with one hand on the seat and the other on the handle bars and see him take off and go, with me standing there smiling. I wanted to take him to a baseball game and smell that sweet spring night air, and watch somebody steal second base. I wanted him to see a good, fast, smart runner, crouch and go, a whir of white going lickety split down that line then, slide cleats up, and hear the umpire holler 'safe.' I wanted to sit out one summer evening, a good blanket under our butts, one you could feel the grass beneath, and I wanted to show him the stars and name them the way my daddy did me. Orion's Belt. Orion's Belt. I wanted to say those words to him. And I do say them out loud, with just me and the old fish listening.'

Adoption cannot cure infertility, but it can cure childlessness. After all you have been through in battling infertility, you deserve success in adoption—and you can obtain it—but *you* have to take the initiative. It will not come looking for you. Success in any venture of life requires education and hard work. Adoption is no exception. Adoptive parents who fully educate themselves about available options and work hard in applying proven techniques will almost always succeed—and succeed quickly. Just as scaling a steep mountain is easy for the trained mountain climber, adoption can be relatively easy for the *trained* adoptive parent. It will only be intimidating if you have not prepared for what you are doing and have not learned the "rules of the game."

If you are considering adoption—whether it be a newborn, toddler or older child; via an agency or independent adoption; from the United States or another country—this book was written expressly for you. It will educate you. It will empower you. It will remove the anxiety that accompanies uncertainty. It will give you a step-by-step plan for quickly locating a child for adoption and planning your adoption.

Basic Terms

Birth mother: The biological mother of the child being placed for adoption.

Birth father: The biological father of the child being placed for adoption.

Adoptive parents: Those who will be adopting the child and becoming the child's legal parents.

Adoptee: The child being adopted.

CHAPTER ONE

Selecting a Method of Adoption that *Works* for You

Normally, when people think of adopting they initially think of adoption agencies. Fortunately for adoptive parents, traditional agency adoption is only one of *twelve* different routes toward adoption. In fact, the world of adoption has changed so dramatically in the last two decades that traditional agency adoptions make up less than half of the adoptions completed within the United States. In some states, more than eight of every ten newborns adopted are not adopted through an adoption agency, rather through *independent* adoption. Unfortunately, most adoptive parents have no knowledge of the extensive number of options available from which to choose the quickest and most economical method to adopt.

In reality, most people seeking to adopt a child can do so within one year, at reasonable cost and without high risk. Furthermore, there is no reason for you to give up your dreams of adopting a healthy, newborn baby of your own ethnic group. Whether you are white, brown or black . . . just out of your teens or both over forty . . . married or single . . . newly married or with several prior marriages behind you . . . whether you have no children or already have several . . . *you can adopt.*

The question for those looking into adoption is not *whether* you can adopt, rather *what method* of adoption is best for you. There are twelve different routes toward adoption:

- Private adoption agencies performing domestic adoptions (American-born children).
- Private adoption agencies performing international adoptions (foreign-born children).
- Private adoption agencies located outside your home state but able to perform domestic and international adoptions within your state *or* in the state where the agency is located.
- Public/County adoption agencies.
- The foster parent *short cut.*
- Independent domestic adoption (American-born children).
- Independent international adoption (foreign-born children).
- Independent adoption initiated by attorneys located outside your home state, but able to assist in domestic and international adoptions by working with an attorney or agency within your home state.
- Independent non-resident adoption which allows adoptive parents to adopt a child in the state where the child is born, even if independent adoption is not permitted in the adoptive parent's home state.
- *Identified* adoptions.
- Facilitator-initiated adoptions.
- Special-needs adoption registries.

Even if you are predisposed to only consider one type of adoption, it is recommended you become familiar with each of the possible methods of adoption. This is not only because false information may have caused you to prematurely reject some types of adoption, but also because many types of adoption have *cross-over* characteristics. These characteristics allow you to start one type of adoption, then change to another type if later determined it would be a better option.

AGENCY ADOPTION

There are two types of adoption agencies—*private* and *public*. As the name implies, private agencies are privately-operated businesses. They are licensed by the state in which they operate to conduct adoptive parent home studies and/or place children for adoption. They are principally supported by the fees they receive from adoptive parents.

Public adoption agencies are operated by the county or state in which they are located and are supported by tax dollars. The main function of public agencies is to find homes for children for whom the county or state has assumed responsibility.

Private and public adoption agencies vary dramatically in what they do—as well as when, and how, they do it. These distinctions will be addressed in detail later in this chapter.

Eligibility Requirements of Adoptive Parents. Although private and public adoption agencies may differ greatly in some ways, they also have a great deal in common.

Each agency will set its own eligibility requirements for adoptive parents who can apply to the agency. However, the

11

following are typical guidelines employed by many adoption agencies:

- Both adoptive parents must be no more than 40 years of age older than the child they will be adopting. This means that many agencies will require those seeking to adopt a newborn to be under 40 years of age. If the child to be adopted were age 8, the adoptive parents must be no more than 48 years of age.
- Married at least three years without an excessive number of prior terminated marriages. (Some agencies will permit only one prior marriage while others will allow several.)
- Be medically unable to conceive a child, or show it is physically unsafe to give birth.
- Live in a home suitable for a child. (Owning a home is not required—renting a house or apartment is usually acceptable as long as the housing is suitable.)
- Be of average good health.
- At least one spouse be securely employed with sufficient income to support a child. Most agencies do not require a full-time, stay-at-home parent once past the child's initial months in the home. It is understood in today's world it is often necessary for both spouses to be employed. However, a permanent stay-at-home parent is often encouraged by some agencies, as one of many factors contributing to the best interests of the child.
- No criminal record or child abuse allegations.
- Have no more than one child already.

If you are one of the many individuals who do not fit within the above guidelines—do not despair! This chapter will be exploring many areas of adoption where traditional restrictions do not apply.

The Home Study. All agency adoptions, whether they are through a private or public agency, require a home study of the adoptive parents. The home study is in two parts. Initially, there is a preplacement home study to determine whether it appears you would be appropriate parents based upon the agency's evaluation of you and your background. The satisfactory completion of the preplacement home study is a prerequisite to having a child placed in your home.

An agency caseworker will be assigned to do the preplacement home study and will want to have several meetings with you, some of which will be in your home. Home visits are often required to see the potential environment for a child. These visits are almost always arranged by appointment, as "surprise visits" are more myth than reality.

The vast majority of agency caseworkers are friendly professionals who are anxious to help you succeed at adoption. Unfortunately, this cannot be said of all caseworkers. A small number may be very judgmental and take advantage of the power they have over whether a child will be placed with you. To avoid such an unpleasant experience, a list of suggested questions will be provided later to help you find the right agency and eliminate disappointment.

Because most agencies operate with almost unlimited discretion regarding with which of their waiting families they will place a child for adoption, it is important to show the agency you are the best waiting adoptive parents. Many adoptive parents waiting for a placement do not realize in many ways they are "in competition" with the agency's other waiting adoptive parents. It is not difficult to rate highly in the eyes of your agency:

- When the agency seeks to make appointments with you for visits to your home or their office, do not ask the caseworker to alter his or her busy schedule to fit your schedule. Show the meeting is important to you by agreeing to the first time they have available. Reschedule any conflicting and less important matters.

- Attend all seminars offered by the agency to teach you about adoptive parenting and related issues. This includes non-mandatory seminars as well.
- When asked by the agency why you wish to adopt, be honest regarding your motivation, instead of saying what you think they want to hear. For example, many caseworkers report they question the motivations of adoptive parents who profess to be interested in adopting only out of "humanitarian desires" to make a home for a child. This motivation may be one of many appropriate factors when discussing adoption, particularly concerning children waiting for an adoptive home, such as special-needs children. Even in those cases, however, many caseworkers feel the primary motivation for adoptive parents should be the desire to share their love with a child and be a parent.
- Read recommended books regarding adoption. It is tremendously impressive to the caseworker handling your preplacement home study if you have read respected adoption books, especially if you have done so voluntarily before the agency even begins your home study. Your advance reading shows you are strongly motivated and truly desire to learn all you can about the most important thing in your life—adoption. Books like James Gritter's *Adoption Without Fear*, Lois Melina's *Raising Adopted Children* and Silber and Speedlin's *Dear Birthmother* are considered basic building blocks to a successful adoption by most adoption professionals. Unfortunately, these books are usually considered too specialized for most bookstores or libraries

to keep in stock. They are easily obtained via the internet, however, at such sites as amazon.com, barnesandnoble.com or adoption101.com (which directs a percentage of its profits to charities benefiting children).

These basic suggestions towards establishing a beneficial relationship with your agency may seem absurdly simple. Surprisingly, however, many caseworkers complain that many of their agency's waiting families fail to show their sincerity and readiness to adopt by such simple acts. Remember, an agency's goal is to find the best homes for the children they place. The more educated and prepared you show yourselves to be can only serve to impress your agency. When a waiting list is not used, the agency has sole discretion regarding with which waiting adoptive parents it will place a child. Make their discretion benefit, not hurt, your chances to adopt quickly.

Of course, there is more to your preplacement home study than visits from your caseworker and the verification of your application information (marriage, employment, health, etc.) The following will also be done in most agency home studies:

- Your fingerprints will be taken and processed through the child abuse registry and federal and state crime index.
- Letters of reference from friends regarding your good character and ability to be excellent parents will be requested.
- You will usually be asked to provide a written biography describing your childhood, your relationship with your parents, the strengths of your marriage and how you resolve conflicts within the marriage, how your extended family feels about your plans to adopt, how you plan to parent your child and how you will discuss adoption with your child.

Post-Placement Procedures. Once the child is born, some agencies will require the child to be placed in a foster care home until the birth parents have relinquished the child by signing a Consent to Adoption, or the child is otherwise freed for adoption (legal issues will be discussed in Chapter Five). This foster home period may be days, weeks or even months, depending upon the circumstances. Once the child is legally free for adoption, the child is then placed with the adoptive parents.

An increasing number of agencies will agree to place the child with the adoptive parents immediately upon the child's discharge from the hospital. Technically this is usually done by making the adoptive parents the child's "foster parents" until the child is technically relinquished for adoption, at which time they officially become "adoptive parents." This new agency option is often called *fost-adopt*. Some agencies refer to these immediate placements as "at risk placements," due to the window of risk which exists until the Consent to Adoption forms have been signed by the birth parents. The practice of placing babies directly with adoptive parents from the hospital is a traditional element of independent adoption, a procedure now duplicated by many agencies.

Regardless of whether the placement is by the traditional delayed method, or the newer fost-adopt method, there will be several post-placement home visits by the agency caseworker to monitor the child's progress in the adoptive home. Usually six months to one year after the child's placement with you the agency is ready to recommend the adoption be granted, allowing a local court to permanently approve the adoption. The adoptive parents normally retain an attorney to prepare the necessary legal documents and appear with them in court, as legal proceedings are usually outside the scope of the adoption agency and are not covered by agency fees. Chapter Five will discuss what happens in court when the adoption is formally granted by the court.

Of course, how you arrive at that moment of completing your adoption will depend upon the type of agency you select: private or public, domestic or international, non-profit or for profit, denominational or nondenominational, open or closed, identified or non-identified. It is easy to see that when you select an agency, there are many decisions to make and a lot to learn. Let's get started!

Private Adoption Agencies

Private adoption agencies have widely different policies and services. In fact, some agencies will differ from other agencies so much the entire nature of the adoption will seem different. This is true even of agencies located in the same city and operating under the same state's laws, as there is much room for flexibility in how adoptions are arranged. Accordingly, it is very important to realize not all adoption agencies are "created equal." The services of one particular agency which are ideal for one couple may not meet the needs and desires of another.

The Agency's Licensing Status. An initial inquiry to make of any agency is to determine exactly what it is licensed to do. For example, some agencies are only licensed to do home studies of adoptive parents hoping to adopt. They are *not* licensed to place children for adoption, meaning the adoptive parents must look to another agency for the actual placement of a child. Other agencies are licensed as full service adoption agencies and are permitted to perform adoptive parent home studies, as well as place children for adoption.

It is also critically important to verify the agency you are considering is licensed as an actual *licensed adoption agency* by the state in which it operates. Some individuals or organizations use names which sound like adoption agencies when in fact they are not. They are generally referred to as *facilitators*. Facilitators are those who render the limited service of finding a baby for a fee. Chapter Two addresses the risks of facilitators.

Most adoptive parents mistakenly only consider adoption agencies located within their home state. There are two situations were out-of-state licensed agencies may be used: when the agency is located out-of-state but licensed by your home state; and when the out-of-state agency is located in a state allowing non-residents to adopt in the state where the agency is located.

Of course, if local private adoption agencies effectively meet the needs of the community, there is little reason to search for out-of-state agencies. For some adoptive parents, however, the use of out-of-state agencies can greatly reduce the time in which they must wait to adopt a child. For example, if the local agencies report a long waiting period to adopt, a particular out-of-state agency may solve that dilemma due to more birth mothers in that agency's geographical region, or its more aggressive approach to locating birth mothers. Depending upon the agency licensing regulations of your state, the out-of-state agency may do every aspect of the adoption, or only handle witnessing the birth mother's consent to the adoption, but have an agency in your home state conduct the home study.

Some adoptive parents consider out-of-state agencies for other reasons. For example, the policies and procedures followed by agencies within your state may be completely different from agencies in other states, due to different state laws. For example, one state may permit the agency to take the birth mother's consent to the adoption immediately after birth and allow the child to be placed with you directly from the hospital. Another state, however, may require a waiting period for the taking of the consent, or a lengthy period in which she may revoke her consent, and a period of foster care before the child can be placed with the adoptive parents.

Although courts normally frown on *forum shopping,* many state's laws permit adoptive parents, who are not residents of the state where the child is born or resides, to complete their entire adoption within that state if the agency having custody of the child is located there. In these out-of-state adoptions, the out- of-state agency which is placing the child for adoption will require a home study from an agency within your state, but will process the adoption through its own court system.

The adoptive parents normally return to their home state after the child is placed in their care, then return months later to appear in court to complete the adoption. This kind of adoption, called *non-resident agency adoption,* can be just as "official" as if it had been completed entirely within the adoptive parents' home state.

To learn more about out-of-state agencies perhaps of interest to you, follow the guidelines provided on page 24.

Religious Affiliation. Private agencies can be divided into *denominational* and *nondenominational* categories. Denominational agencies are those affiliated with a particular religious faith. Generally, these agencies are easy to recognize based upon the agency's name (i.e. Jewish Family Services, Christian Adoption Services, Church of Jesus Christ Latter Day Saints (LDS) Social Services etc.). However, the name can not solely be relied upon, as some agency's names bear little relation to the religious entity to which they are affiliated.

Likewise, some private agencies employ religiously-oriented names with no official association with that faith. For these reasons it is necessary to look beyond the name and question individual agencies to determine their status.

An important fact about denominational agencies not known by most people is that some denominational agencies do not require adoptive parents to be of the faith with which the agency is affiliated. This may be beneficial when the adoptive parents live in a region where there are few agencies from which to choose, or if they find the policies of one particular agency match their desires, even though the agency is affiliated with a different religion.

Fees and Costs. Like other businesses, private adoption agencies offer services for a fee and must make a sufficient profit to remain in operation. Most agencies are *non-profit* agencies. Non-profit agencies may receive financial assistance from charitable entities. Some agencies are operated on a *for-profit* basis. As long as the agency is licensed by the state as an adoption agency, there is usually little difference between the services of a non-profit and for-profit agency, although some view non-profit agencies as more altruistic and reliable. Often, for- profit agencies charge higher fees, as they are solely supported by the fees earned from adoptive parents. Many states require all agencies to be non-profit.

Fees can vary tremendously among private agencies. Depending upon the type of agency, the services being offered, and the state in which it is located, fees may range from approximately $500 to $25,000. The average fees fall between $2,000 and $9,000. Some agencies have a predetermined set fee while others use a sliding scale based upon the adoptive parents' income. This sliding scale fee may vary from 8% to 12% of the adoptive parents' joint pre-tax annual income.

The fee usually covers the adoptive parent preplacement home study, adoption education and counseling for the adoptive parents and birth parents, and post-placement evaluation of the adopted child's progress in the adoptive home. Not all agencies offer these complete services, however, so each agency you are considering must be questioned. Usually a portion of the agency fee is paid when the preplacement home study is started, with the balance due when the child is placed in the adoptive home. Some private agencies request additional funds from the adoptive parents if the birth mother needs assistance with her medical expenses or other birth-related costs. Other agencies may include such costs in their agency fee and forbid any such expenditures by the adoptive parents.

The Children Available. Most private adoption agencies primarily do domestic adoptions, meaning adoptions where the adoptive parents, birth parents and the child are all located within the United States. Some agencies do international adoptions, either exclusively or in addition to domestic adoptions. International adoptions are discussed later in this chapter.

The children available for adoption through private adoption agencies handling domestic adoptions range in age from newborns to older children and are of all ethnic groups. Many agencies also handle the adoption of *special-needs* children. A special-needs child is usually a child the agency feels may require extraordinary parenting due to a physical, emotional or mental disability. Special-needs children may also include children without disabilities, but who fall into a category the agency believes will make an adoptive placement difficult.

Some agencies use the term *hard-to-place* interchangeably with *special-needs*. Other agencies may use the term to describe children without severe handicaps, but who may be difficult to place due to other factors, such as being over the age of six.

Accordingly, it is important to be sure you are using the same terminology as the agency. Special-needs and hard-to-place children are discussed in more detail later in this chapter,

In addition to the emotional rewards which can accompany adopting a special-needs child, adoptive parents usually benefit from the policy of most agencies to speed up special-needs adoptions. This is because many of these children are presently living in foster homes and awaiting an adoptive placement. To encourage special-needs adoptions, most agencies will waive many of their regular restrictions. For example, adoptive parents can often be over the age of forty, be unmarried, and need not be infertile. The agency's fees may also be reduced.

Most private agencies handle only a few special-needs adoptions, as public adoption agencies are usually responsible for most special-needs cases. Most adoptive parents employing a private adoption agency hope to adopt a healthy newborn, oftentimes of their own ethnic group.

Waiting for a Child. Agencies vary in how they determine which child will be placed with which waiting adoptive parents. Historically, all agencies maintained a *waiting list*. Couples would simply wait their turn to reach the top of the list for their turn to adopt, and waiting several years was not uncommon.

Although some agencies still maintain waiting lists, most will now only consider which waiting adoptive parents could most effectively meet the needs of the child to be adopted. This evaluation may include judging the readiness of the adoptive parents, matching the religion, ethnicity and physical characteristics of the child and the adoptive parents, as well as respecting the wishes of the birth parents regarding the type of home they would like for the child.

Regardless whether or not a waiting list is used, or only the child's best interests are considered, one of the most important differences from one agency to another is the time the adoptive parents must wait for a child. Some adoptive parents report waiting five years or more, perhaps even with no results at the end of that time, while others find success within a year or two. Unfortunately, some agencies are so busy adoptive parents must wait years just to start their preplacement home study—then the waiting starts all over again—this time for a child.

Fortunately, some adoption agencies have changed their policies to allow adoptive parents to speed up the process using their own contacts and initiative. These agencies will allow waiting adoptive parents to use their own efforts to locate a birth mother to select them as the planned adoptive parents, then complete the adoption as an agency adoption, even though they met outside the agency.

These adoptions, called *identified, designated* or *collaborative* adoptions, often involve the services of an attorney specializing in adoption as well as the agency. Identified adoptions are discussed later in this chapter.

The Openness of the Adoption. Agencies have changed in other ways as well. Years ago most agencies arranged only *closed* adoptions. A closed adoption is one where the adoptive parents and birth mother would never meet and identities were not disclosed. Although some private agencies still do closed adoptions, many agencies now arrange *open* adoptions. Although the term "open adoption" can mean many things, normally it refers to an adoption where the birth mother and adoptive parents personally meet and exchange personal information before the birth to be sure each wishes to go forward.

Depending upon the policy of the agency and the desires of the birth and adoptive parents, full identities may, or may not, be disclosed. The openness may continue after the birth in a variety of ways. In many adoptions the adoptive parents and birth mother maintain contact by sending pictures and letters once or twice a year. In a small number of adoptions the adoptive parents, birth mother and the child maintain limited face-to-face contact as mutually desired. Such a relationship, called *cooperative* adoption, is found in about ten percent of recent adoptions. It is a trend gaining popularity in the western states and slowly working its way eastward. Cooperative adoption is discussed more fully in Chapter Three.

As can be seen, there are many decisions to be made in selecting the agency best suited for you. The following steps will be helpful in finding the right private agency:

- Compile a list of adoption agencies you may consider. Start with the extensive listing for your home state provided for your state in Chapter Six. If an agency from another state is listed in your state's listings, this should indicate they are perform services within your state, despite being located elsewhere. Ask the agency to be sure, however.
- Learn as much as you can about the agencies on your list from impartial sources. Contact *Resolve* (a national infertility organization) to see if it has a local chapter in your area. Many of their members have adopted and will be an excellent source of reference regarding which agencies are the most, or least, effective. Also speak to your infertility doctor, or if you are not seeing one, your gynecologist. His or her other patients may have talked about good or bad experiences with particular agencies.

You may also wish to join your local adoptive parent association. Other adoptive parents—those who have already gone through the process you are just starting—are often your best source of information. The *Adoptive Families of America*, the *National Adoption Information Clearinghouse* and *Resolve* maintain records of adoptive parent associations throughout the country and can likely provide you with information about a group in your area. To contact these organizations, refer to *Appendix A.*

- Call the agencies you are considering and request written information about their services, policies and fees. Ask if they have free introductory seminars to learn more.

When you have narrowed your list of agencies to a feasible number, obtain specific information by asking the following:

- Are they licensed as an adoption agency by your home state? If they are located out of state and licensed there, will they work in conjunction with certain agencies within your state to make a placement? If so, with which local agencies do they work?
- Are they licensed to do adoption home studies *and* place children for adoption, or do they only do home studies?
- Are they licensed to perform services for adoptive parents in your home county?
- What are the eligibility restrictions they place on adoptive parents (i.e. age, marital status etc.)? Are there any exceptions to those restrictions, such as adopting special-needs children? What kind of children do they place in the special-needs category (older children, minority groups, sibling groups, emotional, mental or physical handicaps).
- How many children did they place for adoption last year? What percentage were newborns? In what percentage of those placements did the agency locate the baby for the adoptive parents, as opposed to "identified" adoptions (discussed later in this chapter) where the adoptive parents locate the birth mother and thereafter have the agency process the adoption?

- From the time of the initial application to adopt, how long do most adoptive parents wait before a child is placed with them? How many families do they have waiting for a child right now?
- Do they put adoptive parents on a waiting list or do they look to other factors in placing a child with adoptive parents? If other factors are used, what are they?
- What are the total agency fees? How much of that amount is for the home study? When do you pay for the home study? If you were honest in your application but are turned down by the agency, what happens to the home study fee you have paid them? Are many people turned down, and if so, for what reason?
- When is the remainder of the fee paid? What happens to your fee to the agency if something goes wrong in the adoption, such as a birth parent changing her mind or other unforeseen legal complication? Do you then get priority for another placement without having to repay any fees or do you start from scratch and pay the agency all over again?
- If the birth mother has no insurance or state-provided Medicaid, do you pay those fees for her or does the agency? What other expenses besides the agency fee could there be? Could this include food or rent expenses for the birth mother if she is unable to work, or other expenses (e.g. maternity clothes, counseling fees, etc.)?
- Does the agency have a staff attorney who prepares and files with the court all the required court documents needed for you to complete the adoption, or do you retain an attorney at your own expense? Can the agency estimate the cost if you must retain an attorney?
- Are most of the adoptions arranged by the agency open or closed (ask for details as these are very vague terms)? Does

the agency encourage open or closed adoptions?

• To speed up the process of having a baby placed with you, does the agency permit identified adoptions, allowing you to find your own birth mother by using an adoption attorney or personally networking to meet someone? If you locate a birth mother in this way, are there any assurances the agency will not place the baby with someone else?

• Can you be listed with other agencies besides theirs to decrease the time required in waiting for a child?

The importance of "checking out" an agency before retaining one can not be overestimated. An example can be seen in the 1992 collapse of one of the nation's largest adoption agencies. After receiving huge "up front" fees from adoptive parents, the agency declared bankruptcy amidst allegations of impropriety. Remember, although an agency's status as "licensed" goes a long way towards demonstrating the agency's reliability, it is not a guarantee. Never ignore your own instincts giving you a feeling of discomfort with a particular agency.

Public Agency Adoption

Each county or state has a government-operated agency to assist in placing children for adoption for whom it has assumed responsibility. These agencies, usually referred to as *public adoption agencies*, are often a branch of your local social services or child welfare office. Chapter Six provides each state's central adoption office, which can direct you to the public adoption agency serving your area.

Although public adoption agencies are usually licensed to accept birth mothers' relinquishment of newborns, their most important function has evolved in recent years to finding homes for special-needs or hard-to-place children. Although some special-needs children are placed through private agencies, most often they are placed through public agencies. Many of these children have been freed for adoption through the court system due to parental abandonment, abuse or severe neglect. These children are of all ethnic groups and of varying ages. Some of these children will need extraordinary parenting due to the problems suffered by the child prior to the adoption, whether it be emotional, physical or intellectual difficulties.

Some children are categorized as special-needs not due to any disability, rather because they fall into a category the agency recognizes will make it more difficult to find an adoptive home. These can include children over a certain age (often age six), sibling groups to be adopted together, or children of an ethnic minority in which there is a scarcity of adoptive parents. Sadly, a disproportionate percentage of minorities live in poverty in our nation, making adoption necessary for a large number of birth parents. Hispanic children are rarely considered hard-to-place solely due to ethnicity. There are normally a sufficient number of hispanic families waiting to adopt, or adoptive parents of other ethnic groups seeking to adopt hispanic children.

For those interested in adopting a special-needs child through a public agency, often there is a substantially shorter waiting period for the adoptive placement once the home study is completed, as many such children are awaiting an adoptive home. Many public agencies are also willing to waive some of their normal restrictions regarding adoptive parents.

For example, if a couple is adopting an older child, the agency will often allow them to be older than forty years of age. Single parents are also considered. In fact, some states report one of every five agency adoptions is by a single parent. Couples who already have several children, or who are not infertile but wish to adopt, are often also considered. Those not interested in adopting a special-needs child can still apply to adopt through the public adoption agency, although often long waits are reported by those waiting for a newborn.

An advantage to adopting through your local public agency is that there is very little cost. Usually, the total fee charged by the county does not exceed several hundred dollars. There are almost never any costs associated with a birth mother's medical or living expenses as most children come into the agency system after having been freed for adoption through the courts. For this reason most of these adoptions are closed, with no contact between the birth and the adoptive parents.

Adoptive parents adopting through a public agency cannot "shop around" as can those working with private agencies, as most public agencies will only accept applications from adoptive parents residing within the county or territory served by the agency. Also, public agencies will normally refuse to offer their services to you if you have located your own birth mother and want the public agency to handle the adoption and take advantage of their low fee. This is because their function is to find homes for children for whom they are already responsible.

The services and policies of each public agency may differ, so adoptive parents are encouraged to attend the free seminars offered by agencies to learn more about their services.

The Foster Parent Short-Cut. Each county or state licenses foster parents to care for children for whom the government has temporary legal custody. Generally, these children have been removed from their families by a Child Protective

29

Services office due to parental abandonment, abuse or neglect, and are awaiting the court's action freeing them for adoption. These children range from infants to older children.

The purpose of placing these children in foster homes is to provide a safe environment for the child, while allowing the child's parents an opportunity to put their lives in order and prove they can provide appropriate parental care. Generally, the parents are provided eighteen months to establish their ability to be adequate parents. Failing to do so, the court may terminate their parental rights and request the county or state adoption agency to find an adoptive home for the child.

Some states wisely recognize the emotional bonds which can form between foster parents and their foster children, thus give special consideration to foster parents wishing to adopt their foster children. Other states do not provide any special treatment or rights to foster parents. In fact, some foster parents are asked to sign a document promising they will never try to adopt their foster children.

The stated purpose of an agency requiring such a promise is the fear foster parents will adopt the children the agency would rather place elsewhere. Fortunately, foster parents' rights are slowly being recognized, as more and more experts recognize the importance in maintaining the relationship formed between foster parents and the children for whom they have been caring.

Foster parenting is certainly not a guaranteed route to adoption, even in states where foster parents are granted special status. Accordingly, it should not be done only for that reason. However, for those families who would enjoy caring for a child and knowing they are providing much needed affection and stability in a child's time of need, it can be a rewarding option. It can also be a learning experience for those individuals who are considering whether adopting an older child is right for them. Both you and the child can benefit from the temporary living arrangements. Foster parents are paid by the county or the state an amount deemed sufficient to care for the child's needs, usually several hundred dollars per month.

Special-Needs Registries. Because of the importance and difficulty of finding homes for hard-to-place children, special *adoption registries* and *photo-listing books* have been created to assist both public and private agencies in placing these children. Some of the principal organizations promoting special-needs adoption are the C.A.P. Book, the National Adoption Center, and the North American Council on Adoptable Children (*Appendix A* provides their contact information), and A.A.S.K. (Aid to Adoption of Special Kids).

The sharing of information via registries may allow an adoptive parent working with a public or private agency in San Francisco to learn of a special-needs child available for adoption through another agency in New Orleans. The two agencies then work together to make the placement.

Adoption registries normally work directly with licensed agencies to find placements for these children. Many registries are willing to speak to you personally regarding the children they have available, in the event you feel your local agency is not exploring this option fully.

Your local public adoption agency, as well as a handful of private agencies, will likely have their own special-needs children in addition to those listed in shared registries. Most registries and public agencies charge a very small fee for their services. Sometimes they waive their fee entirely.

To offset the financial expenses of adopting a special-needs child (possible physical therapy, counseling, special medical care etc.), either at present or anticipated sometime in the future, and to encourage the adoption of these children, the federal government created a program entitled the *Adoption Assistance Program*. This program can provide the adoptive parents monthly funding until the child reaches adulthood to offset special expenses likely to arise in raising a child with special-needs. The granting of funds must be approved by the government on a case-by-case basis before the adoption is finalized. Each state has an office which administers these special funds. Often the amount approved is approximately equal to the amount the county would have been paying had the child remained in foster care.

INDEPENDENT ADOPTION

It seems each year more and more infant adoptions are being completed via *independent* adoption, also referred to as *private* or *direct* adoption. In fact, more than 50% of all infant adoptions completed in the United States are done through independent adoption, rather than through agencies. In some states, almost all newborns are adopted through independent adoption. This popularity is surprising considering most people have never even heard of independent adoption until they explore adoption options in depth.

Despite the largely unfounded reputation of independent adoption being expensive and unreasonably risky, it continues to grow in popularity, so much so that some agencies have begun to alter some of the ways they do adoptions to be more similar to independent adoption. Its popularity with both adoptive parents and birth parents is based upon several factors:

1. It is very flexible, allowing both the adoptive and birth parents to create the type of relationship and adoption they want, without what some may perceive as unnecessary bureaucratic interference.
2. It allows the birth mother to personally meet and select the adoptive parents, rather than relinquish that decision to an adoption agency, thus increasing her confidence in the adoptive placement.
3. The adoptive parents can use their own initiative and enthusiasm to locate and meet a birth mother, rather than perhaps wait several years or more for an agency to do it for them.
4. The child can be placed in the home of the adoptive parents immediately after the birth, rather than be temporarily placed in agency foster care with strangers.

Independent adoption is different from agency adoption in many ways. Some differences are quite subtle, while others are very significant.

Few Eligibility Requirements. Unlike agency adoptions, independent adoption has virtually no eligibility requirements for adoptive parents. Agency restrictions, such as the adoptive parents' age, religion, marital history, number of children and proof of infertility, have little relevance in independent adoption. This is because there are no agency guidelines which must be followed. Instead, the birth mother personally selects the adoptive parents based upon factors *she* deems important.

The Home Study. Although virtually all adoptions require some sort of an investigative home study of the adoptive parents, the home study required in an independent adoption is usually considered much less intrusive and time consuming than in a typical agency adoption. Independent adoption home studies usually consist of fingerprinting the adoptive parents to be sure there is no criminal record or child abuse allegations, the verification of marriage, good health and employment. Instead of the numerous home visits by an adoption agency caseworker, an independent adoption usually involves only one, or a small number, of home visits.

Although each state will have slightly different requirements in the home study, the basic concern is generally whether the proposed adoptive parents appear able to be good parents for a child. Each state varies regarding who may perform an independent adoption home study. In some states a special state adoption office has been staffed to perform all home studies. Other states allow private entities to perform the home study. These may include licensed social workers, licensed private adoption agencies, or other persons approved by the local court.

Some states perform the home study for a relatively small fee, often under $1,000, while others allow private entities to charge what they feel is appropriate. This amount may be as high as several thousand dollars or as inexpensive as several hundred. If a private adoption agency is hired to perform an independent adoption home study, the agency fee is normally significantly less than if the same agency were performing a full traditional agency adoption where it would be performing more services.

Not only is the content of an independent adoption home study less sometimes involved than in most agency adoptions, so is the time frame. Unlike agency adoptions, where a home study is required both before *and* after the placement of the child, many states only require a home study *after* the child's placement into the adoptive parents' home in an independent adoption. The fact no preplacement home study is required by these states allows adoptive parents to adopt immediately, rather than wait for an agency to schedule a preplacement home study which must be completed before even being considered for an adoptive placement. About half the states require a home study of the adoptive parents before a child is placed in the adoptive parents' home, as in agency adoption.

Why are agency and independent adoption home studies so different in many states? The answer likely lies in who is officially placing the child for adoption. In a traditional agency adoption, the birth mother normally relinquishes the child to *the adoption agency.* The agency in turn then officially places the child with the adoptive parents. Because the birth mother is trusting someone other than herself—the agency—to make this tremendously important decision for her, extra scrutiny of the adoptive parents is deemed appropriate.

In most independent adoptions, however, the birth mother is personally selecting the adoptive parents and placing the child into their care. Because states feel they should respect the decision of the birth mother regarding whom she believes will be appropriate adoptive parents, an independent adoption home study is usually limited. Its primary purpose is to be certain the adoptive parents did not provide false information about themselves to the birth mother in convincing her to select them as adoptive parents, and to be sure she did not act negligently in selecting adoptive parents not suitable as parents. Because most birth mothers use excellent judgment selecting adoptive parents, however, it is almost unheard of for a court to deny her choice of adoptive parents.

The Children Available. Although children of all ethnic groups are available, most independent adoptions involve caucasian newborns. Because of the greater availability of minority children with many adoption agencies, particularly public agencies, and the longer waiting time for white newborns, many adoptive parents turn to independent adoption.

35

Similarly, many birth mothers, especially those from a middle and upper-class upbringing, may feel a stigma about approaching an adoption agency. Working with an adoption attorney in an independent adoption setting, however, may allow her to feel more in control.

Waiting for a Child. As in all types of adoption, there is no guarantee of adopting quickly in an independent adoption. A large number of adoptive parents pursuing an independent adoption, however, report they successfully adopt a baby within one year. For some couples the waiting time can be only a few weeks or months. This is due to the fact there are no "waiting lists" and that many states do not require a preplacement home study. Also, because an increasing number of birth mothers are turning to independent adoption to select adoptive parents, fewer children are available through adoption agencies.

The Openness of the Adoption. Independent adoption is often referred to as "open" adoption in many states. Unfortunately, *open* adoption is a vague term and can mean many things. When used to describe independent adoption, it usually refers to the fact many adoptive parents and birth mothers share full or partial identities and become personally acquainted before the birth. For the birth mother, this can be rewarding as she can develop complete confidence in the adoptive parents, greatly enhancing her likelihood of placing the baby for adoption as planned. She can also take pride in her active role in personally selecting the adoptive parents, rather than relinquishing that role to an agency.

The adoptive parents also benefit from becoming acquainted before the birth. They can learn more about their child's biological mother in person, rather than reading about her from an impersonal written analysis. They will be able to share important information about how the adoption occurred and why she felt adoption was her most loving option for the child, issues of great importance to be discussed with an adopted child as he or she grows.

Some states allow for confidentiality in independent adoption, as is done in some agency adoptions. Usually this is done by the use of an intermediary, such as an attorney, who will provide information about the birth mother and adoptive parents to each other, allowing each individual to withhold their identities if they so desire. However, some states require a full and open sharing of identities in independent adoption.

As in any type of adoption, the post-birth relationship can vary dramatically between the adoptive parents and the birth mother. Even if they have become well acquainted before the birth, some birth mothers elect to have complete privacy after the birth and wish no further contact. Many birth mothers desire to remain in indirect contact by receiving updating pictures and letters about the child from the adoptive parents once or twice a year. A small number may wish to remain in face-to-face contact and arrange to get together at prearranged times. Normally, these issues are discussed at the initial stages of the adoption to be sure the birth and adoptive parents desire the same type of adoption.

Fees and Costs. There are several areas of possible expenses in an independent adoption: attorney fees, home study, medical costs and pregnancy-related expenses for the birth mother.

An attorney is usually considered a necessity in an independent adoption as there is no adoption agency overseeing the entire process. Even if adoptive parents do not use an adoption attorney to help them quickly meet and be selected by a birth mother, there are many legal issues to be addressed requiring an attorney's skill and knowledge. Although the attorney's degree of involvement will vary from case to case, thus affecting the cost of the adoption, most adoption specialists charge between $2,500 to $9,000 to handle all aspects of an independent adoption, depending upon many factors.

For this fee the attorney typically does the following: assists the adoptive parents to quickly locate a birth mother; obtains necessary background and health information about the birth parents; provides physician and counseling referrals; examines the case for potential legal or practical difficulties; helps the assigned caseworker process the case; prepares the necessary legal documents and appears in court when required. Chapter Two will discuss fully the role of an adoption attorney and how to locate an ethical and knowledgeable one.

If the birth mother needs financial assistance with expenses related to the birth, such as her medical costs or her living expenses, the adoptive parents can usually assist her by paying some of those expenses. Such assistance allows a birth mother to stay in her own residence, rather than relocating to an agency-style maternity home which may not be comfortable for her. Each state has different regulations regarding what assistance may be provided. A small number of states forbid the adoptive parents to provide any expenses other than medical and legal costs. Generally, however, if the expenses are *pregnancy-related,* they are permitted.

Of course, in some cases, there may be no pregnancy-related expenses required. For example, if a birth mother has health insurance (perhaps through her parents' policy or her own employment) or state-provided Medicaid, there may be no medical expenses for the adoptive parents. Similarly, although some birth mothers are impoverished and desperately need financial help to pay for basic food and rent during the latter stages of the pregnancy, other birth mothers require nothing as they have adequate employment or live with their parents or boyfriend with no rental expenses.

Other less substantial expenses may involve the purchase of some maternity clothes and arranging for adoption counseling to prepare for the birth and adoption experience. These expenses usually total several hundred dollars.

Many adoption professionals estimate the total cost of most attorney-assisted independent adoptions, including attorney fees, home study fees, medical and living expenses (if any), to range between $4,000 and $18,000. Usually costs only go significantly higher if there are medical complications not covered by insurance. Particular expenses, as well as suggestions to reduce or eliminate such critical expenses as medical fees, will be addressed in subsequent chapters.

The practical issues and potential concerns concerning providing financial assistance are addressed in Chapter Two.

Bringing the Baby Home. Independent adoption procedures normally allow the adoptive parents to bring the baby home much quicker than in traditional agency adoption. Most states allow the birth mother to release her child directly into the adoptive parents' physical custody immediately upon the hospital's discharge of the baby, usually when the baby is two or three days old. This allows the adoptive parents to take the baby home right away, with no interim foster home placement.

There are both advantages and disadvantages to immediate placement. The benefit to adoptive parents is taking their baby home immediately. Every new parent, adoptive or otherwise, knows the early days of a child's life are precious and irreplaceable. Naturally, the child also benefits from being with his or her future parents immediately, rather than foster parents.

Of course, there is always a possibility the adoptive parents will bond to a child the birth mother has not yet permanently

39

released for adoption. In fact, the desire to eliminate emotional risk to adoptive parents is the reason some agencies refuse to place the baby with them until the child is irrevocably surrendered for adoption. This protects the adoptive parents emotionally from a potential problem resulting in the removal of the child. However, the days, weeks or even months elapsing during this phase when the child and adoptive parents are separated is a great loss for the adoptive parents and the child.

Interestingly, some agencies now permit immediate placement of the baby with the adoptive parents, even if an irrevocable consent to the adoption has not been signed by the birth mother. In doing so, agencies are duplicating the benefits and risks of the immediate release associated with independent adoption. Many agencies refer to these as "at risk" placements.

Some states' laws permit the birth mother to sign her official consent to the adoption while she is in the hospital, or within several days of the birth. Other states take her consent weeks or even months later (please see Chapter Six's state-by-state review). Although the adoptive parents are normally permitted to bring the baby home during the interim between birth and the signing of the consent to adoption, this leaves a window of risk where the birth mother could change her mind about the adoption. Most adoption experts agree, however, that in professionally arranged adoptions only five percent of birth mothers seek to stop adoption planning once placing the child. In some ways, it seems incongruous adoption is viewed as risky, considering that approximately fifteen percent of pregnancies result in spontaneous miscarriage. Oddly, this makes adoption a less risky venture than pregnancy itself.

Non-resident Independent Adoption

Five states do not permit independent adoption: Colorado, Connecticut, Delaware, Massachusetts and North Dakota. Fortunately, adoptive parents living within these states may still be able to complete an independent adoption without moving to another state through *non-resident independent adoption*. Some states permit adoptive parents to file their Petition for Adoption and complete their adoption in the state where the birth mother lives and gives birth, even if the adoptive parents reside in another state. Some adoptive parents adopt outside their home state even if independent adoption is permitted there, if the child is born in a state permitting non-resident adoption, and the laws and procedures of the other state are more to their liking.

Non-resident independent adoption may be permitted in Alabama, Alaska, California, Hawaii, Iowa, Kansas, Louisiana, Maine, Maryland, Michigan, Missouri, New Hampshire, New Mexico, New York, Ohio, Oregon, Pennsylvania, South Carolina, Texas and Washington. Although the policies of each state allowing non-resident adoption will differ, normally these states will process a non-resident independent adoption as follows:

1. Allow the adoptive parents residing outside the state to file their Petition for Adoption and complete their adoption within the state if the child is born or resides there (or in some cases if the birth parent resides there). The entire adoption is then normally handled completely pursuant to the laws and procedures of the child's state.

2. The adoptive parents would be required to have a home study conducted by an individual or agency as approved by

the court where the case is pending. Based upon the policies of that state, the home study will need to be completed either before or after the child is placed with the adoptive parents. Exceptions are Hawaii and Mississippi, where there are no mandatory requirements for any home study at all, unless one is requested by the court. Usually the home study is performed by an individual or agency in the adoptive parents' home state, although it must be deemed acceptable to the court.

3. The adoptive parents can usually bring the child back to their home state shortly after the child is released from the hospital, even if the adoption has not yet been finalized by the court (assuming the Interstate Compact for the Placement of Children has been complied with, as addressed in Chapter Five). This allows the adoptive parents and the child to reside in the comfort of their own home during the months between the child's birth and the adoption finalization.

4. Some states will require the adoptive parents and the child to return for a final court appearance in which the adoption is formally approved by a judge. Other states do not require them to appear for this final hearing, as the adoption can be approved without their presence.

Nonresident independent adoption is a little-known method of adoption. In some situations adopting out of state will add complications and expense, while in others it may create beneficial options unavailable in your home state. To learn more about this option, consult with an attorney in a state allowing nonresident adoption to learn about the services he or she can offer you. Before working with any attorney, however, whether he or she be local or out-of-state, follow the guidelines recommended in Chapter 2 to find an ethical and knowledgeable one.

Identified Adoptions

Identified adoption, sometimes referred to as *designated* adoption, is a new type of adoption rapidly becoming popular with many adoptive parents seeking to adopt a newborn. An identified adoption is essentially an agency adoption, but with some of the popular elements of independent adoption.

Unlike a traditional agency adoption where the adoptive parents retain an agency and wait to be told the agency is ready to place a baby with them, identified adoption allows the adoptive parents to speed up the process by locating their own birth mother. The adoptive parents often meet the birth mother through a friend, their own networking efforts, or the assistance of an adoption attorney. Once the adoptive parents and the birth mother meet and decide to go forward with adoption planning, the birth mother is referred to the agency for needed services. These services may include adoption education and counseling, obtaining health histories and other important information, and eventually arranging the birth mother's signing of the consent to the adoption.

Some identified adoptions are started by adoptive parents who are already approved and waiting with an agency. The adoptive parents tire of waiting for a child so attempt to hasten a placement by doing the most difficult part of the adoption—finding the birth mother. In other cases, adoptive parents may have met a birth mother before they have even applied to an agency.

Another term often used synonymously with "identified" and "designated" adoption is *collaborative* adoption. A collaborative adoption is one where both an adoption attorney and adoption agency have substantial roles in the adoption.

The adoptive parents have an attorney looking out for their interests, helping them meet a birth mother due to his or her contacts in the adoption community, and offering legal advice and services when required throughout the adoption. The agency is offering their counseling and home study services. Some adoptive parents believe collaborative adoptions offer the best of both independent and agency adoption.

Some agencies will not accept identified adoptions, as they do not like a birth mother and adoptive parents pre-selecting each other and planning their own adoption, removing the agency from any initial decision-making steps. Public adoption agencies will virtually never consider handling an identified adoption. Many private agencies, however, actively pursue identified adoptions and are happy to attempt to cater their services to the desires of birth mothers and adoptive parents.

INTERNATIONAL ADOPTION

International adoptions are those where the child is born outside the United States, but is adopted by adoptive parents living within the United States. Every adoptive parent has heard rumors of one country or another having children awaiting immediate adoption. Most recently this has been (according to 2002 statistics) China leading the way (5,053), Russia (4,939), Guatamala (2,219) and South Korea (1,779).

Adoptive parents sometimes ask why they can't go to a more "pleasant" country, such as Australia or England, to adopt. There are several reasons, both practical and legal. All industrial nations all face the same problem as Americans—

there are more couples waiting to adopt than there are children free for adoption. For that reason, when American adoptive parents travel overseas to their country of choice for their adoption, they are likely to meet other adoptive parents who have travelled there from Germany, Italy, France, England, Sweden, et cetera, who are there with the same goal. International adoption is not just popular with Americans.

Most of the countries with children free for adoption are countries undergoing economic and/or social strife, leading to conditions where they can't offer enough homes for their children. Unlike America, where foster homes are used, foreign nations place children in orphanages until a home is found.

There is also a very important legal reason why international adoptions are from troubled countries, and not countries the equivalent of America. The United States government will only issue a visa, allowing the adopted child to enter America, if the child is parentless. These children, given *orphan* status by our government, are given special consideration in being granted citizenship. Children not meeting this distinction (such as in a voluntary adoption by the birth mother) would not be eligible for this special status to enter our country.

International adoptions are potentially much more legally complex than domestic adoptions, but oddly, are usually completed much faster. Once you are in the child's country (called being "in country") you will complete an adoption in 10-45 days, about ten times faster than domestically.

The procedures you must follow will be determined by many factors: the eligibility restrictions of the adoptive parents set by the adoption program you select and the child's country of origin (age, marital status, etc.); the laws of the child's country governing adoption; the adoption laws of your state governing international adoption; and the USCIS (United States Citizenship and Immigration Service) requirements concerning the admission of the child into the United States and eventual citizenship. (The USCIS was previously known as the INS - the Immigration and Naturalization Service.)

If the preceding list of factors sounds complicated—that is because international adoption *is* complicated. That does not mean an international adoption cannot be done quickly and smoothly, because some can. In fact, many adoptive parents can actually adopt faster internationally than domestically. The potential complications, however, demonstrate the importance of working with a quality international adoption program with an excellent support staff overseas.

All international adoptions require an adoption agency home study by an agency licensed for international home studies. In that sense, every international adoption is an agency adoption. However, the home study requirement is only a very small part of what makes up a completed international adoption. The critical part is the completion of the adoption itself overseas.

In most states, international adoption programs may be operated by either agencies or attorneys, or in some cases even facilitators. Some countries prefer to work with agencies, others with attorneys, while some have no preference. However, as will be explored later in this chapter, the quality, cost and speed of services can vary tremendously among different international programs. Luckily, it is often easy to find an excellent program.

There are several reasons why some adoptive parents prefer international adoption:

- Some adoptive parents are not eligible for a domestic adoption, or fear long waits due to factors (age, marital status, etc.), which are not issues internationally.
- They wish to adopt a caucasian child, which they fear (rightly or wrongly) may be difficult to adopt locally. (In

46

Eastern Europe, virtually all children are caucasian.)

- The adoptive parents may be of an ethnic group where there are few adoptive placements locally, yet they wish a child of their same ethnic group. China is an example.
- The adoptive parents feel they do not need, or in some cases even desire, a newborn (diaper changes and midnight feedings are not for every parent!), and like the idea of adopting a child who is a toddler or older. (Few newborns are available internationally, with the exception of China, as most countries make children available to only their own citizens for at least the first year.)
- They have humanitarian concerns for the children living overseas in orphanages who desperately need homes. This is more compelling for them than the domestic scenario, with many adoptive parents vying for the babies available.
- Some adoptive parents are not comfortable with the open nature of most domestic adoptions. They feel uncomfortable in working closely with a birth mother, and prefer working with a foreign government who has already severed parental rights, and will complete a closed adoption.
- There is fear that a birth parent will seek to reclaim the child under state law. They prefer to adopt a child who is already completely legally free.
- There is concern that even if they are eligible for a domestic adoption, they may wait a long time for a birth mother to select them. They want a definite timetable to have a child in their home, which can be possible in international adoption, but not in domestic.

There are also disadvantages to international adoption. Some adoptive parents describe their trip to the child's country to bring the child home as a nightmare. They complain they arrived in the foreign country only to find the child was not

47

yet free for adoption, or that other adoptive parents were promised that child. The child's photos they were shown may have been years old. There may be an inadequate program staff to assist them overseas in interacting with foreign officials and courts.

Health issues can also be a concern. Due to the lack of quality health care in some nations, some of the children brought home may have minor or major health problems. Some countries have justifiably earned a bad reputation for the poor quality of their orphanages. Other countries, including China and Russia, have orphanages ranging from poor to good.

To avoid these problems before they start, it is critical to find the right international program, and the right country from which to adopt. Happily, there are some countries which dedicate significantly greater resources and energy into their orphanages than is generally found in other countries. It is possible to find orphananges with caring caretakers/teachers; lots of intellectual and physical stimulation; and happy children interacting with each other and their caretakers. The right program can direct you to these select locations. Finding the right program in your area requires a lot of research on the part of the adoptive parent.

To fully understand why some international adoptions can go smoothly, while others become mired in complications, it is necessary to see how the entire international adoption process works. There are two methods to use in doing an international adoption. The USCIS, which oversees part of the process, jokingly calls one "the fast way" and the other "the slow way." Here is a step-by-step review of how the author guides his own clients (aka "the fast way"):

- The adoptive parent must obtain a home study from a licensed adoption agency or specially approved social worker approved to perform international adoptions. This typically takes about three months. The usual home study cost for this "pre-placement" evaluation usually varies from $500 to $1,700.

- *Concurrent* to starting the home study, the adoptive parents should file a USCIS form called the I-600-A (*Application for Advance Processing of Orphan Petition*). The purpose of the I-600-A application process is to receive the USCIS' approval for your international adoption, a required element in every international adoption.

- The I-600-A form must be sent to a specially designated USCIS office serving the adoptive parents' home region, along with their birth certificates or passports; marriage license (if a married couple) and divorce decrees, if any; and the USCIS' fee of $460 (which changes frequently). The adoptive parents will later be fingerprinted as well. It is wise to file the 1-600-A at the same time as starting your home study. This is because the USCIS does not require a copy of the home study when the I-600-A is filed, but it does require the home study before approving the I-600-A. This allows you to start two processes at once, rather than one after the other. Once the USCIS has received your final document, the home study, it will process your fingerprints. Most locations do this by "live scan" taking only a few days for results. Then, the USCIS will usually take from two to eight weeks to approve your *Orphan Petition* by issuing a document called an *I-171-H*.

- Each foreign country requires a *dossier* of the adoptive parents. This is a compilation of all the documents required by the foreign nation. A typical dossier will contain 10-15 documents, such as the home study, USCIS approval (the I-171-H), marriage certificate, letters verifying employment and good health, etc. All these documents must then be *authenticated* or *apostilled*, based upon the foreign country's requirements. Depending upon which is required, some countries will need four government stamps: first notarization or certification; then certification at the state and federal level, followed by the embassy of the foreign nation.

- Now the completed dossier, and the authentication stamps, must be translated into the language of the foreign country, then those translations are authenticated in some manner. Depending upon the requirements of the country from which you are adopting, the cost of the authentications and translations for a complete dossier will be from $1,500-$4,000.

- Depending upon the policies of the country from which you adopt, the dossier may be sent to the foreign country's officials for approval, or it may be hand-carried by the adoptive parents when they travel.

- Adoption programs in some countries will send you a photograph and health history of a child they believe matches your stated desires for a child (age, gender, existence of any special conditions). Some programs can offer multiple children concurrently. It is for the adoptive parent to then determine if they wish to adopt a particular child. Some programs, and the governments with which they work, may present the children's pictures immediately, or take as long as one year. A handful of countries operate in a different way. Rather than force a narrow choice upon the adoptive parents, they confirm they have many children meeting your requirements and invite you to their country to offer several children, to be determined when you arrive.

- Although a small number of countries allow the child to be brought to you via an escort, most countries require the adoptive parents to come to their country, meet the child, then finalize the adoption in their own court. Naturally, these nations want to be sure their children are being properly adopted under their laws.

- A good international adoption program will have a skilled translator, as well as a car and driver, to meet your needs in going to all the official places during your visit. It is this person who will translate for you with foreign officials, interpret health records, and accompany you to the many places you are required to go in completing the adoption (which you could never find alone): the orphanage to meet the child, the court to finalize the adoption a few days later, the birth certificate bureau and passport office to obtain the child's new records reflecting your adoption.
- When the adoption is finalized overseas, you are given a new birth certificate with you listed as parents, and with the child's new name, as you wish it to be.
- Before the child can enter America, a foreign doctor specifically approved by the U.S. government, called a *panel physician*, must conduct a basic examination of the child. The goal is to be sure the adoptive parents know everything that is possible about the child's health. Again showing the varying quality of different country's orphanage systems, the U.S. government requires extensive testing for the children of some countries. With some countries, however, the U.S. government seems to have such confidence in the health system and records of the foreign orphanages that the examination is very cursory.
- All of the above documents are presented to the American Embassy overseas, along with additional USCIS forms, to obtain the needed permission for the child to obtain a *green card* and to enter America as a *legal resident alien*. If the child was fully adopted overseas, he or she is a citizen upon

entering the United States. If only a guardianship or similar status was grated overseas, and the child is then adopted in the United States, citizenship can be applied for.

• Even though the adoption was finalized overseas, many adoptive parents elect to *refinalize* the adoption in their home state court. Depending upon the state in which you reside, this re-adoption home study may be only a cursory home study, a full home study, or may not be required at all. Some international adoption programs include the cost of the legal work in the refinalization.

The above list sounds like a lot—and it is. The good news, however, is that virtually all of the above is the job of your international adoption program. So step number one is to find a program. A good program will know the "ins and outs" of working with the USCIS and foreign governmental officials. The program should also know the exact eligibility requirements of the country with which they are working and what, if anything, you would be required to do in the child's country to legally complete the adoption and bring the child home.

Fees can vary in international adoptions as much as in domestic adoptions. Most programs charge between $10,000-$20,000. Adoptive parents must be *very cautious* in finding out what is covered in the program fee. Some programs do not cover the cost of the translator, car and driver while you are overseas, the dossier, or the orphanage donation. These services can *each* cost thousands of dollars. The better, more straight-forward programs will include all these costs, leaving only the cost of your own travel, home study and USCIS fees.

In selecting an adoption program to complete an international adoption, ask the general agency questions (provided earlier in this chapter) or attorney questions (provided in Chapter 2), as well as the following:

- *Are you a licensed agency or attorney?* (As will be discussed later, some entities are facilitators—viewed with suspicion by many in the adoption field, rather than being a licensed agency or attorney.)
- *With which country do they work?* Adoptive parents may wish to be cautious of programs offering half a dozen countries from which to choose. Often the best programs focus their attention on one or two countries.
- *Does the overseas staff work directly for the program, or are they contracted through another program?* Many programs do not have the staff and funding to travel overseas to set up their own program. Instead, they pay to use the staff of another program. Not only is this a much inferior arrangement, but your cost is higher as a result.
- *How many adoptions have they done with that country this year? Last year?* You want to see a record of reasonable success. However, you may wish to be cautions of those programs which boast completing hundreds of adoptions a year. An adoption is not an assembly-line function. Smaller is often better in many cases.
- *What are the children like which that country has available for adoption (age, ethnic heritage, health, etc.)? What specific health tests are given to the child before you arrive? HIV? Hepatitis B? Syphilis?*
- *Are there children waiting for immediate placement? What is the average time to complete an adoption, from the very start, to bringing your child home?*
- *What are the procedures to adopt from the country with which you will be working? Do you go to the country to bring the child home or does an escort transport the child?*
- *What is the full program fee? Does it include the authentication and translation of our dossier? The home study? A*

53

translator, car and driver to meet us at the airport and bring us to all our official meetings? The translator and driver's food and lodging? The orphanage donation? The translation of the foreign court documents for our embassy? The cost of a lawyer doing our child's re-adoption for us when we get back? If not, what will those fees be?

Oddly, often the best programs are those that are less expensive. This may be because the motivations of those operating the true quality programs are less interested in profit, and more interested in helping form families. Don't be fooled that a high fee indicates better service. In the adoption world, it seems the opposite is often true.

- *Is the adoption completed and approved by the court in the child's country or are we only given guardianship?* The adoption will be simpler and more legally secure if you can legally finalize the adoption overseas, so the child is legally yours from that moment forward. Some countries will only grant guardianship, thus requiring you to adopt the child under your state law when you return home.
- *How long will we be overseas?* Most adoptive parents are required to be overseas for 10-45 days. Most countries require only one visit, although some, like Russia, presently require two. The key is *not* finding the country with the shortest stay overseas, however, as a lifetime addition to your family is being made. The key is finding the right program, the right country, the right child. The horror stories where a couple is stuck overseas for six months are quite rare, and usually indicate they tried a "do it yourself adoption" or an unreliable program.

These questions, coupled with the general questions regarding attorneys and agencies provided earlier, should help you find an excellent program. If you are unable to find a program close to your home with good credentials for international adoptions, remember you can look outside your home state. It is not unusual for adoptive parents in some states, with few existing international options, to select an international program thousands of miles away. The home study is done by someone in the adoptive parents' home region, but the international program is overseen elsewhere.

Some of the above information will be changing in the near future. The Hague Convention on International Adoption, a multi-national treaty, sets new regulations for participating countries. Most significantly, agencies, attorneys, and others involved in adoption programs will need to be approved the the Department of State to handle international adoptions, if the country of both the child and the adoptive parents is a member of the treaty. If not, the treaty's terms will not apply. There is much to do before the United States can meet the terms of the treaty, however. Attorney Irene Steffas, co-chairperson of the International Adoption Committee of the American Academy of Adoption Attorneys, estimates the Hague Treaty will most likely not be effective within the United States until sometime in 2005.

FACILITATORS

Adoption *facilitators* are individuals or organizations whose services are usually centered around efforts to help adoptive parents find a birth mother. Many adoption professionals consider most facilitators a risky avenue toward adoption as many are considered "paid baby finders." Some states, like

New York and New Jersey, make it a crime for a person other than an adoption agency, to receive any compensation for locating a birth mother for adoptive parents to create an adoptive match. Some states have no such criminal sanctions.

Although many facilitators present a risky avenue towards adoption, there are also some ethical and effective facilitators. Facilitators, and the risks of using them, are discussed in Chapter Two.

CHAPTER TWO

Techniques to Quickly Locate a Baby for Adoption

The goal of every waiting adoptive parent is to find a birth mother they like and trust, who will in turn select them as the adoptive parents of her expected child. The days of orphanages—and babies waiting to be adopted—have not existed for six or seven decades in the United States. Now, most adoptive parents locate a baby for adoption by meeting and being selected by a birth mother, usually while she is in the latter stages of her pregnancy.

When adoptive parents are adopting through independent or identified agency adoption, they can beat the *waiting game* of adoption by going out and locating their own birth mother. A common question by those planning to search for a birth mother, however, is "are there any women who want to place their child for adoption?" The answer is an emphatic *"yes."*

How do adoptive parents find a birth mother? It is not as difficult as one would think. In fact, it is often quite easy.

Common sense tells you this is true. Think about all the unplanned pregnancies occurring daily across the United States. Annually, it runs into the millions. It is estimated by many states as many as twenty-five percent of all women giving birth are unmarried.

Although many of these women with unplanned pregnancies will elect to raise the child themselves, or terminate the pregnancy, a large number will select adoption as the best option for themselves and their children. The most common reasons cited in selecting adoption over the other options are:

- Religious reasons preclude terminating the pregnancy.
- Terminating the pregnancy was planned but the birth mother was too far along in her pregnancy.
- The birth mother has terminated a prior pregnancy and feels she cannot emotionally put herself through the process again.
- Although the pregnancy was unplanned, the birth mother has a genuine love for the child she is carrying. She recognizes, however, she cannot provide the lifestyle she wants the child to have. This is often a combination of many factors: being unmarried and wanting her child to have a two-parent home, believing herself too young to be a mother, just starting her education or career and foreseeing financial difficulties supporting herself and a child.

So actually the real question is not *whether* there are any women planning to place their children for adoption, rather *how* can you most effectively arrange for a prospective birth mother to learn about you and select you as the adoptive parents? Many adoptive parents attribute their success in quickly finding a birth mother to their hard work in implementing the techniques discussed below, while others credit simple good luck.

Actually, both hard work and luck play important roles, but likely the old adage "the harder you work, the luckier you are," is accurate. To give yourself the greatest chance of success, not to mention the *quick* success everyone desires, you should use all, or at least most, of the following techniques. The author has found adoptive parents following the full program outlined below generally report being contacted by one or more birth mothers between two to nine months after commencing the full spectrum of techniques, usually with the birth occurring within a few months thereafter.

There are several effective ways to meet a birth mother. These include using an adoption attorney's connections to your advantage, following a detailed guide of *networking* to expose potential birth mothers to you, advertising, and other means of "spreading the word." Let's look at them individually and see how they work.

THE ROLE OF THE ADOPTION ATTORNEY

Generally, when people think of the attorney's role in an adoption, they imagine it to be primarily the preparation of legal documents, making court appearances and offering necessary legal advice. Of course, those are very important elements in an adoption, and if we were speaking of the non-specializing attorney, that would be the limit of his or her services. When the term *adoption attorney* is used, however, it refers to an attorney who *exclusively or primarily does adoptions*, resulting in special knowledge, skill and valuable resources in the adoption community. This special status can result in the attorney quickly locating a birth mother, who in turn can select you as the planned adoptive parents.

Using an adoption attorney over a non-specializing attorney has many advantages, particularly when an independent adoption is being planned:

- As a specialist, he or she will generally know more than an attorney who is a general practitioner, or even a family law specialist (where divorce and child custody are the main part of the practice). Every area of law is becoming more and more complicated and specialized, making it highly advantageous to work with an attorney who knows about the many special laws and legal procedures of adoption *before* they become an issue.

- Because of the extensive experience gained working with birth parents and adoptive parents, an adoption attorney should have greater insight into whether there are any *red flags* to the adoption, whether it involves the birth mother's readiness to start adoption planning or a special legal concern.

- The adoption attorney's expanded knowledge of the adoption community will likely be of tremendous value. For example, who is a counselor you can trust to work with the birth mother? Which local physician and hospital properly handles the emotional issues of adoption, and which ones should you avoid at all costs? What is the personality of the caseworker assigned to do your home study?

- Perhaps the most popular reason why adoptive parents retain an adoption attorney is that a good adoption attorney can often personally introduce you to a birth mother. Established adoption attorneys usually have working relationships with others in pregnancy-related fields, such as physicians, counselors, the clergy etc. When these individuals learn a woman is considering placing a child for adoption, they will often refer her directly to the adoption attorney they have come to trust. There are a small number of states which do not permit attorneys, or any parties but licensed agencies, to locate and introduce birth mothers to adoptive parents. Generally, attorneys in those states advise adoptive parents how to locate a birth mother, then perform the necessary legal work thereafter.

Many adoptive parents reason that since they will eventually need an attorney anyway, why not retain one at the very start of the process, perhaps benefiting by being introduced to a birth mother and having experienced guidance every step of the way.

Selecting an Adoption Attorney

Attorneys are like all professionals: there are good ones and bad ones. Because of the importance of creating your family through adoption, the selection of the attorney handling your adoption is a critical decision. The quality of service, depth of knowledge, fairness of fees, and other important factors can vary dramatically. The state-by-state review in Chapter Six provides the names and biographical information of attorneys who are members of the *American Academy of Adoption Attorneys*. Whether you select an attorney from that listing, or other means, following are some suggested inquiries you may wish to make regarding the qualifications of an attorney:

- *Does the attorney only do adoptions, or is it just one of many areas of practice?* If the attorney is not a specialist, enhanced adoption knowledge may be lacking.

- *How many adoptions does the attorney do annually?* Most adoption attorneys in major metropolitan areas complete thirty or more adoptions per year. Some attorneys complete more than one hundred annually.
- *How long do most of the attorney's clients wait before being selected by a birth mother?* The average waiting time among most successful adoption attorneys is less than one year. Often some couples are lucky and are selected by a birth mother within weeks, while other equally worthy couples wait more than a year.
- *What percentage of birth mothers are found by the attorney through his or her special contacts in the pregnancy and adoption-related fields, rather than the adoptive parents personally locating her?* Most successful adoption attorneys report they locate the birth mothers in about half of the adoptions they handle, while the adoptive parents locate the birth mother in the other half through networking efforts supervised by the attorney.
- *What are the attorney's fees?* Like all professions, the attorneys with the most expertise, leading to consistently successful results, may charge more than less experienced attorneys. However, a high fee is no guarantee of quality. Some adoption attorneys charge by the hour, while many have a predetermined *flat-fee*. Adoption attorney's fees vary tremendously throughout the country. Often fees will be higher in major metropolitan areas than in rural areas where the attorney may be less experienced.

In an independent adoption, where the attorney's role is significant, typical fees range from $2,500 to $9,000. If you are planning an identified agency adoption and the attorney is assisting throughout the adoption, such as helping to locate a birth mother and providing legal assistance, most attorneys will charge between their full fee and half that amount. If the attorney is simply going to court with you to finalize an agency adoption, and all the work has been done by the agency, most attorneys will charge even less.

Caution should be exercised if fees are significantly higher than charged by other adoption attorneys in your area. A higher fee does not always mean the quality of service is higher. Several of the worst attorneys are known to charge excessively high fees. A Beverly Hills or Madison Avenue address is no guarantee of quality.

- *Does the attorney charge his or her entire fee in advance and state it is nonrefundable?* Adoptive parents should be very cautious of attorneys who require their entire fee, or an unjustly large portion, be paid when initially retained if the fee is nonrefundable. Most attorneys charge a fair portion of their fee in advance, sometimes called a *retainer,* and the balance of the fee when further services are rendered.

- *What is the attorney's fee for an initial consultation?* Before deciding if you wish to retain a particular attorney, you will want to meet with him or her to decide if you can work well together. Be cautious if the initial consultation fee is excessive, unless the attorney is in the top of their field, providing grounds for valuing their time more expensively than others. Also be cautious regarding attorneys who attempt to entice you with a "free consultation." You would not expect to spend one or two hours of free time with a leading surgeon or other trained professional. Attorneys are no different.

If someone is offering lengthy free consultations (it normally takes two hours for an attorney to fully explain adoption laws and procedures, it does not necessarily mean the attorney is not competent. However, it may indicate the attorney's practice is lacking in clients, or else why spend hours for no remuneration but the hope of being hired. You may wish to ask yourself why the attorney's practice may be less successful than others.

- *Does the attorney encourage counseling for birth parents?* As will be discussed in Chapter Three, counseling for birth parents, particularly birth mothers, is a critical element to preparing them for the birth and relinquishment process, and giving the adoption the best chance to succeed.

  If the attorney does not encourage counseling it may indicate a basic ignorance about adoption issues, or a predisposition against counseling. Generally, either tendency speaks poorly of the attorney. An exception exists in the small number of states forbidding the adoptive parents to pay any birth expenses other than medical or legal costs, making payments for counseling illegal.

- *Does the attorney seem not only professional, but reasonably emotionally sensitive as well?* Ask yourself if you could work with this person in times of emotional turmoil. Does the attorney check his messages over the weekend if an emergency develops? Can you envision the attorney competently working with a birth mother, or is the attorney so unsympathetic or out of touch with young people that birth mothers will feel uncomfortable and go elsewhere for adoption planning.

- *Has the attorney done anything to distinguish him or herself from other attorneys?* Like other professionals, attorneys can be evaluated by their contributions to their profession. Is the attorney active in membership organizations impacting adoption within your state, such as state bar committees dealing with adoption issues, or similar affiliations? Has the attorney authored any works demonstrating special knowledge? Has the attorney been acknowledged in some way by respected adoption organizations or publications?

Once you have these answers, you have some basic information to use in selecting an attorney. Unfortunately, there is more work remaining in finding the best attorney if you wish to be thorough. Although it may be surprising to learn, it is an unfortunate fact some attorneys may misrepresent their success and stature to potential clients. For example, many unknown "adoption attorneys" appear each year in local yellow page directories, implying they are skilled in adoptions.

Remember, all that is required to place such advertisements is money. Sadly, it is almost impossible to establish that an attorney who tells you he or she has done a large number of adoptions has actually done only one (which was probably for his brother-in-law!). Fortunately, with some diligence you can determine the legitimate attorneys who are successful, knowledgeable, and well respected in the adoption community.

Professionals working within the adoption community (counselors, attorneys, agencies etc.) usually know which attorneys are reputable and which should be avoided, although this information can sometimes be difficult for the general public to obtain. Any inquiry you make will be complicated due to the fact many people do not wish to make negative comments about someone with whom they work, or they may simply feel it is inappropriate to speak poorly of others.

Some individuals will refuse to make even positive comments or recommendations, due to an office policy that forbids providing such information. Often, however, you can obtain some valuable information if you ask in a particular manner, depending upon the individual or group you are contacting.

The following groups and individuals can usually provide you with important insight and *inside information* regarding attorneys you may be considering.

State Adoption Office. Each state has a special adoption office overseeing adoptions within the state. The address and phone number for each state's office is provided in the state-by-state review in Chapter Six. The state adoption office can direct you to any regional offices which may exist within the state handling independent adoptions in your region. In some states the adoption office has a "hands on" approach to the adoptions occurring within its state, while in other states the adoption office leaves case management to the courts.

If you live in a state where the state adoption office has an active role in supervising adoption cases, the caseworkers employed within the office are in an excellent position to know the legal skill and knowledge of the attorneys handling adoptions within the state. Unfortunately, the caseworkers are generally forbidden to make recommendations. Often, however, they will be receptive if you provide the name of a particular attorney and ask if that attorney files many petitions being handled by their office. This may not tell you if the attorney is a good or a bad one. However, it will indicate if the attorney is successful enough to be filing a large number of adoption petitions.

Public Adoption Agencies. As discussed in Chapter One, most counties operate a public adoption agency. Because independent and agency adoptions are normally handled by completely different departments, public adoption agencies may have little contact with adoption attorneys. Regardless, the adoption community is a small one and word often spreads regarding other adoption professionals. Call the county where the attorney you may retain is located and ask for the *officer of the day* or the *duty worker*. As with the state adoption office, public adoption agencies frequently are encouraged not to give outright recommendations. However, if they have even *heard* of the attorney you are considering retaining, you have obtained some helpful information.

Private Adoption Agencies. Private adoption agencies work with attorneys in several ways. In many states, the independent adoption home study may be done by a licensed private adoption agency. Accordingly, these agencies often work closely with attorneys assisting in independent adoptions. Even in states where independent adoption home studies are done by the state adoption office rather than private agencies, local private agencies may have helpful knowledge of adoption attorneys in the region. They are usually much more likely to discuss local attorneys than state or county agencies.

Physicians. The medical profession, particularly infertility specialists, obstetricians and gynecologists, may be familiar with local adoption attorneys. If your personal physicians can not help you, ask friends to inquire of their physicians.

Adoptive Parent Associations. Adoptive parents in many cities or counties have formed adoptive parent associations. These informal groups share information about adoption, most of the members having already adopted. Individuals in these groups can be helpful in many ways, as they have been through the process you are just entering. They can also give you an adoptive parent's view of adoption attorneys. Unlike some of the government offices discussed above, you will likely hear some very frank opinions regarding local attorneys.

To find out if there is a group in your area, contact directory assistance. If there is no listing, a local adoption attorney or agency will likely have the phone number available. The *Adoptive Parents of America, Resolve* and the *National Adoption Information Clearinghouse* also keep records of adoptive parent associations nationally. Please refer to Appendix A to learn about these organizations and how to contact them.

State Bar Association. All attorneys must be licensed to practice law by the state in which they practice. Although there is no formal specialization for adoption in most states, and the State Bar will not recommend attorneys, you can still inquire if there have been any *disciplinary actions* against a particular attorney. Most State Bars do not release records of unsubstantiated complaints, but do maintain records of any official reprimands or suspensions.

Local Bar Associations. Most counties have local bar associations. Unlike the mandatory membership in the State Bar Association, membership in a local bar is purely voluntary. An attorney's membership, or nonmembership, has no direct relationship to legal skills.

Some local bar associations maintain records of client's substantiated complaints against an attorney, although most do not. Most local bar associations have specialty listings in which attorneys can list themselves, to be provided when clients call the bar's referral service for help in finding an attorney. Be advised, however, there is usually no required demonstration of skill for an attorney to list themselves as offering legal services in a particular category, such as adoptions. In fact, many of the attorneys list themselves in such referral services in the hope of garnering more clients.

■ ■ ■ ■ ■

After inquiring of some or all of the above groups and individuals, you should find that some attorney's names will come up repeatedly, leading you to a qualified adoption attorney. If you cannot locate a suitable adoption attorney in your immediate area, you may want to retain one outside your region, but still within your state.

NETWORKING WITH A PHOTO-RESUME LETTER

Networking has become a new popular term, meaning to "get the word out." In the case of adoption, it refers to the need to make as many people as possible aware of your desire to adopt, hopefully leading to a birth mother learning about you. Adoption networking is a science. When done correctly, it can work very effectively. Sadly, many couples make small, but critical errors in their networking campaigns, leading to poor results. The two main issues are *how* to prepare an effective photo-resume letter and *where* to send it. The following networking techniques have proved to be very successful.

Preparing a Photo-Resume Letter

The heart of your networking efforts is the *photo-resume letter*. Although there are key elements to be considered in its preparation, there is no *formula* that should be duplicated. In fact, it is essential your unique personality show through, so birth mothers reading it will see the *real you*.

A photo-resume letter is traditionally a one page, letter-sized, introductory letter in which you describe yourselves, with an affixed photograph. Of course, you can be a bit different and use two pages or multiple photos, but considering you will be duplicating the letter and picture in very large quantities, it is advisable to not get too fancy. A sample photo-resume letter is provided in Appendix B.

There are several important elements in a successful photo-resume letter. These suggestions are based upon comments made to the author by hundreds of birth mothers regarding what attracted them to a particular couple's photo-resume letter:

- Use colored paper (gentle colors or earth tones are best) or attractive stationary. Stay away from odd colors like lime green.
- When you introduce yourselves, it is generally advisable to provide your first and last names. Omitting your last name may make it appear you are being secretive or are nervous about meeting a birth mother. Also, not providing it may make you stand out from other adoptive parents as it is traditional to provide your full names. Even if you live in one of the few states that encourage secrecy in adoption, the reality of modern adoption is that full identities are often voluntarily disclosed. (If you refuse to have your name known by the birth mother at any time in the adoption process you may wish to explore working with an agency which will permit a truly *closed* adoption, or inquire if an attorney can act as a confidential intermediary in an independent adoption.)
- Your salutation should be "Hi," "Hello," "Dear Friend" or something similar, but *not* "Dear Birth Mother." Al-

though there is nothing wrong with the term "birth mother," it may be the first time a woman considering adoption has seen the term and she may resent what she perceives as a label.

- Explain why you are pursuing adoption. Some couples simply state they are unable to conceive children while others give specifics such as describing failed infertility treatments. Whether or not you elect to provide any details of your infertility treatments or difficulties in conception, it is important for birth mothers to see you are adopting because it is the only way for you to start a family. If you are adopting for a reason other than difficulty in conceiving a child, you should explain why.

- Give a brief description of yourselves and what the life of the child you adopt will be like. This may mean touching upon your educational background if you have college degrees or special education, home life, professions, supportive family and friends, etc. Most importantly, talk about your hobbies and fun activities. Often how we spend our leisure time most clearly defines us.

  Furthermore, birth mothers naturally want the child they are placing for adoption to have a wonderful life. Learning about the great parts of your life shows her the child will be sharing in those types of activities.

- If you already have a child, or children, talk about why it is important for you to adopt another child. This could include mentioning the importance of siblings or the fact you came from a large family and desire the same.

- If one of you is, or will be, a full-time parent, by all means mention that.

- If you are an unmarried person—specifically address the issue that you single. Explain why you are seeking to adopt as a single parent. Since most birth mothers are themselves single mothers and envision a two parent family for their child, comment upon your maturity, financial security and readiness to become a parent. Mentioning a supportive network of family and friends is also helpful to demonstrate you will not be facing the difficulties of parenthood alone.

- Any connection you have to adoption should be mentioned as it demonstrates you likely have a special understanding of adoption issues which will make the birth mother feel more comfortable. This could include discussing any family members or close friends who have adopted, are themselves adopted, or once placed a child for adoption.
- Mention you may be willing to assist with birth-related expenses, such as medical and/or living costs, if permitted in your state. Do not presume that a birth mother seeing your photo-resume letter will assume you are willing to help with such expenses unless you specifically mention it.
- Mention the state in which you live, as well as either the city or region. Talk about the benefits of your home town. If you live in a rural setting you can describe the benefits of living in a small town: knowing all your neighbors, clean air, etc. If you live in a major metropolitan area you could talk about the cultural and educational opportunities available. Every region has its benefits—do not be shy about showing pride in your home region.
- If you own your own home, briefly mention it to demonstrate stability.
- If you have already retained an adoption attorney or agency to assist you, provide their name in the photo-resume letter. This lends legitimacy to you and shows you are committed to doing things right. Also, many birth mothers, or the professionals to whom you send your photo-resume letters,

will be leery of being involved with an adoption making no reference to an attorney or agency. This is because they may fear becoming involved in an improperly arranged or illegal adoption.

- Discuss religion if you feel it is appropriate. Many birth mothers will feel the religion of the adoptive parents is a critical factor, while others state they want "good and loving parents," with religion having no bearing.
- Do not feel you must cover your entire life story in this brief photo-resume letter. A birth mother will need to know all about you before officially selecting you as the adoptive parents. However, that does not mean your photo-resume letter must go into great detail. Rather it says, "Hey, here we are, call us and learn more!"
- Provide your home telephone number including the area code. It shows you sincerely want to hear from someone when you state: "Our home telephone number is (909) 555-2221. Please call us collect, night or day." By the way, the last thing you want to do is to miss a call, so *invest in an answering machine*. You may wish to consider making the first words of your machine's message: "Operator, we will accept collect calls."

If you are worried about giving out your home number, knowing the photo-resume letter will be distributed, you can always have a second telephone line installed as your *adoption line*. You can then disconnect it when you have found a birth mother and wish no further calls from other people.

Some phone companies have a special program, such as "smart ring," where you can obtain a second phone number that will ring on your existing phone. When a call comes in on that line your phone will make a ring easily distinguished from the regular ring, allowing you to distinguish adoption calls from your other calls. This program saves the cost of installing a separate new phone line and can easily be terminated when there is no further purpose for the adoption line.

- *Hand-sign each letter.* Do not sign the original letter and then make copies, resulting in photocopied signatures. Each photo-resume letter should have an original signature, as using photocopied signatures makes your photo-resume letter look less personal.
- It is very important to let your personalities come through. If you are funny, do not be afraid to be funny. It you are quiet and sensitive, that is fine too. Remember, the photo-resume letter only opens the door of opportunity. The birth mother will almost always wish to personally meet with you before selecting you as the adoptive parents. If the image presented by your letter is clearly not the real you, she will see that when you meet face-to-face and everyone risks disappointment.
- *The most important part of the photo-resume letter is your picture.* It is from your photograph the birth mother will see the *spark* which attracts her to you. You want a photo where your faces are clearly seen, not so small you are dwarfed by beautiful scenery behind you. Generally, a casual photo is better that a formal one, unless the *real you* is most comfortable in a suit and tie and such formal wear.

It is not necessary to obtain a studio photograph. A typical 35 millimeter or digital camera will usually take sufficiently good photographs. If you have other children, include them. If you have pets, include them, as they are part of your family. Silly as it sounds, your labrador puppy sitting on your lap will likely help, not hurt, your image. Almost everyone loves animals, so why not show you are no different. Most important—smile!

- When you reproduce the photo-resume letters, remember to securely affix the photo to the resume letter with tape or staples. If you use a paper clip your picture may become separated from your letter, perhaps even switched with the photo of another couple's resume letter.
- Make sure the photograph is not too large and is affixed to a part of the letter allowing you to easily fold the photo-resume letter into a standard business-size envelope. Not doing this will add excess costs in mailing your photo-resume letter due to requiring an oversized envelope. Usually, the photograph is sized approximately five inches horizontal by three inches vertical, and placed in the upper right corner.

General Mail-Out Networking

Getting your photo-resume letters out in the community among those who can assist you meet a birth mother is essential to effective networking. To whom you send them, and where, are critical decisions in the success of adoption networking. When the photo-resume letters are mailed to professionals you do not personally know, but hope may be able to indirectly assist you to meet a birth mother, it is called *general mail-out networking*.

The best organizations and individuals to whom to send your photo-resume letters are those likely to come into contact with women with unplanned pregnancies. Generally, these are physicians (particularly obstetricians and gynecologists), counselors (usually listed as Marriage, Family and Child Counselors), birth clinics, abortion clinics, family planning centers and churches. Using your imagination you can likely think of additional categories, although those listed are usually the most effective.

Once you have decided upon the particular categories of organizations and individuals, you must determine the cities and states which your networking campaign will target. As a general rule, it is best to avoid major metropolitan areas with populations over one million. This is because physicians and other popular categories are inundated with photo-resumes from other hopeful adoptive parents. Accordingly, your chance of success in major cities will be diminished. Networking is most effective if you target the categories provided above in less populated areas.

To compile a listing of those to whom you wish to send your photo-resume letters, you need look no further than your local library. Most reasonably-sized libraries maintain an inventory of telephone directories for all counties within your home state, as well as some in other states. Scan the available yellow page directories and see what areas strike you. You may want to select a few regions within your home state, as well as a few out of state.

In addition to looking under the categories mentioned above, also see what is listed under the headings of "pregnancy" and "abortion." Likely there will be some appropriate listings. Also, look in the yellow page directory index. Often you can find a new category in addition to those discussed above.

The goal of this process is to produce a minimum—yes *a minimum*—of 2,000 organizations or individuals to whom to send your photo-resume letter. Naturally, you will increase your likelihood of success if you were to send out even more, but usually a birth mother can be located with this initial mailing within less than one year.

One drawback to compiling your own list via yellow page directories is the accuracy and sufficiency of the addresses provided. For example, telephone directories do not provide the listed party's zip code. Frequently they also omit the suite number (required by the post office for deliveries to office buildings over a certain size). These problems can make delivery of your letters less certain, resulting in half, or more, of your letters not being deliverable, perhaps not even returned to you. Not only does this mean fewer professionals will be receiving your photo-resume letter, but also that you will also be wasting your funds.

For example, if you sent out 2,000 photo-resume letters, and 50% were not received, this means 1,000 photo-resume letters may be forever lost. If the cost of each packet is roughly 65¢ (postage, photograph, resume letter, cover letter and envelope), you have wasted over six hundred dollars. Of equal importance, your time in putting together those packets served no benefit. For this reason it is very important to use up-to-date and accurate listings in compiling your mailing list.

Some adoptive parents feel they are better off buying a professionally prepared mailing list. This may be because they don't have the time to search through phone directories, write down selected names and addresses, then write them again on each envelope. Or, they may feel the likelihood of a high failure rate of delivery due to old or incomplete addresses from phone directories will end up costing them substantially more money than the cost of a mailing list.

Mailing lists are available from several companies. For example, the American Medical Association sells mailing lists of physicians. Also, be aware some mailing lists can even be ordered pre-printed on adhesive mailing labels, thus saving you the time of rewriting each individual's name on a thousand or more envelopes. A company which specializes in pre-printed adoption labels (obstetricians, counselors, etc.) is www.adoption101.com, in their "internet bookstore."

Personal Networking

Naturally you want to get all the help you can from the people you know. But don't stop there. Also get help from the people *they* know. This is called *personal networking.*

Like general mail-out networking, the heart of the program is the photo-resume letter. Instead of sending your photo-resume letters to professionals whom you do not know, you will be directing them to people you personally know, even if they do not work in a pregnancy-related field. Usually, a total of 500 photo-resume letters are necessary for an effective personal networking campaign.

Make a list of friends, relatives and acquaintances, such as old neighbors and co-workers, fraternity brothers, sorority sisters and fellow church members. You may want to start with your Christmas/Hanukkah card list. These people do not have to be your best friends, rather those who simply recognize your name and will be glad to hear from you. You would be shocked how excited people get about the idea of helping someone adopt. Everyone wants to be a *matchmaker* and be an unofficial aunt or uncle. Try to compile a list of at least one hundred names.

Send each one of these people five photo-resume letters. In a a cover letter, you will be asking them to help you by sending a copy of the photo-resume letter to people they know who could assist you, such as their family doctor, personal obstetrician, minister, or friends who work in a hospital, etc.

The point of this type of networking is two-fold. One, you are truly driving home the point to your acquaintances regarding your sincere desire to adopt. Secondly, you are taking advantage of their relationships with others whom, but for your *contact*, otherwise may not consider showing your photo-resume letter to their patients or clients.

For example, if you live in Los Angeles and were to send your photo-resume letter to a local physician whom you do not know personally, your photo-resume letter would likely end up at the bottom of a never-opened drawer. Likely the doctor has his own infertile patients to help, or an adoption agency or attorney to whom he refers.

Imagine, however, if this same physician were to receive your photo-resume letter from one of his regular patients, who tells him you are personal friends, and his help would be appreciated. By approaching the physician through someone he knows, you have avoided the likelihood of your photo-resume letter being ignored. This is a good way to network in large metropolitan areas that are otherwise a poor statistical bet.

The Cover Letter

Whether you are doing general or personal networking, you may wish to consider sending a cover letter with each photo-resume letter you send out. A cover letter helps eliminate any confusion about why you are sending someone your photo-resume letter.

It is a very short letter explaining what you are asking them to do. Like the photo-resume letter it can be mass-produced, so there is little extra work involved by including it in your mail-out campaign, and the only cost is a photocopy. If you are using colored paper or special stationary for your photo-resume letter, you may wish to use matching paper for the introductory letter. Generally, a cover letter should mention the following:

- Briefly explain why you are adopting.
- Explain how adoption works so they feel comfortable with the concept (the idea of searching for a birth mother may be new to them). Briefly describe the procedures for the type of adoption you are planning—independent or agency. If you are using the cover letter for personal networking and want the recipient to send out the copies you have provided to them, explain exactly what you want them to do with the photo-resume letters. For this reason you may have two different cover letters, one for general networking and one for personal networking.
- If you have retained an adoption attorney, mention this in the letter so they know you are doing things right. They may not want to get involved if they anticipate problems.
- Hand-sign each cover letter—no photocopied signatures.

A cover letter is a necessity for personal networking, as you are sending photo-resume letters to people who have never before received one and will need specific instructions regarding how to help you. For general networking, a cover letter is advisable, but not critically necessary. This is because most of the individuals or organizations receiving them from you will have received them before and are familiar with why you have sent them. However, considering the minimal effort involved in adding a cover letter to each photo-resume letter, it is usually advisable to include one with every mailing. *Appendix C* provides a sample cover letter.

Starting Your Networking Campaign

No doubt you have been thinking that addressing all those envelopes and licking all those stamps is a lot of work. Here are two suggestions to make it go quickly. If you are going to do the whole job yourself, set a goal of 50 envelopes per night. The job goes pretty quickly when you are watching television or listening to the radio. If you want to involve your friends—and what better way to get them motivated to help you—have an envelope-addressing, resume-signing pizza party. If you invite ten neighbors and friends, and they each do 50, you have 500 in one day for the cost of a few pizzas.

If neither prospect appeals to you, consider ordering preprinted mailing labels as discussed previously. The important thing is not how you compile your mailing list, rather that your list is up-to-date and accurate. Also, it is critical that all your letters be out in the community working for you. Too many adoptive parents mail a dozen letters every weekend, meaning it will take them years to reach the recommended amount. Send out all your letters right away.

ADVERTISING

In many states it is legal for adoptive parents to place a classified advertisement stating their desire to adopt a child, and asking for women with an unplanned pregnancy to call them to discuss adoption. Some states make it illegal to place such an advertisement, and some only permit advertising by licensed adoption agencies. To see which states permit advertising, see the state-by-state review in Chapter Six, then double-check the permissibility with a local attorney to verify the laws have not changed.

For some adoptive parents, the concept of advertising to meet a birth mother is not agreeable philosophically, feeling smacks of "buying a baby." Sondra Neuburger, editor of the respected *ADOPTNET Magazine* (no longer in publication) and herself an adoptee, is critical of adoption advertising. "The entire adoption plan deserves more dignity than to be listed in the classified section of a newspaper," notes Neuburger, "Newspaper ads can easily be the perfect breeding place for deception and exploitation of innocent people . . . The exchange of sacred parental rights needs to be monitored and counselled by professional people."

Others disagree with this assessment of advertising. They point out that adoptive parents who do not have special contacts with individuals who can help them meet a birth mother, or who live in a region where there are few adoption resources, have few options in telling birth mothers about their desire to adopt. Supporters of advertising also note virtually every adoption agency and attorney advertises in the yellow pages of their local telephone directory, and question the philosophical difference between that and placing their own advertisement.

They argue the key to a viable adoption is the sincerity of the relationship between the birth mother and the adoptive parents, not how they came to learn of each other.

Setting aside the philosophical disagreements surrounding advertising, the bottom line for many adoptive parents will be that advertising *can* work—and work quickly at that. For those considering placing an advertisement, perhaps thinking of it as a *newspaper announcement* makes it more palatable. The principal difference between advertising and networking is you are directing your desire to adopt through a mass market medium, rather than to selected organizations and individuals.

Generally, the advertisement is placed in the *personals* or *classified* section of a community newspaper. Some religious faiths have their own publications which may be advantageous for you, especially if you are of a faith not considered "mainstream."

Even if advertising is permitted in a particular state, individual newspapers may have their own requirements prior to accepting an adoption advertisement. Since you will need to contact the newspaper's classified advertising section to inquire about advertising rates anyway, also ask if there are any special requirements to the newspaper accepting your advertisement. Frequently this is a letter from your attorney or agency to establish the adoption will be done correctly.

The advertisements are usually fairly short, as advertising rates can be substantial for some newspapers. Unlike the distribution of your photo-resume letters, where large metropolitan areas should be avoided, this is not as important in advertising. Often, however, small to medium sized towns are most fruitful.

States economically depressed are generally better as there are usually fewer couples seeking to adopt within those states.

Selecting a state close to your home state will reduce travel costs, as you will likely need to travel to meet the birth mother, or her to you. Either way, the birth mother will expect you to pay the travel costs. Many effective states, however, may be far from you, so travel costs are only one small consideration.

Advertisements can vary tremendously, but most have some common elements, as can be seen below:

ADOPTION. Loving childless couple in Calif. hopes to adopt baby. Can help with doctor bills. Call collect (714) 555-1234.

PREGNANT? Loving college-educated white couple unable to have children seeks to adopt white infant. Secure marriage and beautiful home in quiet Michigan town. Can help with pregnancy costs. Legal and confidential. Please call collect (517) 555-1234.

It is advisable to avoid promissory statements in your advertisement. For example, rather than stating "*Will* pay all birth costs," consider using terms like *can* or *may*. Also, be sure the state in which you are advertising has no prohibition against mentioning financial assistance, and that your home state permits financial assistance to birth mothers (discussed in Chapter Five).

It is strongly recommended you use your special adoption telephone line for your advertisement. You are placing yourselves before a large group of people when you place an advertisement. Of course, this is the whole purpose of placing the advertisement. Be aware, however, you may receive a call from someone whose intent is solely to defraud you or make a *crank* call.

For example, a woman who is not even pregnant may call you to try to obtain a free airline ticket to your home town. Requesting the birth mother send you a confirmation of pregnancy signed by a physician is usually advisable, as well as exchanging appropriate information before investing your emotions and money. Another tip which may be helpful is to inquire of the operator the location of the collect call before you accept the charges. This can usually be done if the call is from outside the state in which you live. For example, if you are told the call originates from the state penitentiary, you may wish to not accept the call!

If you have an attorney, he or she can act as a *screener* to make sure everything appears appropriate. It is not unusual for adoptive parents to speak to a dozen women responding to their advertisement before finding someone who is sincere and mature regarding placing their child for adoption. In the following chapter we will discuss techniques to help distinguish a good from a bad adoption.

Although there are disadvantages to advertising, there is one big advantage—it requires little investment of time. Many couples refuse to take the time to mount a complete networking campaign. For such couples, placing an advertisement is their principal strategy of locating a birth mother. Those who elect to advertise usually only place an advertisement in a few selected newspapers for two weeks each.

Likely the newest method of reaching birth mothers is the internet. It has some of the same advantages and disadvantages as newspaper advertising. There are too many websites to list which list waiting adoptive parents' photo resume letters, to be seen by visiting birth mothers (usually for a fee) who find the sites by searching for information about adoption via search engines like Yahoo, Lycos and Google.

FACILITATORS

Adoption *facilitators* are those who are neither attorneys nor licensed adoption agencies, but who assist with adoption planning. Generally, this assistance is centered around efforts to help adoptive parents find a birth mother. A facilitator can be an individual or an organization (usually using a name sounding like an adoption agency). Some facilitators have some training in adoption, such as a counselor, while many have absolutely no training or experience.

There is controversy among many adoption professionals regarding facilitators. Some feel facilitators provide a legitimate service, while many contend their services are unethical as they essentially "find a baby for money." Of course, adoption attorneys and agencies also help adoptive parents locate a birth mother, but that is usually only a small part of their services. Significantly, some states have enacted laws forbidding facilitators from profiting financially for simply finding a baby.

Nevertheless, where permitted, there are ethical facilitators who can provide assistance to adoptive parents. In fact, some offer assistance for no fee, acting solely for the emotional rewards of helping create families through adoption. Often these are individuals with strong religious motivations or pro-life sentiments.

There are also facilitators who have special training, such as adoption counselors, who may charge a reasonable fee for teaching you to prepare a photo-resume letter and effectively network, as well as offering educational seminars regarding adoption issues. Sometimes the fees for their services are several hundred dollars, which is very reasonable.

However, if the facilitator charges very large fees, such as over one thousand dollars, be sure you know exactly how they will earn those funds. They cannot perform the legal functions of an attorney or agency, thus you may end up paying an attorney or agency anyway, thus duplicating your costs. If an adoption attorney or agency can assist you in locating a birth mother, in addition to their other functions, there may be no need to hire a facilitator to perform that same function. An attorney or agency can perform the same function, usually with much greater training and experience.

Some large facilitator organizations may perform many functions and operate much like an adoption agency, but without the legal power to perform home studies, witness a birth mother's written consent to the adoption, place children for adoption etc. One might ask such organizations if they indeed perform these many functions, why do they not obtain the state's licensing as an adoption agency, permitting them to more effectively perform those services?

One of the reasons many adoption professionals criticize facilitators is the small degree of protection for clients. Both attorneys and adoption agencies must be licensed by the state, usually after a background investigation and demonstration of competency. Facilitators, however, normally do not require any special licensing, other than the basic business license easily obtained for a small fee. Typically, there are no educational or training requirements. As a result, there is often no state licensing body "looking over their shoulders" to be sure they are acting competently.

Before hiring a facilitator consider the following questions:

- What exactly can the facilitator do for you, and or what fee?
- What special training does the facilitator have to be sure he or she can render quality service.

- Are the facilitator's fees reasonable in light of the service they can offer and the training to perform that service?
- If the fees are significant, what services can the facilitator offer which a qualified attorney or agency cannot?

If you have found a facilitator you believe can assist you, it is advisable to follow the same guidelines used in determining an adoption attorney's reputation and qualifications, as discussed earlier in this chapter. Unfortunately, it is more difficult to obtain information about facilitators, as they usually have such a small role in the overall adoption process that their names will often not be recognized by adoption professionals having a more significant role.

THE SUMMARY FOR SUCCESS

If you just read this chapter and did not quite absorb the concept of truly *adopting within one year*, let's review the keys to giving you the best chance to success. You don't do one, or two, of the above strategies. *You do virtually all of them!* Halve your efforts and you halve your chances of success. Here is your essential checklist: 1) Hire a qualified adoption attorney or agency, whose services include assisting you in finding a birth mother; 2) do personal networking, where you send your photo-resume letter to at least 100 acquaintances; 3) do general networking, where you purchase at least 2,000 mailing labels (try multiple states) and; 4) choose either an adoption internet site, or newspaper announcements, and pay for exposure to viewers for at least 60 days. Do *all* these things and your changes of adopting within one year are excellent!

CHAPTER THREE

Arranging a Successful Adoption

Finally, the waiting pays off—you learn that a birth mother has expressed an interest in you and wants to meet in person to determine if you are the right adoptive parents for her child. Your initial excitement is likely immediately followed by nervousness. "Will she like us?" "Will we like her?" "What do we say to each other?"

In some adoptions the birth father will be an active participant and the following suggestions apply equally to him. Unfortunately, most birth fathers elect to not actively participate, leaving the birth mother to face the situation alone.

Of course, if you are planning a completely closed adoption with no contact with the birth parents, or if you are adopting an older child, these issues may be of little assistance to you as your agency or attorney will be handling all direct contact with the birth parents. However, because the majority of infant adoptions involve direct prebirth contact between the birth mother and the adoptive parents, most adoptive parents will benefit from this information.

WORKING WITH A BIRTH MOTHER

The most often asked question regarding birth mothers is a simple and basic one: "What are birth mothers like?" This question can perhaps be best answered by reading a true-life account of one such woman, provided by Michael Spry, in his training manual for pregnancy and adoption counselors, *Towards New Ethical Guidelines for Pregnancy Counseling:*

The moment had finally come. For months—even days—before, it had seemed it would never arrive, but now that the seconds were precious, time seemed to be racing beyond her desperate grasp. Thoughts and emotions flooded through her consciousness, resisting all efforts to control them. Fear, anger, and intense pain swirled inside her as she fought against a vague sense of inevitability. It was as if all of the energy in her young life was pushing toward this single focal point that would change the lives of so many people forever.

Why did it have to hurt so badly? For months she had tried to imagine what it would feel like, but there was no way that she could have anticipated the intensity which now swept over her—she had never faced anything in her eighteen years that could have compared with this.

It wasn't supposed to have been this way. Throughout the make-believe of her childhood and the fantasies of adolescence, she had conjured up a romantic vision of marriage and family life. There was always something special about those dreams of bringing her first child into the world, and of raising that child in a home filled with love and prosperity; it would be among the ultimate experiences in her life. She could picture herself rocking that baby to sleep tightly wrapped in her loving arms, of protecting it from all harm, of nurturing her child to a life of happiness and independence. But now she felt those dreams quickly slipping away.

Part of her was so angry—livid at the audacity of the people waiting to take her baby. What makes them think that they had any right to this beautiful child . . . . This was *her* baby—her precious baby girl—and she was her mommy! But just when the anger would become sharp and crystalline, the stark realities which contained this struggle would assert their presence once again. She had *chosen* this couple— because she liked them, because she felt that they would be exceptional parents for her child. She had attended a birth class with them, allowed them to be at the hospital when her daughter was born; she even invited them to name the baby with her—and it was they who had suggested that her first name be the child's middle name.

Oh, how she had fought with the temptation to keep her baby! It seemed strange that she had once been so committed to making an adoption plan for her child. In the last few days she had considered every conceivable option which could allow her to keep her child, and she had discussed them thoroughly with her mother. The prospective adoptive parents had sensed her deep ambivalence, they had, in fact, told her mother that they were prepared to "bow out gracefully," if necessary. But time and time again, she and her mother kept coming back to the same conclusion—that despite all of her intense desires, she was not really prepared to be a mother at this time in her life, that she could not provide the start for her child that she so desperately wanted. This young mother's heart, clinging to the dream, ached beyond her ability to cope, but her mind kept telling her despite her longings to shut the message out—that this moment was indeed inevitable.

At least she would be discharged from the hospital with her baby—she had insisted upon that. Maybe it was one way that she could hang on to at least a small part of the dream. Because of her desire to be discharged with her baby, however, the hospital would not allow her to give the child over to the care of the adoptive parents within the hospital building. Instead, the adoptive parents would leave their vehicle in front of the main entrance, she would place the child carrier with its delicate cargo in the front seat, then walk away without talking to anyone—she couldn't deal with any more of that. It all sounded straightforward enough, but would she really have the strength to get through it?

As the floor nurse wheeled her out of the elevator, her heart quickened with a sudden surge of panic; the main entrance to the hospital—and the moment she dreaded—lay just around the corner. Could she really find the courage to go on with this? Outside the glass doors, she could see the vehicle of her child's new parents, its engine running to create the warmth necessary for protecting her baby. Everything was in place but her emotions; everyone else was as ready as they could be, waiting only for her to act. The expectations of the moment came crashing down upon her; she was caught between the paralysis that made her want to avoid what was ahead, and a paradoxical desire to get it over with . . . . She drew upon all of the inner courage that she could summon, and with her baby in her arms, took the first step toward the door.

She never really felt the chill, or sensed the billowy snow caught by the biting wind as it kissed her cheeks this February morning. All of that paled in the shadow of the pain which consumed her while she resigned herself to the unfolding fate that lay ahead. Each step that she took toward the climactic moment seemed to amplify the emotional intensity that she could not control. By the time that she placed her hand upon the car's door latch, she was already past the point of no return—even the slightest hesitation now might make it impossible to get through this; she could no longer even allow herself to think about what she was doing.

She opened the car door, gently placed the infant carrier that held her baby in the front seat. Then she took one last look—really little more than a glance; she could not risk more than that or her resolve might crumble. She closed her eyes and swallowed, then turned away and shut the car door; and as she did, she could feel the fabric of her emotions tearing apart, creating a void so great that it seemed nothing could ever fill it. When she walked away, she left behind not just her child, but her childhood, her dream—a big part of herself. . . .

She barely noticed the scene taking place in her wake, of two adoptive parents in tears—not the tears of joy, but of empathy and pain. They ached to reach out to her, to offer some modest comfort to the young woman who had entrusted them with her special gift; but they understood her need to simply walk away. Instead they tried to satisfy their longings by embracing the baby's grandmother who expressed the separating words: "Take good care of her, I know that you will." Then they watched as their baby's shattered family drove away.

Michael Spry's chronicling of this young birth mother's feelings is even more compelling when he reveals he and his wife were the adoptive parents, and the young woman described was the birth mother who placed her child with them.

How did reading the story make you feel? Sad? Nervous? Likely, you felt both. It is hard not to empathize with the pain felt by the birth mother. That feeling may be followed, however, by concerns for yourself as a prospective adoptive parent. It is an understandable worry that a birth mother may stop adoption planning in the face of such emotional pain. In reality, however, it is estimated only a very small number of birth mothers will desire to stop an adoption.

Birth mothers deserve tremendous compassion for their situation, and respect for their emotional strength, especially when considering the age at which most birth mothers are required to face life's realities so harshly. It is tragic the media often presents a negative image of birth mothers—with newspapers, television movies and gossipy talk shows sensationalizing the rare failed adoption, and ignoring the vast majority in which loving families are successfully created.

Understanding a birth mother's perspective of adoption, and her personal emotional needs, is essential to a successful adoption. Although this book shall touch upon some of those issues, there are other books examining the birth mother's role in adoption as their principal focus. Two books virtually considered "required reading" for prospective adoptive parents are *Adoption Without Fear* and *Dear Birthmother*, both discussed later in this book. They should be read *before* even starting an adoption, not later in the process. Visit your local or online bookstore.

Many birth mothers will be advised to read one or both of these particular books by their adoption counselor or attorney. Besides the benefits to you in reading these books, imagine how impressed a birth mother would be if she meets adoptive parents who cared enough to have fully educated themselves by having already read the book she is now reading. Remember, the person who will benefit from a greater understanding of birth mothers is *you*. When you eventually receive a call from a birth mother who has seen your photo-resume letter, or are informed by your adoption attorney or agency that a birth mother wishes to meet with you, you want to be emotionally and intellectually prepared for that very important moment.

Handling a Birth Mother's Initial Call

When your networking campaign pays off, you will be rewarded with a phone call from a birth mother who saw your photo-resume letter or newspaper advertisement. You have been waiting for this moment—so how do you make the most of it? Most importantly, remember she is a person—in many ways no different than you—and likely very nervous about calling you. So relax. In fact, to help yourself relax, it is helpful to have some simple questions outlined next to your phone awaiting the eventual call. Here are some basic suggestions for receiving the initial call:

1. Help her feel at ease by giving her some information about you, rather than starting off with a barrage of questions making her feel she is being cross-examined. You may want to ask her if she has any particular questions about you. Let her know how nice it is to receive her call and how much adoption means to you.
2. Ask about *her*, not just her baby.
3. Some particular initial questions to consider asking are: When is the baby due? How is she feeling? Has she seen a doctor? Where does she live? Does she work? Go to school?

How old is she? Does her family know about the pregnancy and adoption plans? Do they support her decision? Is she married? What are the birth father's feelings? Is this her first child? Why is she considering adoption?

4. Sometimes it can be awkward asking about the ethnicity of a child. However, you might try something similar to "I do not know if you want your child to be raised by someone who has the same general appearance as you. I am white and my husband is hispanic. What about you and the baby's father?" This is a gentler approach than asking "What color are you?" Avoid using the word *caucasian* as some young people will not know what it means. Simply say *white*.

5. Ask for her telephone number so you can get in touch in the future.

6. Tell her you have an attorney or agency who can explain the laws surrounding adoption. Ask if she would prefer to call the attorney or agency or have them call her.

7. Make sure you establish what will happen next. Does she want to think about you and call you back the next day? Does she want you to call her? Does she want to arrange to meet you in person? If so, where and when?

8. Most importantly, do not pressure her. Give her the room she needs to be sure adoption is her best option.

Remember, this is only your initial conversation with the birth mother. Whether you speak by phone or meet in person, you will continue to learn about her, as will she about you. If you have an attorney or agency, they will likely arrange to speak with the birth mother soon after her call, not only to explain adoption laws and procedures she is entitled to know, but also to give you the benefit of his or her opinion whether the adoption appears to be a solid one.

Meeting a Birth Mother in Person

If everything appears appropriate from your initial contact and the birth mother lives in your vicinity, likely you will arrange to meet her with no delay. This will allow you to have the benefits of a face-to-face meeting, as well as learn more about her and her expected baby. If she lives far away or out of your state, and a meeting involves travel expenses, you will want to be extra thorough and get more information, as will be discussed within this chapter.

Some birth mothers seek to maintain a large degree of privacy and do not wish to have more than one or two meetings with you. The majority, however, prefer to become well acquainted with you and have several opportunities to get to know you before the birth. Often, low pressure activities such as meeting for dinner, shopping for maternity clothes, going to a movie together, or similar outings will be planned. Spending all your time with the birth mother sitting across a conference table from you can be intimidating and impersonal. Of course, it is not required that you get well acquainted with the birth mother. Generally, however, most birth mothers will want to get to know you, and you will want to get to know whose child you are adopting. There are benefits to everyone in becoming well acquainted before the birth.

From the birth mother's perspective, she can only have the utmost confidence in her decision to place the child for adoption, if she feels she *truly knows you*. If you can imagine yourself in a situation where you had to place your child for adoption, you can likely imagine the insecurity of placing your baby with virtual strangers. However, truly knowing you— having earned her affection and respect—allows her to make the placement with greater confidence and peace of mind. She will also have great joy in creating a family for you, likely the greatest thing she has ever done for another person. Unless she has come to know you as friends, that joy is often unfocused.

There are also great benefits to you in becoming well acquainted with the birth mother. The insecurities every adoptive parent feels approaching the birth will usually be dramatically lessened when you know you are working with someone who you have come to recognize as a friend.

The biggest beneficiary, however, is the child. It is crucial for an adopted child, when dealing with the issue of adoption, to know he or she was not abandoned or unwanted, rather placed with you as a loving and careful decision by his or her birth mother. This is much more easily understood if he or she can be told about how you got to know each other before making this decision.

You might even want pictures of you and the birth mother together from an outing, or at the hospital, to keep as memories of that special time together. Many adoptive parents ask the birth mother to prepare an album about herself and her family to one day share with the child. This will not only mean a lot to the child to have this healthy understanding of adoption and how he or she came to be in your home, but will also mean a lot to the birth mother to see you honestly care enough to want this information about her for the child.

Some adoptive parents worry that building a close relationship with the birth mother can backfire. You might worry she will mourn the loss of your friendship when you "part ways" after the adoption is finalized. As a general rule, however, birth mothers move on in their lives, as do you in yours. Your closeness was usually a necessity based upon the emotions and mutual needs surrounding the approaching birth. You needed her—she needed you—and the child needed all of you. Later in this chapter the range of post-birth relationships between birth mothers and adoptive parents will be discussed.

Key Issues to Explore

Adoption is a two-way street. Not only is a birth mother deciding if you are the adoptive parents she will select, but you are deciding if she is right for you. Never feel that as adoptive parents you are powerless in the adoption process. You are as entitled to ask questions about a birth mother as she is to ask questions about you.

There are several critical issues to examine when determining the likely success of an adoption, and whether a particular birth mother is emotionally ready and sincere regarding adoption planning. Although the vast majority of birth mothers are very sincere in their interest in adoption, there are a small number who have improper or illegal motivations, thus must be avoided.

Spotting potential problems, or *red flags*, is an important part of planning a trouble-free adoption. Hopefully, you have retained an adoption attorney or agency experienced in making such determinations to assist you in electing whether or not to go forward with a particular birth mother. There are many distinct issues to examine.

The Birth Mother's Due Date. Ideally, you will be contacted by a birth mother in the last few months of her pregnancy. Starting adoption planning too soon in the pregnancy can be risky, as some birth mothers will not have sufficiently come to terms with their pregnancy. This is not to say you should ignore a birth mother who contacts you early in her pregnancy. Rather, it is perhaps appropriate to talk to her and let her know more about you and your desires to adopt, but tell her you feel she should wait until she is later in the pregnancy to make up her mind about pursuing adoption. This is for everyone's benefit and likely she will appreciate your "go slow" approach.

Personal Motivations. There are many good reasons why women turn to adoption. Many birth mothers will mention they are not ready to be a mother, perhaps just starting their education or careers. A relationship with the birth father not expected to result in marriage is often cited, as the birth mother does not wish to be a single parent. Economic hardship is a very real factor, as some women can barely support themselves, not to mention providing the lifestyle and opportunities they want their child to enjoy.

There are also some risky reasons for starting adoption planning. If a birth mother is placing her child for adoption solely to satisfy an angry parent, or to please a boyfriend who does not wish to raise the child, it can be very risky. In such situations she may be suppressing her own desires to raise the child herself in an effort to please others.

Financial Assistance. Approximately fifty percent of birth mothers need some financial assistance during the pregnancy. Financial assistance by adopting parents is legal in almost all states as long as is it pregnancy-related. Often such assistance is to help with medical costs, and in some cases basic food and rent expenses in the latter stages of the pregnancy when she is unable to work.

Many birth mothers will need no financial assistance. They may have adequate employment or live at home with their parents or a boyfriend, thus require no supplemental assistance. Others may have financial problems, but are too proud to accept assistance.

If a birth mother is seeking to greatly enhance her lifestyle to an unreasonably high level at your expense, or request funds for items not related to her basic needs, it may be her motivations regarding adoption are primarily financial. These situations are often a poor risk, as well as bordering on illegality due to the financial assistance not being related to the birth.

Health History. Depending upon the policies of the attorney or agency with whom you are working, the birth parents will almost always be asked to provide a complete health history for themselves and their extended families. This allows you to be fully informed and to share this information with your child's medical providers. You will probably want this information well before the birth, so do not hesitate to request such information. This is a routine inquiry made by adoption attorneys and agencies in most cases. If you are not working with an attorney or agency, however, it will be your responsibility.

The birth mother is usually also asked to sign a *Release of Information* form allowing her physician and the hospital to release medical information surrounding the pregnancy, permitting you to stay fully up to date regarding all medical care. Of course, many adoptive parents accompany the birth mother to her physician appointments at the birth mother's request, so remain informed in that manner.

Opinions of Family and Friends. Although a birth mother's parents and friends generally have no legal right to object to an adoption, they can put emotional pressure upon a birth mother to raise the child herself if they are opposed to adoption.

Interestingly, even a birth mother under the age of eighteen can place her child for adoption without the consent of her parents in virtually all states. The real power of a birth mother's family and friends is not based upon any legal right, however, rather their emotional connection to her.

Usually a birth mother's mother and father are the most influential people in her life, especially if she still lives with them. Accordingly, the younger the birth mother, the more likely she is to be swayed by them. Of course, there is usually at least one particular friend or relative who is against adoption planning. This is usually not a grave concern, as long as there are others supporting the decision.

Counseling. Although some states require that a birth mother be offered counseling before placing a child for adoption, it is normally not required that she actually receive it. In other words, it must be made available to her but she can decline it. Regardless, counseling is often one of the most essential elements of a successful adoption. The goal of counseling should be two-fold. Initially, the counselor should help the birth mother decide for herself if adoption is the best option for her and her child. Secondly, the counselor should prepare the birth mother for the emotions surrounding the birth, and placing the child for adoption.

Many birth mothers feel counseling is unnecessary, stating: "I am sure adoption is what I want to do . . . I don't need counseling." However, no one can anticipate the unexpected emotions that surround giving birth and placing a child for adoption. Counseling prepares her for emotions she does not even know she will be experiencing.

Selecting an adoption counselor is a very important decision. It is essential to find someone neutral, not pressuring the birth mother toward, or away, from adoption. Usually, local adoptive parent groups, adoption education organizations, your attorney, local agencies and other organizations working in the adoption field know where to locate a reputable counselor. If you are planning an agency adoption, your agency likely has staff counselors available.

Counseling is not only for birth mothers. Adoptive parents should also consider meeting with a counselor. Not only does this allow you to discuss your personal emotions surrounding the adoption, but it demonstrates to the birth mother that counseling is indeed so important you are doing it as well.

Oftentimes, after an individual meeting or two with the counselor, it is helpful for the birth mother and adoptive parents to meet jointly with the counselor to work out little details better discussed before the birth. For example, how much contact does she wish to have with you at the hospital? Does she wish to spend time together with both you and the child in her room, or would she prefer private time with the baby? What will your post-birth relationship be like?

Be cautious of anyone who encourages you to not offer counseling to the birth mother, perhaps stating "you are only asking for trouble." Usually these are adoption professionals who either have low ethics, or are simply ignorant. It is true that occasionally a birth mother will go to counseling and immediately stop adoption planning. Actually, this should be seen as a good occurrence. Isn't it better to learn right from the beginning she was not ready for adoption planning—before you have invested your emotions, time and money—than after the adoptive placement when a failed adoption may be truly devastating?

Does She Know Her Options? It is essential for a birth mother to know all her options, in addition to adoption, before committing herself. Not only is providing this information the ethical thing to do, but the practical one as well. Even if you were to not explain certain options she has, she will learn of them later from someone else, whether it be the adoption caseworker or a friend. As was discussed earlier regarding counseling, there is no sense starting an adoption based upon a weak foundation and destined to fail.

The birth mother needs to know she has other options to adoption. She can apply for welfare and obtain some financial assistance in that way. She can investigate temporary foster care programs allowing her to leave the child in another's care until she is sure about what she wants to do. She can talk to her relatives to see if the child would be best suited by being raised by a member of the family. Although it is rare for a birth mother to decide against adoption for one of these reasons, as most have already considered and rejected them, your concern for her welfare will be appreciated by her.

Her Age. Successful adoptions can be completed regardless of the birth mother's age. Be aware, however, when a birth mother is very young, particularly in the 13 to 17 year old age group, she may be less prepared for the emotional burden she will face at the time of the birth. An older woman may be more experienced in life's realities and the difficulties of raising a child under adverse circumstances. For these reasons, counseling and a strong support group of friends and/or relatives are especially important for very young birth mothers.

The Feelings of the Birth Father. Unfortunately, the majority of birth fathers elect to take no, or only a very small, role in adoption planning. For that reason alone, most of the comments within this book are addressed to birth mothers. This does not mean birth fathers have no role in adoption. To the contrary, the birth father represents one-half of the child's biological heritage, and his input should be encouraged. Adopted children will be just as curious about their biological father as they are their biological mother when reaching the point in life when such issues are explored and addressed. For these reasons, virtually every suggestion made within this book regarding birth mothers is equally applicable to a birth father if he wishes to become involved. Fortunately, some birth fathers share the birth mother's interest in personally selecting and meeting the adoptive parents.

In many cases, however, the father makes it known he does not wish to become involved in adoption planning, or the birth mother does not know enough about him to locate him. Many birth fathers fear obligations for child support resulting from making an admission of paternity.

If the birth father is strongly opposed to the adoption, the adoptive parents should consider stopping adoption planning, although many factors go into such a decision. Each state has different laws affecting the rights, or lack thereof, of birth fathers (discussed in Chapter Five). Fortunately, virtually all birth fathers not married to the birth mother make no objection to adoption planning. Treating the birth father as a valuable part of the process, rather than an adversary or inconsequential person, can go a long way to earning his respect and cooperation. Also, be aware a birth father will have his own emotional issues to address. Counseling should be made as available to birth fathers as to birth mothers.

Medical Costs. In addition to possible living expenses, the other major area of birth-related assistance which may need to be provided to a birth mother is medical costs surrounding the birth. This involves the cost of the physician (usually an obstetrician) in providing prenatal care and delivery of the baby, and charges associated with the services of the hospital (the delivery room, nursery costs, lab costs, and other physicians occasionally required if a caesarean section birth occurs).

You will want to estimate these expenses before starting adoption planning to be sure a proposed adoption fits within your budget. Fortunately, some birth mothers have medical insurance, either from their parents' insurance policy, or from their own employment. If they have no insurance, it leaves a potentially large medical bill the adoptive parents will be expected to pay (unless you are working with one of the very few agencies which includes such costs in their set fee).

Unfortunately, the adoptive parents' insurance policy will not cover the birth mother's birth costs, except with a few rare policies. The adoptive parents can eliminate or reduce the medical bills, even without health insurance, by asking the birth mother to apply for her state's Medicaid program. Virtually every state has a Medicaid (or a similarly titled program) where state residents of low economic status and unable to pay for medical care can obtain free medical care. Because the child being born is legally still the birth mother's child at birth, eligibility for Medicaid is usually based solely upon her income, not that of the adoptive parents. Each state, however, will have their own rules of eligibility.

One drawback to Medicaid, however, is the accessibility of doctors and hospitals, as not all physicians and hospitals accept a state's Medicaid program. This is because most state's Medicaid programs have a set fee structure which is less than most physicians and hospitals charge. Some physicians and hospitals refuse to take this lesser fee.

Post-Birth Contact with the Birth Mother

Just as the flexibility of modern adoption allows you and the birth mother to elect the amount of contact prior to the birth, the same is true after the birth and finalization of the adoption. Once the adoption is finalized by the court, your adopted child will be legally yours, and you are in every way the only legal parent the child has. Regardless, you will want to honor any promises you made with the birth parents regarding post-birth contact. Deciding what kind of post-birth relationship is desired by you and the birth mother should be explored *before* the birth, not delayed until after the birth or the end of the adoption process.

Although many adoptions involve little or no contact between birth and adoptive parents, an increasing number of modern-day adoptions have arrangements where the adoptive parents send the birth mother pictures of the child and an updating letter once or twice a year. Of course, in some cases the birth mother wishes no further contact with the adoptive parents or the child, while in others arrangements are made to schedule personal get-togethers with the adoptive parents and the child on an occasional basis. This latter type of adoption is called *cooperative* adoption.

Cooperative *adoption* should not be confused with cooperative *parenting*. Cooperative adoption is an acknowledgment the child will benefit from the greatest possible understanding regarding how he or she came into existence, and remove any mystery surrounding the adoption.

Cooperative adoption is not for everyone, and it requires a solid relationship between birth and adoptive parents. As more and more mental health experts speak in favor of it, however, it is growing in acceptance and popularity. Where ten years ago perhaps one or two percent were cooperative adoptions, at present approximately five to ten percent are now being arranged in this manner. Sharon Kaplan-Roszia, coauthor of *The Open Adoption Experience,* the definitive book on the subject, explains cooperative adoptions as follows:

Sadly, many adoptive parents are fearful of the concept of cooperative adoption, perhaps mistakenly thinking it will somehow weaken their position as parents. What cooperative adoption does is recognize the child as the center of the adoption—and the most important person's interests to protect. The concept of cooperative adoption may be used by each participant differently. It adds options and extends family relationships, rather than eliminate them. It is knowing that children all come into this life whole, with all their rights and relationships intact, with the understanding that no one has the right to interrupt those rights or deprive a child of them.

Too often in the past, birth families and adoptive families were considered to have antagonistic interests. Somehow the fact that they were all human beings with a child's interests at heart got lost. It doesn't matter how this happened and there is no blame. What matters now is that adoption *adds options* to the child's life and to the lives of all relatives. An ideal adoption is one that expands the child's life experiences, not subtracts them.

Secrecy and loss have made traditional adoptions difficult. Cooperative adoption is a positive option, a chance for everyone to celebrate, and a chance for everyone to gain. Just as divorce once left its participants unable to relate, so has adoption. Just as divorce has moved in possibilities from adversary to cooperative, so can adoption.

In defining the limits of an open post-birth relationship some birth and adoptive parents have their attorney draft a "contract" setting forth mutual promises regarding sending photographs, future contact, etc. A handful of states have begun to find these agreements enforceable, while others tend to view them as "gentleman's agreements," with questionable enforceability.

■ ■ ■ ■ ■

As can be seen in this chapter, there are many elements to a successful adoption. In general, however, the most critical elements to a smooth and happy adoption are:

1. *Be honest with the birth mother.* She deserves it—she is entrusting you with her child. Do not pretend to be something you are not in an effort to please her. The right birth mother is out there for you. There is no need to diminish yourself by pretending to be what you are not. You deserve better and so does she.

2. *Do not be afraid.* You are an equal participant in the adoption. Do not be afraid to ask questions or to express your feelings. If something feels wrong, talk about it. If the birth mother is upset by your questions or feelings, perhaps you have not found the right birth mother.

3. *Find a qualified adoption attorney or licensed agency whose philosophy matches your own regarding how adoptions should be done.* There are many legal and procedural pitfalls awaiting you. The right adoption attorney or agency can make all the difference to you and the birth mother in making the many stages of the adoption a smooth one—from your efforts to find a birth mother, pre-birth planning, hospital arrangements, medical care, working with social services during the home study and finally going to court.

4. *Work with an adoption counselor.* Counseling is essential for all the participants to an adoption, but particularly the birth mother. It can help spot a little problem before it becomes a big one. It will help the birth mother with the most emotional moment of her life—saying "goodby" to her baby in the hospital. Besides the benefits to you in helping to make sure the adoption is a successful one, it can also help the birth mother view the adoption with the pride she deserves as she looks back on the moment.

5. *Read available adoption literature.* Often adoptive parents will not hesitate to spend thousands of dollars for adoption fees and expenses, but will hesitate to spend a small fraction of that amount for tremendously helpful books on adoption. It seems incongruous for the average couple to have four or five cookbooks gathering dust in the kitchen, but feel thorough reading on adoption is unnecessary.

There are a select number of books considered *essential* for planning a successful adoption. Some of these books are mentioned and quoted throughout this book, but there are many, many more excellent books. You may wish to see the extensive online selections at amazon.com, barnesandnoble.com or adoption101.com to see more.

CHAPTER FOUR

What Happens at the Hospital

For those adopting a newborn in an adoption in which there is some degree of openness, the hospital arrangements are of great importance. Not only are you dealing with the standard health and medical issues of any birth experience, but you will also be facing the critical emotions arising at the birth of the child for both you and the birth family. By arranging a few key elements in advance, the hospital experience can be greatly enhanced for everyone.

If you are planning to adopt an older child, or do an international adoption, you will normally not need to be involved in hospital planning. This is also true to a lessor extent if you are planning to adopt a newborn in completely closed adoption, where there is no contact with the birth mother. Instead your adoption agency or attorney will be making the necessary arrangements. Even if the arrangements are being handled by others, however, there are many instances where the adoptive parents know they will be responsible for the costs of the birth mother's hospitalizations. Accordingly, the information within this chapter regarding reducing or eliminating medical and hospital costs may be extremely valuable even for those planning a closed adoption.

If you are among the majority of adoptive parents planning to adopt through independent adoption, or a private agency which encourages pre-birth contact between the adoptive parents and the birth mother and the child, the hospital arrangements will be very important to you. Accordingly, this chapter is written for those who plan to be involved in hospital planning to some degree.

WHAT TO DO BEFORE THE BIRTH

There are many decisions for you and the birth mother to make regarding the hospital. Not only do you need to select a particular hospital, but also determine how to make things go as smoothly as possible while you are there. Since the adoptive birth is in many ways a shared experience, these should be decisions you and the birth mother make together, although deference should always be given to the birth mother's feelings as it is she who is giving birth.

Some large communities will have several hospitals from which to choose. Be aware, however, most physicians only deliver at one or two specific hospitals based upon their *delivery privileges*. If the hospital is of importance to you, do not forget to ask any obstetricians you may select which hospitals they use.

Since the procedures and personalities of each hospital staff differ, it is a good idea to visit the hospitals you are considering well in advance of the birth. This is especially true for adoptive births, as some hospitals seem to go out of their way to make everyone feel comfortable in such a special situation, while others treat adoptions as an unwelcome complication to their regular routines.

Most hospitals are willing to give you a brief tour of the facilities. Ask if you can see a hospital room similar to the one the birth mother will be given, as well as a labor and delivery room (where the birth will actually occur). Most rooms have two beds, as private rooms are rare. Often, however, the two-bed rooms end up being the same as a private room, as hospitals usually only put one person in each room, unless they are unusually crowded.

The difference in cost between a two-bed room and a private room is tremendous. Unless the birth mother has strong feelings about being guaranteed a private room, you can reduce your expenditures by booking a standard two-bed room. In most cases the birth mother will have the room all to herself.

Visiting the hospital and meeting key personnel like the staff social worker and/or obstetric staff has many advantages. Seeing the facilities will help everyone feel more comfortable when the time comes to give birth. This is especially true for the birth mother, who will be having her own anxieties about the birth experience itself. Meeting hospital personnel will also allow you to see if they exhibit any apparent biases against adoption. Naturally you would want to consider avoiding a hospital if you perceive negative perceptions about adoption.

You may also wish to ask about any special hospital policies regarding the labor and delivery room. For example, some hospitals will not allow anyone in the labor and delivery room unless they have taken a class on birthing procedures, usually offered at the hospital. This is to reduce the chance the designated labor coach will faint during the birth, giving the hospital two patients instead of one.

Hospitals may limit the number of friends or labor coaches in the labor room to one or two people at one time. Discuss this in advance in case it conflicts with the way you and your birth mother have planned the birth. This policy may be waived by the hospital, as they often understand the special dynamics involved in adoption.

Costs are often an additional factor of importance when selecting a hospital. If your birth mother has insurance, or that state's version of Medicaid (for state citizens of low income), this may not be a major issue. However, if she does not have insurance or Medicaid, it is wise to inquire about hospital fees in advance. Many hospitals have *pre-pay discounts*. These allow patients without insurance to pay a reduced fee if they pay in full by a particular time, usually either before the birth or discharge from the hospital. Often these discounts are substantial, even as high as fifty percent.

Once you and the birth mother have selected a hospital, there are still some decisions to be made. A birth mother can request to be given a room *on* or *off* the maternity ward. Many birth mothers prefer to have a room off the maternity ward so they are not with other mothers who will be bringing their babies home. A birth mother who has a room *off* the maternity ward is still normally allowed to visit with her child as much as she would like, but some hospitals will require her to go to the nursery, rather than having the baby brought to her room if it is too far from the maternity ward.

If the birth mother elects to have a room *on* the maternity ward, she can usually have the child in her room as much as she wishes. The drawback is she may end up sharing her room with a mother who is keeping her child, creating unnecessary emotional hardship for herself. Encourage the birth mother to talk to her counselor about the issue to determine how she will be most comfortable.

Once these decisions have been made, request preregistration forms from the hospital Admissions Department. Having these forms out of the way will allow you and the birth mother to concentrate on each other and the birth when checking into the hospital, rather than filling out forms.

Medical Issues and Potential Costs for the Baby

Medical care for the baby is always an important issue. Fortunately, it is not as financially worrisome as was the case several years ago. Many states have newly-enacted laws regarding health insurance coverage for children being adopted. Although in some states insurance coverage for the child cannot be obtained by the adoptive parents until the child is legally adopted, or until they have legal custody by court order, many other states require insurance carriers to extend the adoptive parent's coverage to the adopted child from the moment the adoptive parents have *physical custody* of the child, or the child is born.

It is recommended you telephone your health insurance carrier well in advance of the birth to be sure you can rely upon coverage, as there can always be rare exceptions. If your insurance company tells you coverage cannot be obtained when you obtain physical custody, stating you must wait until the child is legally adopted, contact your adoption attorney or agency for help. Often, insurance companies are not trying to be deceitful. The clerks who answer such calls may simply not be knowledgeable regarding little-known parts of their state's insurance laws concerning adoption.

There may be some charges for the baby's care at the hospital (usually termed *well-baby* nursery care) that preceded the adoptive parent's physical custody, thus there may be no insurance coverage even if your state allows coverage from the time of physical custody. Fortunately, these charges are usually no more than several hundred dollars per day. Should there be serious medical problems for the child at birth, before the adoptive parent's health insurance applies, there may be alternative protection. Just as a birth mother can be eligible for Medicaid, so can a baby. In fact, if an unforeseen medical problem arises, Medicaid can often be applied for on behalf of the baby by the birth mother after the birth, and have it apply retroactively.

Discussing potential medical problems for the baby brings to mind the issue of the adoptive parents' obligations should an unforeseen severe medical problem develop for the child. Can they decline to adopt the child? The answer is "yes."

Although much is made of the fact a birth mother can change her mind in the early stages of the adoption, this same right is rarely discussed regarding adoptive parents. Actually, the adoptive parents generally have the right to stop the adoption anytime prior to the granting of the adoption by the judge. Of course, it is very rare for adoptive parents to elect to stop adoption planning, even when there is a severe medical problem. Usually, the adoptive parents have looked upon the child as their own from the moment they were selected by the birth mother, even though the child was not yet born. They could no more emotionally walk away from the child than they could if it were their own biological child.

Hospital Notification

Your attorney or agency will normally notify the hospital of adoption planning before the birth by letter. This notification is particularly important if you are planning an open adoption as you will likely be visiting the birth mother and the baby, and the hospital will want to know your identity and right to be present.

It is advisable for you to keep a copy of your attorney or agency's hospital notification identifying you at all times as a means of introduction. The birth mother may go into labor late at night, and the letter may be locked away in the file cabinet of an off-duty hospital staffer. Having your letter handy establishes the appropriateness of your presence.

YOUR ROLE AT THE TIME OF BIRTH

Some adoptive parents and birth mothers become so comfortable with each other before the birth it is decided the adoptive mother, perhaps even the adoptive father as well, will act as the birth mother's labor coach and be present during the birth. It is important, however, for the decision to be solely that of the birth mother, as giving birth is not only an intensely personal moment, but a physically painful one as well. Accordingly, adoptive parents should not feel insulted if they are not asked to be the labor coaches.

Once the child is born, it is unfortunately easy for some adoptive parents to temporarily forget about the birth mother, due to their excitement of seeing and holding the baby. Of course, some birth mothers want little or no contact with the adoptive parents and the child in the hospital. Most birth mothers, however, enjoy the company of the adoptive parents during their hospital stay, and this is a special time to share.

Many birth mothers have the unspoken fear the adoptive parents will not love the child as their own child. Your actions and obvious emotions towards the child will go further in negating that fear than can any words. Also, many adopted children report one of their most prized possessions is a picture of the birth mother and adoptive parents together in the hospital, holding him or her as a newborn infant, making the child's life together.

WHAT HAPPENS AFTER THE BIRTH

Most hospitals will allow the adoptive parents unlimited contact with the child. You are normally allowed to see, hold and feed the child in the nursery, or with the birth mother in her room, depending upon what all of you desire. Remember, however, the birth mother and the baby are the patients of the hospital, not the adoptive parents. Accordingly, the hospital's duty is to them. Be aware of this fact and let the hospital staff know you appreciate their assistance.

Also, remember the birth mother is still the legal parent at this stage of the adoption and only she can authorize any medical procedures regarding the child during the hospitalization, or in some cases until she signs her official consent to the adoption (done while she is still in the hospital in some states). This means a circumcision, if desired during the baby's initial hospitalization, usually needs to be officially authorized by the birth mother. As a practical matter, she will most likely defer such decisions to the adoptive parents. Officially, however, she is the decision-maker.

Although it is understandable adoptive parents would like to spend every available moment with their future child, they must have compassion for the birth mother's desires to be with the child to whom she has just given birth. Try to be happy and supportive of the limited time she has with the baby before her discharge from the hospital, and be respectful for what she is going through.

Many birth mothers report great depression in leaving the hospital without the child to whom they have just given birth. Counselors have referred to this emotion as the *empty-armed syndrome*. They note many birth mothers report their arms literally ache when they think of the child they are not holding.

Although it may seem insignificant in comparison to what the birth mother has just given to you, many birth mothers comment it was helpful to have something—anything—to carry out of the hospital, often a personal gift from the adoptive parents. A few items some birth mothers have said they have enjoyed receiving are a locket with the birth mother and the adoptive parents' picture inside, a photo album filled with pictures of the times the birth mother and adoptive parents shared, or simply a nice bathrobe for her hospital stay. As long as the value of the gift is not excessive, it is normally not considered a violation of the laws surrounding payment of pregnancy-related expenses.

Before the baby is be discharged, the hospital pediatrician will examine the baby and authorize the child's release. Some hospitals have pediatricians on staff who are automatically assigned to examine the baby and give medical authorization for his or her discharge from the hospital. Some hospitals will require you to select your own pediatrician and arrange for them to visit the hospital and examine the baby.

The manner in which the baby is discharged to the adoptive parents varies from state to state. Even within the same state individual hospitals may employ different policies.

In an independent adoption, normally the child is released directly from the hospital to the adoptive parents when discharged by the doctor, often at two days of age, with the birth mother's written permission. Other hospitals will only discharge the baby to an attorney, who in turn places the baby in the care of the adoptive parents. Hospitals within a few states are more formal and require a court order granting custody of the baby to the adoptive parents.

Usually in an agency adoption, the agency has the legal right to make any placement it feels is appropriate after the birth mother has relinquished her rights. This may be to the planned adoptive parents or into a temporary foster home.

The final concern for adoptive parents in the hospital is the baby's birth certificate. Fortunately, this is one function requiring no action by the adoptive parents. The hospital will normally have the birth mother sign a birth certificate before her discharge as part of the hospital's normal procedures. Do not worry if she selects a name for the baby different from the name you have chosen. Your Petition for Adoption will state how you wish to name the child, and a new birth certificate will be issued accordingly after the adoption is approved by the court, replacing the original birth certificate.

CHAPTER FIVE

The Legal Issues in Adoption: Step-by-Step

The easiest way to understand how an adoption works is to approach the entire process in chronological order, as would any adoptive parent who is actually going through an adoption. By understanding how the whole process works before you even start your adoption, you will be able to better analyze your likelihood of success. You can make an informed decision about whether or not there may be a legal problem with your planned adoption, and if so, if it will be a difficult one to overcome.

Be aware, however, this chapter is not written to take the place of retaining an attorney, as obtaining legal advice is essential and is your best protection against an unforeseen problem. Just as you would not consider reading a book on medical care and then acting as your baby's pediatrician, you should not be without the guidance of a skilled attorney or licensed agency.

THE PETITION FOR ADOPTION

The legal document which starts the adoption process in court is the *Petition for Adoption*. The Petition for Adoption is your request for the court to grant the adoption. Each state requires specific information to be provided within the Petition in for the court to accept it. Generally, it identifies the birth and adoptive parents, the child to be adopted, and in fancy legal language lawyers are paid to use, asks the court to grant the adoption when the necessary requirements have been met (signing of consents, completion of the home study etc.).

Preparing the *Petition for Adoption* is only the start of the process, however, and the first of many legal documents. Adopting parents are encouraged not to assume they can handle the adoption without an attorney simply because this initial document may be easy to prepare. It is the equivalent to a mechanic opening the hood of a car to start the necessary work and repairs. Opening the hood is easy. The potential complications that follow are where full knowledge is necessary.

Filing the Petition for Adoption

Once the Petition for Adoption is prepared it must be filed with the court. Most states only permit the Petition for Adoption to be filed in the state and county where the adoptive parents reside, regardless where the birth mother or birth father live or where the child was born.

122

A few states are more flexible and allow the Petition for Adoption to be filed where the baby is born, even if the adoptive parents reside in another state (see page 41). This may allow adoptive parents residing in a state where independent adoption is not permitted to complete an independent adoption in another state. Even if independent adoption is permitted in the adoptive parent's home state, they may elect to complete the adoption in the state where the baby was born if that state's laws and procedures are more to their advantage than those of their home state. This is an option for those adopting through an agency as well (see Chapter 1).

If there is a choice regarding in which of two possible states to file the Petition for Adoption, the relative advantages of each state should be weighed. This is because generally the entire adoption will take place under the jurisdiction of the court where the Petition for Adoption is filed and following that state and county's laws and procedures.

Most states allow the Petition for Adoption to be filed immediately after the child's birth, or after the placement of the child with the adoptive parents if it is an older child is being adopted. A few states do not permit the Petition to be filed until other documents are filed with the court. These documents may include the minor's birth certificate and the birth parents' written consents to the adoption.

When the Petition for Adoption is filed with the court a case number will be assigned to the case and all further documents pertaining to the adoption will bear the same case number. Unlike other types of legal cases, adoption files are kept confidential, so only the court and the parties to the adoption are permitted to see the contents of the file.

THE ROLE OF SOCIAL SERVICES

After the baby is born a copy of the filed Petition for Adoption is usually provided to the individual or agency assigned to conduct your home study and verify the facts alleged in the Petition for Adoption. Also, one or more interviews will be arranged so the child can be observed in the adoptive parent's home to be sure he or she is being well cared for and the environment is appropriate.

If you are planning an agency adoption, or live in a state where a pre-birth home study is required for an independent adoption, the post-birth home study will mainly consist of making sure the baby is being well cared for in your home, as your backgrounds will have already been investigated before the child was placed with you. If you are planning an independent adoption and live in a state where adoptive parents are not required to complete a home study before a child is placed in the adoptive home, the investigation into your backgrounds will occur concurrently with monitoring the child's care. The elements of independent and agency home studies are discussed in Chapter One.

THE BIRTH MOTHER'S
CONSENT TO THE ADOPTION

The birth mother's written consent to the adoption, usually called either a *Consent to Adoption, Surrender, or Relinquishment,* is one of the most important elements of any adoption. Each state has different regulations concerning how soon after the birth the consent may be signed, and who must witness the birth mother's signature. These regulations regarding when, and before whom, the consent may be signed are designed to be sure the birth mother has been fully informed about the adoption process and is not being coerced into consenting to the adoption against her will.

Most states allow the consent to be signed anytime after the birth, assuming the birth mother is free from the effects of medication and duress from the birth. Some states impose a short waiting period, such as requiring 72 hours to elapse after the birth before a consent may be signed. A small number of states prefer she wait several weeks, sometimes even months, before the consent is signed. Some states go to the opposite extreme, such as Alabama and Washington, allowing a birth mother to sign her consent even *before* the birth of the child.

States also differ regarding who is permitted to witness the official consent to the adoption. In most states a specially assigned licensed social worker or similarly trained individual may witness the consent. Some states require the birth mother to appear before a judge to sign the consent, while other states are much more informal and require only a notary public (such as is found in a bank) to act as a witness.

A small number of states will require a birth mother to have the advice of an independent attorney before she signs her consent. Some states only impose this requirement if the birth mother is a minor, usually by the court appointing a *guardian ad litem,* who is a person or attorney making sure the birth mother understands the legal proceedings.

If the adopting parents reside and file their Petition for Adoption in one state, but the birth mother lives in another state, the laws of either state could apply requiring how the consent is signed. Normally, the birth mother's state will allow the procedures of the adoptive parent's home state to be used if the Petition for Adoption is filed there, even if the regulations are different from their own. In some cases, however, the procedures of both states must be complied with. Fortunately, this is a situation commonplace to most attorneys and agencies, thus easily handled.

If the consent to adoption is not properly executed under applicable state law, such as being witnessed by the wrong person or executed too soon, it will likely be deemed completely invalid. To learn the procedures for the state in which you live and where the baby is to be born, refer to the state-by-state review in Chapter Six.

A signed consent to the adoption is critically important because generally the adoption cannot occur without it. Once signed, it usually signals a significant shifting of legal rights concerning the child to the security of the adoptive parents.

Can the Birth Mother Change Her Mind?

It is very rare for a birth mother to sign her consent to the adoption then seek to reclaim her child. Generally, if an adoption is destined to be one of the small number that fail, the birth mother's desire to stop the adoption occurs very early in the adoption process, usually while she is still in the hospital or within a few days thereafter.

Before the birth mother signs her official consent to the adoption, she generally has the automatic right to stop the adoption without the need to go to court to provide an appropriate reason. She simply states she does not elect to start the adoption as planned which is her legal right as the baby's mother. *After* the consent to adoption is signed, however, she generally has given up the right to freely change her mind.

Each state has different regulations regarding what occurs if a birth mother signs her consent to the adoption, then wishes to withdraw her consent and stop the adoption. Most states will provide her with only a limited time in which to stop the adoption.

Some states only allow a consent to be withdrawn upon proof that fraud or duress was used to obtain her signature. Other states are more flexible and require a valid reason to revoke her written consent to the adoption, as well as proof the child's best interests would be served by being with the birth mother rather than the adoptive parents. In looking at what is in a child's best interests, a court will usually compare the two environments, as well as consider whether the child has been living with the adoptive parents long enough to emotionally bond.

Regardless of the specific legal burden established by most states, most judges will be extremely hesitant about removing a child from adoptive parents with whom the child has formed emotional bonds, making it rare for a court to allow a birth mother to withdraw her consent without compelling reasons.

Even within the same state there can be differences regarding the right to withdraw a consent to adoption. This is because some states treat independent adoption differently than agency adoptions.

Virtually all states establish a "cut off" time regarding a birth mother's right to ask to withdraw her signed consent to the adoption, making the consent permanent and irrevocable. In some states this will be the same day the consent to adoption is signed, while other states provide only a set number of days after the consent is signed in which to ask to withdraw it.

The state-by-state review in Chapter Six demonstrates the widely different policies regarding a birth mother's request to withdraw her consent and stop the adoption. Fortunately, virtually all birth mothers are content with their decision towards adoption, making efforts to withdraw consents to adoption very rare.

THE RIGHTS OF THE BIRTH FATHER

The legal rights of birth fathers are one of the more complicated areas of adoption law and subject to much debate. In years past, if a man were not married to the mother of the child, his rights were virtually nonexistent. In recent years, however, nonmarital birth fathers have been accorded greater rights in some states, although generally their rights remain substantially weaker than those of the birth mother.

Technically, most states have created two legal classifications of fathers in adoptions—marital and nonmarital fathers.

Marital Fathers

A man who is married to the birth mother is usually legally referred to as a *presumed* father. This term is used because there is a legal presumption that if a man is married to the child's mother when the birth occurs, then he is the child's father. Generally, a presumed father has the same strong rights as the birth mother. In other words, his consent is required.

Even where the birth mother's husband is not the actual biological father, as could occur due to an extra-marital affair, his rights are still strong due to the marriage. For this reason, adoption planning should normally not even be considered where the birth parents are married, unless they are both in agreement regarding placing the child for adoption.

Nonmarital Fathers

In the vast majority of planned adoptions, the birth father is not married to the birth mother. Instead, he is usually a boyfriend or casual acquaintance. Nonmarital fathers are legally referred to in most states as *putative* or *alleged* fathers, and their legal rights are often weaker than marital fathers.

In fact, many states do not require the written consent of nonmarital fathers. Instead, they simply require proof he has been given written notice that he may be the father of the child for whom adoption is being planned. This written notice is usually called a *Notice of Alleged Paternity* and explains his right to object should he wish to do so.

Likely one of the reasons most states do not require a nonmarital father's written consent to an adoption is the recognition that many of these young men will be fearful of becoming involved in the legal process. For example, a birth father may be concerned he will be obligated to pay child support if he admits he is the child's father.

Of course, many nonmarital fathers happily sign a consent to adoption in the same manner as would a birth mother. Most states also allow him to show his agreement to the adoption, but without admitting he is the father by signing a *Denial of Paternity*.

If a birth father elects not to sign anything, most states have special procedures allowing his rights to be terminated if he has filed no written objection to the adoption within a certain period (often 30 or 60 days) after the baby's birth and his receipt of the *Notice of Alleged Paternity*.

Three situations may arise which complicate the above procedures: 1) Unknown fathers, 2) fathers who can be identified but cannot be located, and 3) situations where more than one man may be the father of the child. Generally, none of these situations are difficult to solve. Let's take a look at these three situations to see how they are resolved.

Unknown Fathers. It is not uncommon for a birth mother to state she had a one-night relationship with a man, and all she knows is his first name. She may have met him at a party and not know his last name, address or telephone number. In cases like this, it is usually impossible to locate the birth father to give him the traditionally required notice of alleged paternity. As a result, most courts will terminate the rights of the "unknown" father and dispense with any further efforts to locate him. The adoption usually can continue without unnecessary delay.

Fathers Who Cannot Be Located. If a birth mother knows the name of the nonmarital father, but does not know his whereabouts, the adoption can also still proceed. The court must usually be satisfied, however, that the adoptive parents have used what is referred to as *due diligence* or *reasonable* *efforts* to try to locate him. Each county and state has different definitions regarding what constitutes reasonable efforts in trying to locate the birth father. Some states may require an independent person to investigate voter registration and other county and state records to see if his whereabouts are listed, or require the publication of a notice of the pending action in the classified section of a newspaper. Other states put the burden on the birth father and have a *registry,* requiring men to check to see if they are listed as a birth father in a pending adoption matter.

If the adoptive parents demonstrate reasonable efforts to try to locate the birth father and he still can not be located, the court will usually issue an order stating further efforts to try to locate him would be futile, and approve the termination of his rights despite the fact he never received notice or made an appearance in court.

Multiple Possible Fathers. Some birth mothers may be unsure about the identity of the biological father because she had sexual relations with more than one man around the time of conception. If this is the case, each of the possible fathers must usually be given notice of alleged paternity, and each must sign a consent to the adoption, denial of paternity, or have his rights terminated by the court.

Blood tests are normally required only if one of the possible birth fathers objects to the adoption, as it would then be necessary for him to establish he is actually the biological father in order to seek to stop the adoption. Fortunately, it is not common for a birth mother to state there are several possible fathers.

A Nonmarital Father's Right to Object

What about the small number of nonmarital fathers who actively object to an adoption? Although each state gives nonmarital fathers different rights, most states' laws provide that a birth father's desires are secondary to those of the birth mother. Based upon the state law controlling your adoption, birth father's rights may range from being much weaker than those of birth mother (with little chance of blocking the adoption against her wishes), to his rights being equal to hers.

Generally, if a nonmarital father desires to object to the adoption, he must prove two separate things to a court. First, he must prove he is the actual biological father. This may be done by the birth mother admitting he is the only possible father, or by blood tests. In most states he must also prove the child's best interests would be served by being raised by him, rather than by the adoptive parents. It is important to note these hearings are not "birth father versus birth mother," rather "birth father versus adoptive parents."

In determining what is in the child's best interests, the court may consider many things: the environment for the child offered by the birth father as compared to the adoptive parents; the birth mother's reasons for not wanting the birth father to raise the child; the length of time the child has been living with the adoptive parents; and the likely effect of removing the child from that secure environment. Courts are usually very hesitant to remove a child from a home environment in which he or she has formed emotional bonds which would be detrimental to break.

The court may also examine the sincerity of the birth father's efforts to object to the adoption. For example, was he objecting even before the birth, or was he apathetic until after the birth, then decided to object? Did he offer to assist the birth mother with her medical expenses and planned child-rearing responsibilities or did he decline to assist the birth mother? Naturally a birth father who has acted responsibly and objected in a timely manner is more impressive to a court.

As a general rule, if the adoptive parents are informed before the birth by the nonmarital father that he will be objecting to the adoption, and it is clear there is no reason why he cannot raise his own biological child, and he is acting responsibly in preparing for parenthood, it may be wise to not even start the adoption for both legal and emotional reasons. Of course, a possible objection from an unreliable or abuse birth father may be a different matter. Litigation is never fun, however, even with you think you will win.

Some birth fathers who are initially opposed to the adoption are swayed by the obvious kindness and sincerity of the adoptive parents. Frequently when a birth father is treated with respect and sees he is not abandoning his child, rather assuring a life of love and oppor-tunity for the child, he will decide adoption is the best option.

Cross-Over Birth Fathers

Determining the legal status and rights of fathers can be a complicated issue. For example, many states have rare but special situations where a man is not married to the birth mother, but due to special circumstances, he is granted the same strong rights as a "presumed" marital father.

Another odd situation can arise when the birth mother is married to one man, but due to an extra-marital affair, another man is the biological father. This results in two types of fathers in the same adoption: the marital "presumed" father, who is not the biological father, and the "alleged/putative" father, who is the actual father.

These issues demonstrate the need to have a competent adoption attorney or agency assist you in determining the legal status of the birth father before starting a planned adoption.

ALTERNATIVES TO CONSENTING TO THE ADOPTION

Normally, an adoption cannot be completed without the written consent of the birth mother, or marital father if one exists. There are exceptions, however.

For example, what happens if the birth mother places the child for adoption, then before signing her consent to the adoption, she disappears and cannot be found? Does that mean that the child and the adoptive parents are left in limbo until she is located and the adoption can not be completed? The answer is generally "no."

Most states allow for a special legal procedure called *abandonment*, which allows adoptive parents to ask the court to waive the requirement that a birth parent sign a consent to the adoption. Although the procedure varies from state to state, usually a period of three to six months must have elapsed since the child was placed with the adoptive parents, and the birth parent has "abandoned" the child by not having any personal contact or providing necessary support for the child. A court may then terminate the rights of the birth parent if it believes the child's best interests would be served by being adopted.

Abandonment proceedings are not common in independent adoptions. They are generally used in adoptions handled by public adoption agencies, which are responsible for children who are wards of the court and needing adoptive homes.

THE INDIAN CHILD WELFARE ACT

The Indian Child Welfare Act is a federal law which overrides state law. It is relatively obscure and only applies to a small number of adoptions, but it is of critical importance when it does apply. It was written by Congress in 1978 to protect American Indian heritage and culture, and stop Child Protective Service workers from removing Indian children from Indian homes due to alleged parental unfitness or other reasons, and placing them in non-Indian homes. Unfortunately, the Indian Act was written so broadly it can sometimes apply to purely voluntary adoptions, and where there is little connection between the Indian birth parent and the tribe.

In simplified terms, the Indian Act states if a child is a member of an Indian tribe, or is the biological child of a member and is therefore eligible for membership, a special written notice of the adoption must be given to the tribe. If the birth parent or the child is living or is domiciled on the reservation, the tribe has the right to block the adoption in order to protect tribal heritage, should it wish to do so. If the child is an Indian, but neither the child nor the birth parent are domiciled on the reservation, notice must still be given to the tribe. However, the tribe's right to object is often not as strong in this case as compared to when the child or parent is actually domiciled on the reservation.

Of course, simply because a child has some Indian heritage does not automatically make the Indian Act apply, as many Americans can point to at least one distant relative who was part Native American. Each tribe has special rules for eligibility, but many tribes require at least 25 percent Indian blood in the child.

Even more important, however, is that even when there is sufficient Indian heritage, most Indian tribes have no desire to object to a planned adoption desired by the birth parents. Only a few tribes are known for trying to block adoptions by non-Indian adoptive parents.

If the Indian Act applies, and the tribe does not object, the adoption can proceed as it would normally, although there are some technical distinctions compared to a regular adoption controlled solely by the laws of the state in which you are adopting. One principal difference under the Indian Act is that an Indian birth parent's consent to adoption must be witnessed by a judge, rather than a social worker or notary as would normally be accepted by many states.

THE INTERSTATE COMPACT
ON THE PLACEMENT OF CHILDREN

If a child is being born in one state and transported into a different state by adoptive parents living in a different state, the *Interstate Compact on the Placement of Children* applies. The Interstate Compact is an agreement between states that they will cooperate with each other to be sure certain protections for the child will be followed when a child is being brought across state lines for adoption. Each state has a specially assigned *Interstate Compact Administrator* as a part of the state adoption office. The compact administrator reviews the interstate adoption application and gives the necessary written approval to the adoptive parents to bring the child home.

To locate the Interstate Compact office of a particular state, contact the state adoption office listed for each state in Chapter Six, which can direct you to the appropriate individual. Be aware some state offices will only work with licensed agencies, attorneys, or other trained individuals, as they lack the manpower to assist those unfamiliar with the process.

Interstate adoptions occur regularly in both independent and agency adoption. For example, if you live and will be adopting in California, but your birth mother will be giving birth in Maine, you must comply with the Interstate Compact before you bring the child into California. Violation of the Interstate Compact is a crime in some states, usually a misdemeanor.

Although complying with the Interstate Compact involves a lot of documentation, perhaps difficult without an attorney, there is normally no tremendous difficulty satisfying the necessary requirements. Other than the paperwork providing the necessary information regarding health and background information about the birth parents and adoptive parents, the principal requirement to satisfy is obtaining a preplacement home study of the adoptive parents.

If you are planning an agency adoption, or an independent adoption in a state where a preplacement home study is required, this home study would likely be satisfactory to meet the Interstate Compact home study requirements. If your state is one of the many requiring no preplacement home study for an independent adoption, you will need a pre-placement home study to satisfy the Interstate Compact Administrator.

Once the home study has been completed, the home study report and other documentation is then sent by the Interstate Compact office in the state where the adoptive parents live to the Interstate Compact office in the state where the child will be born or is presently residing. When both states' Interstate Compact administrators have signed the Interstate Compact forms approving the placement, the child may then be brought home by the adoptive parents.

Each state has different requirements, but many will grant the necessary approval before the birth of the child, allowing the adoptive parents to bring the baby home immediately. Some states will not give their approval until after the child is born. Some will require the birth parents to have signed their consent to the adoption before the child leaves the state.

Usually the only concern surrounding the Interstate Compact is possible time delays. If the child is born, but the Interstate Compact approval is not yet received, the adoptive parents must generally wait in the child's birth state and cannot bring the child into their home state until approval is granted. This is because sometimes it takes both states several weeks, to approve the application. Naturally, the last thing the adoptive parents want to do is be forced to stay in an out-of-state hotel with their new baby until the Interstate Compact approval.

For this reason it is very important for adoptive parents to complete and submit their Interstate Compact application well before the birth, if possible. It is also a good idea early in the adoption to check with the Interstate Compact Administrator of both states to determine if there will be any special requirements which could complicate the adoption. There are some states which impose additional requirements on interstate adoptions. A handful of states may even charge a fee for the services of their Interstate Compact Office, although virtually all states process the application at no cost.

Once the child is legally brought into the home state of the adoptive parents, the adoption is handled as would a regular adoption occurring there. Normally, only that state's laws and procedures will apply to the adoption. Technically, however, the sending state retains some authority in the case should an unforeseen conflict arise between the two states.

FINANCIAL ASSISTANCE
TO THE BIRTH MOTHER

Virtually all states allow the adoptive parents to assist the birth mother with expenses related to the pregnancy. A few states forbid certain areas of assistance, as noted in the state-by-state review in Chapter Six. All expenses are usually itemized for the court to approve before the adoption is finalized. Any payments to a birth mother not related to the birth could be considered buying or selling a child, both of which are a crime.

Financial assistance to a birth mother is considered a gift. This means that if she changes her mind and wishes to stop adoption planning, she cannot be sued to return the financial assistance, as long as she had the bona fide intent to place her child for adoption when she received the funds.

Many birth mothers are self-sufficient and require little, or no, financial assistance. They have good jobs, live with their

139

parents or boyfriends, or may simply have too much pride to accept assistance. There are many women, however, who have true financial problems and need help with basic living expenses. For example, some may have great difficulty paying basic rent and food costs, perhaps existing on welfare or a part-time job, and will ask the adoptive parents to help with those expenses for part of the pregnancy.

As a general rule, it is recommended to provide financial assistance to a birth mother only in the last few months of the pregnancy, unless there is a particular reason why she is not working and requires legitimate assistance. Substantial financial assistance early in the pregnancy is often viewed as risky, as discussed in Chapter Three. Usually, birth-related assistance may legally extend after birth for that period in which the birth mother is incapacitated and unable to work. For a vaginal birth this could be several weeks to more than a month, while a C-section delivery may make a longer period appropriate.

In addition to living costs, the other principal area of financial assistance which may arise is for medical costs associated with the pregnancy. As discussed in Chapter Three, some birth mothers have insurance or Medicaid, so there is little or no contribution necessary from the adoptive parents. Some will not have coverage, however. Before agreeing to the responsibility of paying those bills, investigate what the costs will be, and any way they can be lessened.

Normally, you will not be personally "negotiating" financial issues with your birth mother, making everyone uncomfortable. Your adoption attorney or agency representative does that, speaking to the birth mother regarding her needs, if any, and give the adoptive parents an estimate of any necessary financial assistance. Frequently, attorneys will direct the adoptive parents' assistance to the birth mother through the attorney's client trust account, so all major expenditures are arranged by the attorney's office and proper records maintained for an accounting to the court.

THE FINALIZATION OF THE ADOPTION

When your home study has been completed and the birth parents have signed their consents to the adoption (or the consents have been ordered dispensed with), the agency or person who conducted your home study can recommend the adoption be granted. Only a judge can grant an adoption, however, so a court hearing is set to finalize the adoption.

The final hearing can occur as soon as several weeks after the baby was placed with you, or as long as one year. The state-by-state review in Chapter 6 provides specific information regarding the laws of each state regarding when the finalization can occur.

The final adoption hearing is usually a very casual proceeding, traditionally held in a closed courtroom or the judge's private chambers. Generally, the only persons required to attend the final hearing are the adoptive parents, the child, and the attorney of record for the adoptive parents. The birth parents are not required to attend. Often the adoptive parents will invite family and friends to attend the hearing. Despite the fact taking photographs in court is usually forbidden, many judges will be happy to let your friends take pictures of the proceeding, and in fact, will usually happily join you in a picture. A small number of states do not require the adoptive parents to attend the final hearing, and simply grant the adoption upon review of the final court report prepared by the investigating agency or social worker.

If you are required to attend the final hearing, typically a few basic formal questions are asked by the judge, and then he or she signs the *Decree of Adoption* and other documents prepared by your attorney, thus making the child legally yours. Most judges probably spend more time shaking hands and posing for photos with the adoptive parents and the child than doing expected judicial activities.

A new birth certificate naming you as the child's parents and naming the child as you would like him or her to be named is then prepared by the birth records department in the state where the baby was born. This new birth certificate takes the place of the original birth certificate naming the birth parents. The new birth certificate will list you as the child's natural parents with no mention of adoption.

■　　■　　■　　■　　■

Although many critical legal issues have been explored in this chapter, it is important to recognize this book is not written to take the place of retaining an attorney. Obtaining legal advice is essential in protecting against an unforeseen problem.

If you are planning an independent adoption, an adoption attorney can handle all the many issues discussed above and guide you through the legal process. If you are adopting through an adoption agency, they will either have an attorney on staff, or will instruct you to retain one to handle legal issues outside the scope of the agency.

CHAPTER SIX

State-by-State Review

Each state's laws and procedures vary widely. Accordingly, information is provided for each state individually. Following the summary of each state's laws and procedures is a listing of adoption attorneys practicing within the state, with details about their education and experience. Each state's licensed private adoption agencies are also listed, as well as the supervising state agency. If available, the website and e-mail address is also provided for both attorneys and agencies.

STATE INFORMATION

The following information is provided regarding each state:

General Information

- The name, address, phone and website of the state adoption office which oversees all adoptions within the state is provided. The state adoption office is usually a subdivision of the state's social services or child welfare office.

- Whether independent adoption is permitted within the state.
- The percentage of the state's newborn adoptions completed via independent adoption as compared to agency adoption (percentages not available for all states).
- Whether it is permitted to place an adoption advertisement within the state.
- Requirements for adoptive parents to file a Petition for Adoption in the state. Generally, it is required that the adoptive parents reside within the state, although some states also permit adoptive parents to file their Petition for Adoption when the child is born or resides within that state.
- How long does it take to complete and finalize an adoption after the child's placement with the adoptive parents.
- Are the adoptive parents and the child being adopted required to appear in court when the adoption is finalized by a judge.

Independent Adoption

- Is a preplacement home study of the adoptive parents required before a child can be placed in their home.
- Who may perform the home study.
- What does the home study cost.
- Are birth parents and adoptive parents required by law to meet in person, or is it discretionary.
- Can the adoptive parents assist the birth mother with pregnancy-related expenses.

- May the child be placed with the adoptive parents directly from the hospital.
- How soon after birth may the birth mother legally sign her consent to the adoption.
- As a practical matter how soon after birth do most birth mothers actually sign their official consent to adoption.
- Who may witness the birth mother's signing of the consent to adoption.
- Does the birth mother have the legal right to ask the court to withdraw her written consent to the adoption and seek to stop the adoption.
- How long does the birth mother have the right to ask the court to withdraw her consent to the adoption and what must she prove to successfully do so.

Agency Adoption

- How soon after birth may the birth mother legally sign her consent to the adoption.
- Who may witness the birth mother's signing of the consent to adoption.
- Does the birth mother have the legal right to ask the court to withdraw her written consent to the adoption and seek to stop the adoption.
- How long does a birth mother have the right to ask the court to withdraw her consent to the adoption and what must she prove to successfully do so.
- Do some agencies within the state agree to do "identified" adoptions.

- Are some agencies within the state willing to make "at risk" placements, where the child is placed directly with the adoptive parents from the hospital, before the child is completely free for adoption due to the birth parent's consent being permanent and irrevocable.

Some issues are so complex they cannot be discussed on a detailed state-by-state basis. An example of such an issue is birth fathers' rights. As discussed in Chapter Five, some states provide birth fathers rights equal to the birth mother, and the procedures surrounding the signing of the consent to adoption described in this chapter for birth mothers applies equally to birth fathers. Other states provide nonmarital birth fathers substantially weaker rights and different procedures apply.

Despite the detailed scope of laws and procedures provided for each state, this chapter should only be considered as an overview and a first step toward learning more, not as a substitute for legal assistance. Remember, each state's laws are subject to change, be affected by little-known local or county rules, be interpreted differently by others, or incorrectly summarized within this book. To illustrate the difficulty of verifying researched information, a questionnaire was sent to adoption attorneys within each state regarding the laws and procedures of the state where each attorney practiced law. In some instances, even attorneys within the same state answered the same question differently, demonstrating how identical laws can be interpreted differently, or affected by local court policy.

For these reasons, before beginning formal adoption planning it is critical to consult with an attorney and/or licensed adoption agency to be certain you are receiving accurate and up-to-date information concerning the laws of any state which may be involved in your adoption.

ADOPTION ATTORNEY INFORMATION

The *American Academy of Adoption Attorneys* is a national membership organization of more than 300 attorneys in 50 states and the District of Columbia who have special knowledge of, or interest in, adoption. Each member was sent a questionnaire requesting information about the nature of their practice and adoption experience. The following information is provided regarding each attorney for whom a questionnaire was available:

- The attorney's name, address, telephone and fax number, as well as their website and e-mail address.
- The year the attorney began practicing law.
- States in which the attorney is licensed to practice law, in addition to the state in which he or she is listed.
- The law school from which the attorney graduated.
- Whether the attorney limits his or her practice to adoptions. If not, the percentage of their practice consisting of adoptions.
- The number of adoptions the attorney has completed in his or her career.
- The number of adoptions completed annually.
- The percentage of adoptions completed each year being independent or agency adoptions.
- The percentage of adoptions where he or she personally located the birth mother and introduced her to the adoptive parents, resulting in an adoptive match.
- Any additional information the attorney elected to provide, such as being an adoptive parent, birth parent or adoptee, and other points of interest to adoptive parents.

To see additional or new AAAA members, you may visit the AAAA website at www.adoptionattorneys.org.

LICENSED PRIVATE ADOPTION AGENCIES

The name, address and phone number of every licensed private adoption agency within each state is provided, as well as their website and e-mail address. A primary source for this information is The National Adoption Information Clearinghouse. Its website is naic.acf.hhs.gov. Agencies handling international adoption (exclusively or in addition to domestic) are indicated with the * symbol. Their services may range from offering a full fledged international adoption program, or simply performing international home studies.

Some of the agencies listed below may inform you they do not place children for adoption, even though they are licensed by the state to do so. This is because sometimes certain agencies will elect to limit their services to arranging foster care or similar services.

Public adoption agencies are not listed as they are too numerous to list. To locate the public agency serving your county or region, contact the state adoption office, or consult a local telephone directory.

It is important to follow the suggestions provided in Chapter One concerning selecting a qualified and experienced agency. Simply because an agency is listed below is not a guarantee they offer quality service or are presently licensed by the state.

■　■　■　■　■

Alabama

State Adoption Office: (334) 242-1374
Department of Human Resources
Family Services Partnership—Office of Adoptions
50 N. Ripley Street
Montgomery, AL 36130   www.dhr.state.al.us/fsd/adopt.asp

General Information. Alabama permits both independent and agency adoption. Approximately 60% of Alabama's infant adoptions are completed via independent adoption; 40% via agencies. Advertising is permitted. To file a Petition for Adoption within Alabama either the adoptive parents *or* the child to be adopted must reside there. If it is an agency adoption the Petition can additionally be filed where the agency having custody of the child is located. Normally, independent adoptions are finalized three months after the child is placed with the adoptive parents; six months for some agency adoptions. The adopting parents and the child are usually required to appear at the final court hearing.

Independent Adoption. A preplacement home study of the adoptive parents is normally required before a child may be placed in their home, although a court has the authority in some circumstances to allow a child to be placed before the home study is completed. The home study may be conducted by the state adoption office, a licensed adoption agency or an individual licensed by the state as an *private independent practitioner* (usually a licensed social worker). The fee for the state office is $300. Private agency home studies are typically less than $1,500.

The birth mother and the adoptive parents are not required by law to meet and share identities, although about half elect to do so voluntarily. The adoptive parents are permitted to assist the birth mother with pregnancy-related expenses, such as medical, legal and living costs. The child may be placed with the adoptive parents directly upon his or her release from the hospital. Most hospitals have a special form for the birth mother to sign allowing the child's release to the adoptive parents. Normally no court order is required.

The birth mother may sign her consent to the adoption before or after the birth. If signed before the birth it must be signed before a probate judge. If signed after the birth it may be witnessed by a probate judge, a representative of a licensed adoption agency or a notary public. Most birth mothers sign their consents before, or within a few days after, the birth. If the birth mother is under the age of 19 she must be appointed a guardian ad litem before she signs her consent, to be sure she understands her rights. This individual is usually an attorney whose fees, usually paid by the adoptive parents, average $200.

There is a five day period after the consent is signed, or the birth occurs, whichever is later, in which the birth mother has the automatic right to withdraw her consent. After the five days have elapsed, but within 14 days of the signing or the birth (whichever occurs first), the consent can only be withdrawn by the birth mother proving to a court the child's best interests would be served by being removed from the adoptive parents. After the 14 day period has elapsed, the consent can only be withdrawn upon proof of fraud, duress or legal mistake.

Agency Adoption. There is no difference regarding the process in which a birth mother signs her consent to adoption in an independent or agency adoption. The information provided above regarding independent adoption (e.g. when it can be signed, before whom, legal burden to seek to withdraw a signed consent, requirement for guardian ad litem) is identical regarding agency adoption.

Some agencies within Alabama agree to do identified adoptions. Some agencies will also agree to make immediate hospital "at risk" placements.

Adoption Attorneys

David P. Broome   Tel (251) 432-9933
155 Monroe Street   Fax (251) 432-9706
Mobile, AL 36602

Mr. Broome began practicing law in 1977 and is a graduate of the University of Alabama School of Law. Approximately 30% of his practice consists of adoptions. He estimates he has completed more than 100 adoptions in his career and presently completes 27 annually. Of these, 90% are independent adoptions and 10% are international. He reports the majority of his clients locate their own birth mother to select them as adoptive parents. He is also available to be retained in contested adoption cases. He is an adoptee.

Bryant A. Whitmire Jr.   Tel (205) 324-6631
215 Richard Arrington Jr. Blvd., #501   Fax (205) 324-6632
Birmingham, AL 35203

Mr. Whitmire began practicing law in 1972 and is a graduate of the University of Alabama School of Law. Approximately 80% of his practice consists of adoptions. He estimates he has completed several hundred in his career and presently completes 150 annually. Of these, 80% are independent adoptions and 20% are international. He is also available to be retained in contested adoption cases.

Licensed Private Adoption Agencies (* Offers intercountry programs)

Alabama Baptist Children's Homes and Family Ministries, Inc.
PO Box 361767; Birmingham, AL 35236-1767; (205) 982-1112; Toll Free: (888) 720-8805; Fax: (205) 982-9992;
World Wide Web: http://www.abchome.org/;
Association for Guidance, Aid, Placement and Empathy (AGAPE) of North Alabama, Inc.; P.O. Box 3887; Huntsville, AL 35810; (256) 859-4481; Mobile: (334) 343-4875; Montgomery: (334) 272-9466; World Wide Web: http://www.agape-nal-inc.org; E-mail: info@agape-nal-inc.org
Catholic Family Services; P.O. Box 745; Huntsville, AL 35804
(256) 536-0041; Tuscaloosa: (205) 533-9045; South
Birmingham: (205) 324-6561
Catholic Social Services; 4455 Narrow Ln Road; Montgomery, AL 36116-2953; (334) 288-8890; Mobile; (334) 434-1550
*Children of the World; 110 South Section Street; Fairhope, AL 36532;
(251) 990-3550; Fax: (251) 990-3494
World Wide Web: http://www.childrenoftheworld.com
E-mail: adoption@childrenoftheworld.com
Children's Aid Society; 181 West Valley Avenue, Suite 300;
Homewood, AL 35209; (205) 251-7148; Fax: (205) 252-3828
World Wide Web: www.childrensaid.org/; E-mail: cas@childrensaid.org;
Family Adoption Services; 529 Beacon Parkway West, Suite 108; Birmingham, AL 35209; (205) 290-0077
Lifeline Children's Services; 2908 Pumphouse Road; Birmingham, AL 35243; (205) 967-0919
Southern Social Works, Inc.; PO Box 8084; Anniston, AL 36202; (256) 237-4990
Fax: (256) 240-9808; World Wide Web:
http://www.southernsocialworks.com; E-mail: sosocwrks@aol.com

Special Beginnings Inc.; 1301 Azalea Road, Suite 108; Mobile, AL 36693; (334) 666-6703; Fax: (334) 343-7173; World Wide Web: http://www.specialbeginnings.org; E-mail: flora@specialbeginnings.org
United Methodist Children's Home; 1712 Broad Street, PO Box 830; Selma, AL 36702-0830; (334) 875-7283; Fax: (334) 875-5161; World Wide Web: http://www.umch.net; E-mail: umchalwf@bellsouth.net
*Villa Hope International Adoption; 6 Office Park Circle, Suite 218; Birmingham, AL 35223; (205) 870-7359; Fax: (205) 871-6629; World Wide Web: http://www.villahope.org; E-mail: villahope@villahope.org

Alaska

State Adoption Office:*   (907) 465-2145
Division of Family and Youth Services
Department of Health and Social Services
P.O. Box 110630
Juneau, AK 99811   www.hss.state.ak.us/dfys

General Information. Alaska permits both independent and agency adoption. Approximately 50% of Alaska's infant adoptions are completed via independent adoption; 50% via agencies. Advertising is permitted. To file a Petition for Adoption within Alaska either the adopting parents, or the child being adopted, must reside there. Normally, adoptions are finalized approximately three to six months after the child is placed in the adoptive parents' custody. The adoptive parents and the child being adopted are required to appear at the final court hearing, but this can often be done telephonically.

Independent Adoption. A preplacement home study of the adoptive parents is usually required before a child may be placed in their home. The pre and post-placement home study is done by a licensed social worker at a usual fee of approximately $500.

   The birth mother and adoptive parents are not required by law to meet and share identities, although some do so voluntarily. The adoptive parents are permitted to assist the birth mother with pregnancy-related medical, legal and living expenses. The child may be placed with the adoptive parents directly upon his or her release from the hospital, although each hospital has its own forms and policies.

The birth mother may sign give her consent in two ways: a consent or a relinquishment. If the consent method is used, once it is signed, the birth mother has ten days in which she has the automatic right to withdraw it, should she wish to do so. The consent can be witnessed by a judge or notary public. After the initial ten days have elapsed, she can only withdraw it by proving to a court the child's best interests would be served by being removed from the adoptive parents. Once the adoption is finalized by a judge, the consent is basically irrevocable. If the relinquishment method is used, the birth mother has ten days in which she has the automatic right to withdraw the consent, should she wish to do so. However, once the ten days have elapsed, it is irrevocable. The relinquishment must be witnessed by a judge.

Agency Adoption. An agency adoption always requires an adoptive parent pre-placement home study. The information provided above regarding independent adoption is identical regarding agency adoption.

Some agencies within Alaska agree to do identified adoptions. Few agencies agree to make immediate hospital "at risk" placements.

Adoption Attorneys

Robert B. Flint	Tel (907) 276-1592
717 K Street	Fax (907) 277-4352
Anchorage, Alaska 99501	

Mr. Flint began practicing law in 1963 and is a graduate of Georgetown University.

Licensed Private Adoption Agencies (* Offers intercountry programs)

Adopt An Angel Child' 308 G Street, Suite 225; Anchorage, AK 99501
*Adoption Advocates International; 218 Martin Drive; Fairbanks, AK 99712; (907) 457-3832; World Wide Web: http://www.adoptionadvocates.org/alaska; E-mail: aai@adoptionadvocates.org
*Alaska International Adoption Agency; 3705 Artic Blvd, Suite 1177; Anchorage, AK 99503-5789; (907) 243-6212
Fax: (907) 274-5941; World Wide Web: http://www.akadoptions.com; E-mail: info@akadoptions.com

Catholic Social Services; 225 Cordova Street; Anchorage, AK 99501; (907) 276-2554; Fax: (907) 272-7370; World Wide Web: http://www.cssalaska.org; E-mail: catholicsocialservices@css-ak.org
*Circle of Hope International Adoption Agency; 407 Hemlock Street; Sitka, AK 99835; (907) 966-2606; E-mail: coh@acsalaska.net
*Fairbanks Counseling and Adoption; 912 Barnette Street
Fairbanks; AK 99707; (907) 456-4729; Fax: (907) 456-4623
World Wide Web: http://www.ptialaska.net/ ~ fca;
E-mail: fca@ptialaska.org
World Association for Children and Parents (WACAP); 4704 Kenai Avenue; Anchorage, AK 99508;

Arizona

State Adoption Office: (602) 542-2359
Arizona Department of Economic Security
Box 6123
Phoenix, AZ 85005   www.de.state.az.us/links/foster/index.html

General Information. Arizona permits both independent and agency adoption. Approximately 65% of Arizona's infant adoptions are completed through independent adoption; 35% via agencies. Advertising is permitted. To file a Petition for Adoption in Arizona the adoptive parents must be residents of the state, generally for at least 90 days. Normally, adoptions are finalized approximately six months after the Petition for Adoption is filed. The adoptive parents and the child being adopted are required to appear at the final court hearing.

Independent Adoption. A preplacement home study of the adoptive parents, resulting in "certification" of the adoptive parents, is usually required before a child is placed in the adoptive parents' home. In some cases where there is no certification, a placement with the adoptive parents may be made, provided a temporary custody order is obtained within 5 days of the placement. The home study may be conducted by the state adoption office or a licensed private agency. The cost of the home study varies. Once the home study is completed it must be filed with the juvenile court, allowing the adoptive parents to be certified as adoptive parents, after which time the adoptive placement can occur. If the adoptive parents were unable to complete a preplacement home study, they may request a court to issue a temporary custody order, allowing them to have immediate custody of the child and complete their home study after the placement.

The birth mother and adoptive parents are not required by law to meet and share identities, although most do so voluntarily. The adoptive parents are permitted to assist the birth mother with pregnancy-related expenses, but the payment of her living expenses (such as food and rent) requires advance court approval if the total expenses are in excess of $1,000. The child may be placed with the adoptive parents directly upon his or her release from the hospital, but some hospitals require that the release be made directly to the attorney or agency handling the adoption. A small number of hospitals require a copy of the birth mother's consent to the adoption.

The birth mother may sign her consent to the adoption no sooner than 72 hours after the birth. It must be witnessed by a notary public or two witnesses over the age of 18. Most consents to are signed three to four days after the baby's birth. Once the consent to adoption is signed it is basically irrevocable, unless the birth mother can prove it was signed based upon fraud, duress or undue influence.

Agency Adoption. There is no difference regarding the process in which a birth mother signs her consent to adoption in an independent or agency adoption. The information provided above regarding independent adoption (e.g. when it can be signed, before whom, legal burden to withdraw a signed consent) is identical regarding agency adoption.

Some agencies within Arizona agree to do identified adoptions. Some agencies will also agree to make immediate hospital "at risk" placements.

Adoption Attorneys

Phillip "Jay" McCarthy Jr.	Tel: (928) 774-1453
Hufford, Horstman, Mongini, Parnell & McCarthy	Fax (928) 779-3621
120 N. Beaver Street	
Flagstaff, AZ 86001	

Mr. McCarthy began practicing law in 1980 and is a graduate of Creighton University School of Law. Approximately 30% of his practice consists of adoptions. He estimates he has completed more than 250 adoptions in his career and he presently completes 40 annually. Of these, 90% are independent; 10% are agency. Of the adoptions he has handled, he reports 50% of her clients meet a birth mother through her office; 50% locate their own birth mother. He is also available to handle contested adoption cases and reports special emphasis on the Indian Child Welfare Act.

Scott E. Myers   Tel (520) 327-6041
3180 East Grant Road   Fax (520) 326-9097
Tucson, AZ 85716

Mr. Myers began practicing law in 1975 and is a graduate of Louisiana State University. Approximately 80% of his practice consists of adoptions. He estimates he has completed more than 400 adoptions in his career and presently completes in excess of 100 annually. Of these, 50% are independent; 50% are agency. Of the adoptions he has handled, he reports 50% of his clients locate a birth mother through his office; 50% locate their own birth mother.

Kathryn A. Pidgeon   Tel: (602) 522-8700
3131 E. Camelback Road, Suite 200 Fax: (602) 522-8706
Phoenix, Arizona 85016

Ms. Pidgeon began practicing law in 1989 and is a graduate of University of Miami College of Law. Approximately 95% of her practice consists of adoptions. She completes approximately 100 adoptions annually. Of these 75% are independent; 25% agency. Of the adoptions she has handled, she reports 50% of her clients meet a birth mother through her office; 50% locate their own birth mother.

Daniel I. Ziskin   Tel (602) 234-2280
P.O. Box 7447   Fax (602) 274-9297
Phoenix, Arizona 85011

Mr. Ziskin began practicing law in 1975 and is a graduate of Arizona State University School of Law. Approximately 45% of his practice consists of adoptions. He has completed more than 700 adoptions in his career, and presently completes 35 annually. Of these, 90% are independent; 8% are agency; and 2% are international. Of the adoptions he has handled he reports 15% of his clients locate a birth mother through his office; 85% find their own birth mother. He is an adoptive parent.

Licensed Private Adoption Agencies (* Offers intercountry programs)

Adoption Care Center; P.O. Box 5659; Scottsdale, AZ 85261-5659; (480) 322-8838; Fax: (480) 922-8873; World Wide Web: http://www.geocities.com/heartland/forest/1574/index.html
*Adoption Journeys of Arizona, Inc.; 4065 East Roberts Place; Tuczon, AZ 85711; (520) 327-0899; Fax: (520) 327-0899; E-mail: http://www.adoptionjourneys.org
Aid to Adoption of Special Kids (AASK) of Arizona; 501 East Thomas Rd, # 100; Phoenix, AZ 85012; (602) 254-2275; Toll Free: (800) 370-2275; Fax: (602) 212-2564; World Wide Web: http://www.AASK-AZ.org
American Adoptions; 8676 West 96th Street, Suite 140; Overland Park, KS 66212; (913) 383-9804; Fax: (913) 383-1615
Arizona Baptist Children's Services; PO Box 39239; Phoenix, AZ 85069-9239; (602) 943-7760; World Wide Web: http://www.abcs.org
*Arizona Family Adoption Services, Inc.; 346 East Palm Lane; Phoenix, AZ 85004-1531; (602) 254-2271; Fax: (602) 254-1581; World Wide Web: http://www.azadoptions.com; E-mail: office@azadoptions.com
Arizona's Children Association; 2700 South Eighth Avenue; Tucson, AZ 85725; (520) 622-7611; Fax: (520) 624-7042
World Wide Web: http://www.arizonaschildren.org
Birth Hope Adoption Agency, Inc.; 3225 N. Central Avenue, Suite 1217; Phoenix, AZ 85012; (602) 277-2860
Black Family and Children's Services, Inc.; 2323 North Third Street, Suite 202; Phoenix, AZ 85004; (602) 256-2948; Fax: (602) 276-1984
Casey Family Program; Tucson Division; 1600 North Country Club; Tucson, AZ 85716; (520) 323-0886; Fax: (520) 323-6819
Catholic Community Services in Western Arizona; Yuma Office; 690 East 32nd Street; Yuma, AZ 85365; (520) 341-9400; Toll Free: (888) 514-3482; World Wide Web: http://www.ccs-soaz.org/ccswa.htm
Catholic Community Services of Southeastern Arizona
Bisbee Office; P.O. Box 1777; Bisbee, AZ 85603; (520) 432-2285; Toll Free: (800) 338-2474; World Wide Web: http://www.ccssoaz.org/csssea.htm
Catholic Social Services of Central and Northern Arizona; 1825 West Northern Avenue; Phoenix, AZ 85021; (602) 997-6105; World Wide Web: http://www.diocesephoenix.org/css/; Flagstaff Office; (928) 774-9125; Prescott Office; (928) 778-2531; Mesa Office; (480) 964-8771; Tucson; (520) 623-0344; Toll Free: (800) 234-0344; World Wide Web: http://www.ccs-soaz.org/css.htm

Christian Family Care Agency; 1102 South Pantano Road; Tucson, AZ 85710; (520) 296-8255; Fax: (520) 296-8773;
World Wide Web: http://www.cfcare.org; Phoenix; (602) 234-1935; Fax: (602) 234-0022; World Wide Web: http://www.cfcare.org; E-mail: info@cfcare.org
*Commonwealth Adoptions International, Inc.; 4601 East Ft. Lowell, Suite 200; Tucson, AZ 85712; (520) 327-7574
Fax: (520) 327-8640; World Wide Web:
http://www.commonwealthadoption.org; E-mail:
info@commonwealthadoption.org
*Dillon Southwest; 3014 North Hayden Road, Suite 101;
Scottsdale, AZ 85251; (480) 945-2221; Fax: (480) 945-3956
World Wide Web: http://www.dillonsouthwest.org;
E-mail: info@dillonsouthwest.org
Family Service Agency; 1530 East Flower Street; Phoenix, AZ 85014; (602) 264-9891; World Wide Web: http://www.fsaphoenix.org;
E-mail: fsaphoenix@aol.com
*Hand in Hand International Adoptions; 931 East Southern Avenue, Suite 103; Mesa, AZ 85204; (480) 892-5550
Fax: (480) 381-1725; World Wide Web: http://www.hihiadopt.org/; E-mail: arizona@hihiadopt.org
Home Builders For Children, Inc.; 3014 North Hayden Road;
Scottsdale, AZ 85251; (480) 429-5344; Fax: (480) 945-3956
LDS Family Services; 5049 E. Broadway Boulevard, Suite 126; Tucson, AZ 85711; (520) 745-0459; Fax: (520) 512-0647;
Mesa; (480) 968-2995; Fax: (480) 967-4103; Snowflake; (520) 536-4117; Fax: (520) 536-7626; World Wide Web: http://www.itsaboutlove.org
*MAPS Arizona; 7000 North 16th Street, Suite 120 #438;
Phoenix, AZ 85020; (602) 277-9243; Fax: (602) 279-9469
World Wide Web: http://www.mapsadopt.org
Oasis Adoption Services, LLC.; 4420 West Oasis Drive; Tucson, AZ 85742; (520) 579-5578; Fax: (520) 579-5578

Arkansas

State Adoption Office: (501) 682-8462
Department of Human Services
Division of Children and Family Services
P.O. Box 1437, Slot 808
Little Rock, AR 72203   www.state.ar.us/dhs/adoption/adoption.html

General Information. Arkansas permits both independent and agency adoption. Approximately 40% of Arkansas' infant adoptions are completed via independent adoption; 60% via agencies. Advertising is permitted but some newspapers place restrictions on whom may place ad. To file a Petition for Adoption within Arkansas either the adopting parents, *or* the legal parent of the child being placed for adoption, must be residents of the state (at least 4 months pre-birth for a birth mother). If it is an agency adoption the Petition can also be filed where the adoption agency having custody of the child is located. Normally, adoptions are finalized approximately 14 days after the child's placement with the adoptive parents. The adopting parents are required to appear in court for the final hearing.

Independent Adoption. A preplacement home study of the adoptive parents is not required before a child is placed in their home. The postplacement home study may be performed by a representative of the state adoption office, private adoption agency or licensed social worker. The state adoption office's maximum fee is $200, but its services are usually limited to finding homes for children who are wards of the state. Fees for home studies by private agencies and social workers average $400.

The birth mother and the adoptive parents are not required by law to meet and share identities, although most share at least first names voluntarily. The adoptive parents are permitted to assist the birth mother with pregnancy-related medical, legal and living expenses. The child may be placed with the adoptive parents directly upon his or her discharge from the hospital. Each hospital has different policies regarding releasing the child, however. Most require either a court order authorizing the release, a copy of the birth mother's consent to the adoption, or a similar formal authorization to release the child.

The birth mother may sign her consent both before or after the birth. If signed before the birth, it is called a *relinquishment*. It must be witnessed by a judge or notary public. If the birth mother is under the age of 18 she must be appointed a guardian ad litem prior to her signing of the consent to be sure she understands her rights. Most consents are signed within several days of the birth. Once the consent or relinquishment is signed the birth mother has ten days from the birth, or the date she signed the consent/relinquishment, whichever occurs later, to revoke the consent with no legal burden. After the ten days have elapsed, the consent may only be withdrawn if the birth mother proves to a court the child's best interests would be served by being removed from the adoptive parents. Once the adoption is finalized the consent is basically irrevocable.

Agency Adoption. There is no difference regarding the process in which a birth mother signs her consent to adoption in an independent or agency adoption. The information provided above regarding independent adoption (e.g. when the consent can be signed, legal burden to withdraw a signed consent) is identical regarding agency adoption, although the consent may be witnessed by a representative of the adoption agency and a notary.

Some agencies agree to do identified adoptions. Some agencies also agree to make immediate hospital "at risk" placements.

Adoption Attorneys

Sandra Coody Bradshaw   Tel (870) 364-2111
Griffin, Rainwater & Draper   Fax (870) 364-3126
P.O. Box 948
Crossett, AR 71635

Ms. Bradshaw began practicing law in 1992 and is a graduate of University of Mississippi School of Law. Of the adoptions she completes, all are independent adoptions. She is also admitted to practice law in Mississippi.

Kaye H. McLeod   Tel (501) 663-6224
210 Linwood Court   Fax (501) 663-5393
Little Rock, Arkansas 72225

Ms. McLeod began practicing law in 1981 and is a graduate of University of Arkansas School of Law at Little Rock. Approximately 90% of her practice consists of adoptions. She estimates she has completed more than 1,000 adoptions in her career and presently completes 40 annually. Of these, 90% are independent; 5% are agency; 5% are international. Of the adoptions she has completed, she reports 15% of her clients locate a birth mother through her office; 85% locate their own birth mother.

Licensed Private Adoption Agencies (* Offers intercountry programs)

Adoption Advantage; 1014 West 3rd Street; Little Rock, AR 72201; (501) 376-7778;

Adoption Choices; 1616 East 19th Street, Suite 101; Edmond, OK 73120; (405) 715-1991; Fax: (405) 715-2640; World Wide Web: http://www.adoptionchoices.org; E-mail: info@adoptionchoices.org

Adoption Services, Inc.; 2415 North Tyler; Little Rock, AR 72207; (501) 664-0340; Fax: (501) 664-9186

*Bethany Christian Services; 1100 North University Avenue, Suite 66; Little Rock, AR 72207-6344; (501) 664-5729; Fax: (501) 664-5740; World Wide Web: http://www.bethany.org/arkansas; E-mail: bcslittlerock@bethany.org; Fayetteville; (501) 442-8381; Fax: (501) 442-8568; World Wide Web: http://www.bethany.org/arkansas; E-mail: bcsfayetteville@bethany.org

Children's Home, Inc.; Church of Christ; 1502 E Kiehl Avenue, Suite B; Sherwood, AR 72120; (501) 835-1595; Paragould; (870) 239-4031

*Dillon International, Inc.; 17 Greenview Circle; Sherwood, AR 72120; (501) 791-9300; Fax: (501) 791-9303; World Wide Web: http://www.dillonadopt.com; E-mail: dillonarkansas@dillonadopt.com

Families Are Special; 2200 Main Street, P.O. Box 5789; North Little Rock, AR 72119; (501) 758-9184

Family Life Connections; P.O. Box 2645; Russellville, AR 72811; (501) 968-5400

*Gladney Center for Adoption; P.O. Box 94615; North Little Rock, AR 72190-4615; (501) 791-3206; World Wide Web: http://www.gladney.org/; E-mail: info@gladney.org

Highlands Child Placement Services; 5506 Cambridge, P.O. Box 300198; Kansas City, MO 64130-0198; (816) 924-6565

Fax: (816) 924-3409; World Wide Web: http://www.ag.org/benevolences/highlands/index_highlands.cfm; E-mail: highlands@ag.org

*Holt International Children's Services; 5016 Western Hills Avenue; Little Rock, AR 72204; (501) 568-2827;

Fax: (501) 568-2827; World Wide Web: http://www.holtintl.org; E-mail: info@holtinternational.org

*Integrity, Inc.; 6124 North Moor Drive; Little Rock, AR 72204; (501) 614-7200

LDS Social Services of Oklahoma; 4500 S. Garnett, Suite 425;
Tulsa, OK 74146; (918) 665-3090

Mississippi Children's Home Society; 1900 North West Street, P.O. Box 1078; Jackson, MS 39215; (601) 352-7784; Toll Free: (800) 388-6247; World Wide Web: http://www.mchsfsa.org/adoption.html;

Porter-Leath Children's Center; 868 North Manassas Street;
Memphis, TN 38107-2516; (901) 577-2500; Fax: (901) 577-2506; World Wide Web: http://www.porter-leath.org; E-mail: porterleath@porter-leath.org

Searcy Children's Home Church of Christ; 900 North Main Street; Searcy, AR 72143; (501) 268-5383

Senior Services Stepping Stone; 1400 West Markham Street, Suite 403; Little Rock, AR 72201; (501) 375-5808

*Ventures for Children International; 1621 Starr Drive;
Fayetteville, AR 72701; (479) 582-0305; Fax: (208) 248-7181;
World Wide Web: http://www.venturesforchildren.org;
E-mail: info@venturesforchildren.org

Volunteers of America of North Louisiana; 360 Jordan Street;
Shreveport, LA 71101; (318) 221-2669; World Wide Web:
http://www.voanorthla.com; E-mail: lisa@voanorthla.org

California

State Adoption Office: (916) 323-2921
State Department of Social Services, Adoption Branch
744 P Street; M.S. 19-31
Sacramento, CA 95814   www.childsworld.ca.gov

General Information. California permits both independent and agency adoption. Approximately 85% of California's infant adoptions are completed via independent adoption; 15% via agencies. Advertising is permitted only by licensed adoption agencies. To file a Petition for Adoption in California the adopting parents must reside there *or* the placing birth parent must reside there when either the *Adoption Placement Agreement* is signed, or the Petition for Adoption is filed. Normally, adoptions are finalized 8 to 10 months after the placement of the child with the adoptive parents. The adopting parents and child being adopted are required to appear in court for the final hearing.

Independent Adoption. A preplacement home study of the adoptive parents is not required before a child is placed in their home. The post-placement home study may be conducted by the State Department of Social Services or a county adoption agency designated by the Department of Social Services to perform independent adoption services for that county. The state fee for the home study is $2,950. (Alternatively, a private agency can be retained to perform an Preplacement Evaluation, which can be turned over the designated state or county office handling independent adoptions in the adoptive parents' county, and the state or county fee is reduced from $2,950 to $775.)

The birth mother is required by law to personally select the adoptive parents with full sharing of identities. Although it is not required by law that they meet in person, this is done in virtually all adoptions. The adoptive parents are permitted to assist the birth mother with pregnancy-related expenses. The child may be placed with the adoptive parents directly from the hospital upon the birth mother's signature upon a standard hospital form entitled the *Health Facility Minor Release*.

The birth mother must receive advice and information, called an *Advisement of Rights*, from a licensed social worker approved by the state as an *Adoption Services Provider* (often referred to as an "ASP"), or a licensed adoption agency acting as an ASP, at least ten days before she signs her consent to adoption. The consent form is called the *Adoption Placement Agreement*, which is also signed by the adoptive parents, and outlines the rights and duties of each party. It may only be signed after the birth mother's medical discharge from the hospital. The Adoption Services Provider then sends the birth mother's consent and related documents to the State Department of Social Services (or its designated county entity) which will assign an adoption caseworker who will oversee the remainder of the adoption.

The *Adoption Placement Agreement* is normally signed hours or days after the hospital discharge. However, it is not an effective forfeiture of rights by the birth mother until one of two events occur, whichever occurs first: 1) The birth mother can sign a *Waiver of Right to Revoke Consent* in the presence of the State Department of Social Services or designated county agency anytime after signing the *Adoption Placement Agreement* (at which point her consent to adoption then immediately becomes irrevocable) except upon proof of fraud or duress; or 2) if the birth mother does not elect to sign a *Waiver of Right to Revoke Consent*, her consent to adoption becomes permanent and irrevocable automatically on the 31st day after the signing of the *Adoption Placement Agreement* (if the birth mother has not previously withdrawn her consent during that period).

Agency Adoption. The birth mother may sign a consent to adoption, called a *relinquishment* in agency adoptions, anytime after the birth of the child. It must be witnessed by a representative of a licensed adoption agency. Once the relinquishment it signed and satisfactorily filed with the State Department of Social Services the relinquishment is irrevocable, except when revoked with the agreement of the adoption agency, or proof of fraud or duress. A birth mother may request the adoption agency to delay the effective date of her signed relinquishment for a period, usually up to 30 days, in which case it can be withdrawn automatically within the stated time.

Most agencies agree to do *identified* adoptions. Most will also make "at risk" placements directly to the adoptive parents from the hospital.

Adoption Attorneys

G. Darlene Anderson   Tel (760) 743-4700
127 E. Third Avenue, Suite 202   Fax (760) 743-6218
Escondido, California 92025

Ms. Anderson began practicing law in 1983 and is a graduate of the University of San Diego School of Law. Approximately 85% of her practice consists of adoptions. She estimates she has completed more than 500 adoptions in her career and presently completes 54 annually. Of these, 90% are independent; 10% are agency. Of the adoptions she has handled, she reports 60% of her clients locate a birth mother through her office; 40% locate their own birth mother.

Randi G. Barrow   Tel (310) 395-1723
610 Santa Monica Blvd., Suite 223   Fax (310) 395-0096
Escondido, California 92025

Ms. Barrow began practicing law in 1988 and is a graduate of the Loyola School of Law, Los Angeles. Her pratice is limited to adoptions. She estimates she completes 30 adoptions annually. Of these, 95% are independent; 5% are agency. Of the adoptions she has handled, she reports 5% of her clients locate a birth mother through her office; 95% locate their own birth mother. She is the author of *Somebody's Child: Stories from the Private Files of an Adoption Attorney.*

David H. Baum   Tel (818) 501-8355
16255 Ventura Blvd., Suite 704   Fax (818) 501-8465
Encino, California 91436   e-mail: adoptlaw@ix.netcom.com

Mr. Baum began practicing law in 1978 and is a graduate of Loyola University School of Law. Approximately 85% of his practice consists of adoptions. He estimates he has completed more than 600 adoptions in his career and presently completes up to 75 annually. Of these, 85% are independent; 15% are agency. Of the adoptions he has handled, he reports 75% of his clients locate a birth mother through his office; 25% locate their own birth mother. He is an adoptive parent. His website is www.adoptlaw.com.

ADOPTING IN AMERICA

D. Durand Cook
8383 Wilshire Blvd., Suite 1030
Beverly Hills, CA 90211

Tel (323) 655-2601
Fax (323) 852-0871
e-mail: durand@adoption-option.com

Mr. Cook began practicing law in 1969 and is a graduate of California Western School of Law. His practice is limited to adoptions. He estimates he has completed 3,000 adoptions in his career and presently completes 100 annually. Of these, 85% are independent; 14% are agency and 1% is international. Of the adoptions he has handled, he reports 98% of his clients meet a birth mother through his office; 2% locate their own birth mother. His website is www.adoption-option.com

Douglas R. Donnelly
427 E. Carrillo Street
Santa Barbara, CA 93101

Tel (805) 962-0988
Fax (805) 966-2993
e-mail: DDonnelly@adoptionattorneys.org

Mr. Donnelly began practicing law in 1977 and is a graduate of Loyola University School of Law of Los Angeles. His practice is limited to adoptions. He estimates he has completed more than 1,200 adoptions in his career and presently completes 95 annually. Of these, 95% are independent; 5% are agency. Of the adoptions he has handled, he reports 65% of his clients meet a birth mother through his office; 35% locate their own birth mother. Additionally, Mr. Donnelly has earned a distiguished reputation in handling contested adoption litigation. He authored the Code of Ethics of the American Academy of Adoption Attorneys. He is an adoptive parent. His website is www.adoptionlawfirm.com

Randall B. Hicks
6690 Alessandro Blvd., Suite D
Riverside, CA 92506

Tel (909) 789-6800
Fax (909) 789-6802
e-mail: ranhicks@aol.com

Orange CountyCounty client line:

Tel (714) 544-1289

Mr. Hicks began practicing law in 1986 and is a graduate of Pepperdine University School of Law. His practice is limited to adoptions. He estimates he has completed more than 800 adoptions in his career and presently completes 60 annually. Of these, 70% are independent; 10% are agency and 20% are international adoptions. (He is the director of an Eastern European international program.) Of the adoptions he has handled, he reports 85% of his clients locate a birth mother through his office; 15% locate their own birth mother. He is the author of *Adopting In America: How To Adopt Within One Year, Adopting in California: How To Adopt Within One Year* and *Adoption*

166

Stories for Young Children. He was the host of the 1991 P.B.S. educational series *Adoption Forum.* His website is randallhicks.com

Joy L. Kolender	Tel (858) 485-9823
11348 Monticook Court	Fax (858) 485-5503
San Diego, CA 92127	e-mail: adoptionatty@aol.com

Ms. Kolender began practicing law in 1984 and is a graduate of the University of San Diego School of Law. Her practice is limited to adoptions. She estimates she completes 60 adoptions annually. Of these, 95% are independent; 5% are agency. She reports 3% of her clients locate a birth mother through her office; 97% find their own birth mother. She is an adoptive parent.

David J. Radis	Tel (310) 552-0536
1901 Avenue of the Stars, Suite 1900	Fax (310) 552-0713
Los Angeles, California 90067	e-mail: radis@radis-adopt.com

Mr. Radis began practicing law in 1974 and is a graduate of Southwestern University School of Law. Approximately 98% of his practice consists of adoptions. He estimates he has completed more than 2,500 adoptions in his career and presently completes 115 annually. Of these, 65% are independent; 35% are agency. Of the adoptions he has handled, he reports 60% of his clients locate a birth mother through his office; 40% locate their own birth mother. His website is www.radis-adopt.com.

Susan Romer	Tel (415) 363-4523
Law Offices of Adams & Roper	Fax (415) 643-6421
1191 Church Street	
San Francisco, CA 94114	

Ms. Romer began practicing law in 1991 and is a graduate of Golden Gate University College of Law. Her practice is limited to adoptions. She estimates she has completed more than 300 adoptions in her career and presently completes 50 annually. Of these, 40% are independent; 60% are agency. of the adoptions she has handled, she reports 70% of her clients locate a birth mother through her office; 30% locate their own birth mother. Her website is www.1-800-U-ADOPT-US.com

Felice Webster
4525 Wilshire Blvd., Suite 201
Los Angeles, CA 90010

Tel (323) 664-5600
Fax (323) 664-4551
e-mail: fwebster@adoptionattorneys.org

Ms. Webster began practicing law in 1974 and is a graduate of Loyola Law School. Approximately 90% of her practice consists of adoptions. She estimates she has completed more than 500 adoptions in her career and presently completes 50 annually. Of these, 70% are independent; 30% are agency. Of the adoptions she has handled, she reports 70% of her clients locate a birth mother through her office; 30% locate their own birth mother.

Marc D. Widelock
1801 Oak Street
Bakersfield, CA 93390

Tel (800) MrStork
Fax (661) 396-7393
e-mail: widelock@thestork.com

Mr. Widelock began practicing law in 1986 and is a graduate of Western State University Law School. Approximately 90% of his practice consists of adoptions. Of the adoptions he handles, 98% are independent; 2% are agency. He is available to handle contested adoption cases.

Nancy R. Worchester
1253 High Street
Auburn, CA 95603

Tel (530) 888-1311
Fax (530) 888-7529

Ms. Worchester began practicing law in 1981 and is a graduate of Southwestern University School of Law. Her practice is limited to adoptions. She estimates she completes approximately 65 adoptions annually. Of these, 90% are independent; 10% are agency. Of the adoptions she has handled, she reports 60% of her clients locate a birth mother through her office; 40% locate their own birth mother. She is an adoptive parent.

Licensed Private Adoption Agencies (* Offers intercountry programs)

AASK (Adopt A Special Kid); 7700 Edgewater Drive, Suite 320; Oakland, CA 94621; (510) 553-1748; Toll Free: (888) 680-7349; Fax: (510) 553-1747; World Wide Web: http://www.adoptaspecialkid.org; E-mail: andrea@adoptaspecialkid.org
*ACCEPT (An Adoption and Counseling Center); 339 South San Antonio Road, Suite 1A; Los Altos, CA 94022; (650) 917-8090; Fax: (650) 917-8093; World Wide Web: http://www.acceptadoptions.org; E-mail: acceptadoptions@aol.com

*Across the World Adoptions; 399 Taylor Boulevard, Suite 102; Pleasant Hill, CA 94523; (925) 356-6260; Toll Free: (800) 610-5607; Fax: (925) 827-9396; World Wide Web: http://www.adopting.com/atwa; E-mail: atwakids@pacbell.net

*Adopt International; 121 Springdale Way; Redwood City, CA 94062; (650) 369-7300; Fax: (650) 369-7400; World Wide Web: http://www.adopt-intl.org/; E-mail: adoptinter@aol.com;

Oakland; (510) 653-8600; Fax: (510) 653-8603; World Wide Web: http://www.adopt-intl.org; E-mail: adoptinter@aol.com

Adoption Connection; Jewish Family and Children Services; 1710 Scott Street, 2nd Floor; San Francisco, CA 94115-3004;

(415) 359-2492; Toll Free: (800) 972-9225; Fax: (415) 359-2490; World Wide Web: http://www.adoptionconnection.org/

Adoption Horizons; 302 Fourth Street, 2nd Floor; Eureka, CA 95501-0302; (707) 444-9909; Toll Free: (800) 682-3678; Fax: (707) 442-6672; E-mail: adoptnow@humboldt1.com

*Adoption Options, Inc.; 4025 Camino Del Rio South, Suite 300; San Diego, CA 92108-4108; (619) 542-7772; Toll Free: (877) 542-7772; Fax: (619) 542-7773; World Wide Web: http://www.child4me.com; E-mail: info@adoption-options

*Adoptions Unlimited, Inc.; 4091 Riverside Drive, Suite 115 and 116; Chino, CA 91710; (909) 902-1412; Fax: (909) 902-1414; World Wide Web: http://www.adopting.com/aui/; E-mail: auica@aol.com

Alternative Family Services Adoption Agency; 25 Division Street, Suite 201; San Francisco, CA 94103; (415) 626-2700;

Fax: (415) 626-2760; E-mail: afssanfran@aol.com

*Angels' Haven Outreach; 370 West Grand Blvd, Suite 207; Corona, CA 92882; (909) 735-5400; Fax: (909) 371-0161;

World Wide Web: http://www.angels-haven.com;

E-mail: sherry@angels-haven.com

Aspira Foster & Family Services; 333 Gellert Bouldevard, Suite 203; Daly City, CA 94015-2614; (650) 758-0111; Fax: (650) 758-0122; World Wide Web: http://www.aspirafostercare.org

*Bal Jagat Children's World, Inc.; 9311 Farralone Avenue; Chatsworth, CA 91311; (818) 709-4737; Fax: (818) 722-6377;

World Wide Web: http://www.baljagat.org/; E-mail: bjcw@earthlink.net

*Bay Area Adoption Services, Inc.; 465 Fairchild Drive, Suite 215; Mountain View, CA 94043; (650) 964-3800; Fax: (650) 964-6467; World Wide Web: http://www.baas.org/;

E-mail: baas@baas.org

Bethany Christian Services - North Region; 3048 Hahn Drive; Modesto, CA 95350-6503; (209) 522-5121; Toll Free: (800) 454-0454; Fax: (209) 522-1499; World Wide Web: http://www.bethany.org/modesto; E-mail: bcsmodesto@bethany.org

Bethany Christian Services - South Region; 11929 Woodruff Avenue; Downey, CA 90241-5601; (562) 803-3454; Fax: (562) 803-6674; World Wide Web: www.bethany.org/downey; E-mail: bcsdowney@bethany.org

Bethany Christian Services, Inc.; 14125 Telephone Avenue, Suite 12; Chino, CA 91710-5771; (909) 465-0057; Fax: (909) 628-8294; World Wide Web: http://www.bethany.org/downey; E-mail: bcschino@bethany.org

Better Life Children Services; 1337 Howe Avenue, Suite 107; Sacramento, CA 95825; (916) 641-0661; Fax: (916) 614-0664

Black Adoption Placement and Research Center; 125 Second Street; Oakland, CA 94607; (510) 839-3675; Toll Free: (800) 299-3678; Fax: (510) 839-3765; World Wide Web: http://www.baprc.org; E-mail: family@baprc.org

Catholic Charities Adoption Agency; 349 Cedar Street; San Diego, CA 92101-3197; (619) 231-2828; Fax: (619) 232-3807; E-mail: dsables@ccdsd.org

Catholic Charities of the Archdiocese of San Francisco; 98 Bosworth Street, 3rd Floor; San Francisco, CA 94112; (415) 406-2358; Fax: (415) 406-2386; World Wide Web: http://www.ccasf.org; E-mail: twatters@ccasf.org

Catholic Youth Organization; 1 St. Vincent Drive; San Rafael, CA 94903; (415) 507-2000

Children's Bureau of Southern California; Palmdale Office; 1529 East Palmdale Blvd, Suite 210; Palmdale, CA 93550-2029; (661) 272-9996

Children's Bureau of Southern California; 3910 Oakwood Avenue; Los Angeles, CA 90004-3487; (323) 953-7356, Ext: 201; Fax: (323) 661-7306; World Wide Web: http://www.all4kids.org

*Chrysalis House; 4025 North Fresno Street, Suite 106; Fresno, CA 93726; (559) 229-9862; Fax: (559) 229-9863; World Wide Web: http://www.chrysalishouse.com; E-mail: contact-us@chrysalishouse.com

*East West Adoptions, Inc.; 2 Parnassus Road; Berkeley, CA 94708; (510) 644-3996; Fax: (510) 548-0740

Ettie Lee Youth and Family Services; 13139 Ramona Blvd, #C; Irwindale, CA 91706; (626) 960-8381

Excel Family Intervention Program; 8616 Latijera Blvd, #412; Los Angeles, CA 90045; (310) 337-7053

Families First; Hercules Office; 825 Alfred Nobel Drive, Suite F; Hercules, CA 94547; (510) 741-3100; Fax: (510) 741-3120;
World Wide Web: http://www.familiesfirstinc.org; Davis; (530) 753-0220; Sacramento Office; (916) 641-9595; Toll Free: (800) 495-9559; Fax: (916) 641-9599; World Wide Web: http://www.familiesfirstinc.org; E-mail: SacramentoPFC@familiesfirstinc.org
Families for Children; 2990 Lava Ridge Court, Suite 170; Roseville, CA 95661-3077; Modesto Office; (209) 548-9854;
Benicia Office; (707) 748-4150; Fax: (707) 748-4159
Family Builders By Adoption; 528 Grand Avenue; Oakland, CA 94610; (510) 272-0204; Fax: (510) 272-0277; World Wide Web: http://www.familybuilders.org; E-mail: kids@familybuilders.org
*Family Connections; Ventura Office; 577 E. Thompson Blvd; Venture, CA 93001; (805) 641-1121; Fax: (805) 641-2487; Southern California Office (Oceanside); (760) 754-0200; Fax: (760) 754-0201; Central Valley Office; (559) 325-9388; Fax: (559) 325-9373; E-mail: fresnofc@pacbell.net;
Modesto; (209) 524-8844; Fax: (209) 578-9823; E-mail: familycn@pacbell.net; Northern California Office; (916) 568-5966; Fax: (916) 568-6005; E-mail: fcadoptsac@msn.com
Future Families, Inc.; 3233 Valencia Avenue, Suite A-6; Aptos, CA 95003; Toll Free: (888) 922-5437; World Wide Web: http://www.futurefamilies.org; E-mail: graham@futurefamilies.org; South Bay Office; (408) 298-8789
E-mail: contactme@futurefamilies.org
*God's Families International Adoption Services; P.O. Box 320; Trabuco Canyon, CA 92678; (949) 858-7621; Fax: (949) 858-5431; World Wide Web: http://www.godsfamilies.org/;
E-mail: director@godsfamilies.org
Hand in Hand Foundation; 2401 Robertson Road; Soquel, CA 95073; (408) 476-1866
*Heartsent Adoptions, Inc.; 15 Altarinda Road, Suite 100; Orinda, CA 94563; (925) 254-8883; Fax: (925) 254-8866; World Wide Web: http://www.heartsent.org
*Holy Family Services - Counseling and Adoption; Santa Ana Office; 1403 South Main Street; Santa Ana, CA 92707-1790; (714) 835-5551; Fax: (714) 973-4971; World Wide Web: http://www.hfs.org; E-mail: contact@hfs.org
*Holy Family Services - Counseling and Adoption; San Bernardino Office; 1441 N. D Street; San Bernardino, CA 92405-4738; (909) 885-4882; Fax: (626) 578-7321; World Wide Web: http://www.hfs.org; E-mail: contact@hfs.org; Thousand Oaks Office; (805) 464-2367; World Wide Web: http://www.hfs.org; E-mail: contact@hfs.org; Pasadena Office; (626) 432-5680; World Wide Web: http://www.hfs.org; E-mail: contact@hfs.org

Independent Adoption Center; Los Angeles Office; 5777 Century Boulevard, Suite 1240; Los Angeles, CA 90045
(310) 215-3180; Toll Free: (800) 877-6736; Fax: (310) 215-3252; World Wide Web: http://www.adoptionhelp.org;
E-mail: iacorg@earthlink.net; Los Angles; (310) 215-3180;
Fax: (310) 215-3252; World Wide Web: http://www.adoptionhelp.org; Central Office, Headquarters;
(925) 827-2229; Toll Free: (800) 877-6736; Fax: (925) 603-0820; World Wide Web: http://www.adoptionhelp.org;
E-mail: iacorg@earthlink.net
Indian Child and Family Services; 29377 Rancho California Road, Suite 200; Temecula, CA 92591-5206; (909) 676-8832; Toll Free: (800) 969-4237; Fax: (909) 676-3950
Infant of Prague; 6059 N. Palm Avenue; Fresno, CA 93704; (559) 447-3333; Fax: (559) 447-3322; World Wide Web: http://www.infantofprague.org;
Inner Circle Foster Care and Adoption Services; 7120 Hayvenhurst Avenue, Suite 204; Van Nuys, CA 91406; (818) 988-6300; Fax: (818) 988-7087; World Wide Web: http://www.fosterfamily.org; E-mail: Icffa@aol.com
Institute for Black Parenting; 1299 East Artesia Blvd, Suite 200; Carson, CA 90746; (310) 900-0930; Toll Free: (800) 367-8858; Fax: (310) 900-0948; World Wide Web: http://www.instituteforblackparenting.com; E-mail: info@instituteforblackparenting.org
*International Christian Adoptions; 41745 Rider Way, #2; Temecula, CA 92590; (909) 695-3336; Fax: (909) 308-1753;
World Wide Web: http://www.4achild.com; E-mail: ICA1@gte.net
Kern Bridges Adoption Agency; 1615 V Street; Bakersfield, CA 93301; (661) 322-0421; World Wide Web: http://www.www.kernbridges.com
*Kinship Center; 22 Lower Ragsdale Drive, Suite B; Monterey, CA 93940; (831) 649-3033; Fax: (831) 646-4843; World Wide Web: http://www.kinshipcenter.org/; E-mail: kinship@redshift.com; Santa Ana Office; (714) 979-2365; Fax: (714) 979-8135; World Wide Web: http://www.kinshipcenter.org/; E-mail: kinship@redshift.com
LDS Family Services; Concord Office; 2120 Diamond Boulevard, Suite 120; Concord, CA 94520-5704; (925) 685-2941; Fax: (925) 685-2958; Colton Office; (909) 824-0480;
Fax: (909) 824-0487; World Wide Web: http://ldssocal.org
Fresno Office; (559) 255-1446; Fax: (559) 255-4876; Fountain Valley Office; (714) 444-3463; Fax: (714) 444-1768; San Jose Office; (408) 243-1688; Fax: (408) 243-3926; California North Agency; (916) 725-5032; California South Agency; (858) 467-9170; Fax: (858) 467-9183
*Life Adoption Services; 440 West Main Street; Tustin, CA 92780; (714) 838-

5433; Fax: (714) 838-1160; World Wide Web: http://www.lifeadoption.com; E-mail: lifeadoption@fea.net

Lilliput Children's Services; Chico Office; 8 Williamsburg Lane; Chico, CA 95826; (530) 896-1920; World Wide Web: http://www.lilliput.org; Redding Office; (530) 722-9092; Stockton; (209) 943-0530; Toll Free: (800) 408-2533; Fax: (209) 943-6829; Sacramento Office; (916) 923-5444; Toll Free: (800) 325-5359; Fax: (916) 923-2365; San Leandro Office; (510) 483-2030; Toll Free: (800) 408-2533; Fax: (510) 483-2084

McKinley Children's Center; 762 West Cypress; San Dimas, CA 91773; (909) 599-1227; World Wide Web: http://www.mckinleycc.org; E-mail: support@mckinleyCC.org

*Nightlight Christian Adoptions; 801 East Chapman Avenue, Suite 106; Fullerton, CA 92831; (714) 278-1020; Fax: (714) 278-1063; World Wide Web: http://www.toadoptkids.org/;
E-mail: info@toadoptkids.org

*North Bay Adoptions; 444 Tenth Street, 3rd Floor; Santa Rosa, CA 95401; (707) 570-2940; Fax: (707) 570-2943;
World Wide Web: http://www.northbayadoptions.com;
E-mail: infor@northbayadoptions.com

Olive Crest Adoption Services; 2130 E. Fourth Street, Suite 200; Santa Ana, CA 92705; (714) 543-5437; Toll Free: (800) 743-6783; World Wide Web: http://www.olivercrest.org;
E-mail: info@olivercrest.org

Partners For Adoption; 4527 Montgomery Drive, Suite A;
Santa Rosa, CA 95409; (707) 539-9068; Fax: (707) 539-9466;
World Wide Web: http://www.sonic.net/adoptpfa;
E-mail: adoptpfa@sonic.net

Sierra Adoption Services; Sacramento Office; 8928 Volunteer Lane, Suite 240; Sacramento, CA 95826; (916) 368-5114;
Fax: (916) 368-5157; World Wide Web: http://www.sierraadoption.org; E-mail: sassac@jsierradoption.org; Nevada County Center; (530) 272-9600; Fax: (530) 272-9101; E-mail: sasgv@sierradoption

Southern Calfornia F.F.A.-Adoption Program; 155 N. Occidental Boulevard; Los Angeles, CA 90026; (213) 365-2900

Special Families Adoptions; 3002 Armstrong Street; San Diego, CA 92111; (858) 277-9550

*The Family Network, Inc.; 307 Webster Street; Monterey, CA 93940; (831) 663-5428; Toll Free: (800) 888-0242; Fax: (408) 655-3811; World Wide Web: http://www.adopt-familynetwork.com; E-mail: thefamilynetwork@eartlink.net

The Sycamores Adoption Agency; 210 South DeLacey Avenue, Suite 110; Pasadena, CA 91105-2006; (626) 395-7100; Fax: (626) 395-7270; World Wide Web: http://www.sycamores.org

Trinity Children and Family Services; 1111 Howe Avenue, Suite 455; Sacramento, CA 95825; (916) 646-2032;
World Wide Web: http://www.trinitycfs.org

Trinity Foster Care; 3530 Atlantic Avenue, Suite 100; Long Beach, CA 90807-4569; (562) 424-6888; World Wide Web: http://www.trinitycfs.org

True to Life Children's Services; 1800 North Gravenstein Highway; Sebastopol, CA 95472; (707) 823-7300; Fax: (707) 823-3410; World Wide Web: http://www.tlc4kids.org;
E-mail: information@tlc4kids.org

Valley Teen Ranch; 2610 W. Shaw, Suite 105; Fresno, CA 93711; (559) 437-1144; Fax: (559) 438-5004

*Vista Del Mar Child Care Services; 3200 Motor Avenue; Los Angeles, CA 89934; (310) 836-1223; Toll Free: (888) 228-4782; Fax: (310) 204-4134; World Wide Web: http://www.vistadelmar.org; E-mail: adoptions@vistadelmar.org

Westside Children's Center; 12120 Wagner Street; Culver City, CA 90230; (310) 390-0551; Fax: (310) 397-2213; World Wide Web: http://www.westsidechildrens.org; E-mail: hopem@westsidechildrens.org

Colorado

State Adoption Office: (303) 866-3209
Department of Social Services
1575 Sherman Street-Adoption Unit
Denver, CO 80203   www.cdhs.state.co.us/cyf/cwelfare/cwweb.html

General Information. Colorado permits only agency adoption, although "direct" adoption is permitted where the child is placed with a close family relative (known as "kinship adoption"). Accordingly, virtually all adoptions within Colorado are agen- cy adoptions. Advertising is generally permitted. To file a Petition for Adoption within Colorado the adopting parents are not required to reside there. Normally, adoptions are finalized six months after the placement of the child with the adoptive parents.

Agency Adoption. A preplacement home study of the adopting parents is required before a child can be placed in their home. The home study may be performed by the state adoption office (usually where the child is a ward of the state) or a licensed adoption agency. The cost varies.

Although birth mothers and adoptive parents are not required by law to meet in person, many elect to do so voluntarily. Adopting parents are permitted to assist with pregnancy-related expenses. The child may not be released directly to the adoptive parents from the hospital. Instead, the child is released to the custody of the adoption agency. Often, however, the agency will elect to immediately place the child with the adoptive parents, who have been licensed as temporary foster parents. Identified adoptions are common.

There are two methods to terminate a birth mother's parental rights. The traditional mentod is where the consent to adoption signed by the birth mother is actually entitled a *Petition for Relinquishment,* which may be signed and filed with the court anytime after the birth and the birth mother's receipt of counseling from the state adoption office or a licensed adoption agency. It need only be witnessed by a notary public. A court hearing is then scheduled, usually within several weeks of the birth, to confirm the adoption will be in the child's best interests, at which time the court may give an *Order of Relinquishment.* The consent cannot be withdrawn after the Order of Relinquishment has been made, except upon proof of fraud or duress.

Effective 2003, there is an alternative pre-birth relinquishment method. Using this new method, the birth mother may sign an *affidavit* establishing her desire to relinquish parental rights before the birth, if the child is under one year of age, she is being assisted by a licensed adoption agency, has received counseling. The affidavit must be witnessed by a notary, and two witnesses, one of whom must be a representative of a licensed adoption agency. Upon filing of the affidavit, the court is permitted to terminate the birth mother's rights, upon filing of the affidavit, without a hearing, no more than seven days after the filing of the affidavit and accompanying *Petition for Relinquishment.*

Most agencies within Colorado agree to do identified adoptions. Most agencies also agree to make immediate hospital "at risk" placements directly from the hospital before the consents are irrevocable.

Adoption Attorneys

Seth A. Grob   Tel (303) 679-8266
31425 Forestland Drive   Fax (303) 679-8266
Evergreen, CO 80439   e-mail: sgrob@adoptionattorneys.org

Mr. Grob began practicing law in 1991 and is a graduate of the University of California at Los Angeles. Approximately 80% of his practice consists of adoptions. He estimates he completes 45 adoptions annually. Of these, 50% are independent; 50% are agency.

Susan Price   Tel (303) 893-3111
Wedgle & Kukreja   Fax (303) 893-0842
730 17th Street, Suite 230
Denver, CO 80202

Ms. Price began practicing law in 1978 and is a graduate of the University of Denver School of Law. She estimates she completes more than 50 adoptions annually. Of these, 50% are independent; 50% are agency. She is an adoptive parent.

Daniel A. West   Tel (719) 473-4444
Beltz & West   Fax (719) 444-0156
729 S. Cascade Avenue
Colorado Springs, CO 80903

Mr. West began practicing law in 1996 and is a graduate of the University of Denver College of Law. Approximately 33% of his practice consists of adoptions. He estimates he completes 20 adoptions annually. Of these, 80% are independent; 20% are agency.

Licensed Private Adoption Agencies (* Offers intercountry programs)

*AAC Adoption and Family Network; P.O. Box W, 735 East Hwy 56; Berthoud, CO 80513; (970) 532-3576; Fax: (303) 442-2231; World Wide Web: http://rainbowkids.com/aac.html; E-mail: aacadopt@frii.com
*Adoption Alliance; 2121 South Oneida Street, Suite 420; Denver, CO 80224; (303) 584-9900; Fax: (303) 337-5481;
http://www.adoptall.com/home.html; E-mail: info@adoptall.com
Adoption Connection; 702 S. Nevada Street; Colorado Springs, CO 80903; (719) 442-6880

Adoption Options; 2600 South Parker Road, #2-320; Aurora, CO 80014; (303) 695-1601; Fax: (303) 695-1626

Adoption Services, Inc.; 1108 Northstar Drive; Colorado Springs, CO 80906; (719) 632-9941

*Bethany Christian Services of Colorado; 9185 E. Kenyon Avenue, Suite 190; Denver, CO 80237-1856; (303) 221-0734;
Toll Free: (800) 986-4484; Fax: (303) 221-0960;
World Wide Web: http://www.bethany.org; E-mail: info@bethany.org

Catholic Community Services of Colorado; 825 E Pikes Peak Avenue; Colorado Springs, CO 80903; (719) 578-1222

*Chinese Children Adoption International; 6920 South Holly Circle, Suite 100; Englewood, CO 80112; (303) 850-9998;
Fax: (303) 850-9997; World Wide Web: http://www.chinesechildren.org; E-mail: info@chinesechildren.org

Christian Family Services; 1399 S. Havana Street, Suite 204;
Aurora, CO 80012; (303) 337-6747

Christian Home for Children, Inc.; 1880 S. Cascade Avenue;
Colorado Springs, CO 80906-2590; (719) 632-4661

Colorado Adoption Center; 1136 E. Stuart Street, Suite 2040;
Fort Collins, CO 80525; (970) 493-8816

Colorado Christian Services; 1100 West Littleton Blvd, Suite 105; Littleton, CO 80120; (303) 761-7236; World Wide Web: http://www.christianservices.org

Creative Adoptions; 2329 W. Main Street, Suite 220;
Littleton, CO 80120; (303) 730-7791; World Wide Web: http://www.creativeadoptions.com/; E-mail: Krac010@aol.com

Designated Adoption Services of Colorado, Inc.; 1420 Vance Street, Suite 202; Lakewood, CO 80215; (303) 232-0234

*Friends of Children of Various Nations; 1562 Pearl Street;
Denver, CO 80203; (303) 837-9446; Fax: (303) 837-9848;
E-mail: fcvn@WebAccess.Net

*Hand in Hand International Adoptions; 453 East Wonderview Avenue, PMB #333; Estes Park, CO 80517; (970) 586-6866;
Fax: (970) 577-9452; World Wide Web: http://www.hihiadopt.org/; E-mail: colorado@hihiadopt.org

*Hope's Promise; 309 Jerry Street, Suite 202; Castle Rock, CO 80104; (303) 660-0277; World Wide Web: http://www.hopespromise.com/; E-mail: hopes@henge.com

LDS Family Services; 3263 Fraser Street, Suite 3; Aurora, CO 80011; (303) 371-1000

*Littlest Angels International; 2191-2225 Drive, #1; Cedaredge, CO 81413; (970) 856-6177; Toll Free: (800) 875-4253; Fax: (970) 928-2020; World Wide Web: http://www.co-biz.com/angelsinternational; E-mail: ltlst@aol.com

Loving Homes; 212 West 13th; Pueblo, CO 81003; (719) 545-6181; E-mail: lhomes@aol.com

Loving Homes; 4760 Oakland Street, Suite 700; Denver, CO 80239-1022; (303) 371-9185; Fax: (303) 371-1193; E-mail: lhomes@aol.com

Lutheran Family Services of Colorado; Northern Area Office; 3800 Automation Way, Suite 200; Ft. Collins, CO 80525; (970) 266-1788; Fax: (970) 266-1799; World Wide Web: http://www.lfsco.org/; E-mail: Newhomesn@lfsco.org; Southern Area Office; (719) 227-7571; Fax: (719) 227-7581; Central Area Office; (303) 922-3433; Fax: (303) 922-7335;

*One Light Adoptions, Inc.; 2336 Canyon Boulevard, Suite 102; Boulder, CO 80302; (303) 442-8880; Toll Free: (888) 442-8885; Fax: (303) 442-8889; World Wide Web: http://www.onelightadoptions.org; E-mail: info@onelightadoptions.org

Professional Adoption Services; 1210 S. Parker Road, Suite 104; Denver, CO 80231; (303) 755-4797

*Rainbow House International; 19676 Highway 314; Belen, NM 87002; (505) 861-1234; Fax: (505) 864-8420; World Wide Web: http://www.rhi.org; E-mail: rainbow@rhi.org

Small Miracles; 5555 Denver Tech Center Parkway, Suite B-2100; Englewood, CO 80111; (303) 220-7611; Fax: (303) 694-2622; World Wide Web: http://www.smallmiracles.org; E-mail: smallmiracles@smallmiracles.org

Top of the Trail; 543 South 2nd Street; Montrose, CO 81401 (970) 249-4131; Fax: (970) 249-4218;

Connecticut

State Adoption Office: (860) 550-6659
The Department of Children and Families
Adoption Resource Exchange
Whitehall, Building 2
Undercliff Road
Meridan, Connecticut 06451   state.ct.us/dcf

General Information. Connecticut only permits agency adoption. However, identified adoptions are permitted, where the birth mother was located outside the agency, as long as the attorney or intermediary did not receive a fee for locating the birth mother. Accordingly, all adoptions within Connecticut are agency adoptions. Advertising is not permitted. To file a Petition for Adoption within Connecticut the adopting parents must reside there. Normally, adoptions are finalized 6 to 12 months after the placement of the child with the adoptive parents. The adoptive parents are required to appear in court for the final hearing, although many courts waive this requirement.

A preplacement home study of the adopting parents is required before a child can be placed in their home. The home study may be performed by the Department of Children and Youth Services or a licensed adoption agency. The Department of Children Services charges no fee for their home study services, but their services are usually limited to children being adopted who are wards of the state. The fees of private agencies are typically $10,000.

Birth mothers and adoptive parents are not required by law to meet in person, although some elect to do so voluntarily. Normally, full identities are not disclosed. Adopting parents are permitted to assist with pregnancy-related expenses, such as medical, legal and living costs, although any assistance must be paid through the agency and not directly to the birth mother. Assistance living expenses cannot exceed $1,500 without special court approval. The child may not be released directly to the adoptive parents from the hospital. Instead, the child is released to the custody of the adoption agency. In some cases the agency will elect to immediately place the child with the adoptive parents as an "at risk" placement before the child is permanently free for adoption.

ADOPTING IN AMERICA

The consent to adoption process is made by the birth mother or the agency filing a voluntary *Petition to Terminate Parental Rights* with the court. This petition to voluntarily terminate parental rights may not be signed by the birth mother until at least 48 hours have elapsed after the birth and must be witnessed by a notary public. The birth mother later signs a *Consent to Termination of Parental Rights,* also witnessed by a notary, which is presented in a court hearing approximately four weeks later. The birth mother need not appear at that hearing.

If the birth mother is under the age of 18 a guardian ad litem, usually an attorney, shall be appointed prior to her signing of the consent to termination of parental rights to be sure she understands her legal rights. The consent may also not be signed until the birth mother has received mandatory counseling. The consent can not be withdrawn once the court has approved the consent and resulting termination of parental rights, except upon proof of fraud or coercion.

Adoption Attorneys

No biographies are available for adoption attorneys in Connecticut.

Licensed Private Adoption Agencies (* Offers intercountry programs)

Boys Village Youth and Family Services, Inc.; 528 Wheelers Farm Road; Milford, CT 06460; (203) 877-0300; Toll Free: (888) 922-5528; Fax: (203) 876-0076; http://www.boysvill.org/; E-mail: sylviak@boysvill.org
Casey Family Services; Hartford Division; 43 Woodland Street; Hartford, CT 06105; (860) 727-1030; Fax: (860) 727-9355; World Wide Web: http://www.caseyfamilyservices.org;
Bridgeport Division; (203) 372-3722; Fax: (203) 372-3558
*Catholic Charities of Fairfield County; 238 Jewett Avenue
Bridgeport, CT 06606; (203) 372-4301; http://www.ccfc-ct.org/; E-mail: CCFCADPTN@aol.com
Catholic Charities, Catholic Family Services Archdiocese of Hartford; 467 Bloomfield Avenue; Bloomfield, CT 06002;
(860) 242-9577; Fax: (860) 286-2800
Catholic Charities, Hartford District Office; 896 Asylum Avenue; Hartford, CT 06105-1991; (860) 522-8241; New Haven District Office; (203) 787-2207; Waterbury District Office; (203) 755-1196

Child Adoption Resource Association, Inc.; 2 Union Plaza;
New London, CT 06320; (860) 442-0553; World Wide Web:
http://www.adoptacarakid.org
*Children's Center; 1400 Whitney Avenue; Hamden, CT 06514; (203) 248-
2116; Fax: (203) 786-6408
Community Residences, Inc.; 732 West Street, #2; Plainville, CT 06489; (860)
621-7600; Fax: (860) 747-2506
Connection, Inc.; 955 South Main Street; Middletwon, CT 06457; (860) 343-
5500; Fax: (860) 343-5517
Curtis Home Foundation; 380 Crown Street; Meriden, CT 06450; (203) 237-
9526; Fax: (203) 630-2121;
DARe Family Services, Inc.; 1184 Burnside Avenue; East Hartford, CT 06108;
(860) 291-8688; Fax: (860) 291-2689; World Wide Web:
http://www.darect@juno.com
Devereux Foundation; 81 Sabbady Lane; Washington, CT 06793; (860) 868-
7377; Fax: (860) 868-7894; World Wide Web:
http://www.theglenholmeschool.org
Downeyside; 2264 Silas Deane Hwy, Suite 100; Rocky Hill, CT 06067-2333;
(860) 296-3310; Fax: (860) 257-1698; World Wide Web:
http://www.downeyside.org
*Family and Children's Agency Inc.; 9 Mott Avenue; Norwalk, CT 06850;
(203) 855-8765; Fax: (203) 838-3325; http://www.fcadopt.org; E-mail:
adoption@fcagency.org
Family Services, Inc.; 92 Vine Street; New Britain, CT 06052;
(860) 223-9291;
Franciscan Family Care Center, Inc.; 271 Finch Avenue; Meriden, CT 06450;
(203) 237-8084; Fax: (203) 639-1333
Healing the Children Northeast, Inc; 21 Main Street, P.O. Box 129; New
Milford, CT 06776; (860) 355-1828; Fax: (860) 350-6634; World Wide Web:
http://www.htcne.org
Highland Heights; St. Francis Home for Children, Inc.; 651 Prospect Street,
Box 1224; New Haven, CT 06505; (203) 777-5513
Institute of Professional Practice, Inc.; 1764 Litchfield Turnpike; Woodbridge,
CT 06525; (203) 389-6956; Fax: (203) 392-2113
International Alliance for Children, Inc.; 2 Ledge Lane; New Milford, CT
06776; (203) 354-3417; Fax: (203) 354-4451
Jewish Family Service of New Haven; 1440 Whalley Avenue; New Haven, CT
06515; (203) 389-5599; Fax: (203) 389-5904
Jewish Family Services Inc.; 2370 Park Avenue; Bridgeport, CT 06604; (203)
366-5438; Fax: (203) 366-1580; World Wide Web: http://www.jfsnh.org;

Jewish Family Services Infertility Center; 740 North Main Street; West Hartford, CT 06117; (860) 236-1927; Fax: (860) 236-6483;
Klingberg Family Centers, Inc.; 370 Linwood Street; New Britain, CT 06052; (860) 224-9113; Fax: (860) 826-1739;
World Wide Web: http://www.klingberg.com
LDS Social Services; 34 Jerome Street, Suite 319, P.O. Box 378; Bloomfield, CT 06004; Toll Free: (800) 735-0149; Fax: (860) 889-4358; Nashua, NH (603) 889-0148; Toll Free: (800) 735-0419; Fax: (603) 889-4358
*Lutheran Social Services of New England; 2139 Silas Deane Hwy, #201; Rocky Hill, CT 06067; (860) 257-9889; Toll Free: (800) 286-9889; Fax: (860) 257-0340; http://www.adoptlss.org; E-mail: LSSadoptct@aol.com
New Opportunities for Waterbury, Inc.; 232 North Elm Street; Waterbury, CT 06702; (203) 575-9799; Fax: (203) 755-8254
North American Family Institute; 10 Waterchase Drive; Rocky Hill, CT 06067; (860) 529-1522; Fax: (860) 529-1802
Rainbow Adoptions International, Inc.; 80 Garden Street; Wethersfield, CT 06109; (860) 721-0099
Thursday's Child; 227 Tunxis Avenue; Bloomfield, CT 06002; (860) 242-5941; Fax: (860) 243-9898; World Wide Web: http://www.tcadoption.org
United Services, Int.; 303 Putnam Road, P.O. Box 387; Wauregan, CT 06387; Toll Free: (800) 953-0295; Fax: (203) 564-6110; World Wide Web: http://www.usmhs.org
Waterford Country School; 78 Hunts Brook Road, P.O. Box 408; Quaker Hill, CT 06751; (860) 442-9454; Fax: (860) 442-2228
Wellspring Foundation; 21 Arch Bridge Road, P.O. Box 370; Bethlehem, CT 06751; (203) 266-7235; Fax: (860) 266-5830
Wheeler Clinic, Inc.; 91 Northwest Drive; Plainville, CT 06062; (860) 646-6801; Fax: (860) 793-3520
*Wide Horizons for Children; 776 Farmington Avenue; West Hartford, CT 06119; (860) 570-1740; Fax: (860) 570-1745; http://www.whfc.org; E-mail: info@whfc.org

Delaware

State Adoption Office: (302) 633-2655
Delaware Dept. of Services for Children, Youth & Families
1825 Faulkland Road
Wilmington, DE 19805

General Information. Delaware permits only agency adoption, although independent adoption (with no preplacement home study requirement) is permitted if the child being adopted is a close relative. Identified agency adoption is also permitted. Advertising is only permitted by adoption agencies. To file a Petition for Adoption within Delaware either the adopting parents must reside there or the child must be born there. Adoptions are normally finalized six months to one year after the birth or the placement of the child with the adoptive parents. The adopting parents and the child are generally not required to appear in court for the final hearing.

A preplacement home study of the adopting parents is required before a child may be placed in their home. The home study must be conducted by a licensed adoption agency. The fee varies but may range from $2,000 to $15,000. The birth mother and adoptive parents are not required by law to meet in person and share identities, although some elect to do so voluntarily. Adopting parents are permitted to assist with pregnancy-related expenses, such as medical, legal and living costs, although they must be paid through the agency and not directly to the birth mother.

The child may not be released directly to the adoptive parents from the hospital. Instead, the child is released to the custody of the adoption agency. In some cases the agency will elect to immediately place the child with the adoptive parents as an "at risk" placement where the child is not yet permanently free for adoption. Approximately half of Delaware's infant adoptions are identified adoptions.

The birth mother may sign her consent to adoption anytime after the birth. (A birth father may sign before the birth.) The consent to adoption must be witnessed by a notary public and must be taken before approved individuals designated by statute, including a judge, court approved individual, adoption agency employee, hospital social worker or an attorney not representing the adoptive parents or adoption agency. The consent is signed and filed with the court, in conjunction with a voluntary *Petition for Termination of Parental Rights*. A birth mother has the right to revoke her consent to adoption within 14 days of signing, by written instrument. Once the 14 days have elapsed, the consent is basically irrevocable.

Identified adoptions are common and most agencies will agree to make them. Many agencies will also agree to make immediate hospital "at risk" placements.

Adoption Attorneys

Ellen Shaffer Meyer   Tel (302) 429-0344
521 West Street   Fax (302) 429-8806
Wilmington, DE 19801

Ms. Meyer began practicing law in 1982 and is a graduate of Widener University School of Law. Approximately 80% of her practice consists of adoptions. She estimates she has completes 100 annually. Of these, 80% are agency; 20% are intercountry.

Licensed Private Adoption Agencies (* Offers intercountry programs)

Adoption House; 3411 Silver Side Road, Suite 101; Webster
Wilmington, DE 19180; (302) 477-0944; http://www.adoptionhouse.org; E-mail: adopt@adopthouse.org
*Adoptions From The Heart; 18-A Trolley Square; Wilmington, DE 19806; (302) 658-8883; Fax: (302) 658-8873; World Wide Web: http://www.adoptionsfromtheheart.org/;
E-mail: adoption@adoptionsfromtheheart.org
*Bethany Christian Services; 1661 S. Dupont Highway, Suite 1; Dover, DE 19901-5129;
Catholic Charities; P.O. Box 2610, Fourth Street and Greenhill Avenue; Wilmington, DE 19805; (302) 655-9624; Fax: (302) 655-9753; Dover: (302) 674-1600
*Child and Home Study Associates; 242 N James Street, Suite 202; Wilmington, DE 19804-3168; (302) 475-5433
Children and Families First; 2005 Baynard Blvd; Wilmington, DE 19802; (302) 422-9013;

Children's Choice of Delaware, Inc.; University Office Plaza,; Bellevue Building, Suite 102; Newark, DE 19702; (302) 731-9512

Children's Choice of Delaware, Inc.; 1151 Walker Road; Dover, DE 19904-6539; (302) 678-0404

LDS Family Services; 500 West Chestnut Hill; Newark, DE 19713; (302) 456-3782

*Madison Adoption Agency; 1009 Woodstream Drive; Wilmington, DE 19810; (302) 475-8977; Fax: (302) 529-1976

*Tressler Adoption Services of Delaware; Diakon Lutheran Social Ministries; 1679 South DuPont Hwy; Dover, DE 19901;

(302) 730-1205; Fax: (302) 730-1208; http://www.tressler.org; E-mail: hsaunders@tressler.org

Tressler Lutheran Services; 836 South Geoirge Street; York, PA 17403; (717) 845-9113; Fax: (717) 852-8439

Welcome House Adoption Program; 520 Dublin Road, PO Box 181; Perkasie, PA 18944; (215) 249-0100; Fax: (215) 249-0125; www.pearlsbuck.org; E-mail: mtomlinson@pearlsbuck.org

Welcome House, Inc.; 910 Barley Drive; Wilmington, DE 19807; (302) 654-7683; Fax: (302) 654-7683

District of Columbia

District Adoption Office: (202) 727-4733
District of Columbia Child & Family Services
400 6th Street SW
Washington, D.C. 20024

General Information. The District of Columbia permits both independent and agency adoption. Approximately 75 % of the District of Columbia's infant adoptions are completed via independent adoption; 25 % via agencies. Advertising is permitted. To file a Petition for Adoption in the District of Columbia the adoptive parents must have resided there for one year. If it is an agency adoption the Petition may also be filed there if the adoption agency having custody of the child is located there. Usually, adoptions are finalized approximately eight months after the child's placement with the adoptive parents. The adoptive parents and the child are normally required to appear in court for the final hearing.

Independent Adoption. A preplacement home study is not required of the adoptive parents before a child may be placed in their home. The postplacement home study may be conducted by the state adoption office or a licensed adoption agency. The cost varies.

The adoptive parents and the birth mother are not required by law to meet in person and share identities, although many do so voluntarily. The adoptive parents are permitted to assist the birth mother with pregnancy-related medical and legal expenses. Living expense assistance is not permitted. The child may be released from the hospital upon his or her discharge directly to the adoptive parents, although each hospital has different policies. Some hospitals will accept a release form while others require a court order.

The birth mother may sign her consent anytime after the birth. It may be witnessed by a person authorized to take acknowledgments, such as a notary public, or in some cases an adoption agency representative or representative of the Mayor of the District of Columbia. Absent proof of fraud or undue influence, the consent is generally considered irrevocable upon signing, assuming the child has been placed in the custody of the adoptive parents.

Agency Adoption. A birth mother may not sign her consent to the adoption, called a *relinquishment* in an agency adoption, until 72 hours have elapsed following the birth. She must also have received counseling prior to the signing of the relinquishment. Once the relinquishment is signed, there is a ten day period in which the birth mother may automatically withdraw her consent by written request. After the ten days have elapsed, the relinquishment can only be withdrawn upon proving to a court that fraud or undue influence was used. Once the adoption is finalized the relinquishment is basically irrevocable.

Many adoption agencies within the District of Columbia do identified adoptions. Many will also agree to make "at risk" placements of the child with the adoptive parents directly from the hospital before relinquishments are irrevocable.

186

State-by-State Review

Adoption Attorneys

Note: Many attorneys listed in Virginia also practice in the District of Columbia.

Mark T. McDermott
Joseph, McDermott & Reiner
1050 17th Street N.W., Suite 700
Washington, D.C. 20036

Tel (202) 331-1955
Fax (202) 293-2309

Mr. McDermott began practicing law in 1974 and is a graduate of Indiana University School of Law. He is also licensed to practice law in California, Indiana, Maryland and Virginia. Approximately 70% of his practice consists of adoptions. He estimates he has completed 1,200 adoptions in his career and presently completes 100 annually. Of these, 80% are independent; 20% agency. His clients locate their own birth mother. His office also agrees to handle contested adoptions where litigation is required. He is an adoptive parent and is a past president of the American Academy of Adoption Attorneys.

Peter J. Wiernicki
Joseph, McDermott & Reiner
1050 17th Street N.W., Suite 700
Washington, D.C. 20036

Tel (202) 331-1955
Fax (202) 293-2309

Mr. Wiernicki began practicing law in 1986 and is a graduate of the Universityy of Baltimore School of Law. He is also licensed to practice law in California, Maryland and Virginia. Approximately 80% of his practice consists of adoptions. He estimates he has completes more than 100 adoptions annually. Of these, 80% are independent; 20% agency. His clients locate their own birth mother. His office also agrees to handle contested adoptions where litigation is required.

Licensed Private Adoption Agencies (* Offers intercountry programs)

*Adoption Center of Washington; 1726 M Street NW, Suite 1101; Washington, DC 20036; (202) 452-8278; (800) 452-3878; Fax: (202) 452-8280; http://www.adoptioncenter.com; E-mail: info@adoptioncenter.com;
*Adoption Service Information Agency, Inc. (ASIA); 7720 Alaska Avenue NW; Washington, DC 20012; (202) 726-7193; Fax: (202) 722-4928; http://www.asia-adopt.org; E-mail: ASIAadopt@aol.com;
*Adoptions Together Inc.; 419 7th Street NW, Suite 201; Washington, DC 20004; (202) 628-7420; http://www.adoptionstogether.org; E-mail: adoptionworks@adoptionstogether.org;

Barker Foundation, 4400 MacArthur Boulevard, Suite 200; Washington, DC 20818; (202) 363-7751; Toll Free: (800) 673-8489; http://www.barkerfoundation.org; E-mail: info@barkerfoundation.org;
*CASI Foundation For Children; 816 Connecticut Avenue, N.W., 1st Floor; Washington, DC 20003; (202) 974-0970; Fax: (202) 974-0975; World Wide Web: http://www.adoptcasi.org; Catholic Charities Archdiocese of Washington D.C.; Pregnancy and Adoption Services; The James Cardinal Hickey Center, 924 G Street NW; Washington, DC 20001; (202) 772-4327; Fax: (202) 772-4409; Satellite offices: (202) 581-3630;
(202) 526-4100; World Wide Web: http://www.catholiccharities.org;
*Datz Foundation; 311 Maple Avenue West, Suite E; Vienna, VA 22180; (703) 242-8800; Fax: (703) 242-8804; World Wide Web: http://www.datzfound.com; E-mail: markeckman@hotmail.com;
Family and Child Services of Washington D.C., Inc.; 929 L Street NW; Washington, DC 20001; (202) 289-1510; Fax: (202) 371-0863; World Wide Web: http://www.familyandchildservices.org;
Family and Child Services of Washington, D.C., Inc.; 929 L Street, NW; Washington, DC 20001; (202) 289-1510; Fax: (202) 371-0863; World Wide Web:http://www.familyandchildservices.org;Satelliteoffice:(202)289-1510; Fax: (202) 371-0863;
*International Families, Inc.; 5 Thomas Circle, N.W.; Washington, DC 20005; (202) 667-5779; Fax: (202) 667-5922; World Wide Web: http://www.ifichild.com; E-mail: ifichild@aol.com;
*Lutheran Social Services of the National Capital Area; 4406 Georgia Avenue NW; Washington, DC 20011-7124; (202) 723-3000; Fax: (202) 723-3303; World Wide Web: http://www.lssnca.org; E-mail: greenberg@lssnca.org; Progressive Life Center; 1123 11th Street, N.W.; Washington, DC 20001; (202) 842-2016;

Florida

State Adoption Office: (850) 487-2383
Department of Children & Families—Adoptions Branch
1317 Winewood Blvd.
Tallahassee, FL 32399
 www5.myflorida.com/cf_web/myflorida/healthhuman/adoption

General Information. Florida permits both independent and agency adoption. Approximately 60% of Florida's infant adoptions are completed via independent adoption; 40 % via agencies. Advertising is permitted when placed by an attorney or agency. To file a Petition for Adoption within Florida the adoptive parents or the child must reside there. Normally, independent adoptions are finalized three to six months after the child's placement with the adoptive parents. The adoptive parents may be required to appear in court for the final hearing in some regions, but in others are not required to appear in person.

Independent Adoption. A preplacement home study of the adoptive parents is required before a child may be placed in their home. The home study may be conducted by the state adoption office, a licensed private adoption agency or a licensed social worker. The cost varies.

The adoptive parents and birth mother are not required by law to meet in person and share identities, although some do so voluntarily. The adoptive parents are permitted to assist the birth mother with pregnancy-related expenses, although they may not continue beyond six weeks after the birth. If the expenses for legal or living costs exceed $5,000, court approval is required for the excess. The child may be released from the hospital directly to the adoptive parents, usually by means of a release form to the attorney who in turns places the child with the adoptive parents.

When the child being adopted is under the age of six months, the birth mother may sign her consent 48 hours after the birth or the day she is medically discharged from the hospital, whichever is sooner. It must be witnessed by two witnesses and a notary public. Most birth mothers sign their consents about three days after birth. Once signed, the consent is irrevocable unless fraud or duress is proven. However, if the child being adopted was over the age of six months when adopted, there is a three day revocation period.

Agency Adoption. There is no difference regarding the process in which a birth mother signs her consent to adoption in an independent or agency adoption. The information provided above regarding independent adoption (e.g. when it can be signed, before whom, legal burden to seek to withdraw a signed consent) is identical regarding agency adoption.

Some agencies within Florida agree to do identified adoptions, as well as agree to make immediate hospital "at risk" placements.

ADOPTING IN AMERICA

Adoption Attorneys

Madonna Finney Hawken   Tel (850) 577-3077
660 E. Jefferson Street   Fax (850) 577-3079
Tallahassee, FL 32201   e-mail: mfhawken@aol.com

Ms. Hawken began practicing law in 1988 and is a graduate of the University of Florida College of Law. Her practice is limited to adoptions. She estimates she completes 25 adoptions annually. Of these, 95% are independent; 5% are agency. She reports 95% of her clients locate a birth mother through her office; 5% find their own birth mother. Her website is www.madonnahawken.com

Brian T. Kelly   Tel (904) 348-6400
Shorstein & Kelly   Fax (904) 348-6424
3821 Atlantic Blvd.
Jacksonville, FL 32207

Mr. Kelly began practicing law in 1983 and is a graduate of the University of Florida College of Law. He estimates he completes 30 adoptions annually. Mr. Shorstein additionally represents a Florida child-placing agency. Of these, 70% are independent; 30% are agency. He reports 75% of his clients find a birth mother through his office; 25% find their own birth mother.

Linda McIntyre   Tel (954) 344-0990
2929 University Drive, Suite 204
Coral Springs, FL 33065

Ms. McIntyre began practicing law in 1984 and is a graduate of Nova University School of Law. Approximately 95% of her practice consists of adoptions. She estimates she has completed more than 900 adoptions in her career. Of these, 90% are independent; 5% are agency; and 5% are intercountry. She is past co-chariperson of the Florida Bar Family Law Section Committee on Adoption.

Michael A. Shorstein   Tel (904) 348-6400
Shorstein & Kelly   Fax (904) 348-6424
3821 Atlantic Blvd.
Jacksonville, FL 32207

Mr. Shorstein began practicing law in 1985 and is a graduate of Florida State Univesity College of Law. He estimates he has completed more than 1,000 adoptions in his career and presently completes 100 annually. Of these, 70%

are independent; 30% are agency. Of the adoptions he has handled, he reports 75% of his clients locate a birth mother through his office; 25% locate their own birth mother.

Jeanne T. Tate   Tel (813) 258-3355
418 W. Platt Street, Suite 3   Fax (813) 258-3373
Tampa, FL 33606

Ms. Tate began practicing law in 1982 and is a graduate of the University of Florida College of Law. She estimates she completes 100 adoptions annually. Of these, 50% are independent; 40% are agency; 10% are international. Of the adoptions she has handled, he reports 65% of her clients locate a birth mother through her office; 35% locate their own birth mother.

Licensed Private Adoption Agencies (* Offers intercountry programs)

A Bond of Love Adoption Agency, Inc.; 1800 Siesta Drive;
Sarasota, FL 34239; (941) 957-0064; Fax: (941) 957-0064
Adoption Advisory Associates; 1111 East Boca Raton Road;
Boca Raton, FL 33432; (561) 362-5222; E-mail: adoptadv@aol.com
Adoption Advocates, Inc.; 11407 Seminole Boulevard; Largo, FL 33778; (727) 391-8096; Fax: (727) 399-0026; World Wide Web:
http://adoptionadvocatesinc.com/; E-mail: Adoptme@gte.net
Adoption Agency of Central Florida; 1681 Maitland Avenue; Maitland, FL 32751; (407) 831-2154
Adoption By Choice; St. Andrew's Square, 4102 West Linebaugh Avenue, Suite 200; Tampa, FL 33624; (813) 960-2229; Toll Free: (800) 421-2229; Fax: (813) 969-2339; E-mail: melisa@abcadopt.com
*Adoption Placement, Inc.; 1840 North Pine Island Road; Ft. Lauderdale, FL 33322; (954) 474-8494; http://www.adoptionplacement.com; E-mail: api@adoptionplacement.com
*Adoption Resources of Florida; 112 South Armenia Avenue; Tampa, FL 33609; (813) 251-3388; Toll Free: (888) 726-3555; Fax: (813) 251-4187; http://www.adoptionfl.com; E-mail: adoption@adoptionfl.com
Advocates for Children and Families; 16831 NE 6th Avenue; North Miami Beach, FL 33162-2408; (305) 653-2474; Toll Free: (800) 348-0467; Fax: (305) 653-2746; World Wide Web: http://www.adoptionflorida.org; E-mail: info@adoptionflorida.org
All About Adoptions, Inc.; 505 East New Haven Avenue; Melbourne, FL 32901; (321) 723-0088; Fax: (321) 952-9813;
E-mail: grassadopt@aol.com

American Adoptions; National Offices; 8676 West 96th Street, Suite 140; Overland Park, KS 66212; Toll Free: (800) 236-7846; World Wide Web: http://www.americanadoptions.com; E-mail: adoptions@americanadoptions.com

*Arbor Family Center; 1416C West 16th Street; Panama City, FL 32405; (850) 215-2232; Fax: (850) 785-4059; World Wide Web: http://www.arborfamilycenter.org; E-mail: arborfc1@cs.com

Catholic Charities; 1801 East Memorial Blvd; Lakeland, FL 33801-2226; (941) 686-7153; Wilton Manors: (954) 630-9404; West Palm Beach:(561) 842-2406; Stuart: (561) 283-0541

Catholic Charities Bureau; 134 E. Church Street, Suite 2; Jacksonville, FL 32202-3130; (904) 354-3416; St. Augustine:

(904) 829-6300

Gainesville: (352) 372-0294;

Catholic Charities of Tallahassee; 855 W. Carolina Street; Tallahassee, FL 32309; (850) 222-2180

Catholic Charities of the Diocese of Venice, Inc.; 4930 Fruitville Road; Sarasota, FL 34232-2206; (941) 484-9543

Catholic Social Service of Bay County; 3128 E. 11th Street; Panama City, FL 32404; (850) 785-8935

Catholic Social Services; 817 Dixon Blvd, #16; Cocoa, FL 32922; (407) 636-6144; Orlando: (407) 658-1818; Ft. Walton:

(850) 244-2825

Catholic Social Services of Pensacola; 222 E. Government Street; Pensacola, FL 32501; (850) 436-6410

Children's Home Society of Florida; 3535 Lawton Road, Suite 260; Orlando, FL 32803; (407) 895-5800; Fax: (407) 895-5801; World Wide Web: http://www.chsfl.org; E-mail: kim.brien@chsfl.org; Pensacola: (850) 494-5990; Toll Free: (800) 235-2229; Fax: (850) 494-5981; E-mail: cynthia.blacklaw@chsfl.org; Tallahassee: (850) 921-0772; Fax: (850) 921-0726; E-mail: Janice.Kane@chsfl.org;

West Palm Beach: (561) 844-9785; Toll Free: (800) 433-0010; Fax: (561) 848-0195; E-mail: south.coastal@chsfl.org; Jacksonville: (904) 348-2811; Fax: (904) 348-2818; E-mail: rjohnson@chsfl.org; Fort Myers: (941) 334-0222; Fax: (941) 334-0244; e-mail: chsswra@aol.com; Fort Pierce: (561) 489-5601, Ext: 212; Toll Free: (800) 737-5756; Fax: (561) 489-5604; E-mail: larry.wilms@chsfl.org; Melbourne: (407) 752-3170; Fax: (407) 752-3179; E-mail: Kene.Ledford@chsfl.org;

Daytona Beach: (904) 304-7600; Fax: (904) 304-7620; E-mail: Donna.Marietta@chsfl.org; Miami: (305) 324-1262; Fax: (305) 326-7430; E-mail: carla.penn@chsfl.org;

Children's Home Society of Florida (cont'd)
Panama City: (850) 747-5411; Fax: (850) 747-5662; E-mail: michelle.flaat@chsfl.org; Gainesville: (352) 334-0955; E-mail: rjohnson@chsfl.org; Ft. Lauderdale: (954) 763-6573; Fax: (954) 764-6458; E-mail: annie.luther@chsfl.org

Children's Home, Inc.; 10909 Memorial Hwy; Tampa, FL 33615; (813) 855-4435

Christian Family Services; 2720 SW 2nd Avenue; Gainesville, FL 32607; (352) 378-6202

Everyday Blessings; 13129 St. Francis Lane; Thonotosassa, FL 33592; (813) 982-9226

*Family Creations, Inc.; 5550 26th Street West, Suite 8A; Bradenton, FL 34207; (941) 727-9630; Toll Free: (866) 322-9630; World Wide Web: http://www.familycreationsinc.com;
E-mail: familycreationsadoption@msn.com

*Flordia Home Studies and Adoption, Inc.; 3945 Hidden Glen Drive; Sarasota, FL 34241; (941) 342-8189; E-mail: susan@flhomestudies.com

Florida Baptist Children's Home; 8415 Buck Lake Road; Tallahassee, FL 32311-9522; (850) 878-1458; Miami: (305) 271-4121; Cantonment: (850) 494-9530

Florida Baptist Family Ministries; 1015 Sikes Boulevard; Lakeland, FL 33815; (941) 687-8811

Gift of Life, Inc.; 4437 Park Blvd; Pinellas Park, FL 33781-3540; (727) 549-1416; Toll Free: (800) 216-5433; Fax: (727) 548-8174; World Wide Web: http://www.giftoflifeinc.org; E-mail: giftoflifeadoptions@email.msn.com

Given in Love Adoptions; 151 Mary Esther Blvd., Suite 305; Mary Esther, FL 32569; (850) 243-3576

Gorman Family Life Center, Inc.; dba Life for Kids; 315 N. Wymore Road; Winter Park, FL 32789; (407) 628-5433

*International Adoption Resource, Inc.; 9900 W Sample Road, Suite 300; Coral Springs, FL 33065; (954) 825-0470; Fax: (954) 825-0469; World Wide Web: http://www.iaradopt.com; E-mail: IARebecca@aol.com

Jewish Adoption and Foster Care; 10001 West Oakland Park Blvd, Suite 200; Sunrise, FL 33351; (954) 749-7230; Fax: (954) 749-7231; World Wide Web: http://www.jafco.org/index.html; E-mail: info@jafco.org

Jewish Family & Community Services, Inc.; (AKA First Coast Adoption Professionals); 3601 Cardinal Point Drive; Jacksonville, FL 32257; (904) 448-1933

Jewish Family Services; 300 41st Street, Suite 216; Miami Beach, FL 33145; (305) 672-8080

Jewish Family Services, Inc., of Broward County; 100 S. Pine Island Boulevard, Suite 130; Plantation, FL 33324; (954) 370-2140

LDS Family Services; 10502 Satellite Blvd, Suite D; Orlanda, FL 32837; (407) 850-9141; Fax: (407) 850-9687
*Lifelink Child and Family Services Corporation; 1031 South Euclid Street; Sarasota, FL 34237; (941) 957-1614; World Wide Web: http://www.lifelink.org; E-mail: alladopt@lifelink.org
*New Beginnings Family & Children's Services; 1301 Seminole Blvd, Suite 111; Largo, FL 33773; (727) 584-5262
Fax: (727) 585-6322; World Wide Web: http://www.new-beginnings.org; E-mail: newbeginn@aol.com
One World Adoption Services, Inc.; 1030 South Federal Highway, Suite 100; Hollywood, FL 33019; (954) 922-8400; Fax: (954) 922-4575; E-mail: adoptbaby@aol.com;
Open Door Adoption Agency; 220 Alba Avenue; Quincy, FL 32351; (850) 627-1420; World Wide Web: http://www.opendooradoption.com; E-mail: pendoor@rose.net;
Shepherd Care Ministries; dba Christian Adoption Services; 5935 Taft Street; Hollywood, FL 33021; (954) 981-2060;
St. Vincent Adoption Center; 18601 S.W. 97th Avenue; Miami, FL 33157; (305) 445-5714;
*Suncoast International Adoptions, Inc.; 12651 Walsingham Road, Suite C; Largo, FL 33774; (727) 596-3135; Fax: (727) 593-0106; E-mail: suncoastadoption@aol.com
*Tedi Bear Adoptions Inc.; 1415 Atlantic Boulevard; Neptune Beach, FL 32266; (904) 242-4995; Fax: (904) 242-8951; E-mail: info@tedibearadoptions.org
The Southwest Florida Children's Home; 4551 Camino Real Way; Fort Myers, FL 33912; (941) 275-7151
*Universal Aid for Children; Cypress Village East, 167 SW 6th Street; Pompano Beach, FL 33060; (954) 785-0033; Fax: (954) 785-7003; World Wide Web: http://www.uacadoption.org; E-mail: uacadopt@aol.com

Georgia

State Adoption Office:*   (404) 657-3558
Department of Human Resources
Office of Adoptions
2 Peachtree Street, N.W. Suite 8-400
Atlanta, Georgia 30303

General Information. Georgia permits both independent and agency adoption. Approximately 75 % of Georgia's infant adoptions are completed via independent adoptions; 25 % via agencies. Attorneys are not permitted to locate birth mothers for adoptive parents to start adoption planning. Advertising is not permitted, except by licensed adoption agencies. To file a Petition for Adoption in Georgia the adoptive parents must reside there for six months. Normally, adoptions are finalized within four months of the placement of the child and filing of the Petition for Adoption. The adoptive parents and the child are required to appear at the final court hearing.

Independent Adoption. A preplacement home study of the adoptive parents is not required of the adoptive parents before a child is placed in their home. The postplacement home study may be conducted by a licensed private adoption agency or other court appointed individual. The fee varies.

    The adoptive parents and birth mother are not required by law to meet in person and share identities, although many do so voluntarily. The adoptive parents are permitted to assist the birth mother with medical expenses only. The child may be placed with the adoptive parents immediately upon discharge from the hospital, usually through the attorney by means of a "Third Party Discharge" form.

    The birth mother may sign her consent (called a *surrender*) anytime after the birth. It must be witnessed by a notary public and an additional witness. Most consents are signed within several days of the birth. There is a ten day period after the signing of the consent in which the birth mother has the automatic right to withdraw her consent. After the ten day period has expired the consent is irrevocable, except upon proof of fraud or duress.

Agency Adoption. There is no difference regarding the process in which a birth mother signs her surrender in an independent or agency adoption, although agencies must wait until at least 24 hours after birth and an agency representative acts as an additional witness.

Many agencies within Georgia agree to do identified adoptions. Many agencies agree to make immediate hospital "at risk" placements.

Adoption Attorneys

Rhonda L. Fishbein	Tel (404) 248-9205
17 Executive Park Drive, Suite 290	Fax (404) 248-0419
Atlanta, Georgia 30329	

Ms. Fishbein began practicing law in 1982 and is a graduate of the Benjamin N. Cardozo School of Law. She is also licensed to practice law in New York. Her practice is limited to adoptions. She estimates she has completed several hundred adoptions in her career and presently completes 100 annually. Of these, 40% are independent; 50% are agency; and 10% are intercountry. She is an adoptive parent.

Jerrold W. Hester	Tel (770) 446-3645
3500 Parkway Lane, Suite 230	Fax (770) 840-9725
Norcross, GA 30092	

Mr. Hester began practicing law in 1975 and is a graduate of the University of Georgia School of Law. Approximately 70% of his practice consists of adoptions. He estimates he has completed more than 1,300 adoptions in his career and presently completes 65 annually. Of these, 70% are independent; 25% are agency; 5% are international.

Licensed Private Adoption Agencies (* Offers intercountry programs)

AAA Partners in Adoption; 3440 Francis Road, Suite B; Alpharetta, GA 30004; (770) 740-0045; Fax: (770) 704-8189; http://www.aaapia.org; E-mail: clause@aaapia.org
*Adopt An Angel International; 10391 Big Canoe; Jasper, GA 30143; (706) 268-1841; Fax: (706) 268-3471; http://www.AdoptAnAngel.org; E-mail: AdoptAnAngel@aol.com

Adoption Planning, Inc.; 17 Executive Park Drive, Suite 480; Atlanta, GA 30329; (404) 248-9105; Toll Free: (800) 367-3203; Fax: (404) 248-0419; World Wide Web: http://www.adoptionplanning.org; E-mail: wecare@adoptionplanning.org

Adoption Services, Inc.; P.O. Box 155; Pavo, GA 31778; (912) 859-2654

All God's Children, Inc; 1120 Athens Road; Winterville, GA 30683; (706) 742-7420

*Bethany Christian Services; 15 Dunwoody Park Drive, Suite 200; Atlanta, GA 30341-1316; (770) 455-7111; Toll Free: (800) 238-4269; Fax: (770) 455-7118; World Wide Web: http://www.bethany.org/atlanta; E-mail: bcsatlanta@bethany.org

Catholic Social Services, Inc.; Adoption Program; 680 W. Peachtree Street, N.W.; Atlanta, GA 30308; (404) 881-6571

Edgewood Baptist Church, Inc.; New Beginning Adoption and Counseling Agency; 1316 Wynnton Ct., Ste. A; Columbus, GA 31906; (706) 571-3346

Families First; 1105 W. Peachtree Street, NE; Atlanta, GA 30309; (404) 853-2800; World Wide Web: http://www.familiesfirst.org;

Family Counseling Center/CSRA, Inc.; 603 Ellis Street; Augusta, GA 30901; (706) 722-6512

*Genesis Adoptions; 3440 Preston Ridge Road, Suite 400; Alpharetta, GA 30005; (770) 521-5552; Fax: (678) 393-7333; http://www.GenesisAdoptions.org; E-mail: genesis@abraxis.com

Georgia Association for Guidance, Aid, Placement and Empathy (AGAPE), Inc.; 3094 Mercer University Drive, Suite 200; Atlanta, GA 30341; (404) 452-9995;

Georgia Baptist Children's Home and Family Ministries North Area (Palmetto); 9250 Hutchison Ferry Road; Palmetto, GA 30268; (770) 463-3344

Georgia Youth Advocate Program, Inc.; 343 Telfair Street; Augusta, GA 30901; Toll Free: (800) 722-3912; World Wide Web: http://www.gyap.org; E-mail: kawad@nyap.org

Greater Chattanooga Christian Services and Children's Home; 744 McCallie Avenue, Suite 329; Chattanooga, TN 37403; (423) 756-0281; Fax: (423) 265-7326;

*Hope for Children, Inc.; 1515 Johnson Ferry Road, Suite 200; Marietta, GA 30062; (770) 977-0813; Toll Free: (800) 522-2913; Fax: (770) 973-6033; World Wide Web: http://www.hopeforchildren.org; E-mail: ShawnDeal@hopeww.org

*Illien Adoptions International Inc.; 1250 Piedmont Ave NE; Atlanta, GA 30309; (404) 815-1599; Fax: (404) 876-0483; World Wide Web: http://www.illienadopt.com; E-mail: illienusa@aol.com

197

Independent Adoption Center; 3774 Lavista Road, Suite 100; Tucker, GA 30084; (404) 321-6900; Toll Free: (800) 877-6736; Fax: (404) 321-6600; http://www.adoptionhelp.org; E-mail: iacorg@earthlink.net
Jewish Family Services, Inc.; Cradle of Love Adoption; Counseling and Services; 4549 Chamblee-Dunwoody Road; Atlanta, GA 30338-6210; (770) 955-8550
LDS Family Services; 4823 North Royal Atlanta Drive; Tucker, GA 30084; (404) 939-2121
Lutheran Ministries of Georgia Inc.; 756 West Peachtree Street;NW; Atlanta, GA 30308; (404) 607-7126; Fax: (404) 875-9258; World Wide Web: http://www.lmg.org/programs/adoptions.htm; E-mail: lmgadoption@mindspring.com;
*Open Door Adoption Agency, Inc.; 403B North Broad Street, P.O. Box 4; Thomasville, GA 31799-0004; (229) 228-6339; Toll Free: (800) 868-6339; Fax: (229) 228-4726; http://www.opendooradoption.com; E-mail: opendoor@rose.net;
ROOTS Adoption Agency; 1777 Phoenix Parkway, Suite 108; Atlanta, GA 30349; (770) 907-7770; Fax: (770) 907-7726; World Wide Web: http://www.rootsadopt.com; E-mail: radopt@hotmail.com;
The Giving Tree, Inc; 1842 Clairmont Road; Decatur, GA 30033; (404) 633-3383; Fax: (404) 633-3348; http://www.thegivingtree.org; E-mail: director@thegivingtree.org;
*World Partners Adoption, Inc; 2205 Summit Oaks Court; Lawrenceville, GA 30043; (770) 962-7860; Toll Free: (800) 350-7338; Fax: (770) 513-7767; http://www.worldpartnersadoption.org; E-mail: WPAdopt@aol.com

Hawaii

State Adoption Office: (808) 586-5698
Department of Human Services
Lynne Kazama 810 Richards Street, Suite 400
Honolulu, HI 96813   www.state.hi.us/dhs/index.html

General Information. Hawaii permits both independent and agency adoption. The majority of Hawaii's infant adoptions are completed via independent adoption. Advertising is permitted by law but most Hawaii newspapers refuse to accept advertising by adoptive parents. To file a Petition for Adoption in Hawaii either the adopting parents must reside there, *or* the child to be adopted must have been born there or reside there. If it is an agency adoption the Petition for Adoption can additionally be filed in Hawaii if the agency having custody of the child is located there. Normally, adoptions are finalized two to six months after the placement of the child with the adoptive parents. At least one of the adopting parents and the child are required to appear at the final hearing.

Independent Adoption. A preplacement home study of the adoptive parents is not required before a child may be placed in their home. In fact, there is no requirement for even a postplacement home study, although the court has discretion to require one. If a home study is required, it may be conducted by any person or organization approved by the court, usually a licensed social worker. The fee for the home study is typically $1,200-$1,500.

The birth mother and adoptive parents are not required by law to meet in person and share identities, although most elect to do so voluntarily. The adopting parents are permitted by law to assist with the birth mother's pregnancy-related medical, legal and living expenses. The child may be released from the hospital directly to the adoptive parents, usually by the birth mother signing a hospital form authorizing the release.

The birth mother may sign her consent to the adoption anytime after the birth. It may be witnessed by a notary or a judge. Once the consent is signed and the child has been placed with the adoptive parents, the consent can only be withdrawn if the best interests of the child would be served by being removed from the adoptive parents. Once the adoption is finalized by the court, there is a one year period where the adoption can be "set aside" and the consent revoked if fraud or duress is proved.

Agency Adoption. There is no difference regarding the process in which a birth mother signs her consent to adoption in an independent or agency adoption. The information provided above regarding independent adoption (e.g. when it can be signed, before whom, legal burden to seek to withdraw a signed consent) is identical regarding agency adoption.

Many agencies in Hawaii agree to do identified adoptions, as well as make immediate "at risk" placements before consents are irrevocable.

Adoption Attorneys

Laurie A. Loomis   Tel (808) 524-5066
1001 Bishop Street, Pacific Tower, Suite 2010   Fax (808) 531-3553
Honolulu, HI 96813

Ms. Loomis began practicing law in 1985 and is a graduate of Catholic University School of Law. She reports 99% of her practice consists of adoptions. She estimates she has completed 600 adoptions in her career and presently completes 50 annually. Of these, 95% are independent; 5% are agency. Of the adoptions she has completed, she reports 50% of her clients locate their birth mother through her office; 50% locate their own birth mother.

Licensed Private Adoption Agencies (* Offers intercountry programs)

*AdoptInternational; 820 Mililani Street, Suite 401; Honolulu, HI 96813; (808) 523-1400; http://www.adopt-intl.org/; E-mail: adoptinter@aol.com;
Casey Family Programs; 1848 Nuuanu Avenue; Honolulu, HI 96817; (808) 521-9531; Fax: (808) 961-4913; http://www.casey.org; E-mail: info@casey.org;
Catholic Services to Families; 200 North Vineyard Boulevard, Suite 302; Honolulu, HI 96817; (808) 537-6321;
*Child and Family Services; 200 North Vineyard Blvd, Building B; Honolulu, HI 96817; (808) 521-2377;
*Crown Child Placement International, Inc.; PO Box 26419; Honolulu, HI 96825-6419; (808) 946-0443;
*Hawaii International Child Placement and Family Services, Inc.; 1168 Waimanu Street, Suite B; Honolulu, HI 96814; (808) 589-2367; http://www.h-i-c.org;
LDS Family Services Hawaii Honolulu Agency; 1500 South Beretania Street, Suite 403; Honolulu, HI 96826; (808) 945-3690;

Idaho

State Adoption Office: (208) 334-5700
Department of Health and Welfare
Division of Family and Community Services
450 West State Street
Boise, Idaho 83720   www2.state.id.us/dhw/Adoption

General Information. Idaho permits both independent and agency adoption. Approximately 75 % of Idaho's infant adoptions are completed via independent adoption; 25 % via agencies. Advertising is not permitted. To file a Petition for Adoption in Idaho the adoptive parents must reside there, usually for a minimum of six months prior to filing the Petition for Adoption. Normally, independent adoptions are finalized approximately three months after the placement of the child with the adoptive parents, while agency adoptions take seven months. The adopting parents and the child are required to appear in court for the final hearing.

Independent Adoption. A preplacement home study of the adopting parents is required before a child can be placed in their home. The home study is usually performed by a licensed private adoption agency or licensed social worker approved to perform home studies. The fee averages $600 to $900.

The adoptive parents and birth mother are not required by law to meet in person and share identities, although it is sometimes done voluntarily. The adopting parents are permitted to assist the birth mother with medical and legal expenses related to the pregnancy. Living expense assistance is permitted not to exceed $2,000. The child may be released to the adoptive parents directly from the hospital upon discharge, although the forms and procedures among hospitals varies. Some hospitals require the attorney to be present at the discharge.

The birth mother may sign her consent to the adoption anytime after the birth, although some judges prefer birth parents wait at least 48 hours after birth before signing. If the consent is signed before a notary it is revocable by the birth mother. If the consent is signed before a judge, it is irrevocable. Most consents are signed several days after the birth.

Agency Adoption. There is no difference regarding the process in which a birth mother signs her consent to adoption in an independent or agency adoption. The information provided above regarding independent adoption (e.g. when it can be signed, before whom, legal burden to seek to withdraw a signed consent) is identical regarding agency adoption.

Most agencies within Idaho agree to do identified adoptions. Most agencies will also agree to make immediate hospital "at risk" placements.

ADOPTING IN AMERICA

Adoption Attorneys

Alfred E. Barrus   Tel (208) 678-1155
P.O. Box 487   Fax (208) 678-1166
Boise, Idaho 83702

Mr. Barrus began practicing law in 1974 and is a graduate of the University of Idaho School of Law. Approximately 25% of his practice consists of adoptions. He estimates he completes 20 adoptions annually. Of these, 50% are independent; 50% are agency. Of the adoptions he has completed he reports 20% of his clients locate their birth mother through his office; 80% find their own birth mother.

John T. Hawley Jr.   Tel (208) 336-6686
202 N. Ninth Street, Suite 205   Fax (208) 336-2088
Boise, Idaho 83702   e-mail: hawley@hpmlawyers.com

Mr. Hawley began practicing law in 1980 and is a graduate of the Gonzaga University School of Law. Approximately 85% of his practice consists of adoptions. He estimates he completes 40 adoptions annually. Of these, 95% are independent; 5% are agency; 5% are international. Of the adoptions he has completed he reports 30% of his clients locate their birth mother through his office; 70% find their own birth mother.

Licensed Private Adoption Agencies (* Offers intercountry programs)

Casey Family Program; 6441 Emerald; Boise, ID 83704; (208) 377-1771; http://www.casey.org; E-mail: info@casey.org;
*CASI Foundation For Children; 2308 North Cole Road, Suite E; Boise, ID 83704; (208) 376-0558; Toll Free: (800) 376-0558; Fax: (208) 376-1931; World Wide Web: http://www.adoptcasi.org; E-mail: info@adoptcasi.org;
Idaho Youth Ranch Adoption Services; 7025 Emerald; P.O. Box 8538; Boise, ID 83707; (208) 377-2613; Fax: (208) 377-2819; http://www.youthranch.org; E-mail: mhoward@youthranch.org;
LDS Family Services; 1070 Hiline, Suite 200; Pocatello, ID 83201; (208) 232-7780;
LDS Family Services; 1420 E. 17th, Suite B; Idaho Falls, ID 83404; (208) 529-5276; Burley: (208) 678-8200; Boise: (208) 376-0191;
*New Hope Child and Family Agency; 700 West Riverview Drive; Idaho Falls, ID 83401; (208) 523-6930; Toll Free: (800) 574-7705; World Wide Web: http://www.newhopekids.org; E-mail: info@newhopekids.org;

Illinois

State Adoption Office: (217) 524-2422
Department of Children and Family Services
Adoption Division
406 East Monroe St, Section 225
Springfield, Illinois 62701   www.state.il.us/dcts
(Or call *The Adoption Information Center of Illinois* at (312) 346-1516)

General Information. Illinois permits both independent and agency adoption. Approximately 70% of Illinois' infant adoptions are completed via independent adoption; 30% via agencies. Advertising is permitted. To file a Petition for Adoption within Illinois the adopting parents must reside there, usually for a minimum of six months prior to the filing of the Petition for Adoption. If it is an agency adoption, the Petition for Adoption can additionally be filed within Illinois if the adoption agency having custody of the child is located there. Normally, adoptions are finalized six months after the placement of the child with the adoptive parents. The adoptive parents and the child are usually required to appear in court for the final hearing.

Independent Adoption. A preplacement home study of the adoptive parents is normally not required before a child may be placed in their home. A few counties, however, may require a preplacement interview (e.g. Cook County). The postplacement home study may be conducted by the state adoption office, a licensed private adoption agency or other court approved individual. The fee varies.

The adoptive parents and the birth mother are not required by law to meet in person, although it is done voluntarily in most cases. The adopting parents are permitted to assist the birth mother with her pregnancy-related expenses, including living costs, although such expenses require advance court approval. The child may be placed directly with the adopting parents immediately upon hospital discharge, although a court order giving temporary legal custody to the adopting parents is normally required.

The birth mother may sign her consent to the adoption no sooner than 72 hours after the birth. It must be witnessed by a judge or other individual authorized by the court to act as a witness. Once signed, the consent is irrevocable.

Agency Adoption. The birth mother may sign her consent to adoption, called a *surrender*, after 72 have elapsed after the birth. It may be witnessed by a representative of the adoption agency and a notary public. Once signed, the consent is irrevocable, except upon proof of fraud or duress.

Some agencies within Illinois agree to handle identified adoptions. Many agencies also agree to make "at risk" placements.

Adoption Attorneys

Shelley B. Ballard   Tel (312) 673-5312
Ballard, Desai, Bush-Joseph & Horwich   Fax (312) 673-5318
208 S. LaSalle Street, Suite 2079
Chicago, IL 60604   e-mail: sballard@infertility-law.com

Ms. Ballard began practicing law in 1987 and is a graduate of Northwestern University School of Law. Her practice is limited to adoptions. She estimates she completes 150 adoptions annually. Of these, 24% are independent; 35% are agency; 41% inter-country. Of the adoptions she has handled, she reports 5% of her clients locate a birth mother through her office; 95% locate their own birth mother.

Deborah Crouse Cobb   Tel (618) 692-6300
Crouse, Cobb & Bays   Fax (618) 692-9831
2 Sunset Hills, Executive Park, Suite 4-C
Edwardsville, Illinois 62025   e-mail: debcobb@sbcglobal.net

Ms. Cobb began practicing law in 1984 and is a graduate of Washington University School of Law of St. Louis. Approximately 80% of her practice consists of adoptions. She estimates she completes more than 150 adoptions annually. Of these, 35% are independent; 40% are agency; 25% inter-country. Of the adoptions she has handled, she reports 20% of her clients locate a birth mother through her office; 80% locate their own birth mother.

H. Joseph Gitlin   Tel (815) 338-0021
Gitlin, Haaff & Kasper   Fax (815) 338-0544
111 Dean Street
Woodstock, IL 60098

Mr. Gitlin began practicing law in 1959 and is a graduate of De Paul University College of Law. He estimates he has completed 2,000 adoptions. 15% of his practice consists of adoptions. Of the adoptions he has completed, 90% are independent; 5% are agency; 5% are international. Of the adoptions he has completed, he reports 10% of his clients locate a birth mother through her office; 90% locate their own birth mother.

Susan F. Grammer   Tel (618) 259-2113
2 Terminal Drive, Suite 17-B; P.O. Box 111   Fax (618) 259-2111
Bethalto, IL 62010   e-mail: sgrammer@adoptionattorneys.org

Ms. Grammer began practicing law in 1983 and is a graduate of Washington University School of Law. Her practice is limited to adoptions. She estimates has completed 800 adoptions in her career. Of these, 25% are independent; 70% are agency; 5% are international. Of the adoptions she has completed, she reports 30% locate their office through her office; 70% locate their own birth mother.

Theresa Rahe Hardesty   Tel (309) 692-1087
7513 N. Regent Place   Fax (309) 692-5334
Peoria, Illinois 61614

Ms. Hardesty began practicing law in 1977 and is a graduate of De Paul University College of Law. Her practice is limited to adoptions. She estimates she completes 150 adoptions annually. Of these, 15% are independent; 50% are agency; 35% are international. She reports 5% of her clients locate a birth mother through her office; 95% locate their own birth mother.

Michelle M. Hughes   Tel (312) 857-7287
221 N. LaSalle, Suite 2020   Fax (312) 658-0114
Chicago, IL 60601

Ms. Hughes began practicing law in 1989 and is a graduate of the University of Chicago School of Law. She estimates 90% of her practice consists of adoptions. She reports she completes more than 200 adoptions annually. Of these, 20% are independent; 75% are agency; 5% are international. Of the adoptions she has completed, she reports 1 % of her clients locate a birth mother through her office; 99 % locate their own birth mother.

Kimberly Kuhlengel-Jones	Tel (618) 327-3093
255 E. St. Louis St., P.O. Box 186	Fax (618) 327-3905
Nashville, IL 62263	

Ms. Kuhlengel-Jones began practicing law in 1995 and is a graduate of the Southern Illinois University School of Law. She estimates 90 % of her practice consists of adoptions. She reports she completes more than 45 adoptions annually. Of these, 25 % are independent; 50 % are agency; 25 % are international. Of the adoptions she has completed, she reports 80 % of her clients locate a birth mother through her office; 20 % locate their own birth mother.

Sheila A. Maloney	Tel (630) 570-5050
928 Warren Avenue, Suite 3	Fax (630) 570-5006
Downers Grove, IL 60515	e-mail: stmesq@msn.com

Ms. Maloney began practicing law in 1986. She estimates 90 % of her practice consists of adoptions. She reports she completes 75 adoptions annually. Of these, 10 % are independent; 70 % are agency; 20 % are international. Of the adoptions she has completed, she reports 85 % of her clients locate a birth mother through her office; 15 % locate their own birth mother. She is an adoptive parent. Her website is iladoptionlawyer.com.

Denise J. Patton	Tel (847) 995-7003
401 Woodcroft Lane	
Schaumburg, IL 60173	e-mail: attypatton@aol.com

Ms. Patton began practicing law in 1996. She estimates 99 % of her practice consists of adoptions. She reports she completes more than 100 adoptions annually. Of these, 40 % are independent; 40 % are agency; 20 % are international. All of her clients locate their own birth mother. She is available for contested adoption litigation. Her website is ILAdoptionAttorney.com.

Licensed Private Adoption Agencies (* Offers intercountry programs)

Adoption-Link, Inc.; 1145 Westgate, Suite 104; Oak Park, IL 60301; (708) 524-1433; Fax: (708) 524-9691; http://www.adoptionlinkillinois.com;
Aunt Martha's Youth Services; 233 West Joe Orr Road; Chicago Heights, IL 60411-1744; (708) 754-1044;

Aurora Catholic Social Services; 1700 N Farnsworth Avenue Suite 18; Aurora, IL 60505; (708) 892-4366;

*Bethany Christian Services; 9718 South Halsted Street; Chicago, IL 60628-1007; (773) 233-7600; Fax: (773) 233-7617; World Wide Web: http://www.bethany.org; E-mail: bcschicago@bethany.org;

Catholic Charities, Joliet Diocese; 203 N. Ottawa Street, 2nd Floor, Suite A; Joliet, IL 60432; (815) 723-3053;

Catholic Charities, Springfield Diocese; 120 S. 11th Street; Springfield, IL 62703; (217) 525-0500;

Catholic Social Services, Belleville Diocese; 8601 W. Main Street, Suite 201; Belleville, IL 62220; (618) 394-5900; World Wide Web: http://cssil.org; E-mail: adoption@cssil.org;

Catholic Social Services, Peoria Diocese; 413 N.E. Monroe; Peoria, IL 61603; (309) 671-5720; Fax: (309) 671-0257; E-mail: AdoptCSSA@aol.com; Rockford: (815) 965-0623;

Center for Family Building, Inc.; 1740 Ridge Avenue, Suite 208; Evanston, IL 60201; (847) 869-1518; Fax: (847) 869-4108; World Wide Web: http://www.centerforfamily.com; E-mail: info@centerforfamily.com;

Chicago Child Care Society; 5467 S. University Avenue; Chicago, IL 60615; (773) 643-0452; World Wide Web: http://www.cccsociety.org;

Chicago Youth Centers; 10 W. 35th Street; Chicago, IL 60616; (312) 225-8200; Fax: (312) 225-9008; World Wide Web: http://www.chicagoyouthcenters.org; E-mail: sbooker@cycyws.org;

Children's Home and Aid Society of Illinois; 1819 S. Neil, Suite D; Champaign, IL 61820; (217) 359-8815; World Wide Web: http://www.chasisystems.org;

Children's Home and Aid Society of Illinois; 910 Second Street; Rockford, IL 61104; (815) 962-1043; Fax: (815) 962-1272;

Counseling and Family Service; 330 S.W. Washington; Peoria, IL 61602; (309) 676-2400;

*Cradle Society; 2049 Ridge Avenue; Evanston, IL 60201; (847) 475-5800; Fax: (847) 475-5871; World Wide Web: http://www.cradle.org; E-mail: cradle@cradle.org;

*Evangelical Child and Family Agency; 1530 North Main Street; Wheaton, IL 60187; (630) 653-6400; Toll Free: (800) 526-0844; World Wide Web: http://www.evancfa.org; E-mail: EvanCFA@aol.com;

*Family Resource Center; 5828 North Clark Street; Chicago, IL 60660; (773) 334-2300; Toll Free: (800) 676-2229; Fax: (773) 334-8228; World Wide Web: http://www.adoptillinois.org; E-mail: adoption@adoptillinois.org;

Family Service Agency of Adams County; 915 Vermont Street; Quincy, IL 62301; (217) 222-8254; Sangamon County: (217) 528-8406; Fax: (217) 528-8542; http://www.service2families.com; E-mail: fscsfld@fgi.net;

*Finally Family; 161 West Harrison, Suite C-102; Chicago, IL 60605; (312) 939-9399; Toll Free: (800) 917-1199; Fax: (312) 692-1922; World Wide Web: http://www.finallyfamily.com; E-mail: michelle@finallyfamily.com;

Glenkirk; 2501 N. Chestnut; Arlington Heights, IL 60004; (847) 998-8380; World Wide Web: http://www.glenkirk.org/services/adoption.html; E-mail: adopt@glenkirk.org;

*Hobby Horse House; P.O. Box 1102; Jacksonville, IL 62651-1102; (217) 243-7708;

Hope for the Children; 1530 Fairway Drive; Rantoul, IL 61866; (217) 893-4673; Fax: (217) 893-3126;

World Wide Web: http://www.hope4children.org; E-mail: h4tc@soltec.net;

Illinois Baptist Children's Home; 4243 Lincolnshire Drive; Mt. Vernon, IL 62864; (618) 242-4944; World Wide Web: http://www.bchfs.com/mtvernon.html; E-mail: carladonoho@bchfs.com;

Illinois Children's Christian Home; P.O. Box 200; St. Joseph, IL 61873; (217) 469-7566;

Jewish Children's Bureau of Chicago; 1 South Franklin Street; Chicago, IL 60606; (312) 444-2090; World Wide Web: http://www.jcbchicago.org;

*Journeys of the Heart Adoption Services; P.O. Box 28; Glen Ellyn, IL 60138; (630) 469-4367; Fax: (630) 469-4382; World Wide Web: http://www.journeysoftheheart.net; E-mail: JOHChicago@aol.com;

*Lifelink/Bensenville Home Society; 331 South York Road; Bensenville, IL 60106; (630) 521-8262; World Wide Web: http://www.lifelink.org; E-mail: alladopt@lifelink.org;

Lutheran Child and Family Services; 2408 Lebanon Avenue; Belleville, IL 62221; (618) 234-8904; Mt. Vernon: (618) 242-3284; Fax: (618) 242-3288; World Wide Web: http://www.lcfs.org; Oak Park: (708) 763-0700; Fax: (708) 763-0747; Springfield: (217) 544-4631; Fax: (217) 544-0412;

Lutheran Social Services of Illinois; 1144 West Lake Street, 3rd Floor; Oak Park, IL 60301; (708) 445-8341; Fax: (708) 445-8351; World Wide Web: http://www.lssi.org; Chicago: (773) 371-2700; Fax: (773) 239-5296;

*New Life Social Services; 6316 North Lincoln Ave; Chicago, IL 60659; (773) 478-4773; Fax: (773) 478-7646; http://www.nlss.org; E-mail: info@nlss.org;

Pathways Child Placement Services, Inc.; 4109 Sylvan Drive; Floyds Knobs, IN 47119-9603; (502) 459-2320; Fax: (502) 459-2345;

Saint Mary's Services; 717 West Kirchoff Road; Arlington Heights, IL 60005; (847) 870-8181;

*Sunny Ridge Family Center, Inc.; 2 South 426 Orchard Road; Wheaton, IL 60187; (630) 668-5117; Fax: (630) 668-5144; http://www.sunnyridge.org;

United Methodist Children's Home; 2023 Richview Road; Mt. Vernon, IL 62864; (618) 242-1070, Ext: 239; E-mail: audreyb@umchome.org;

*Uniting Families Foundation; 95 West Grand Avenue, Suite 206, P.O. Box 755; Lake Villa, IL 60046; (847) 356-1452; Fax: (847) 356-1584; http://members.aol.com/UnitingFam/index.html;E-mail:UnitingFam@aol.com; Volunteers of America of Illinois; 224 N. Desplaines Street, Suite 500; Chicago, IL 60661; (312) 707-9477; World Wide Web: http://www.voaillinois.com/; E-mail: tammyreed@earthlink.net;
Volunteers of America of Illinois; 4700 State Street, #2; East St. Louis, IL 62205; (618) 271-9833; World Wide Web: http://www.voaillinois.com;

Indiana

State Adoption Office: (317) 233-1743
Division of Family and Children
Bureau of Family Protection and Preservation
402 W. Washington Street, Room W364
Indianapolis, IN 46204   www.in.gov/fssa/adoption/index.html

General Information. Indiana permits both independent and agency adoption. Approximately 65% of Indiana's infant adoptions are completed via independent adoption; 35% via agencies. Advertising is permitted. To file a Petition for Adoption within Indiana the adopting parents must reside within the state. Normally, adoptions are finalized three months to one year after the placement of the child with the adoptive parents. The adoptive parents are required to appear in court for the final hearing.

Independent Adoption. A preplacement home study of the adoptive parents is not required before a child can be placed in their home, although the home study may voluntarily be done in advance. The postplacement home study may be done by the state adoption office or a licensed private adoption agency. The fee varies.

Adoptive parents and birth mothers are not required to meet in person and share identifying information, although it is sometimes done voluntarily. The adoptive parents are permitted to assist the birth mother with pregnancy-related expenses. The child may be placed directly with the adoptive parents from the hospital, although generally a court order is required.

The birth mother may sign her consent to the adoption anytime after the birth. It must be witnessed by a judge or a notary public. Most consents are signed within several days of the birth. Once the consent is signed it may be withdrawn with 30 days only by proving the child's best interests would be served by being removed from the adoptive parents, or that fraud or duress existed. However, if the birth mother elects to appear in court to confirm her consent, the consent becomes irrevocable immediately at the time of the court appearance.

Agency Adoption. There is no difference regarding the process in which a birth mother signs her consent to adoption in an independent or agency adoption. The information provided above regarding independent adoption (e.g. when it can be signed, before whom, legal burden to seek to withdraw a signed consent) is identical regarding agency adoption.

Some agencies in Indiana agree to do identified adoptions. Some agencies will also agree to make immediate hospital "at risk" placements.

Adoption Attorneys

Steven M. Kirsh
Kirsh & Kirsh
2930 E. 96th Street
Indianapolis, Indiana 46240

Tel (317) 575-5555
Fax (317) 575-5631
e-mail: skirsh@kirsh.com

Mr. Kirsh began practicing law in 1979 and is a graduate of Indiana University School of Law. He limits his practice to adoptions. He estimates he has completed more than 2,500 adoptions in his career and presently completes 135 annually, almost all of them independent. Of the adoptions he has handled, he reports 40% of his clients locate a birth mother through his office; 60% locate their own birth mother. He has served as president of the American Academy of Adoption Attorneys and is a member of the American Bar Association Adoption Committee. Mr. Kirsh practices law with his brother, Joel D. Kirsh, who also limits his practice to adoptions. Mr. Kirsh's website is www.Indianaadoption.com

Joel Kirsh
Kirsh & Kirsh
2930 E. 96th Street
Indianapolis, Indiana 46240

Tel (317) 575-5555
Fax (317) 575-5631
e-mail: jkirsh@kirsh.com

Mr. Kirsh began practicing law in 1984 and is a graduate of Indiana University School of Law. His practice is limited to adoptins. He estimates he completes

140 adoptions annually (not counting step-parent adoptions), all of them independent adoptions. Of the adoptions he has handled, he reports 75% of his clients locate a birth mother through his office; 25% locate their own birth mother. Mr. Kirsh practices law with his brother, Steven Kirsh, who also limits his practice to adoptions. Mr. Kirsh's website is www.Indianaadoption.com.

Keith M. Wallace   Tel (812) 426-1231
Law Offices of Bowers & Harrison   Fax (812) 464-1287
25 NW Riverside Drive   e-mail: kwallace@ftia.org
Evansville, IN 47706

Mr. Wallace began practicing law in 1983 and is a graduate of Valparaiso University School of Law. He limits his practice to adoptions and estimates he completes 250 adoptions annually. Of these, 5% are independent; 95% are agency. Of the adoptions he has handled, he reports 100% of his clients locate their own birth mother, rather than through his office.

Licensed Private Adoption Agencies (* Offers intercountry programs)

AD-IN (Adoption of indiana, Inc.); 1980 East 116th Street, Suite 325; Carmel, IN 46032; (317) 574-8950; Toll Free: (888) 573-0122; World Wide Web: http://www.ad-in.org; E-mail: msterchi@iquest.net;
Adopt America Network; 1020 Manesville Road; Shippensburg, PA 17257; (717) 532-9005; Fax: (717) 532-3423; E-mail: main1020@pix.net;
Adoption Resource Services, Inc.; 218 South Third Street, #2; Elkhard, IN 46516; (800) 288-2499; Fax: (574) 293-2210; E-mail: rcmarco@yahoo.com;
Adoption Services, Inc.; 3050 North Meridian Street; Indianapolis, IN 46208; (317) 926-6338;
*Adoption Support Center; 6331 North Carrolton Avenue; Indianapolis, IN 46220; (317) 255-5916; Toll Free: (800) 274-1084;
*Americans for African Adoptions, Inc.; 8910 Timberwood Drive; Indianapolis, IN 46234-1952; (317) 271-4567; Fax: (317) 271-8739; World Wide Web: http://www.africanadoptions.org; E-mail: info@africanadoptions.org;
Baptist Children's Home; 354 West Street; Valparaiso, IN 46383; (219) 462-4111; Fax: (219) 464-9540; http://www.baptistchildrenshome.org/;
Bethany Christian Services; 830 Cedar Parkway; Schererville, IN 46375-1200; (219) 864-0800; Fax: (219) 864-1865; http://www.bethany.org; E-mail: bcsschererville@bethany.org; Indianapolis: (317) 254-8479; Fax: (317) 254-8480; E-mail: bcsindianapolis@bethany.org;
Catholic Charities; 973 West Sixth Avenue; Gary, IN 46402; (219) 882-2723; http://www.catholic-charities.org/programs.html; E-mail: garycfs@netnitco.net;

Fort Wayne: (260) 422-5625; Toll Free: (800) 686-7459; Fax: (260) 422-5657; E-mail: fwoffice@diocese.fwsb.org; South Bend: (574) 234-3111; Toll Free: (800) 686-3111; Fax: (574) 289-4831; E-mail: sboffice@fw.diocesefwsb.org; Evansville: (812) 423-5456;

Catholic Family Services of Michigan City; 1501 Franklin Street; Michigan City, IN 46360-3709; (219) 879-9312; World Wide Web: http://catholic-charities.org/prgorams.html; E-mail: mccfs@netnitco.net;

Center for Family Building, Inc.; 8231 Hohman Avenue, Suite 200, #3; Munster, IN 46321; (219) 836-0163; World Wide Web: http://www.centerforfamily.com; E-mail: info@centerforfamily.com;

Childplace, Inc.; 2420 Highway 62; Jeffersonville, IN 47130; (812) 282-8248; Fax: (812) 282-3291; World Wide Web: http://www.childplace.org; E-mail: nathans@childplace.org;

Children Are the Future; 504 Broadway, Suite 725; Gary, IN 46402; (219) 881-0750;

Children's Bureau of Indianapolis; 615 North Alabama Street, Suite 426; Indianapolis, IN 46204; (317) 264-2700; Fax: (317) 264-2714; World Wide Web: http://www.childrensbureau.org; E-mail: cbinfo@childrensbureau.org;

*Coleman Adoption Agency; 615 North Alabama Street, Suite 319; Indianapolis, IN 46204; (317) 638-0965; Toll Free: (800) 886-3434; Fax: (317) 638-0973; World Wide Web: http://www.colemanadopt.org;

*Compassionate Care; Highway 69 West, Route 3, Box 12B; Wilder Center; Oakland City, IN 47660; (812) 749-4152; Toll Free: (800) 749-4153; Fax: (812) 749-8190; World Wide Web: http://www.compassionatecareadopt.org; E-mail: icomcare@gibsoncounty.net;

*Families Thru International Adoption; 400 Bentee Wes Court; Evansville, IN 47715; (812) 479-9900; Toll Free: (888) 797-9900; http://www.ftia.org; E-mail: adopt@ftia.org;

Family and Children's Services; 655 South Hebron Avenue; Evansville, IN 47414; (812) 471-1776;

G.L.A.D.; P.O. Box 9105; Evansville, IN 47724; (812) 424-4523;

*Hand In Hand International Adoptions; 201A N. Orange St.; Albion, IN 46701; (260) 636-3566; http://www.hihiadopt.org/; E-mail: Indiana@hihiadopt.org;

Independent Adoption Center; 537 Turtle Creek Drive South, Suite 23; Indianapolis, IN 46227; (317) 788-1039; Toll Free: (800) 877-6736; Fax: (317) 788-1094; World Wide Web: http://www.adoptionhelp.org; E-mail: iacorg@earthlink.net;

Indiana Youth Advocate Program; 2626 East 46th Street, Suite 140; Indianapolis, IN 46205; (317) 475-9294; Toll Free: (800) 471-4795; Fax: (317) 475-0081; World Wide Web: http://www.seidata.com/ ~ aurplib/iyap/index.html;

Jeremiah Agency; 3021 Stella Dr.; Greenwood, IN 46142-0864; (317) 887-2434;

LDS Family Services; Indiana Agency; 3333 Founders Road, Suite 200; Indianapolis, IN 46268-1397; (317) 872-1749; Toll Free: (877) 872-1749; Loving Option; 206 S. Main St.; Bluffton, IN 46714; (219) 824-9077; Lutheran Child and Family Services; 1525 North Ritter Avenue; Indianapolis, IN 46219; (317) 359-5467; Lutheran Social Services; P.O. Box 11329; Fort Wayne, IN 46857-1329; (219) 426-3347; Northwest Regional Office: 219) 838-0996; Fax: (219) 838-0999; Open Arms Christian Homes; Route 2, Box A; Bloomfield, IN 47424; (812) 659-2533; Paralegal on Call, Inc; P.O. Box 652; Greenwood, IN 46142; (317) 888-6707; E-mail: paroncall@aol.com; Pathways Child Placement Services, Inc.; 4109 Sylvan Drive; Floyds Knobs, IN 47119-9603; (502) 459-2320; Fax: (502) 459-2345; Specialized Alternatives for Families and Youth of America (SAFY); 661 West Superior St. #200; Ft. Wayne, IN 46802; (260) 422-3672; http://www.safy.org; St. Elizabeth's; 2500 Churchman Avenue; Indianapolis, IN 46203; (317) 787-3412; Toll Free: (800) 499-9113; World Wide Web: http://www.stelizabeths.org; E-mail: stelizabeths@stelizabeths.org; St. Elizabeth's of Southern Indiana; 621 East Market; New Albany, IN 47150; (812) 949-7305; *Sunny Ridge Family Center, Inc.; 900 Ridge Road, Suite H; Munster, IN 46321; (219) 836-2117; Fax: (219) 836-2621; World Wide Web: http://www.sunnyridge.org; E-mail: info@sunnyridge.org; The Villages, Inc.; 652 N. Girl's School Road, Suite 240; Indianapolis, IN 46214-3662; Toll Free: (800) 874-6880; World Wide Web: http://www.villages.org; Valley Children's Services; One Professional Center, 1801 North Sixth Street, Suite 800; Terre Haute, IN 47804; (812) 234-0181;

Iowa

State Adoption Office: (515) 281-5358
Department of Human Services
Hoover State Office Building, 5th floor
Des Moines, Iowa 50319   www.dhs.state.ia.us/acfs/acfs.asp

General Information. Iowa permits both independent and agency adoption. Approximately 50% of Iowa's infant adoptions are completed via independent adoption; 50% via agencies. Advertising is permitted.

To file a Petition for Adoption within Iowa either the adoptive parents must reside there *or* the child is born and resides there. Normally, adoptions are finalized seven months after the placement of the child with the adoptive parents. The adopting parents and the child are required to appear in court for the final hearing, although many courts will waive the requirement for out-of-state residents and allow them to appear with their attorney by telephone.

Independent Adoption. A preplacement home study of the adoptive parents is required before a child can be placed in their home. The home study is performed by a *certified adoption investigator* (a person certified by the state to perform home studies) or a licensed adoption agency. The fee varies from approximately $600 to $1,000.

The adoptive parents and birth mother are not required by law to meet in person and share identities, although in some cases it is done voluntarily. The adoptive parents are permitted to assist the birth mother with pregnancy-related medical, legal and living expenses, although if she is receiving welfare, she may be required to reimburse the welfare office the amount she received from the adoptive parents. The birth mother must also be offered three counseling sessions, although she may waive them. Children may be placed directly with the adoptive parents from the hospital, although many hospitals require a court order. Occasionally a short-term foster home placement is made until the birth mother's consent is irrevocable.

Normally, the juvenile court will appoint a custodian for the child, who will witness the birth mother signing her consent to adoption, called a *Release of Custody*. The birth mother cannot sign the *Release of Custody* until at least 72 hours after the birth. Once signed, there is a 96 hour period in which the birth mother has the automatic right to withdraw it. A termination of parental rights hearing is then scheduled after the expiration of the 96 hour period. After the 96 hour period, but before the termination of parental rights hearing, the birth mother can withdraw her consent if she can show good cause to do so, usually proof of fraud or duress. After the court order terminating parental rights, the consent is basically irrevocable.

Agency Adoption. There is no difference regarding the process in which a birth mother signs her consent to adoption in an independent or agency adoption. The information provided above regarding independent adoption (e.g. when it can be signed, before whom, legal burden to seek to withdraw a signed relinquishment) is identical regarding agency adoption. Some agencies within Iowa agree to do identified adoptions. Few agencies agree to make immediate hospital "at risk" placements.

Adoption Attorneys

Lori L. Klockau	Tel (319) 338-7968
Bray & Klockau	Fax (319) 354-4871
402 S. Linn Street	
Iowa City, IA 52240	

Ms. Klockau began practicing law in 1991 and is a graduate of the University of Iowa. She estimates 50% of her practice consists of adoptions. She reports she has completed more than 100 adoptions in her career, and presently completes approximately 25 annually. Of these, 75% are independent; 20% are agency; 5% are international. Of the adoptions she has completed, 50% of her clients locate a birth mother through her office; 50% locate their own birth mother.

Licensed Private Adoption Agencies (Offers intercountry programs)

*Bethany Christian Services; 617 Franklin Street, Suite 201; Pella, IA 50219-1522; (641) 628-3247; World Wide Web: http://www.bethany.org/desmoines; E-mail: bcspella@bethany.org; Orange City: (712) 737-4831; Toll Free: (800) 238-4269; Fax: (712) 737-3238; E-mail: bcsorangecity@bethany.org; Cedar Rapids: (319) 832-2321; Toll Free: (800) 238-4269; E-mail: bcscedarrapids@bethany.org; Des Moines: (515) 270-0824; Toll Free: (800) 238-4269; Fax: (515) 270-0605; E-mail: bcsdesmoines@bethany.org;

Catholic Charities of Sioux City; 1601 Military Road; Sioux City, IA 51103; (712) 252-4547; Fax: (712) 252-3785;

Catholic Charities of the Archdiocese of Dubuque; P.O. Box 1309; Dubuque, IA 52004-1309; (563) 588-0558; Toll Free: (800) 772-2758;

Children and Families of Iowa; 1111 University Avenue; Des Moines, IA 50314; (515) 288-1981; Fax: (515) 288-9109; World Wide Web: http://www.cfiowa.org; E-mail: agencyinfo@cfiowa.org;

Children's Square U.S.A. Child Connect; 541 Sixth Avenue, Box 8-C; Council Bluffs, IA 51502-3008; (712) 322-3700;

Families of North East Iowa; P.O. Box 806; Maquoketa, IA 52060; (319) 652-4958;

First Resources Corporation; 109 C East Marion, P.O. Box 107; Sigourney, IA 52591; (515) 622-2543;

Four Oaks, Inc.; 5400 Kirkwood Boulevard; Cedar Rapids, IA 52406-5216; (319) 364-0259; Fax: (319) 364-1162; World Wide Web: http://www.fouroaks.org;

*Gift of Love International Adoptions, Inc.; 7405 University Boulevard, Suite 8; Des Moines, IA 50325; (515) 255-3388; Toll Free: (877) 282-8015; Fax: (515) 279-3017; World Wide Web: http://www.giftoflove.org; E-mail: adoption@giftoflove.org;

Healing the Children; 412 E. Church Street; Marshalltown, IA 50158; (515) 753-7544;

*Hillcrest Family Services; 4080 1st Avenue NE; Cedar Rapids, IA 52402; (319) 362-3149;

*Holt International Children's Services; 10685 Bedford Avenue, Suite 300; Omaha, NE 68134; (402) 934-5031; Fax: (402) 934-5034; World Wide Web: http://www.holtintl.org; E-mail: info@holtintl.org;

Keys to Living; 463 Northland Avenue; Cedar Rapids, IA 52402-6237; (319) 377-2161;

Lutheran Family Service; 230 Ninth Avenue, North; Fort Dodge, IA 50501; (515) 573-3138;

Lutheran Social Service of Iowa; 3116 University Avenue; Des Moines, IA 50311; (515) 277-4476; World Wide Web: http://www.lssia.org; E-mail: info@lssia.org;

Ralston Adoption Agency; 2208 S. Fifth Avenue; Marshalltown, IA 50158-4515; Toll Free: (800) 304-0219;

Tanager Place; 2309 C Street, SW; Cedar Rapids, IA 52601; (319) 365-9164;

Young House, Inc.; P.O. Box 845; Burlington, IA 52601; (319) 752-4000;

Kansas

State Adoption Office: (785) 296-0918
Department of Social and Rehabilitation Services
Children and Family Policy Division
915 SW Harrison, 5th floor
Topeka, Kansas 66612   www.srskansas.org

General Information. Kansas permits both independent and agency adoption. Approximately 85 % of Kansas' infant adoptions are completed via independent adoption; 15 % via agencies. Advertising is permitted if done by a licensed adoption agency, although many newspapers will accept an advertisement if accompanied by a letter from an attorney. To file a Petition for Adoption within Kansas either the adoptive parents must reside there *or* the child is born there and the birth mother resides there. If it is an agency adoption the Petition for Adoption can also be filed there if the adoption agency having custody of the child is located there. Normally, independent adoptions are finalized one to two months after the child's placement with the adoptive parents; one to six months for agency adoptions. The adopting parents are required to appear in court for the final hearing, but some judges will waive this requirement.

Independent Adoption. A preplacement home study of the adoptive parents is required before a child can be placed in their home, although the court has discretion to waive this requirement. The home study may be conducted by a licensed clinical social worker or licensed private adoption agency. Most home study fees total approximately $500.

Adoptive parents and birth mothers are not required by law to meet in person and share identities, although it is sometimes done voluntarily. The adoptive parents are permitted to assist with pregnancy-related expenses, such as medical, legal and living costs. The child may be released from the hospital directly to the adoptive parents, but often a court order granting the adoptive parents temporary custody is required.

The consent to adoption may be signed no sooner than 12 hours after the birth. It may be witnessed by a judge or a notary public. Most consents are signed within several days of the birth. If the birth mother is under the age of 18 she must have her own attorney prior to signing the consent to adoption. Usually the attorney's fees, typically only several hundred dollars, are paid by the adoptive parents. Once signed, the consent is irrevocable, except upon proof of fraud or duress.

Agency Adoption. There is no difference regarding the process in which a birth mother signs her consent to adoption in an independent or agency adoption, although agencies call the consent a *relinquishment*. The information provided above regarding independent adoption (e.g. when it can be signed, before whom, legal burden to seek to withdraw a signed consent) is identical regarding agency adoption.

Some agencies within Kansas agree to do identified adoptions. Some agencies will agree to make immediate hospital "at risk" placements.

217

ADOPTING IN AMERICA

Adoption Attorneys

Jill Bremyer-Archer   Tel (620) 241-0554
Bremyer & Wise   Fax (620) 241-7692
P.O. Box 1146
McPherson, KS 67460

Ms. Bremyer-Archer began practicing law in 1980 and is a graduate of Washburn University School of Law. She estimates 40% of her practice consists of adoptions. She reports she she has completed more than 100 adoptions in her career and presently completes more than 20 adoptions annually. Of these, 80% are independent; 20% are agency. Of the adoptins she has completed, 15% of her clients locate their birth mother through her office; 85% locate their own birth mother.

Allan A. Hazlett   Tel (785) 232-2011
1608 S.W. Mulvane Street   Fax (785) 232-5214
Topeka, Kansas 66604

Mr. Hazlett began practicing law in 1967 and is a graduate of the University of Kansas College of Law. Approximately 95% of his practice consists of adoptions. His practice is limited to adoptions. He reports he has completed several hundred adoptions in his career and presently completes 60 annually. Of these, 75% are independent; 24% are agency; 1% are internatinoal. Of the adoptions he has completed, 20% of his clients locate a birth mother through his office; 80% locate their own birth mother. He is a past president of the American Academy of Adoption Attorneys.

Licensed Private Adoption Agencies (*Offers intercountry programs)

A Child's Dream; 413 South 10th Street; Atchison, KS 66002; E-mail: amadoption@aol.com;
A.C.T. (Adoption, Consultation and Training Services, Inc); 4717 McCormick Court; Lawrence, KS 66047; (913) 727-2288;
*Adoption and Beyond, Inc.; 10680 Barkley, Suite 230; Overland Park, KS 66323; (913) 381-6919; Fax: (913) 831-6909; World Wide Web: http://www.adoption-beyond.org; E-mail: adopt@adoption-beyond.org;
Adoption Centre of Kansas, Inc.; 1831 Woodrow Avenue; Wichita, KS 67203; (316) 265-5289; Toll Free: (800) 804-3632; Fax: (316) 265-3953; World Wide Web: http://www.adoptioncentre.com; E-mail: casemanager@adoptioncentre.com;

*Adoption of Babies and Children, Inc. (ABC Adoption); 9230 Pflumm; Lenexa, KS 66215; (913) 894-2223; Toll Free: (800) 406-2909; Fax: (913) 894-2839; World Wide Web: http://www.abcadoption.org/; E-mail: jagee1@msn.com; Adoption Option; 7211 W. 98th Terrace, #100; Overland Park, KS 66212; (913) 642-7900;

American Adoptions; 8676 West 96th Street, Suite 140; Overland Park, KS 66212; http://www.americanadoptions.com; E-mail: adoptions@americanadoptions.com; Overland Park: (913) 383-9804;

Catholic Charities, Diocese of Dodge City; 2546 20th Street; Great Bend, KS 67530; (316) 792-1393; Salina: (785) 825-0208; Toll Free: (888) 468-6909; http://www.catholiccharitiessalina.org; E-mail: ccharsal@salhelp.org;

Catholic Community Services; 2220 Central Avenue; Kansas City, KS 66102; (913) 621-1504; Fax: (913) 621-4507;

Catholic Social Service; 425 N. Topeka; Wichita, KS 67202; (316) 264-8344;

Christian Family Services of the Midwest, Inc.; 10550 Barkley, Suite 100; Overland Park, KS 66212; (913) 383-3337; World Wide Web: http://srweb.com/cfs; E-mail: adoption@swbell.net;

Family Life Services of Southern Kansas; 305 S. Summit; Arkansas City, KS 67005-2848; (316) 442-1688;

Hagar Associates; 115 SW 7th Street; Topeka, KS 66614; (913) 271-6045;

Heart of America Adoption Center; 108 East Poplar; Olathe, KS 66061; (913) 342-1110;

Inserco, Inc.; 5120 E. Central, #A; Wichita, KS 67208; (316) 681-3840;

Kansas Children's Service League; Wichita; 1365 North Custer; Wichita, KS 67201; (316) 942-4261; http://www.kcsl.org; E-mail: tlong@kcsl.org;

Kansas City-Black Adoption Program & Services: (913) 621-2016; Manhattan: (785) 539-3193;

Kaw Valley Center; 4300 Brenner Rd.; Kansas City, KS 66104; (913) 334-0294;

Lutheran Social Services; 1855 North Hillside; Wichita, KS 67214-2399; (316) 686-6645; Fax: (316) 686-0453; World Wide Web: http://www.lss-ksok.org;

Lutheran Social Services of Kansas; 2942 SW Wanamaker Drive, Building B, Suite 1C; Topeka, KS 66614; (785) 272-7883; Toll Free: (800) 210-5387; Fax: (785) 228-9405; E-mail: bkarstensen@lss.org;

Special Additions, Inc.; P.O. Box 10, 19055 Metcalf Avenue; Stilwekk, KS 66085; (913) 681-9604; Fax: (913) 681-0748; World Wide Web: http://www.specialad.org; E-mail: specialadd@aol.com;

St. Francis Academy, Inc.; 10985 W. 175th Street; Olathe, KS 66062; (913) 681-9604;

Sunflower Family Services; 1503 Vine Street, Suite E; Hays, KS 67601; (913) 625-4600; Toll Free: (800) 555-4614; World Wide Web: http://www.sunflowerfamily.org; E-mail: teresaw@sunflowerfamily.org;

The Villages, Inc.; 2209 SW 29th Street; Topeka, KS 66611; (785) 267-5900;

Kentucky

State Adoption Office: (502) 564-2147
Cabinet for Families and Children
275 E. Main Street, 6 West
Frankfort, KY 00004   http://cfc.state.dy.us/help/adoption.asp

General Information. Kentucky permits both independent and agency adoption. Approximately 80 % of Kentucky's infant adoptions are completed via independent adoption; 20 % via agencies. Advertising is not permitted. To file a Petition for Adoption within Kentucky the adopting parents must reside there. Normally, adoptions are finalized three to four months after the place-ment of the child with the adopting parents. The adoptive parents and the child to be adopted are required to appear in court for the final hearing.

Independent Adoption. A preplacement home study of the adoptive parents is required before a child can be placed in their home. The home study is conducted by either the state adoption office or a licensed agency. The fee, in the form of a "filing fee," is $150 if done by the state adoption office. The state will not start the preplacement home study until the adoptive parents have been selected by a birth mother or they otherwise know of a particular child they plan to adopt.

The adopting parents and the birth mother are not required to meet in person and share identities, although some do so voluntarily. The adoptive parents are permitted to assist the birth mother with pregnancy-related expenses, such as medical, legal and living costs. The child may be released directly from the hospital to the adoptive parents if they have a preapproved home study from a Kentucky licensed adoption agency. Each hospital has different forms and procedures regarding the child's release.

The birth mother may assent to the adoption in one of two ways—either by signing a *Voluntary and Informed Consent*, or by filing a voluntary *Petition to Terminate Parental Rights* with the court. The former is less complicated, although it does not become irrevocable until 20 days after signing and approval of the adoption placement. The latter option is more secure, as it is irrevocable upon the judge signing the order terminating the birth mother's rights. If the birth mother is a minor a guardian ad litem is appointed for her. Neither the *Voluntary and Informed Consent* nor the voluntary *Petition to Terminate Parental Rights* can be signed and filed until at least 72 hours after birth.

Depending upon the courty the hearing upon the *Petition to Terminate Parental* rights may be scheduled immediately after this 72 hour period or within 30 days, and if the birth mother appears with her attorney, and a guardian ad litem is appointed for the child, the court can often issue its order terminating her rights, provided the adoption placement has been approved by the Cabinet for Human Resources.

Agency Adoption. There is no difference regarding the process in which a birth mother signs her consent to adoption in an independent or agency adoption, except that the simpler *Voluntary and Informed Consent* method is unavailable in agency adoptions. Otherwise, the information provided above regarding independent adoption (e.g. when it can be signed, before whom, legal burden to seek to withdraw a signed consent, etc.) is identical regarding agency adoption.

Although adoption agencies in Kentucky sometimes arrange "open" adoptions, identified adoptions (where the adoptive parents and birth parents initially became acquainted outside the agency) are not permitted. Some agencies will agree to make immediate hospital "at risk" placements.

Adoption Attorneys

Carolyn S. Arnett   Tel (502) 585-4368
One Riverfront Plaza, Suite 1708   Fax (502) 585-5369
Louisville, KY 40202

Ms. Arnett began practicing law in 1984 and is a graduate of the University of Louisville School of Law. Her practice is limited to adoptions. She estimates she has completed several hundred adoptions in her career and presently completes 50 annually. Of these, 10% are independent; 90% are agency. Of the adoptions she has completed, she reports 90% of her clients locate a birth mother through her office; 10% locate their own birth mother.

ADOPTING IN AMERICA

Elisabeth Goldman   Tel (859) 252-2325
118 Lafayette Avenue   Fax (859) 252-2325
Lexington, Kentucky 40502

Ms. Goldman began practicing law in 1975 and is a graduate of University of Kentucky College of Law. Approximately 95% of her practice consists of adoptions. She estimates she has completed several hundred adoptions in her career and presently completes more than 25 annually. Of these, 60% are independent; 30% are agency; 10% are international. Of the adoptions she has completed, she reports 20% of her clients locate a birth mother through her office; 80% find their own birth mother.

Licensed Private Adoption Agencies (* Offers intercountry programs)

*A Helping Hand Adoption Agency; 501 Darby Creek Road, Suite 17; Lexington, KY 40509; (859) 263-9964; Toll Free: (800) 525-0871; Fax: (859) 263-9957; World Wide Web: http://www.ahh.to; E-mail: info@ahh.to;
Adopt! Inc.; 135 Lackawana Road; Lexington, KY 40503; (859) 276-6249; Fax: (859) 276-5570; World Wide Web: http://www.adoptinc.org; E-mail: info@adoptinc.org;
Adoptions of Kentucky; One Riverfront Plaza, Suite 1708; Louisville, KY 40202; (502) 585-3005; Fax: (502) 585-5369; World Wide Web: http://www.adoptionsofkentucky.com;
Bluegrass Christian Adoption Services; 1517 Nicholasville Road, Suite 405; Lexington, KY 40503; (859) 276-2222; Fax: (859) 277-7999; World Wide Web: http://www.iglou.com/kac/bluegrass.html; E-mail: bcas@prodigy.net;
Catholic Social Service Bureau; 1310 Leestown Road; Lexington, KY 40508; (859) 253-1993; Fax: (859) 254-6284; World Wide Web: http://www.iglou.com/kac/cathsocsvcbureau.html;E-mail:Lhainley@cdlex.org; Northern Kentucky: (859) 781-8974; Fax: (859) 581-9595;
Childplace, Inc.; 4500 Westport Road; Louisville, KY 40207; (502) 363-1633; World Wide Web: http://www.childplace.org; E-mail: nathans@childplace.org;
*Children's Home of Northern Kentucky; 200 Home Road; Covington, KY 41011; (859) 261-8768; Fax: (859) 291-2431; World Wide Web: http://www.iglou.com/kac/childrenshome.html; E-mail: shamilton.cinoh@juno.com;
*Chosen Children Adoption Services, Inc.; 5427 Bardstown Road, Suite One; Louisville, KY 40291; (502) 231-1336; Fax: (502) 231-4098; E-mail: chosenchildren@kyadoptions.com;
Cumberland River Region; MH-MR Board; 1203 American Greeting Road; Corbin, KY 40702; (606) 528-7010;

Holston United Methodist Home for Children; 503 Maple Street; Murray, KY 42071; (270) 759-5007; World Wide Web: http://www.holstonhome.org;
Home of the Innocents; 10936 Dixie Highway; Louisville, KY 40272; (502) 995-4402; Fax: (502) 995-4420; World Wide Web: http://www.homeoftheinnocents.org;
Hope Hill Children's Home; 10230 Hope Means Road; Hope, KY 40334; (859) 498-5230; Fax: (859) 498-2606; World Wide Web: http://www.familyconnectioninc.org/hopehill/index.html;
Jewish Family and Vocational Service; 3587 Dutchmans Lane; Louisville, KY 40205; (502) 452-6341; Fax: (502) 452-6718; World Wide Web: http://www.jfvs.com; E-mail: jfvs@jfvs.com;
*Kentucky Baptist Homes for Children; 10801 Shelbyville Road; Louisville, KY 40243; (502) 568-9117; Toll Free: (800) 928-5242; World Wide Web: http://www.kbhc.org/; E-mail: adoption@kbhc.org;
Kentucky One Church One Child Adoption Agency; 170 West Chesnut Street; Louisville, KY 40203; (502) 561-6827; Toll Free: (800) 248-8671; Fax: (502) 561-1899; World Wide Web:http://www.iglou.com/kac/ky1chrch1child.html; E-mail: kococ@bellsouth.net;
*Kentucky United Methodist Homes for Children or Youth; Mary Kendall Campus; 193 Phillips Court; Owensboro, KY 42303; (270) 683-3723; Toll Free: (877) 887-4481; World Wide Web: http://www.kyumh.org/; E-mail: drrankin@kyumh.org;
LDS Social Services; 1000 Hurstbourne Lane; Louisville, KY 40224; (502) 429-0077;
Shoemakers Christian Homes for Children and Adolescents; 1939 Goldsmith Lane, Suite 136; Louisville, KY 40218; (502) 485-0722;
Specialized Alternatives for Families and Youth of America; 3150 Custer Drive, Suite 103; Lexington, KY 40517; (859) 971-2585; World Wide Web: http://www.safy.org;
St. Joseph's Children's Home; 2823 Frankfort Avenue; Louisville, KY 40206; (502) 893-0241; Fax: (502) 896-2394; World Wide Web: http://www.sjkids.org/; E-mail: Elizabet@stjosephchildrenshome.org;
The Villages; 109 North Main Street; Henderson, KY 42420; (502) 827-9090;
Treatment Foster Care and Adoption Services; 116 Buckhorn Lane; Buckhorn, KY 41721; (606) 398-7245;

Louisiana

State Adoption Office: (225) 342-4086
Department of Social Services—Office of Community Services
P.O. Box 3318; 5700 Florida Blvd, 8th floor
Baton Rouge, Louisiana 70821 www.dss.state.la.us/offocs/index.htm

General Information. Louisiana permits both independent and agency adoption. Approximately 50 % of Louisiana's infant adoptions are completed via independent adoption; 50 % via agencies. Advertising is not permitted, except by licensed adoption agencies. To file a Petition for Adoption within Louisiana the adoptive parents must reside there, *or* the birth parent relinquishing custody must be domiciled for at least eight months in Louisiana and surrender the child there. Normally, independent adoptions are finalized 14 months after the placement of the child; agency adoptions are usually finalized in eight months. The adoptive parents are required to appear in court for the final hearing.

Independent Adoption. A preplacement home study of the adoptive parents is required before the child can be placed in their home, unless a court specifically approves a direct placement without a home study. Upon completion of a preplacement home study the adoptive parents receive a *Certification for Adoption.* The home study may be conducted by a licensed private adoption agency, licensed social worker, psychologist or psychiatrist. The individual or agency which conducts the home study also issues the Certification—for Adoption. The cost of the pre and post-placement home study services typically varies from $1,000 to $1,500.

    The birth mother and adoptive parents are not required to meet in person, but the name of the adoptive parents or their attorney must be provided on the consent form signed by the birth mother. The adoptive parents are permitted to assist the birth mother with pregnancy-related medical, legal and living expenses. The child may be released directly from the hospital to the adoptive parents, usually by releasing the child to the attorney handling the adoption.

    The birth mother may sign her consent to adoption, called a *surrender,* no sooner than five days after the birth. She must have her own attorney to advise her. The consent must be witnessed by a notary and two witnesses, as well as her attorney. If the birth mother is under the age of eighteen, she must also have her parent, or a guardian (called a *tutor*) sign the consent as well. Once signed, the consent is irrevocable, but for proof of fraud or duress.

Agency Adoption. There is no difference regarding the process in which a birth mother signs her consent to adoption in an independent or agency adoption, except that a birth mother need not have her own attorney. The information provided above regarding independent adoption (e.g. when it can be signed, before whom, legal burden to seek to withdraw a signed consent) is identical regarding agency adoption.

Some agencies agree to do identified adoptions. Some agencies will also agree to make immediate hospital "at risk" placements.

Adoption Attorneys

Edith H. Morris	Tel (504) 524-3781
Morris, Lee & Bayle	Fax (504) 561-0028
1515 Poydras Street, Suite 1870	
New Orleans, LA 70112	

Ms. Morris began practicing law in 1985 and is a graduate of Loyola University School of Law. Approximately 20% of her practice consists of adoptions. She estimates she has completed in excess of 100 adoptions in her career and she presently completes 25 annually, all of them independent. Of the adoptions she has handled, she estimates 20% of her clients locate a birth mother through her office; 80% locate their own birth mother. She handles contested adoptions requiring litigation.

Licensed Private Adoption Agencies (* Offers intercountry programs)

Acorn Adoption, Inc.; 3350 Ridgelake Drive, Suite 259; Metairie, LA 70002; (504) 838-0080; Toll Free: (888) 221-1370; World Wide Web: http://www.acornadoption.org; E-mail: acornadoption@msn.com;
*Beacon House Adoption Services, Inc; 15254 Old Hammond Hwy, Suite C-2; Baton Rouge, LA 70816; (225) 272-3221; http://www.beaconhouseadoption.com; E-mail: BeaconHouse@worldnet.att.net;

Catholic Charities Archdiocese of New Orleans; 1000 Howard Avenue, Suite 1200; New Orleans, LA 70113-1916; (504) 523-3755; World Wide Web: http://www.catholiccharities-no.org; E-mail: ccano@archdiocese-no.org; Catholic Social Services of Houma – Thibodaux; P.O. Box 3894; Houma, LA 70361; (985) 876-0490; Fax: (985) 876-7751; E-mail: rgorman@htdiocese.org; Lafayette: (337) 261-5654; Toll Free: (800) 256-7222; World Wide Web: http://www.dol-louisiana.org;

Children's Bureau of New Orleans; 210 Baronne Street, Suite 722; New Orleans, LA 70112; (504) 525-2366;

D. Missy Everson, LCSW, DCSW - A Professional Corporation; 2020 East 70th Street, Suite #205; Shreveport, LA 71105; (318) 798-7664; Fax: (318) 861-1710; World Wide Web: http://www.adoptinla.com; E-mail: dmeapc@aol.com;

*Gladney Center for Adoption; 6300 John Ryan Drive; Fort Worth, TX 76132-4122; (817) 922-6088; Toll Free: (800) 452-3639; Fax: (817) 922-6040; World Wide Web: http://www.gladney.org; E-mail: info@gladney.org;

Holy Cross Child Placement Agency, Inc.; 910 Pierremont Road, Suite 356; Shreveport, LA 71106; (318) 865-3199;

Jewish Family Service of Greater New Orleans; 3330 W. Esplanade Avenue S., Suite 600; Metairie, LA 70002-3454; (504) 831-8475;

LDS Social Services; 2000 Old Spanish Trail, Pratt Center, Suite 115; Slidell, LA 70458; (504) 649-2774;

Louisiana Baptist Children's Home; P.O. Box 4196; Monroe, LA 71211; (318) 343-2244; World Wide Web: http://www.lbch.org; E-mail: home@lbch.org;

Mercy Ministries of America; P.O. Box 3028, 804 Spell Street; West Monroe, LA 71210; (318) 388-2040;

St. Elizabeth Foundation; 8054 Summa Avenue, Suite A; Baton Rouge, LA 70809; (225) 769-8888;

St. Gerard's Adoption Network, Inc.; P.O. Drawer 1260; Eunice, LA 70535; (318) 457-1111;

Sunnybrook Children's Home, Inc.; 2101 Forsythe Avenue; Monroe, LA 71201; (318) 329-8161;

Volunteers of America; Greater Baton Rouge at Lake Charles; 340 Kirby Street; Lake Charles, LA 70601; (318) 497-0034;

Metairie: (504) 835-3005; Alexandria: (318) 442-8026; World Wide Web: http://www.voanorthla.com; E-mail: lisa@voanorthla.org; Shreveport: (318) 221-2669

Maine

State Adoption Office: (207) 287-5060
Department of Human Services—Bureau of Child and Family Services
State House, Station 11
Augusta, ME 04333   www.adopt.org/me/

General Information. Maine permits both independent and agency adoption. Advertising is permitted by licensed adoption agencies. To file a Petition for Adoption within Maine the adoptive parents, *or* the child to be adopted, must reside there. If it is an agency adoption, the Petition for Adoption may also be filed in Maine if the adoption agency having custody of the child is located there. Normally, independent adoptions are finalized one to two months after the placement of the child with the adoptive parents. Agency adoptions are typically finalized six months after placement. The adoptive parents are required to appear in court for the final hearing, although the court may waive this requirement.

Independent Adoption. A preplacement home study of the adoptive parents is required before a child can be placed in their home. The home study may be performed by a licensed private adoption agency. The fee varies but is typically $1,600. There is no requirement for a post-birth home study.

The birth parents and adoptive parents are not required to meet and share identities, although it is sometimes done voluntarily. Adoptive parents may assist the birth mother by paying pregnancy-related medical, legal and living expenses. The child may be released to the adoptive parents directly from the hospital, usually upon the birth mother's signature on hospital release forms.

The consent to adoption may be signed any time after the birth. It must be witnessed by a probate judge. It may be withdrawn only within three days of signing the consent. After the three day period has elapsed, the consent can only be withdrawn upon proof of fraud or duress.

Agency Adoption. There is little difference regarding the process in which a birth mother signs her consent to adoption in an independent or agency adoption, although the consent form employed by adoption agencies is called a *Consent and Surrender*. Unlike independent adoption, agency adoptions do require a post-birth home study. The remaining information provided above regarding independent adoption (e.g. when the consent can be signed, before whom, legal burden to seek to withdraw a signed consent) is identical regarding agency adoption.

Some agencies within Maine do identified adoptions. Few agree to do immediate hospital "at risk" adoptions.

Adoption Attorneys

Judith M. Berry   Tel (207) 839-7004
28 State Street   Fax (207) 839-9848
Gorham, ME 04038

Ms. Berry began practicing law in 1991 and is a graduate of the Universidy of Maine School of Law. Her practice is limited to adoptions and she estimates she completes more than 200 adoptions annually. Of these, 70% are independent; 20% are agency; 10% international. Of the adoptions she has handled, she estimates 10% of her clients locate a birth mother through her office; 90% locate their own birth mother. She handles contested adoptions requiring litigation. She is an adoptive parent.

Licensed Private Adoption Agencies (* Offers intercountry programs)

C.A.R.E. Development; P.O. Box 2356; Bangor, ME 04401; (207) 945-4240;
*Good Samaritan Agency; 100 Ridgewood Drive; Bangor, ME 04401; (207) 942-7211;
*International Adoption Services Centre; 432 Water Street, P.O. Box 56; Gardiner, ME 04345; (207) 582-8842; E-mail: 105342.2617@compuserve.com;
*Maine Adoption Placement Service (MAPS); International Office; 277 Congress Street; Portland, ME 04101; (207) 775-4101; Fax: (207) 775-1019; World Wide Web: http://www.mapsadopt.org; E-mail: info@mapsadopt.org;
Portland: (207) 772-3678; Fax: (207) 773-6776;
E-mail: maps306@mapsadopt.org; Bangor Office: (207) 941-9500; Fax: (207) 941-8942; E-mail: mapsbangor@mapsadopt.org; Main Office: 58 Pleasant Street; Houlton, ME 04730; (207) 532-9358; Fax: (207) 532-4122;
Maine Children's Home for Little Wanderers; 11 Mulliken Court; Augusta, ME 04330; (207) 622-1552; http://www.mint.net/mainechildrenshome; Waterville: (207) 872-0261; E-mail: info@midmainechamber.com;

SMART; P.O. Box 547; Windham, ME 04062; (207) 893-0386;
St. Andre Home, Inc.; 283 Elm Street; Biddeford, ME 04005; (207) 282-3351;

Maryland

State Adoption Office: (410) 767-7506
Maryland Department of Human Resources
311 Saratoga Street
Baltimore, MD 21201

General Information. Maryland allows both independent and agency adoption. Approximately 75% of Maryland's infant adoptions are completed through independent adoption; 25% via agency. Advertising is permitted. Intermediaties, other than licensed adoption agencies, are not permitted to receive compensation for locating a birth mother to create an adoptive match for adoptive parents. Adoptive parents can file their Petition for Adoption in Maryland if they reside there *or* if the baby was born there. Adoptions are usually finalized 3 to 6 months after the filing of the Petition for Adoption. The adoptive parents and the child to be adopted are required to appear at the final court hearing.

Independent Adoption. Adoptive parents are not required to have a home study completed before a child is placed in their home. After the child's placement with the adoptive parents, the home study may be performed by a licensed adoption agency, court investigator, social worker or county social services department. The fee for the home study varies from free to approximately $1,500 based upon who performs the home study, and the county in which the adoptive parents live.

The birth parents and adoptive parents are not required to meet and share identities. However, many voluntarily agree to meet in person. Identities are shared in many cases. Adoptive parents may assist the birth mother by paying her pregnancy-related medical and legal expenses. Assistance with living costs is not permitted. The child may be placed with the adoptive parents directly from the hospital, but a court order granting the adoptive parents temporary legal custody is required.

The birth mother may sign her consent to the adoption anytime after the birth. There are no particular witnessing requirements. Most consents

229

are signed one to four days after the birth. The birth mother has the automatic right to withdraw the consent for a period of 30 days after signing. Once the 30 day period has passed her consent is irrevocable.

Agency Adoption. There is no difference regarding the process in which a birth mother signs her consent to adoption in an independent or agency adoption. The information provided above regarding independent adoption (e.g. when the consent can be signed, before whom, legal burden to seek to withdraw a signed consent) is identical regarding agency adoption.

Some agencies agree to do identified adoptions. Some agencies also agree to do immediate hospital "at risk" placements.

Adoption Attorneys

Mark T. McDermott   Wash D.C. office: Tel (202) 331-1955
Joseph, McDermott & Reiner   Fax (202) 293-2309
30 Courthouse Square, Suite 300
Rockville, MD 20850

Mr. McDermott began practicing law in 1974 and is a graduate of Indiana University School of Law. He is also licensed to practice law in California, the District of Columbia, Indiana, Maryland and Virginia. Approximately 70% of his practice consists of adoptions. He estimates he has completed 1,200 adoptions in his career and presently completes 100 annually. Of these, 80% are independent adoptions; 20% agency. His office also agrees to handle contested adoptions where litigation is required. He is an adoptive parent and is a past president of the American Academy of Adoption Attorneys.

Margaret E. Swain   Tel (410) 583-0688
6301 N. Charles Street, Suite 2   Fax (410) 321-4718
Baltimore, MD 21212   e-mail: artlawmes@aol.com

Ms. Swain began practicing law in 1988 and is a graduate of the University of Baltimore. Approximately 50% of her practice consists of adoptions. She estimates she has completed 175 adoptions in her career and presently completes more than 25 annually. Of these, 75% are independent; 15% are agency; 10% are international.

Licensed Private Adoption Agencies (* Offers intercountry programs)

*Adoption Resource Center, Inc.; 6630 Baltimore National Pike, Suite 205-A; Baltimore, MD 21228; (410) 744-6393; Fax: (410) 744-1533; World Wide Web: http://www.adoptionresource.com/; E-mail: adoptrc@aol.com;
*Adoption Service Information Agency, Inc. (ASIA); 7720 Alaska Avenue NW; Washington, DC 20012; (202) 726-7193; Fax: (202) 722-4928; World Wide Web: http://www.asia-adopt.org; E-mail: ASIAadopt@aol.com;
*Adoption Service Information Agency, Inc. (ASIA); 8555 16th Street, Suite 600; Silver Spring, MD 20910; (301) 587-7068; Fax: (301) 587-3869; World Wide Web: http://www.asia-adopt.org; E-mail: ASIAadopt@aol.com;
*Adoptions Forever; 5830 Hubbard Drive; Rockville, MD 20852; (301) 468-1818; Fax: (301) 881-7871; World Wide Web: http://www.adoptionsforever.com; E-mail: adopt@adoptionsforever.com;
*Adoptions Together Inc.; 5750 Executive Drive, Suite 107; Baltimore, MD 21228; (410) 869-0620; Fax: (410) 869-8419; World Wide Web: http://www.adoptionstogether.org; E-mail: adoptionworks@adoptionstogether.org;
*Adoptions Together Inc.; 10230 New Hampshire Avenue, Suite 200; Silver Spring, MD 20903; (301) 439-2900; Fax: (301) 439-9334; World Wide Web: http://www.adoptionstogether.org; E-mail: adoptionworks@adoptionstogether.org;
*America World Adoption Association; 6723 Whittier Avenue, Suite 406; McLean, VA 22101; (703) 356-8447; Toll Free: (800) 429-3369; World Wide Web: http://www.america-world.org; E-mail: info@awaa.org;
Associated Catholic Charities; Archdiocese of Baltimore; 1 E. Mt. Royal Avenue; Baltimore, MD 21202; (410) 659-4031; Fax: (410) 659-4060;
*Barker Foundation, The; 7945 MacArthur Boulevard, Room 206; Cabin John, MD 20818; (301) 229-8300; Toll Free: (800) 673-8489; Fax: (301) 229-0074; World Wide Web: http://www.barkerfoundation.org; E-mail: info@barkerfoundation.org;
*Bethany Christian Services; 2130 Priest Bridge Drive, Suite 9; Crofton, MD 21114-2466; (410) 721-2835; Fax: (410) 721-5523; World Wide Web: http://www.bethany.org/maryland
E-mail: bcscrofton@bethany.org;
Board of Child Care; 3300 Gaither Road; Baltimore, MD 21244; (410) 922-2100; Fax: (410) 922-7830; World Wide Web: http://www.boardofchildcare.org; E-mail: info@boardofchildcare.org;
Catholic Charities Archdiocese of Washington D.C.; 1438 Rhode Island Avenue NE; Washington, DC 20018; (202) 526-4100; World Wide Web: http://www.catholiccharities.org;

Catholic Charities, Inc.; Delaware Diocese; 1405 Wesley Drive; Salisbury, MD 21801; (410) 749-1121; Fax: (410) 543-0510; E-mail: ccsal@ce.net;
*Cradle of Hope Adoption Center, Inc.; 8630 Fenton Street, Suite 310; Silver Spring, MD 20910; (301) 587-4400; Fax: (301) 588-3091; World Wide Web: http://www.cradlehope.org/; E-mail: cradle@cradlehope.org;
*Creative Adoptions, Inc.; 10750 Hickory Ridge Road, Suite 108; Columbia, MD 21044; (301) 596-1521; Fax: (301) 596-0346; World Wide Web: http://www.creativeadoptions.org/; E-mail: cai@creativeadoptions.org;
*Datz Foundation; 16220 Frederick Road; Gaithersburg, MD 20877; (301) 258-0629; Fax: (301) 921-6689; World Wide Web: http://www.datzfound.com; E-mail: markeckman@hotmail.com;
Family and Child Services of Washington, D.C., Inc.; 5301 76th Avenue; Landover Hills, MD 20784; (301) 459-4121, Ext: 334; Fax: (202) 371-0863; World Wide Web: http://www.familyandchildservices.org;
Family and Children's Society; 204 West Lanvale Street; Baltimore, MD 21217; (410) 669-9000; Fax: (410) 728-2972;
Family Building Center; The Mercantile-Towson Building; 409 Washington Avenue, Suite 920; Towson, MD 21204-4903; (410) 494-8112;
*Frank Adoption Center; 9 East Church Street; Frederick, MD 21701; (301) 682-5025; Fax: (301) 682-5026;
*Holy Cross Child Placement Agency, Inc.; St. John's Episcopal Church; 6701 Wisconsin Avenue; Chevy Chase, MD 20815; (301) 907-6887; Fax: (202) 237-2846;
*International Children's Alliance; 7029 River Oak Court; Clarksville, MD 21029; (443) 535-9020; Fax: (443) 535-9019;
*International Children's Alliance; 8807 Colesville Road, 3rd Floor; Silver Spring, MD 20910; (301) 495-9710; Fax: (301) 495-9790; World Wide Web: http://www.adoptica.org; E-mail: adoptionop@aol.com;
*International Families, Inc.; 613 Hawkesburg Lane; Silver Spring, MD 20904; (301) 622-2406; World Wide Web: http://www.ifichild.com; E-mail: ifichild@aol.com;
*International Social Service; American Branch, Inc.; 700 Light Street; Baltimore, MD 21230-3850; (410) 230-2734; Fax: (410) 230-2741; World Wide Web: http://www.iss-usa.org; E-mail: jselinske@lirs.org;
Jewish Family Services - Adoption Alliances; 6 Park Center Court, McDonogh Crossroads, Suite 211; Owings Mills, MD 21117; (410) 466-9200; Fax: (410) 664-0551; World Wide Web: http://www.jfs.org; E-mail: jfs@jfs.org;
Jewish Social Services Agency of Metropolitan Washington; 6123 Montrose Road; Rockville, MD 20852-4880; (301) 881-3700; Fax: (301) 770-8471;
LDS Family Services; 172 Thomas Johnson Drive, #200; MD; (301) 434-0080;

*Lutheran Social Services of the National Capital Area
Zion Evangelical Lutheran Church; 7410 New Hampshire Avenue; Takoma Park, MD 20912; (301) 434-0080; Fax: (202) 723-3303; World Wide Web: http://www.lssnca.org; E-mail: greenberg@lssnca.org; Washington: (202) 723-3000; Fax: (202) 723-3303; World Wide Web: http://www.lssnca.org;
*New Family Foundation; 5537 Twin Knolls Road, Suite 440; Columbia, MD 21045; (410) 715-4828;
Rainbow Christian Services; 6000 Davis Blvd; Camp Springs, MD 20746; (301) 899-3200;
The Kennedy Krieger Institute; 2901 East Biddle Street; Baltimore, MD 21213; (410) 502-9533; Fax: (410) 502-8160;
*Tressler Adoption Services of Maryland; Maritime Center 1 at Pointe Breeze, 2200 Broening Highway, Suite 110; Baltimore, MD 21224; (410) 633-6900; http://www.tressler.org; E-mail: rhoyle@tressler.org;
Tressler Lutheran Services; 836 South Geoirge Street; York, PA 17403; (717) 845-9113; Fax: (717) 852-8439;
*World Child International; 9300 Colombia Boulevard; Silver Spring, MD 20910; (301) 588-3000; Fax: (301) 585-7879; World Wide Web: http://www.worldchild.org/; E-mail: info@worldchild.org;
*World Child International; 207 Brooks Avenue; Gaithersburg, MD 20877; (301) 977-8339; Fax: (301) 608-2425; World Wide Web: http://www.worldchild.org/; E-mail: info@worldchild.org;

Massachusetts

State Adoption Office: (617) 748-2267
Department of Social Services
24 Farnsworth Street
Boston, MA 02210
                www.state.ma.us/dss/Adoption/AD_Overview.htm

General Information. Massachusetts permits only agency adoption. Accordingly, all of Massachusetts' infant adoptions are completed via agency adoption. Advertising is permitted only by licensed adoption agencies. To file a Petition for Adoption within Massachusetts either the adoptive parents, *or* the child, must reside there. Normally, adoptions are finalized seven to twelve months after the placement of the child with the adoptive parents. The adoptive parents and the child are required to appear in court for the final hearing.

ADOPTING IN AMERICA

A preplacement home study of the adoptive parents is required before a child can be placed in their home. The home study must be performed by a licensed adoption agency. The fee varies among private agencies for pre and post-placement home study services from $2,500 to $12,000, depending upon the services rendered.

It is not required that the birth mother and adoptive parents meet in person and share identities, although it is done voluntarily in many cases. Many agencies do identified adoptions, where meetings between the parties occur and identities are usually shared. The adoptive parents are permitted to assist with pregnancy-related medical, legal and living expenses. The child may be released directly from the hospital to the adoptive placement as an "at risk" placement if the agency authorizes the release. Massachusetts agencies usually refer to this as a "trust placement."

The consent to adoption, called a *adoption surrender,* may be signed no sooner than the fourth day after birth. It must be witnessed by a notary and two witnesses. The consent is irrevocable upon signing, but for proof of fraud and duress.

Adoption Attorneys

Paula Mackin   Tel (617) 332-0781
233 Needham Street, 5th floor   Fax (617) 244-6511
Newton, MA 02464   e-mail: mackinpb@aol.com

Ms. Mackin began practicing law in 1975 and is a graduate of the George Washington University School of Law. Approximately 95% of her practice consists of adoptions. She estimates she completes more than 100 adoptions annually. Of these, 80% are agency; 20% are international. She is available to handle contested adoption litigation matters. She is an adoptive parent. Her website is www.adoptinmassachusetts.cm

Licensed Private Adoption Agencies (* Offers intercountry programs)

A Red Thread Adoption Services; 681 Washington Street, Suite 12; Norwood, MA 02062; (781) 762-2428; E-mail: redthreadadopt@aol.com;
Act of Love Adoptions; 734 Massachusetts Avenue; Boston, MA 02476; Toll Free: (800) 277-5387;
*Adoption Resource Center at Brightside; 2112 Riverdale Street; West Springfield, MA 01089; (413) 827-4315; http://www.brightsideadoption.org;

Adoption Resources; 1340 Centre Street; Newton Centre, MA 02159; (617) 332-2218;

AdoptionLink; Jewish Family Services of Greater Springfield, Inc.; 15 Lenox Street; Springfield, MA 01108; (413) 737-2601;

Adoptions With Love, Inc.; 188 Needham Street, Suite 250; Newton, MA 02164; (617) 965-2496; Toll Free: (800) 722-7731;

*Alliance for Children, Inc.; 55 William Street, Suite G10; Wellesley, MA 02481-3902; (781) 431-7148; Fax: (781) 431-7474; World Wide Web: http://www.allforchildren.org; E-mail: info@allforchildren.org; Wellesley: (781) 431-7148; Fax: (781) 431-7474;

*American-International Children's Alliance (AICA); PO Box 858; Marblehead, MA 01945; Toll Free: (866) 862-3678; Fax: (603) 658-6579; World Wide Web: http://www.adopting.com/aica; E-mail: adopt@mattbi.com;

*Angel Adoptions, Inc.; 11 Dix Street; Waltham, MA 02453; (781) 899-9222; World Wide Web: http://www.angel-adoptions.org; E-mail: adoption@angel-adoptions.org;

Beacon Adoption Center, Inc.; 66 Lake Buel Road; Great Barrington, MA 01230; (413) 528-2749; Fax: (413) 528-4311;

Berkshire Center for Families and Children; 480 West Street; Pittsfield, MA 01201; (413) 448-8281;

*Bethany Christian Services; 1538 Turnpike Street; North Andover, MA 01845-6221; (978) 794-9800; Toll Free: (800) 941-4865; Fax: (978) 683-5676; World Wide Web: http://www.bethany.org; E-mail: bcsnandover@bethany.org;

Boston Adoption Bureau, Inc.; 14 Beacon Street, Suite 620; Boston, MA 02108; (617) 277-1336; Toll Free: (800) 338-2224;

Bright Futures Adoption Center, Inc.; 5 Broadview Street; Acton, MA 01720; (978) 263-5400; Toll Free: (877) 652-6678; Fax: (978) 266-1909; World Wide Web: http://www.bright-futures.org/; E-mail: adopt@comap.com;

*Cambridge Family and Children's Services; 929 Massachusetts Avenue; Cambridge, MA 02139; (617) 876-4210; Toll Free: (800) 906-4163; World Wide Web: http://www.helpfamilies.org; E-mail: adoption@helpfamilies.org;

Catholic Charities Center of the Old Colony Area; 686 N. Main Street; Brockton, MA 02301; (508) 587-0815; Somerville: (617) 625-1920; Worcester: (508) 798-0191; Fax: (508) 797-5659; Fitchburg: (978) 343-4879;

Catholic Social Services of Fall River, Inc.; 783 Slade Street, PO Box M South Station; Fall River, MA 02720; (508) 674-4681; Fax: (508) 675-2224;

Children's Aid and Family Services of Hampshire County, Inc.; 8 Trumbull Road; Northampton, MA 01060; (413) 584-5690; Fax: (413) 586-9436;

Children's Friend; 21 Cedar Street; Worcester, MA 01609; (508) 753-5425;

Children's Services of Roxbury, Inc.; 504 Dudley Street; Roxbury, MA 02119; (617) 542-2366; Fax: (617) 542-2369;

ADOPTING IN AMERICA

*China Adoption With Love, Inc; 251 Harvard Street, Suite 17; Brookline, MA 02446; Toll Free: (800) 888-9812; Fax: (617) 232-8288; World Wide Web: http://www.chinaadoption.org; E-mail: cawli@aol.com;
Concern; 1 W. Main Street; Fleetwood, PA 19522; (610) 944-0445; Fax: (610) 944-1195; World Wide Web: www.concern4kids.org; E-mail: concerngbo@fast.net; *Concord Family Service Society, Inc.; 111 Old Road to Nine; Acre Cor., Suite 2002; Concord, MA 01742-4174; (978) 369-4909; Fax: (978) 371-1463;
DARE Family Services; 17 Poplar Street; Roslindale, MA 02131; (617) 469-2311; Fax: (617) 469-3007; Danvers: (978) 750-0751; Fax: (978) 750-0749; Family and Children's Services of Catholic Charities; 53 Highland Avenue; Fitchburg, MA 01420; (978) 343-4879;
*Florence Crittenton League; 119 Hall Street; Lowell, MA 01854-9671; (978) 452-9671; Fax: (978) 970-0070; World Wide Web: http://www.fcleague.org/; E-mail: info@fcleague.org;
Full Circle Adoptions; 39 Main Street; Northampton, MA 01060; (413) 587-0007; Toll Free: (888) 452-3678; Fax: (413) 584-1624; World Wide Web: http://www.fullcircleadoptions.org; E-mail: adoption@fullcircleadoptions.com;
*Gift of Life Adoption Services, Inc.; 1087 Newman Avenue; Seekonk, MA 02771; (508) 761-5661; World Wide Web: http://www.giftoflife.cc; E-mail: giftoflife@giftoflife.cc;
Hope Adoptions, Inc.; 21 Cedar Street; Worcester, MA 01609; (508) 753-5425;
*Interfaith Social Services; 776 Hancock Street; Quincy, MA 02170; (617) 773-6203; Fax: (617) 472-4987; E-mail: iss@interfaithsocialserv.org;
Jewish Family and Children's Services Adoption Resources; 1340 Centre Street; Newton, MA 02159; (617) 332-2218;
*Jewish Family Service of Metrowest; 475 Franklin Street, Suite 101; Framingham, MA 01702; (508) 875-3100; Fax: (508) 875-4373; World Wide Web: http://www.jfsmw.org; E-mail: info@jfsmw.org; Worcester: (508) 755-3101; E-Mail: info@jfsworcester.org;
*Love the Children of Massachusetts; 2 Perry Drive; Duxbury, MA 02332; (781) 934-0063;
*Lutheran Social Services of New England; 74 Elm Street, 2nd Floor; Worcester, MA 01609-2833; (508) 791-4488; Toll Free: (800) 286-9889; Fax: (508) 753-8051; http://www.adoptlss.org/; E-mail: LSSadoptma@aol.com;
*Maine Adoption Placement Service (MAPS); Boston - International Office; 400 Commonwealth Avenue; Boston, MA 02115; (617) 267-2222; Fax: (617) 267-3331; World Wide Web: http://www.mapsadopt.org/; E-mail: mapsboston@aol.com;
Merrimack Valley Catholic Charities; 439 South Union Street, Suite 4210; Lawrence, MA 01843; (978) 452-1421;

*New Bedford Child and Family Services; 1061 Pleasant Street; New Bedford, MA 02740; (508) 996-8572; World Wide Web: http://www.cfservices.org; E-mail: crocha@cfservices.org;
Special Adoption Family Services; A Program of Communities for People; 418 Commonwealth Avenue; Boston, MA 02215-2801; (617) 572-3678; Fax: (617) 572-3611;
*The Home for Little Wanderers; 271 Huntington Avenue; Boston, MA 02115; (617) 267-3700; Toll Free: (888) 466-3321; Fax: (617) 267-8142; World Wide Web: http://www.thehome.org; E-mail: mjanisch@thehome.org; United Homes for Children; 90 Cushing Avenue; Dorchester, MA 02125; (617) 825-3300; United Homes for Children; 1147 Main Street, Suite 209-210; Tewksbury, MA 01876; (978) 640-0089; Fax: (978) 640-9652;
*Wide Horizons For Children; Main Office; 38 Edge Hill Road; Waltham, MA 02451; (781) 894-5330; Fax: (781) 899-2769; World Wide Web: http://www.whfc.org/; E-mail: info@whfc.org;

Michigan

State Adoption Office: (517) 373-4553
Department of Social Services—Adoption Services Division
P.O. Box 30037, Suite 514
Lansing, Michigan 48909

General Information. Michigan permits both independent and agency adoptions. Independent adoptions were illegal in Michigan until 1995. It is now estimated approximately 25% of Michigan's newborn adoptions were completed via independent adoption; 75% via agency. Advertising is permitted. To file a Petition for Adoption in Michigan, either the adoptive parents must reside there, or the child to be adopted must be physically present there. Normally, adoptions are finalized about six months after placement with the adoptive parents.

Independent Adoption. A preplacement home study of the adoptive parents is required before a child can be placed in their home. The home study must be performed by a licensed adoption agency. The fee usually ranges from $850 to $3,000.

It is not required by law for the birth mother and adoptive parents to meet in person and share identities, but it is usually done. The adoptive parents are permitted to assist the birth mother with pregnancy-related medical and living expenses if of reasonable amount and supported by receipts. The child may be released directly to the adoptive parents directly from the hospital with the birth mother's signature o a *Temporary Placement Agreement.*

The consent to adoptions can be signed anytime after the birth. It must be taken in court at a hearing, which is usually scheduled by the court anywhere from four days to three weeks later, depending upon the county. Once signed, the consent is irrevocable and can only be witndrawn upon proof of fraud or duress.

Agency Adoption. There is no difference regarding the process in which a birth mother signs her consent to adoption in an independent or agency adoption, with the exception that in most cases a birth mother relinquishes her child directly to the agency, rather than making a direct placement to the adoptive parents. Either form of consent is irrevocable upon signing in court.

Most agencies in Michigan agree to do identified adoptions. Many will do immediate "at risk" placements with the adoptive parents before the irrevocable consents are taken if the adoptive parents are properly licensed.

Adoption Attorneys

There are no attorney biographies avialable for AAAA members in the state of Michigan.

Licensed Private Adoption Agencies (* Offers intercountry programs)

*Adoptees Help Adopt International; 5955 N. Wayne Road; Westland, MI 48185; (734) 467-6222; Fax: (734) 467-8020; E-mail: nleu37A@prodigy.com;
*Adoption Associates, Inc; 13535 State Road; Grand Ledge, MI 48837; (517) 627-0805; http://www.adoptassoc.com; E-mail: adopt@adoptassoc.com; St. Clair Shores: (810) 294-1990; Jenison: (616) 667-0677;
Adoption Consultants; 22749 Michigan Avenue; Dearborn, MI 48124; (248) 737-0336; Fax: (248) 737-0349; World Wide Web: http://www.aciadoption.com; E-mail: aciadopt@core.com;
Adoptions of the Heart; 4295 Summerwind Avenue, NE; Grand Rapids, MI 49525; (616) 365-3166; Fax: (616) 365-2955;

Alliance for Adoption/Jewish Family Service; 24123 Greenfield Road; Southfield, MI 48075; (248) 559-0117; Fax: (248) 559-5403;
Alternatives for Children and Families; P.O. Box 3038; Flint, MI 48502; (810) 235-0683; Fax: (810) 235-4619;
*Americans for International Aid and Adoption; 2151 Livernois, Suite 200; Troy, MI 48083; (248) 362-1207; Fax: (248) 362-8222; World Wide Web: http://www.rainbowkids.com/aiaa.html; E-mail: info@aiaadopt.com;
Anishnabek Community Family Services; 2864 Ashmun Street; Sault Ste. Marie, MI 49783; (906) 632-5250; Fax: (906) 632-5266;
*Bethany Christian Services; 2041 30th Street; Allegan, MI 49010-9514; (616) 686-0157; Fax: (616) 686-8133; http://www.bethany.org; E-mail: bcsallegan@bethany; Fremont: (231) 924-3390; Madison Heights: (248) 414-4080; Fax: (248) 414-4085; E-mail: bcmadisonhts@bethany.org; Holland: (616) 396-0623; Fax: (616) 396-2315; E-mail: bcsholland@bethany.org; Kalamazoo: (616) 372-8800; World Wide Web: http://www.bethany.org/kalamazoo; E-mail: bcskalamazoo@bethany.org; Grand Rapids: (616) 224-7617; Toll Free: (800) 652-7082; Fax: (616) 224-7619; E-mail: info@bethany.org; East Lansing: (517) 336-0191; Fax: (517) 336-0101; E-Mail: bcselansing@bethany.org; Paw Paw: (616) 657-7096; Fax: (616) 657-4642; E-mail: bcspawpaw@bethany.org;
Binogii Placement Agency; 2864 Ashmun Street, Third Floor; Sault Ste. Marie, MI 49783; (906) 632-5250; Fax: (906) 632-5266;
Catholic Family Services; 1819 Gull Road; Kalamazoo, MI 49001; (616) 381-9800; Fax: (616) 381-2932;
Catholic Family Services of the Diocese of Saginaw; 915 Columbus Avenue; Bay City, MI 48708; (517) 892-2504; Fax: (517) 892-1923; Midland: (517) 631-4711; Fax: (517) 832-5525; Saginaw: (517) 753-8446; Fax: (517) 753-2582;
Catholic Human Services; 154 S. Ripley Boulevard; Alpena, MI 49707; (517) 356-6385; Gaylord: (517) 732-6761; Traverse City: (231) 947-8110; Fax: (231) 947-3522;
Catholic Social Services of Flint; 901 Chippewa Street; Flint, MI 48503; (810) 232-9950; Fax: (810) 232-7599; E-mail: ccsflint@gfn.org; Kent County: (616) 456-1443; Fax: (616) 732-6391; Macomb County: (810) 416-2311; Toll Free: (888) 422-2938; Fax: (810) 416-2311; E-mail: csmacomb@teleweb.net; Marquette: (906) 228-8630; Fax: (906) 228-2469; E-mail: lkearney@dioceseofmarquette.org; Monroe County: (734) 847-1523; Monroe: (734) 242-3800; Fax: (734) 242-6203; Muskegon: (231) 726-4735; Fax: (231) 722-0789; E-mail: cssmusk@aol.com; Oakland County: (248) 333-3700; Fax: (248) 333-3718; Port Huron: (810) 987-9100; Fax: (810) 987-9105; Iron Mountain: (906) 774-3323; Ann Arbor: (734) 971-9781; E-mail: loisplant@aol.com; Detroit: (313) 883-2100; Lansing: (517) 323-4734;

Child and Family Services; 1352 Terrane Street; Muskeyon, MI 49442; (616) 726-3582;

*Child and Family Services of Michigan; 2806 Davenport; Saginaw, MI 48602-3734; (517) 790-7500; Fax: (517) 790-8037; World Wide Web: http://www.cfsm.org; E-mail: cfsm@cfsm.org;

Child and Family Services of Michigan, State Office; 2157 University Park Drive, PO Box 348; Okemos, MI 48805; (517) 349-6226; Toll Free: (800) 878-6587; Fax: (517) 349-0969;

Child and Family Services of Northeast Michigan; 1044 Us-23 North, PO Box 516; Alpena, MI 49707; (989) 356-4567; Toll Free: (800) 779-0396; Fax: (517) 354-6100; World Wide Web: http://www.cfsm.org; E-mail: alpena@cfsm.org; Traverse City:

(231) 946-8975; Fax: (231) 946-0451; E-mail: traversecity@cfsm.org; St. Joseph; (616) 983-5545; Toll Free: (888) 237-1891; Fax: (616) 983-4920; E-Mail: stjoseph@cfsm.org; Marquette: (906) 226-2516; Fax: (906) 226-2297; E-mail: cfsm@cfsm.org; Houghton: (906) 482-4488; Fax: (906) 482-4401; Holland: (616) 396-2301; Fax: (616) 396-8070; Grand Haven: (616) 846-5880; E-mail: holland@cfsm.org;

Child and Family Services, Capital Area; 4287 Five Oaks Drive; Lansing, MI 48911; (517) 882-4000; Fax: (517) 699-2749; World Wide Web: http://www.childandfamily.org; E-mail: info@childandfamily.org; St.Joseph: (616) 983-5545;

Child and Parent Services; 30600 Telegraph Road, Suite 2215; Bingham Farms, MI 48025; (248) 646-7790; Toll Free: (800) 248-0106; Fax: (248) 646-4544;

Children's Center of Wayne County; 100 W. Alexandrine; Detroit, MI 48201; (313) 831-5520; Fax: (313) 831-5520;

*Children's Hope Adoption Services; 7823 South Whiteville Road; Shepherd, MI 48883; (517) 828-5842; Fax: (517) 828-5799;

Christ Child House; 15751 Joy Road; Detroit, MI 48228; (313) 584-6077; Fax: (313) 584-1148;

Christian Care Maternity Ministries; Baptist Children's Home; 214 N. Mill Street; St. Louis, MI 48880; (517) 681-2172;

Christian Cradle; 535 N. Clippert, Suite 2; Lansing, MI 48912; (517) 351-7500; Fax: (517) 351-4810;

Christian Family Services; 17105 W. 12 Mile Road; Southfield, MI 48076; (248) 557-8390; Fax: (248) 557-6427;

D.A. Blodgett Services; 805 Leonard NE OFC; Grand Rapids, MI 49503-1184; (616) 451-2021; Fax: (616) 451-8936; World Wide Web: http://www.dablodgett.org/; E-mail: GeneralEmail@dablodgett.org;

Developmental Disabilities; 420 W. 5th Avenue; Flint, MI 48503; (810) 257-3714;

Eagle Village Family Living Program; 4507 170th Avenue; Hersey, MI 49639; (231) 832-2234; Toll Free: (800) 748-0061; Fax: (231) 832-0385; World Wide Web: http://www.eaglevillage.org; E-mail: info@eaglevillage.org;
*Eastern European Adoption Services; INC 22233 Genesis; Woodhaven, MI 48183; (734) 479-2348; Fax: (734) 479-6330;
Ennis Center for Children; 91 S. Telegraph Road; Pontiac, MI 48341; (248) 333-2520; Fax: (248) 333-3410;
Ennis Center for Children; 2051 Rosa Parks Boulevard; Detroit, MI 48216; (313) 963-7400; Fax: (313) 963-7424; Flint: (810) 233-4031; Fax: (810) 233-0008; Detroit: (313) 342-2699; Fax: (313) 342-2180;
Evergreen Children's Services; 10421 W. Seven Mile Road; Detroit, MI 48221; (313) 862-1000; Fax: (313) 862-6464; E-mail: ecsnew@aol.com;
*Family Adoption Consultants; 45100 Sterritt, Suite 204; Utica, MI 48317; (810) 726-2988; Fax: (810) 726-2599; World Wide Web: http://www.facadopt.org; E-mail: Mpara@sprynet.com; Kalamazoo: (616) 343-3316; Fax: (616) 343-3359; E-mail: melissa@facadopt.org;
Family and Children's Service of Calhoun; 632 North Avenue; Battle Creek, MI 49017; (616) 965-3247; Fax: (616) 966-4135; World Wide Web: http://www.cfsm.org/; E-mail: battlecreek@csfm.org; Hastings: (616) 948-8465; E-mail: battlecreek@csfm.org; Midland: (517) 631-5390; Fax: (517) 631-0488; E-mail: midland@csfm.org; Kalamazoo: (616) 373-0248; Fax: (616) 344-0285; E-mail: kalamazoo@csfm.org;
Family Counseling and Children's Service of Lenawee County; 213 Toledo Street; Adrian, MI 49221; (517) 265-5352; Fax: (517) 263-6090; World Wide Web: http://www.fccservices.org; E-mail: adrian@cfsm.org;
Family MatchMakers; 2544 Martin, SE; Grand Rapids, MI 49507; (616) 243-1803; E-mail: fammatch@iserv.net;
Family Services and Child Aid, Jackson; 330 W. Michigan Avenue; Jackson, MI 49204; (517) 787-2738;
Forever Families Inc.; 42705 Grand River Avenue, Suite 201; Novi, MI 48375; (248) 344-9606; Fax: (248) 344-9604; E-mail: foreverfamilies@ameritech.net;
*Hands Across the Water; 2890 Carpenter Street, Suite 600; Ann Arbor, MI 48108; (734) 477-0135; Fax: (734) 477-0213; World Wide Web: http://www.hatw.org; E-mail: info@hatw.org;
HelpSource; 201 North Wayne Road; Westland, MI 48185-3689; (734) 422-5401; Fax: (734) 422-7893;
Homes for Black Children; 511 E. Larned Street; Detroit, MI 48226; (313) 961-4777; Fax: (313) 961-2994;
Interact Family Services; 1260 Woodkrest Drive; Flint, MI 48532;
*International Adoption Association; 517 Baldwin Avenue; Jenison, MI 49428; (616) 457-6537; http://www.adoptionpros.com; E-mail: AdoptPros@aol.com;

241

Judson Center/Washtenaw County; 4925 Packard Road, Suite 200; Ann Arbor, MI 48108; (734) 528-1720; Fax: (734) 528-1695;

Keane Center for Adoption; 930 Mason; Dearborn, MI 48124; (313) 277-4664; Fax: (313) 278-1767; E-mail: cbrail@provide.net;

LDS Social Services; 37634 Enterprise Court; Farmington Hills, MI 48331; (248) 553-0902; Fax: (248) 553-2632;

Lula Belle Stewart Center; 11000 W. McNichols, Suite 116; Detroit, MI 48221; (313) 862-4600; Fax: (313) 864-2233;

Lutheran Adoption Service; 21700 Northwestern Highway, Suite 1490; Southfield, MI 48075-4901; (248) 423-2770; Fax: (248) 423-2783; World Wide Web: http://www.lssm.org/service/adoption/adoption.asp; Grandville: (616) 532-8286; Fax: (616) 532-8919;

Lutheran Adoption Service Bay City Branch; 6019 West Side; Bay City, MI 48706; (517) 686-3170; http://www.lssm.org/service/adoption/adoption.asp; Lansing: (517) 886-1380; Fax: (517) 886-1586;

Lutheran Social Service of Wisconsin and Upper Michigan; 1009 West Ridge Street, Suite A; Marquette, MI 49855; (906) 226-7410; Fax: (906) 226-9800; World Wide Web: http://www.lsswis.org;

Methodist Children's Home Society; 26645 W. 6 Mile Road; Detroit, MI 48240; (313) 531-3140; Fax: (313) 531-1040;

Michigan Indian Child Welfare Agency; 6425 S. Pennsylvania Avenue, Suite 3; Lansing, MI 48911; (517) 393-3256; Fax: (517) 393-0838; Baraga: (906) 353-6178; Fax: (906) 353-7540;

Wilson: (906) 466-9221; Sault Ste. Marie: (906) 632-8062; Toll Free: (800) 562-4957; Fax: (906) 632-1810; Grand Rapids: (616) 454-9221;

Morning Star Adoption Resource, Inc.; 3311 West Twelve Mile; Berkley, MI 48072; (248) 399-2740;

Oakland Family Services; 114 Orchard Lake Road; Pontiac, MI 48341; (248) 858-7766; Fax: (248) 858-8227; E-mail: ofs@ofsfamily.org;

*Orchards Children's Services; 30215 Southfield Road; Southfield, MI 48076; (248) 258-0440; Fax: (248) 258-0487; World Wide Web: http://www.orchards.org; E-mail: adopt@orchards.org; Sterling Heights: (810) 997-3886; Fax: (810) 997-0629;

Sault Tribe Binogii Placement Agency; 2864 Ashmun Street; Sault St. Marie, MI 49783; (906) 632-5250;

Spaulding for Children; 16250 Northland Drive, Suite 120; Southfield, MI 48075; (248) 443-7080; Fax: (248) 443-7099; World Wide Web: http://www.spaulding.org; E-mail: sfc@Spaulding.org;

Spectrum Human Services; 23077 Greenfield Road, Suite 500; Southfield, MI 48075; (248) 552-8020; Fax: (248) 552-1135;

Westland: (734) 458-8736; Fax: (734) 458-8836;

St. Francis Family Services; 17500 W. 8 Mile Road; Southfield, MI 48075; (248) 552-0750; Fax: (248) 552-9019;

St. Vincent-Sarah Fisher Center; 27400 W. 12 Mile Road; Farmington Hills, MI 48334; (248) 626-7527; Fax: (248) 539-3584; World Wide Web: http://www.home-sweet-home.org
E-mail: svs@aol.com;

Starfish Family Services; 30000 Hivley Road; Inkster, MI 48141-1089; (734) 728-3400; Fax: (734) 728-3500; World Wide Web: http://www.sfish.org; E-mail: ocash@sfish.org;

Teen Ranch - Port Huron; 3815 Lapeer Road; Port Huron, MI 48060; (810) 987-6111; Fax: (810) 987-6116; World Wide Web:
http://www.netonecom.net/ ~ christal/ranch/; E-mail:
teenranch@centuryinter.net; Marlette: (517) 635-7511; Fax: (517) 635-3324; World Wide Web: http://www.centuryinter.net/teenranch.m/; Southfield: (248) 443-2900; Fax: (248) 443-1695;

Whaley Children's Center; 1201 N. Grand Traverse; Flint, MI 48503; (810) 234-3603; Fax: (810) 232-3416;

Minnesota

State Adoption Office: (651) 296-3740
Department of Human Services, Adoption Section
444 Lafayette Road North
St Paul, MN 55155
    www.dhs.state.mn.us/childint/programs/Adoption/default.htm

General Information. Minnesota permits both independent (technically called *direct placement* in Minnesota) and agency adoption. Approximately 80 % of Minnesota's infant adoptions are completed via independent adoption; 20 % via agencies. Advertising is permitted. Attorneys are not permitted to locate birth mothers for adoptive parents. To file a Petition for Adoption within Minnesota the adoptive parents must reside there for a minimum of one year, although a court may waive this requirement. Normally, adoptions are completed no sooner than three months after the child's placement with the adoptive parents. The adoptive parents and the child are required to appear in court for the final hearing.

Independent ("direct placement") Adoption. A preplacement home study of the adoptive parents is required before a child can be placed in their home, although in emergency situations exceptions may be permitted. The home study must be conducted by a licensed private adoption agency. The fee varies but is usually $2,200 to $6,000.

It is not required for the adoptive parents and birth mother to meet in person and share identities, although some elect to do so voluntarily. The adoptive parents are permitted to assist with the birth mother's pregnancy-related expenses. The child may be released directly from the hospital to the adoptive parents. Normally, however, the child's release must by court order, through an adoption agency, or the birth mother must be discharged with the child then personally give the child to the adoptive parents outside the hospital.

The consent may be signed no sooner than 72 hours after the birth. It may be witnessed by a judge or a representative of the state adoption office or a licensed adoption agency if that agency provided counseling services to her. If the birth mother did not receive counseling, her consent must be witnessed by a judge. Birth mothers must be offered an independent attorney at the adoptive parents' expense. If the birth mother is a minor, her custodial parent must also sign a consent, and if that parent refuses, a guardian ad litem can be appointed to do so. Most consents are signed within one to two weeks after the birth. Once the consent is signed, the birth mother has the automatic right to withdraw the consent for a period of ten working days. Once the ten days have elapsed, the consent may only be withdrawn upon proof of fraud.

Agency Adoption. There is no difference regarding the process in which a birth mother signs her consent to adoption in an independent or agency adoption (e.g. when the consent can be signed, before whom, legal burden to seek to withdraw a signed consent) is identical regarding agency adoption, except there is no right to her own attorney at the adoptive parents' expense.

Some agencies in Minnesota agree to do identified adoptions, as well as make immediate "at risk" placements before consents are irrevocable.

State-by-State Review

Adoption Attorneys

Gary A. Debele
Walling & Berg
121 S. 8th Street, Suite 1100
Minneapolis, MN 55402

Tel (612) 335-4288
Fax (612) 340-1154

Mr. Debele began practicing law in 1987 and is a graduate of the University of Minnesota School of Law. Approximately 40% of his practice consists of adoptions. He estimates he has completed several hundred adoptions in his career and presently completes more than 25 annually. Of these, 60% are independent; 30% are agency; 10% are international. He is an adoptive parent.

Jody Ollyver DeSmidt
Walling & Berg
121 S. 8th Street, Suite 1100
Minneapolis, MN 55402

Tel (612) 335-4284
Fax (612) 340-1154

Ms. DeSmidt began practicing law in 1982 and is a graduate of William Mitchell College of Law. Approximately 75% of her practice consists of adoptions. She estimates she has completed more than 500 adoptions in her career and presently completes 30 annually. Of these, 55% are independent; 35% are agency; 10% are international.

Judith D. Vincent
111 Third Ave. #240, Mill Place
Minneapolis, MN 55401

Tel (612) 332-7772
Fax (612) 332-1839

Ms. Vincent began practicing law in 1978 and is a graduate of University of Minnesota School of Law. Approximately 97% of her practice consists of adoptions. She estimates she has completed 1,500 adoptions in her career and presently completes 107 annually. Of these 60% are independent; 35% are agency; 5% are international. She is an adoptive parent.

Wright S. Walling
Walling & Berg
121 S. 8th Street, Suite 1110
Minneapolis, MN 55402

Tel (612) 335-4283
Fax (612) 340-1154
e-mail: wsw@walling-berg.com

Mr. Walling began practicing law in 1972 and is a graduate of the University of Minnesota School of Law. Approximately 85% of his practice consists of adoptions. He estimates he has completed more than 1,000 adoptions in his career and presently completes 75 annually. Of these, 60% are independent; 35% are agency; 10% are international. He is available to be retained in contested adoption cases. He is an adoptive parent. His website is walling-berg.com.

Licensed Private Adoption Agencies (* Offers intercountry programs)

*Adoption Miracle International, Inc.; 19108 Kingswood Terrace; Minnetonka, MN 55345; (952) 470-6141; Fax: (612) 677-3453; World Wide Web: http://www.adoptionmiracle.org;
E-mail: info@adoptionmiracle.org;
*Bethany Christian Services; 3025 Harbor Lane, Suite 223; Plymouth, MN 55447-5138; (612) 553-0344; Fax: (612) 553-0117; World Wide Web: http://www.bethany.org/plymouth; E-mail: bcsplymouth@bethany.org;
Caritas Family Services; 305 Seventh Avenue North; St. Cloud, MN 56303; (320) 252-4121;
Catholic Charities of the Archdiocese of Winona; 111 Market Street, P.O. Box 3; Winona, MN 55987-0374; (507) 454-2270;
Catholic Charities/Seton Services; 1276 University Avenue; St. Paul, MN 55104-4101; (651) 603-0225; Fax: (651) 641-1005;
*Child Link International; 6508 Stevens Ave S.; Richfield, MN 55423; (612) 861-9048; Fax: (612) 869-2004; World Wide Web: http://www.child-link.com; E-mail: ChildLink1@aol.com;
*Children's Home Society of Minnesota; 1605 Eustis Street; St. Paul, MN 55108-1219; (651) 646-7771; Toll Free: (800) 952-9302; Fax: (651) 646-0436; World Wide Web: http://www.chsm.com; E-mail: info@chsm.com;
Chosen Ones Adoption Agency; 1622 East Sandhurst Drive; Maplewood, MN 55109; (651) 770-5508;
Christian Family Life Services; 203 South 8th Street; Fargo, ND 58103; (701) 237-4473; Fax: (701) 280-9062;
*Crossroads Adoption Services; 4620 West 77th Street, Suite 105; Minneapolis, MN 55435; (612) 831-5707; Fax: (612) 831-5129; World Wide Web: http://www.crossroadsadoption.com;E-mail:kids@crossroadsadoption.com;
Downey Side; 400 Sibley Street, Suite 20; St. Paul, MN 55101; (651) 228-0117; St. Cloud: (320) 240-1433; Fax: (320) 240-1532;
*European Children's Adoption Services; 6050 Cheshire Lane North; Plymouth, MN 55446; (763) 694-6131; http://www.ecasus.org; E-mail: zina@ecasus.org;
Family Alternatives; 416 East Hennepin Avenue; Minneapolis, MN 55414; (612) 379-5341;
*Family Resources; 2903 Euclid Avenue; Anoka, MN 55303; (763) 323-8050; http://www.familyres.net; E-mail: familyresources@msn.com;

Hand in Hand International Adoptions; 1076 Charles Avenue; St. Paul, MN 55104; (651) 917-0384;

Holy Family Adoption Agency; 525 Thomas Avenue; St. Paul, MN 55103; (651) 220-0090;

*HOPE Adoption & Family Services International, Inc.; 5850 Omaha Avenue North; Oak Park Heights, MN 55082; (651) 439-2446; Fax: (651) 439-2071; World Wide Web: http://www.hopeadoptionservices.org; E-mail: hope@hopeadoptionservices.org;

*International Adoption Services; 4940 Viking Drive, Suite 388; Minneapolis, MN 55435; (952) 893-1343; Fax: (952) 893-9193;

LDS Social Services; 3120 Earl Brown Drive, Suite 210; Brooklyn Center, MN 55430; (763) 560-0900;

*Love Basket, Inc.; 3902 Minnesota Avenue; Duluth, MN 55802; (218) 720-3097; Fax: (218) 722-0195; World Wide Web: http://www.lovebasket.org/; E-mail: lovebskt@theriver.net;

Lutheran Home Christian Family Services; 611 West Main Street; Belle Plain, MN 56011; (612) 873-2215;

Lutheran Social Services; 2485 Como Avenue; St. Paul, MN 55108; (651) 642-5990; Fax: (651) 696-2360; Moorhead: (218) 236-1494; Fax: (218) 236-0836; St. Cloud: (320) 251-7700; Fax: (320) 251-8898; Duluth: (218) 726-4888;

Lutheran Social Services of Minnesota; 2414 Park Avenue; Minneapolis, MN 55404; (612) 879-5334; Fax: (612) 871-0354;

New Horizons Adoption Agency, Inc.; Frost Benco Building, Highway 254; Frost, MN 56033; (507) 878-3200; Fax: (507) 878-3132;

New Life Family Services; 1515 E. 66th Street; Minneapolis, MN 55423-2674; (612) 866-7643;

New Life Family Services; 902 North Broadway; Rochester, MN 55904; (507) 282-3377;

North Homes Inc; 1880 River Road; Grand Rapids, MN 55744-4085;

PATH (Professional Association of Treatment Homes); Redwood Falls; 231 East 2nd Street, Box 364; Redwood Falls, MN 55343; (507) 637-5147;

PATH (Professional Association of Treatment Homes); Duluth Office; 500 Alworth Building, 306 West Superior Street; Duluth, MN 55802; (218) 722-6106; Rochester: (507) 282-6909; Marshall: (507) 532-4635; St. Paul: (612) 646-3221; Fergus Falls: (218) 739-3074; Fax: (218) 739-2063; St. Cloud: (320) 654-8807; Fax: (320) 654-8875; Bemidji: (218) 751-7515; Fax: (218) 751-0253;

Permanent Family Resource Center; 1220 Tower Road; Fergus Falls, MN 56537; (218) 998-3400;

*Reaching Arms International, Inc.; 3701 Winnetka Avenue North; New Hope, MN 55427; (763) 591-0791; http://www.raiadopt.org; E-mail: raiadopt@raiadopt.org;

Summit Adoption Home Studies, Inc.; 1389 Summit Avenue; St. Paul, MN 55105; (651) 645-6657; Fax: (651) 645-6713; World Wide Web: http://www.summitadoption.com; E-mail: summitadopt@uswest.net;
Upper Midwest American Indian Center; 1035 West Broadway; Minneapolis, MN 55411; (612) 522-4436; Fax: (612) 522-8855;
Village Family Services Center; 715 11th Street, Suite 302; Moorhead, MN 56560; (218) 291-1214; Fax: (218) 233-7930;
Wellspring Adoption Agency; 1219 University Avenue SE; Minneapolis, MN 55414; (612) 379-0980; Fax: (612) 332-1839;

Mississippi

State Adoption Office: (601) 359-4981
Department Human Services—Family and Children Services
750 North State Street
Jackson, MS 39202   www.mdhs.state.msus/fcs_adopt/html

General Information. Mississippi permits both independent and agency adoption. Advertising is permitted. To file a Petition for Adoption within Mississippi the adoptive parents must be residents, usually for at least 90 days. Normally, adoptions are finalized approximately six months after the placement of the child with the adoptive parents. The adoptive parents and the child to be adopted are required to appear in court for the final hearing.

Independent Adoption. A preplacement home study of the adoptive parents is not required before a child is placed in their home. In fact, the court may waive even a postplacement home study. If a home study is required, it is usually conducted by a licensed social worker at a cost of $750.

It is not required by law that the adoptive parents and birth mother meet in person and share identities, although some do so voluntarily. The adoptive parents are permitted by law to assist the birth mother with pregnancy-related medical and legal expenses. Living expenses are not permitted. The child may be released directly to the adoptive parents from the hospital, usually through an attorney.

The consent to adoption cannot be signed sooner than 72 hours after the birth. There are no state statutory laws governing the possible withdrawal of a consent to adoption, but case law indicates that once the consent is signed it is irrevocable, except for proof of fraud or duress. The state statute also does not mention who, if anyone, must act as a witness to the signing of the consent. As a practical matter, however, all consents are normally witnessed by a notary public.

Agency Adoption. There is no difference regarding the process in which a birth mother signs her consent to adoption in an independent or agency adoption, except that a pre-placement home study is routinely done at a cost of $750. The other information provided above regarding independent adoption (e.g. when the consent can be signed, before whom, legal burden to seek to withdraw a signed consent) is identical regarding agency adoption.

Some agencies in the state agree to do identified adoptions, as well as make immediate "at risk" placements before consents are irrevocable.

Adoption Attorneys

No attorney biographies are available for Mississippi.

Licensed Private Adoption Agencies (* Offers intercountry programs)

Acorn Adoptions, Inc.; 113 South Beach Boulevard, Suite D; Bay St. Loius, MS 39520; Toll Free: (888) 221-1370; World Wide Web: http://www.acornadoption.org; E-mail: acornadoption@msn.com;
*Bethany Christian Services; 7 Professional Parkway, #103; Hattiesburg, MS 39402-2637; (601) 264-4984; Toll Free: (800) 331-5876; Fax: (601) 264-2648; World Wide Web: http://www.bethany.org/mississippi; E-mail: bcshattiesburg@bethany.org; Columbus: (662) 327-6740; Toll Free: (800) 331-5876; Jackson: (601) 366-4282; Toll Free: (800) 331-5876; Fax: (601) 366-4287;
Catholic Charities, Inc.; P.O. Box 2248; Jackson, MS 39226-2248; (601) 355-8634;
Catholic Social and Community Services; P.O. Box 1457; Biloxi, MS 39533-1457; (228) 374-8316;
Harden House Adoption Agency; 110 North Gaither Street; Fulton, MS 38843; (601) 862-7318;
Jewish Family Services, Inc.; 6560 Poplar Avenue; Memphis, TN 38138; (901) 767-8511; Fax: (901) 763-2348;
LDS Social Services; 2000 Old Spanish Trail, Pratt Center, Suite 115; Slidell, LA 70458; (504) 649-2774;

Lutheran Ministries of Georgia Inc.; 756 West Peachtree Street NW; Atlanta, GA 30308; (404) 607-7126; http://www.lmg.org/programs/adoptions.htm; E-mail: lmgadoption@mindspring.com; Mississippi Children's Home Society; 1900 North West Street, P.O. Box 1078; Jackson, MS 39215; (601) 352-7784; Toll Free: (800) 388-6247; World Wide Web: http://www.mchsfsa.org/adoption.html; E-mail: jstrickland@mchsfsa.org; New Beginnings of Tupelo; 1445 East Main Street; Tupelo, MS 38804; (662) 842-6752; *Southern Adoption; 12511 Marty Stuard Drive; Philadelphia, MS 39350; Toll Free: (800) 499-6862; Fax: (602) 656-6561;

Missouri

State Adoption Office: (573) 751-0311
Department of Social Services—Division of Family Services
P.O. Box 88
Jefferson City, MO 65103 www.dss.state.mo.us/dfs/adopt.htm

General Information. Missouri permits both independent and agency adoption. Approximately 60 % of Missouri's infant adoptions are completed via independent adoption; 40 % via agencies. Advertising is permitted. To file a Petition for Adoption within Missouri either the adoptive parents, the birth mother, or the child to be adopted, must reside there. Normally, adoptions are finalized approximately seven months after the placement of the child with the adoptive parents. The adoptive parents and the child are usually required to appear in court for the final hearing.

Independent Adoption. A preplacement home study of the adoptive parents is required before a child is placed in the adoptive home. It may be conducted by a licensed adoption agency or licensed social worker. The fees vary but typical pre and post-placement home study fees total $1,000 to $5,000.

Adoptive parents and birth mothers are not required by law to meet in person or share identities, although it is done voluntarily in a some cases. The adoptive parents are permitted to assist with pregnancy-related medical, living, counseling and legal expenses. The child may be released directly from the hospital to the adoptive parents, although hospital policies vary. Some hospitals accept a Power of Attorney form while others require a court order called an *Order of Transfer of Custody*.

The consent to adoption of the birth mother can be signed no sooner than 48 hours after the birth. It must be witnessed by a notary or two witnesses. Most consents are signed within several days of the birth. After signing, the consent must then be filed with the court so a judge may approve the consent and issue an order approving the consent. Before the court enters this order the birth mother has the automatic right to withdraw her consent. After the court's order, the consent may only be withdrawn upon proof of fraud or duress.

Agency Adoption. There is no difference regarding the process in which a birth mother signs her consent to adoption in an independent or agency adoption. The information provided above regarding independent adoption (e.g. when the consent can be signed, before whom, legal burden to seek to withdraw a signed consent) is identical regarding agency adoption.

Some agencies in Missouri agree to do identified adoptions. Some agencies also agree to make immediate hospital "at risk" placements with the adoptive parents before the consents are irrevocable.

Adoption Attorneys

Catherine W. Keefe   Tel (314) 726-6242
130 S. Bemiston, Suite 602   Fax (314) 726-5155
Clayton, MO 63105

Ms. Keefe began practicing law in 1986 and is a graduate of St. Louis University School of Law. Approximately 40% of her practice consists of adoptions. She estimates she completes about 45 adoptions annually. Of these, 50% are independent; 25% are agency; and 25% are intercountry. Her clients find their own birth mother. She is available to be retained in contested adoption cases.

Sanford Kriegel   Tel (816) 756-5800
Krigel & Krigel   Fax (816) 756-1999
4545 Belleview
Kansas City, MO 64111

Mr. Kriegel began practicing law in 1976 and is a graduate of St. Louis University School of Law. Approximately 25% of his practice consists of adoption. He estimates he completes more than 100 adoptions annually. Of these, 75% are independent; 20% are agency; and 5% are intercountry. His clients find their own birth mother. He is available to be retained in contested adoption cases.

Kay A. VanPelt   Tel (417) 886-9080
VanPelt & VanPelt   Fax (417) 886-8563
1524 E. Primrose, Suite A
Springfield, MO 65804

Ms. VanPelt began practicing law in 1983 and is a graduate of University of Missouri at Columbia School of Law. Approximately 90% of her practice consists of adoptions. She estimates she completes about 30 adoptions annually. Of these, 50% are independent; 30% are agency; and 20% are intercountry. Her clients find their own birth mother. She is available to be retained in contested adoption cases.

F. Richard "Rick" VanPelt   Tel (417) 886-9080
VanPelt & VanPelt   Fax (417) 886-8563
1524 E. Primrose, Suite A
Springfield, MO 65804

Mr. VanPelt began practicing law in 1983 and is a graduate of University of Missouri at Columbia School of Law. Approximately 35% of his practice consists of adoptions. He estimates he completes about 25 adoptions annually. Of these, 70% are independent; 20% are agency; and 10% are intercountry. His clients find their own birth mother. He is available to be retained in contested adoption cases.

Licensed Private Adoption Agencies (* Offers intercountry programs)

Action for Adoption; 1015 Locust Street; St. Louis, MO 63101; (816) 490-0198;
Adop Kids, Incorporated; 109 West Jefferson; Kirkwood, MO 63122; (314) 725-1917;
*Adoption Advocates; 3100 Broadway, Suite 218; Kansas City, MO 64111; (816) 753-1881;
*Adoption and Beyond, Inc.; 401 West 89th Street; Kansas City, MO 64114; (816) 822-2800; World Wide Web: http://www.adoption-beyond.org; E-mail: adopt@adoption-beyond.org;
Adoption and Counseling Services for Families; 7611 State Line, Suite 140; Kansas City, MO 64111; (816) 942-8440;

*Adoption and Fertility Resources; 144 Westwoods Drive; Liberty, MO 64068; (816) 781-8550;
Adoption and Fertility Resources; Seaport Professional Complex; Liberty, MO 64068; (816) 781-8550;
Adoption By Family Therapy of the Ozarks, Inc;
Stoneridge Center; Kimberling, MO 65686; (417) 882-7700;
Adoption Counseling, Inc.; 1420 West Lexington Avenue; Independence, MO 64052; (816) 507-0822;
Adoption of Babies and Children; 4330 Bellview, Suite 200; Kansas City, MO 64111; Toll Free: (800) 406-2909;
Adoption Option; 1124 Main; Blue Springs, MO 64015; (816) 224-1525;
Affordable Adoption Solutions, Inc.; 122 1/2 Madison Street, Suite A; Jefferson City, MO 65101; (573) 632-6646;
Alternatives Opportunities, Inc. dba Gateway Youth & Family Services; 222 East Water; Springfield, MO 65806; (417) 869-8911;
American Adoption; 306 East 12th Street, Suite 908; Kansas City, MO 64106; Toll Free: (800) 875-2229; World Wide Web: http://www.americanadoptions.com/; E-mail: adoptions@americanadoptions.com;
*Americans Adopting Orphans; 8045 Big Bend Boulevard; Webster Groves, MO 63119; (314) 963-7100; World Wide Web: http://www.orphans.com/; E-mail: aao@orphans.com;
Annie Malone Children & Family Service Center; 2612 Annie Malone Drive; St. Louis, MO 63113; (314) 531-0120; *Bethany Christian Services; 1 Mcbride & Son Corporate Center Drive; Chesterfield, MO 63005-1406; (636) 536-6363; http://www.bethany.org/missouri; E-mail: bcschesterfield@bethany.org;
BFT Holding Corporation dba Bringing Families Together, LLC.; 7151 N Lindberg Boulevard; Hazelwood, MO 63042; (314) 731-3969;
Boys and Girls Town of Missouri; 13160 County Road 3610; St. James, MO 65559; (573) 265-3251;
Butterfield Youth Services; 11 West Eastwood; Marshall, MO 65340; (660) 886-2253;
Catholic Charities of Kansas City; 1112 Broadway; Kansas City, MO 64111; (816) 221-4377;
Catholic Services for Children and Youth; #20 Archbishop May Drive; St. Louis, MO 63119; (314) 792-7400;
Central Baptist Family Services; 1015 Locust Street, Suite 900; St. Loius, MO 63101; (314) 241-4345; Fax: (314) 241-4330;
Children of the World, Inc.; 16 N Central; Clayton, MO 63105; (314) 721-2130;
Children's Home Society of Missouri; 9445 Litzsinger Road; Brentwood, MO 63144; (314) 968-2350;

253

*Children's Hope International dba China's Children; 9229 Lackland Road; St. Louis, MO 63114; (314) 890-0086; Fax: (314) 427-4288; World Wide Web: http://www.ChildrensHope.com; E-mail: adoption@childrenshopeint.org;

*Christian Family Life Center; 141 North Meremec, Suite 201; Clayton, MO 63105; (314) 862-6300; Fax: (314) 862-2540; World Wide Web: http://www.cflcenter.org;

Christian Family Services of the Midwest, Inc.; 5703 North Flora; Gladstone, MO 64118; (816) 452-2077;

Christian Family Services, Inc.; 7955 Big Bend Boulevard; Webster Groves, MO 63119; (314) 968-2216;

Christian Salvation Services; 4390 Lindell Boulevard; St. Louis, MO 63108; (314) 535-5919;

Creative Families, Inc.; 9378 Olive Boulevard, Suite 320; St. Louis, MO 63122; (314) 567-0707;

Crittenton St. Luke's Health Care System; 10918 Elm Avenue; Kansas City, MO 64134; (816) 765-6600;

*Dillon International, Inc.; 1 First Missouri Center, Suite 115; St. Louis, MO 63141; (314) 576-4100; Fax: (314) 453-9975; World Wide Web: http://www.dillonadopt.com; E-mail: dillonkids@aol.com;

Downey Side Families for Youth; 6500 Chippewa, Suite 324; St. Louis, MO 63109; (314) 457-1358;

Edgewood Children's Home; 330 North Gore Avenue; Webster Groves, MO 63119; (314) 968-2060;

Faith House; 5355 Page; St. Louis, MO 63112; (314) 367-5400;

Family Builders, Inc.; 203 Huntington Road; Kansas City, MO 64113; (816) 822-2169;

Family Care Center; 14377 Woodlake Drive, Suite 308; Chesterfield, MO 63017; (314) 576-6493;

Family Resource Center; 3309 S Kingshighway; St. Louis, MO 63116; (314) 534-9350;

FARM, INC (THE) dba KYDS,INC; 3549 Broadway; Kansas City, MO 64111; (816) 931-4703;

Friends of African-American Families and Children Service Center; 3920 Lindell Boulevard, Suite 102; St. Louis, MO 63108; (314) 535-2453;

Future Inc.; 643 Wynn Place; St. Louis, MO 63021; (314) 391-8868;

*Hammerman & Deveraux Counseling and Adoption Services; 16 North Central, Suite 206; Clayton, MO 63015; (314) 725-0551; Fax: (509) 757-7474;

Heart of America Adoption Center, Inc.; 306 East 12th Street, Suite 908; Kansas City, MO 64106; (636) 625-2266;

*Heart of America Family Services; 3100 N.E. 83rd Street; Suite 1401; Kansas City, MO 64119; (816) 436-0486;

Highlands Child Placement Services; 5506 Cambridge, P.O. Box 300198; Kansas City, MO 64130-0198; (816) 924-6565; Fax: (816) 924-3409; E-mail: highlands@ag.org;

Hope N. Heller, Ph.D. Adoption Services, Inc.; 11330 Olive Boulevard, Suite 225; St. Louis, MO 63141; (314) 567-7500;

Kansas Children's Service League; 3200 Wayne, Suite W-104; Kansas City, MO 64109; (816) 921-0654;

Kaw Valley Center; 3210 Lee's Summit Road; Independence, MO 64055; (816) 350-1901;

LDS Family Services; 517 West Walnut; Independence, MO 63044; (816) 461-5512;

Light House (The); 7110 Wyandotte; Kansas City, MO 64114; (816) 361-2233;

*Love Basket, Inc.; 10306 State Highway 21; Hillsboro, MO 63050; (636) 797-4100; Fax: (636) 789-4978; World Wide Web: http://www.lovebasket.org/; E-mail: lovebasket.@jcn.net;

Lutheran Family and Children's Services; 8631 Delmar Boulevard; University City, MO 63124; (314) 534-1515; Fax: (314) 534-1588;

Mattie Rhodes Memorial Society; 5001 Independence Avenue; Kansas City, MO 64124; (816) 471-2536;

Missouri Alliance for Children and Families L.L.C.; 724 Heisinger; Jefferson City, MO 65109;

Missouri Baptist Children's Home/MBCH Children & Family Ministries; 11300 St. Charles Rock Road; Bridgeton, MO 63044; (314) 739-6811; Fax: (314) 739-6325; World Wide Web: http://www.mbch.org;

*New Family Connection; 201 North Kingshighway; St. Charles, MO 63301; (636) 949-0577;

Niles Childrens Home; 1911 East 23rd Street; Kansas City, MO 64127; (816) 241-3448;

Our Little Haven; 4326 Lindell Boulevard; St. Louis, MO 63108; (314) 533-2229;

Presbyterian Children's Services, Inc. dba Farmington Children's Home (A); 608 Pine Street; Farmington, MO 63640
(573) 756-6744;

Professional Adoption Resources; P.O. Box 11; Troy, MO 63379; (636) 528-2499;

Reaching Out Thru International Adoption, Inc.; 11715 Administration Drive, Suite 101; St. Louis, MO 63146; (314) 971-3073;

Respond, Inc.; 4411 N. Newstead Avenue; St. Louis, MO 63115; (314) 383-4243;

Salvation Army Children's Shelter; 101 West Linwood; Kansas City, MO 64111; (816) 756-2769;

Salvation Army Hope Center; 3740 Marine Avenue; St. Louis, MO 63118; (314) 773-0980;

*Seek International; 4583 Chestnut Park Plaza, Suite 205; St. Louis, MO 63129-3100; (314) 416-9723; Fax: (314) 416-7880; World Wide Web: http://www.seekinc.org; E-mail: seekinc@seekinc.org;

*Small World Adoption Foundation, Inc.; 15480 Clayton Road, Suite 101; Ballwin, MO 63011; (636) 207-9229; Fax: (636) 207-9055; World Wide Web: http://www.swaf.com; E-mail: staff@swaf.com;

Special Additions, Inc.; 701 Berkshire Drive; Belton, MO 64012; (816) 421-3737;

Spofford – Cornerstone; 9700 Grandview Road; Kansas City, MO 64134; (816) 508-3400;

St. Louis Christian Home, Inc. d/b/a Echo; 3033 N Euclid Avenue; St. Louis, MO 63115; (314) 381-3100;

Universal Adoption Services; 124 East High Street; Jefferson City, MO 65101; Toll Free: (800) 934-9733;

Urban Behavioral Healthcare Institute; 912 Allen Avenue; St. Louis, MO 63104; (314) 577-5000;

Montana

State Adoption Office: (406) 444-5919
Department of Public Health and Human Services
P.O. Box 8005
Helena, Montana 59604   www.dphhs.state.mt.us

General Information. Montana permits both independent and agency adoption. Approximately 50% of Montana's infant adoptions are completed via independent adoption; 50% via agencies. Advertising is not permitted. To file a Petition for Adoption within Montana the adoptive parents must be residents of the state. Normally, independent adoptions are finalized approximately one month after the child's placement with the adoptive parents; agency adoptions normally six months. The adoptive parents and the child are required to appear in court for the final hearing.

Independent Adoption. A preplacement home study of the adoptive parents is preferred by Montana courts before a child is placed in the adoptive parents' home, although the court may waive a preplacement home study and require only a postplacement home study. The home study may be conducted by the state adoption office or a licensed adoption agency. The fee may be $750.00 or more.

It is required by law that the adoptive parents and birth mother share identities, and virtually all meet each other in person. The adoptive parents are allowed by law to assist the birth mother with pregnancy-related expenses, including living expenses. The child can be released to the adoptive parents directly from the hospital, although usually only after a *Notice of Parental Placement* has been filed. This is a document signed by the birth mother and filed with the local court (either before or after birth) which identifies the adoptive parents she has selected.

The consent may be signed no sooner than 72 hours after the birth. It may be witnessed by a notary or representative of the court or a licensed adoption agency. A birth mother may only withdraw her consent if she can prove to a court the child's best interests would be served by being with her, rather than the adoptive parents. However, once the court issues an *Interlocutory Decree of Adoption,* (usually issued several weeks after the child's placement), the consent can only be withdrawn upon proof of fraud or duress.

Agency Adoption. There is little difference regarding the process in which a birth mother signs her consent to adoption in an independent or agency adoption. However, in an agency adoption, the consent is irrevocable once it is signed and the court has entered an *Order Terminating Parental Rights.* The information provided above regarding independent adoption (e.g. when the consent can be signed and before whom) is identical regarding agency adoption.

Some agencies in Montana agree to do identified adoptions. Some agencies also agree to make immediate hospital "at risk" placements with the adoptive parents before the consents are irrevocable.

Adoption Attorneys

There are no attorney biographies available for Montana.

Licensed Private Adoption Agencies (* Offers intercountry programs)

*A New Arrival; 804 Bayers Lane; Silver Star, MT 59751; (406) 287-2114; http://www.anewarrival.com; E-mail: info@anewarrival.com;

257

Catholic Social Services for Montana; Box 907, 25 South Ewing; Helena, MT 59624; (406) 442-4130; Fax: (406) 442-4192;
Lutheran Social Services; PO Box 1345; Great Falls, MT 59403; (406) 761-4341;

Nebraska

State Adoption Office: (402) 471-9331
Department of Health and Human Services
P.O. Box 95044
Lincoln, Nebraska 68509   www.hhs.state.ne.us/adp/adpindex.htm

General Information. Nebraska permits both independent and agency adoption. Advertising is permitted. To file a Petition for Adoption within Nebraska the adoptive parents must reside there. Normally, adoptions are finalized approximately seven months after the child's placement with the adoptive parents. The adoptive parents and the child are required to appear in court for the final hearing.

Independent Adoption. A preplacement home study of the adoptive parents is required before a child can be placed in their home. The home study may be performed by a licensed adoption agency or the Nebraska Department of Social Services (which serves only certain counties in an independent adoption). The fees for pre and post-placement home study services usually ranges from $1,500 to 2,500.

It is not required by law for the birth mother and adoptive parents to meet in person or share identities, although some elect to do so voluntarily. The adoptive parents are permitted to assist the birth mother with pregnancy-related medical, legal and living expenses. The child may be released to the adoptive parents directly from the hospital, although many hospitals will only arrange the release through an attorney.

The consent can be signed anytime after the birth, although most adoption professionals wait at least 48 hours. It must be witnessed by a notary and one witness. There are no state statutes governing the withdrawal of a consent to adoption, but case law indicates a signed consent can only be withdrawn by proof to the court fraud or duress was used, or the child's best interests would be served by being removed from the adoptive parents. Once the adoption is finalized the consent becomes basically irrevocable.

State-by-State Review

Agency Adoption. There is no difference regarding the process in which a birth mother signs her consent to adoption in an independent or agency adoption, with the exception that the consent is irrevocable once: it is signed; the child has been placed with the adoptive parents; and the agency has accepted the consent. The information provided above regarding independent adoption (e.g. when the consent can be signed and before whom) is identical regarding agency adoption.

Some agencies in Nebraska agree to do identified adoptions. Some agencies also agree to make immediate hospital "at risk" placements with the adoptive parents before the consents are irrevocable.

Adoption Attorneys

There are no attorney biographies available for Nebraska.

Licensed Private Adoption Agencies (* Offers intercountry programs)

*Adoption Links Worldwide; 6901 Dodge Street, Suite 101; Omaha, NE 68132; (402) 556-2367; http://www.alww.org;
American Adoptions; National Offices; 8676 West 96th Street, Suite 140; Overland Park, KS 66212; http://www.americanadoptions.com; E-mail: adoptions@americanadoptions.com;
*Catholic Charities; 3300 N. 60th Street; Omaha, NE 68104; (402) 554-0520; World Wide Web: http://www.ccomaha.org; E-mail: catholiccharities@ccomaha.org;
Child Saving Institute; 115 South 46th Street; Omaha, NE 68132; (402) 553-6000; Toll Free: (888) 588-6003; http://www.childsaving.org;
*Holt International Children's Services; 10685 Bedford Avenue, Suite 300; Omaha, NE 68134; (402) 934-5031; Fax: (402) 934-5034; World Wide Web: http://www.holtintl.org; E-mail: info@holtintl.org;
Jewish Family Services; 333 South 132nd Street; Omaha, NE 68154; (402) 330-2024;
LDS Family Services; 517 West Walnut; Independence, MO 63044; (816) 461-5512;
Lutheran Family Services; 120 South 24th Street; Omaha, NE 68102; (402) 342-7007;
Nebraska Children's Home Society; 3549 Fontenelle Boulevard; Omaha, NE 68104; (402) 451-0787; http://www.nchs.org; E-mail: adopt@nchs.org;
Nebraska Christian Services, Inc.; 2600 South 124th Street; Omaha, NE 68144; (402) 334-3278;

259

Nevada

State Adoption Office: (702) 486-7633
Department of Human Resources—Division of Child and Family Services
6171 W. Charleston Blvd.
Las Vegas, NV 89102   http://dcfs.state.nv.us/

General Information. Nevada permits both independent and agency adoption. Advertising is not permitted. To file a Petition for Adoption within Nevada the adopting parents must reside there. Normally, adoptions are finalized approximately six to seven months after the child's placement with the adoptive parents. The adopting parents and the child are required to appear in court at the final hearing.

Independent Adoption. A preplacement home study of the adoptive parents is required before a child can be placed in their home. The home study may be conducted by the state adoption office (which usually limits its services to foster homes and special needs adoptions) or a licensed adoption agency. The fee varies but is usually under $8,500.

It is not required by law that adoptive parents and birth mothers meet in person, although it is usually done voluntarily. It is required that full identities be shared. The adoptive parents are permitted to assist the birth mother with pregnancy-related expenses. The child may be released directly from the hospital to the adoptive parents, if the consent to adoption has been signed.

The consent to adoption can be signed no sooner than 72 hours after the birth. It must be witnessed by three witnesses, one of whom must be a social worker, and one who must be a notary public. The state statutes provide that once the consent is signed it cannot be automatically withdrawn, but no details are provided regarding the legal burden to successfully withdraw a con-sent. Case law indicates proof would be required to prove the child's best interests would be served by being removed from the adoptive parents.

Agency Adoption. There is no difference regarding the process in which a birth mother signs her consent to adoption in an independent or agency adoption. The information provided above regarding independent adoption (e.g. when it can be signed, before whom, legal burden to seek to withdraw a signed consent) is identical regarding agency adoption.

Most agencies within Nevada do not agree to do identified adoptions where full identities have been shared. Some agencies will agree to make immediate hospital "at risk" placements.

Adoption Attorneys

There are no attorney biographies for attorneys in Nevada.

Licensed Private Adoption Agencies

Catholic Charities of Southern Nevada; 808 South Main Street; Las Vegas, NV 89101; (702) 385-2662; Fax: (702) 384-0677; World Wide Web: http://www.catholiccharities.com; E-mail: CCSN@CatholicCharities.com; Catholic Community Services of Northern Nevada; 500 East 4th Street, P.O. Box 5099; Reno, NV 89512; (775) 322-7073; World Wide Web: http://heather.greatbasin.com/ ~ ccsnn2/index.htm;
LDS Social Services; 513 S. Ninth Street; Las Vegas, NV 89101; (702) 385-1072;

New Hampshire

State Adoption Office: (603) 271-4707
Department of Health and Human Services
Division for Children, Youth and Families
129 Pleasant Street
Concord, New Hampshire 03301

General Information. New Hampshire permits both independent and agency adoption. Approximately 60% of New Hampshire's infant adoptions are completed via independent adoption; 40% via agencies. Advertising is permitted. To file a Petition for Adoption in New Hampshire either the adoptive parents, *or* the child to be adopted, must be residents of the state. If it is an agency adoption the Petition for Adoption may also be filed there if the agency having custody of the child is located in New Hampshire. Normally, adoptions are finalized approximately seven months after the child's placement with the adoptive parents.

ADOPTING IN AMERICA

Independent Adoption. A preplacement home study of the adoptive parents is required before a child can be placed in their home. The home study may be conducted by a licensed adoption agency. The fee varies.

It is not required by law that the adoptive parents and the birth mother meet in person and share identities, although some elect to do so voluntarily. The adoptive parents are permitted to assist the birth mother with pregnancy-related expenses, including living expenses. The child can be released directly to the adoptive parents from the hospital, although each hospital may employ different release forms.

The consent to adoption can be signed no sooner than 72 hours after the birth. It may be witnessed by a judge or a person authorized by the court to act as a witness. If the birth mother is under the age of 18 the court may require the consent of one of her parents as well. Once signed, the consent can only be withdrawn prior to the court granting an *Interlocutory Decree of Adoption,* upon proof the child's best interests would be served by being removed from the adoptive parents. After the Interlocutory Decree of Adoption, the consent is irrevocable but for proof of fraud or duress.

Agency Adoption. There is no difference regarding the process in which a birth mother signs her consent to adoption in an independent or agency adoption, although the consent form is usually referred to as a *relinquishment* in an agency adoption. The information provided above regarding independent adoption (e.g. when the consent can be signed and before whom) is identical regarding agency adoption.

Some agencies in New Hampshire agree to do identified adoptions. Some agencies also agree to make immediate hospital "at risk" placements with the adoptive parents before the consents are irrevocable.

Adoption Attorneys

Margaret Cunnane Hall   Tel (603) 673-8323
37 High Street   Fax (603) 672-2348
Milford, NH 03055

Ms. Hall began practicing law in 1979 and is a graduate of the New England School of Law. Approximately 40 % of her practice consists of adoptions. She estimates she has completed 400 adoptions in her career and presently completes 32, all of them independent. Of the adoptions she has completed, she reports

90% of her clients locate a birth mother through her office; 10% find their own birth mother.

Patricia B. Quigley   Tel (603) 644-8300
Quigley Law Office   Fax (603) 626-1740
67 Central Street   e-mail: patriciaquigley@adoptionnh.com
Manchester, NH 03101

Ms. Quigley began practicing law in 1982 and is a graduate of Northeastern University School of Law. Approximately 40% of her practice consists of adoptions. She estimates she completes about 20 adoptions annually. Of these, 90% are independent; 10% are agency. She is available to be retained in contested adoption cases. Her website is www.adoptionhn.com.

Licensed Private Adoption Agencies (* Offers intercountry programs)

Adoptive Families for Children; 26 Fairview Street; Keene, NH 03431; (603) 357-4456; Fax: (603) 352-8543;
*Bethany Christian Services of New England; P. O. Box 320; Candia, NH 03034-0320; (603) 483-2886; Fax: (603) 483-0161; World Wide Web: http://www.bethany.org; E-mail: bscandia@bethany.org;
Boston Adoption Bureau, Inc.; 14 Beacon Street, Suite 620;
Boston, MA 02108; (617) 277-1336; Toll Free: (800) 338-2224;
Casey Family Services; Building 2, 105 Loudon Rd; Concord, NH 03301; (603) 224-8909; World Wide Web: http://www.caseyfamilyservices.org;
Child and Family Services of New Hampshire; 99 Hanover Street; Manchester, NH 03105; (603) 668-1920; Toll Free: (800) 640-6486; Fax: (603) 668-6260; World Wide Web: http://www.cfsnh.org/;
Creative Advocates for Children and Families; 817 Lincoln Street #209; Manchester, NH 03103; (603) 623-5006;
LDS Social Services; 547 Amherst Street, Suite 404; Nashua, NH 03063-4000; (603) 889-0148; Toll Free: (800) 735-0419; Fax: (603) 889-4358;
*Lutheran Social Services of New England; 261 Sheep Davis Road, Suite A-1; Concord, NH 03301; (603) 224-8111; Toll Free: (800) 286-9889; Fax: (603) 224-5473; http://www.adoptlss.org/; E-mail: Intladopt@aol.com;
*New Hampshire Catholic Charities, Inc.; 215 Myrtle Street, P.O. Box 686; Manchester, NH 03105-0686; (603) 669-3030; Toll Free: (800) 562-5249; Fax: (603) 626-1252; World Wide Web: http://www.catholiccharitiesnh.org;
*New Hope Christian Services; 210 Silk Farm Road; Concord, NH 03301; (603) 225-0992; Fax: (603) 225-7400; World Wide Web: http://www.peekaboo.net/nh/adopt; E-mail: NewhopeAd@aol.com;

*Vermont Children's Aid Society; 207 West Main Street, PO Box 4085; Bennington, VT 05201; (802) 422-7901
Toll Free: (802) 422-0974; Fax: (802) 773-8757; World Wide Web: http://www.vtcas.org/; E-mail: vtcasman@sover.net;
*Vermont Children's Aid Society; 79 Weavers Street; Winooski, VT 05404; (802) 655-0006; Toll Free: (800) 479-0015; Fax: (802) 655-0073; World Wide Web: http://www.vtcas.org/; E-mail: mainadmn@vtcas.org;
*Wide Horizons for Children; 11 Powers Street, PO Box 176; Milford, NH 03055; (603) 672-3000; World Wide Web: http://www.whfc.org;

New Jersey

State Adoption Office: (609) 984-2380
Department of Human Services—Division of Youth and Family Services
50 East State Street, 5th floor, CN717
Trenton, NJ 08625
www.state.nj.us/humanservices/adoption/adopt.html

General Information. New Jersey permits both independent and agency adoption. Advertising is permitted. To file a Petition for Adoption within New Jersey the adoptive parents must reside there, or the child must be born there, although out-of-state residents may file their Petition for Adoption there if the child was surrendered to a New Jersey adoption agency. Normally, independent adoptions are finalized nine months after the placement of the child with the adoptive parents. Agency adoptions are usually finalized six months after placement. The adoptive parents are required to appear in court for the final hearing.

Independent Adoption. Birth mothers can be introduced to adoptive parents by intermediaries only if the adoptive parents have a completed home study. The intermediary (which includes attorneys) cannot charge a fee for this service. This home study can be conducted by a licensed adoption agency. The fee varies.

It is not required by law that the adoptive parents and birth mother meet and share identities, although it is often done voluntarily. The adoptive parents are permitted by law to assist the birth mother with pregnancy-related living and medical expenses. The child can be placed with the adoptive parents directly from the hospital, but usually the birth mother must be discharged with the baby, then personally place the child with the adopting parents outside the hospital.

The consent to adoption can be signed anytime after birth. The consent is not irrevocable until one of two situations occur. The birth parent can appear before a judge and agree to the termination of parental rights. If this is done, usually it is approximately two weeks after the birth. If this is not done, the consent cannot be made permanent until a preliminary hearing, which normally occurs several months after the birth and filing of the *Complaint for Adoption.*

Agency Adoption.   A birth mother's consent to adoption, called a *surrender*, can be taken no sooner than 72 hours after birth. Once executed, it is irrevocable, except for fraud or duress. A birth parent must also be offered, but is not required to accept, three counseling sessions.

Many agencies in New Jersey agree to do identified adoptions. Some agencies will agree to do immediate hospital "at risk" placements.

Adoption Attorneys

Donald C. Cofsky	Tel (856) 429-5005
Cofsky & Zeidman	Fax (856) 429-6328
209 Haddon Avenue	
Haddonfield, NJ 08033	

Mr. Cofsky began practicing law in 1973 and is a graduate of Temple University School of Law. Approximately 35 % of his practice consists of adoptions. He estimates he has completed more than 1,000 adoptions in his career and presently completes 100 annually. Of these, 20 % are independent; 65 % are agency; 15 % are international. His clients locate their own birth mother. He is available to be retained in contested adoption cases. His website is www.209law.com

Chana Mesberg	Tel (201) 833-1170
450 Churchill Road	Fax (201) 833-1613
Teaneck, NJ 07666	

Ms. Mesberg began practicing law in 1986 and is a graduate of Pace University School of Law. Her practice is limited to adoptions. She estimates she completes 40 annually. Of these, 80 % are independent; 10 % are agency; 10 % are international. Of the adoptions she has handled, she reports 75 % find a birth mother through her office; 25% find their own birth mother. She is an an adoptive parent.

Deborah Steincolor   Tel (973) 743-7500
295 Montgomery Street
Bloomfield, NJ 07003

Ms. Steincolor began practicing law in 1987 and is a graduate of the Delaware Law School. Her practice is limited to adoptions. She estimates she has completed more than 1,600 adoptions in her career and she presently completes 50 annually. Of the adoptions she has completed, 65% are independent; 35% are agency.

Licensed Private Adoption Agencies (* Offers intercountry programs)

Adoption ARC, Inc.; 4701 Pine Street, J-7; Philadelphia, PA 19143; (215) 844-1082; Toll Free: (800) 884-4004; Fax: (215) 842-9881; World Wide Web: http://www.adoptionarc.com; E-mail: taralaw@aol.com;
Adoption Services Associates; 5370 Prue Road; San Antonio, TX 78240; Toll Free: (800) 648-1807; Fax: (210) 691-8836; World Wide Web: http://www.adoptionservicesassociates.org;
E-mail: adopt@adoptionservicesassociates.org;
*Adoptions From the Heart; 451 Woodland Avenue; Cherry Hill, NJ 08002; (609) 665-5655; World Wide Web: http://www.adoptionsfromtheheart.org; E-mail: adoption@adoptionsfromtheheart.org;
American Adoptions; National Offices; 8676 West 96th Street, Suite 140; Overland Park, KS 66212; Toll Free: (800) 236-7846; World Wide Web: http://www.americanadoptions.com; E-mail:
adoptions@americanadoptions.com;
BASES; Monument Road; Philadelphia, PA 19131; (215) 877-1925; Fax: (215) 877-1942; E-mail: randerson@bases.org; Bethanna; 1030 Second Street Pike; Southampton, PA 18966; (215) 849-8815; Fax: (215) 849-8957;
*Bethany Christian Services; 445 Godwin Avenue; Midland Park, NJ 07432; (201) 444-7775; Fax: (201) 444-5420; World Wide Web: http://www.bethany.org/newjersey; E-mail: bcshawthorne@bethany.org; Lancaster: (717) 399-3213; Fax: (717) 399-3543; E-mail: mdemastus@bethany.org;
Better Living Services; 560 Springfield Avenue, Suite C, P.O. Box 2969; Westfield, NJ 07090-2969; (908) 654-0277; Fax: (908) 654-0414;
Brookwood Child Care; 25 Washington Street; Brooklyn, NY 11201; (718) 596-5555, Ext: 510; Fax: (718) 596-7564; World Wide Web: http://www.brookwoodchildcare.org;

Catholic Charities; Diocese of Metuchen; P.O. Box 191; Metuchen, NJ 08840; (732) 562-1990; Trenton: (609) 406-7400; Web: http://www.dioceseoftrenton.org;

Catholic Community Services of Newark; 499 Belgrove Drive, Suite 2; Kearny, NJ 07032; (201) 991-3770; Fax: (201) 991-3771;

Catholic Family and Community Services; 476 17th Avenue; Paterson, NJ 07501; (973) 523-9595; Fax: (973) 523-0930;

Catholic Home Bureau for Dependent Children; 1011 First Avenue, 12th Floor; New York, NY 10022; (212) 371-1000; Fax: (212) 755-4233;

Catholic Social Services of the Diocese of Camden; 810 Montrose Street; Vineland, NJ 08360; (856) 691-1841; Fax: (856) 692-6575;

*Child and Home Study Associates; 1029 Providence Road; Media, PA 19063; (610) 565-1544; Fax: (610) 565-1567;

*Children of the World; 685 Bloomfield Avenue, Suite 201; Verona, NJ 07044; (973) 239-0100; Fax: (973) 239-3443;

Children's Aid and Family Services, Inc.; 200 Robin Road; Paramus, NJ 07652; (201) 261-2800; Fax: (201) 261-6013; World Wide Web: http://www.cafsnj.org; E-mail: info@cafsnj.org;

Children's Aid and Family Services, Inc.; 60 Evergreen Place; East Orange, NJ 07019; (973) 673-6454; World Wide Web: http://www.cafsnj.org; E-mail: info@cafsnj.org;

Children's Choice; International Plaza Two, Suite 325; Philadelphia, PA 19113; (610) 521-6270; Fax: (610) 521-6266; World Wide Web: www.childrenschoice.org; E-mail: chichoice@aol.com;

Children's Choice, Inc.; 151 Fries Mill Road, Suite 205-206; Turnersville, NJ 08012; (856) 228-5223; Fax: (610) 521-6266;

Children's Home Society of New Jersey; 21 Main Street; Clinton, NJ 08809; (908) 735-9458; World Wide Web: http://www.chsofnj.org; Trenton: (609) 695-6274; Fax: (609) 394-5769; E-mail: kwestbrook@chsofnj.org;

*Chosen Children Adoption Services, Inc.; 5427 Bardstown Road, Suite One; Louisville, KY 40291; (502) 231-1336; Fax: (502) 231-4098; E-mail: chosenchildren@kyadoptions.com;

*Christian Homes for Children; 275 State Street; Hackensack, NJ 07601; (201) 342-4235; Fax: (201) 342-0246;

Downey Side Families for Youth; 146 U.S. Route 130; Bordentown, NJ 08505; (609) 291-2784; Fax: (609) 291-2787;

Family and Children's Service; 1900 Route 35; Oakhurst, NJ 07755; (732) 531-9111; Fax: (732) 531-8507;

Family and Children's Services; 40 North Avenue; Elizabeth, NJ 07207; (908) 352-7474; Fax: (908) 965-3227;

*Family Options; 19 Bridge Avenue; Red Bank, NJ 07701; (732) 936-0770;

*Gladney Center for Adoption; 6300 John Ryan Drive; Fort Worth, TX 76132-4122; (817) 922-6088; Toll Free: (800) 452-3639; Fax: (817) 922-6040; World Wide Web: http://www.gladney.org; E-mail: info@gladney.org;
*Golden Cradle; 1050 North Kings Highway, Suite 201; Cherry Hill, NJ 08034; (856) 667-2229; Fax: (856) 667-2229; World Wide Web: http://www.goldencradle.org; E-mail: adoptions@goldencradle.org;
Graham-Windham Child Care; 33 Irving Place; New York, NY 10003; (212) 529-6445, Ext: 386; Fax: (212) 614-9811;
*Growing Families Worldwide Adoption Agency, Inc.; 178 South Street; Freehold, NJ 07728; (732) 431-4330; Fax: (908) 431-3884;
Harlem-Dowling Children Services; 2090 7th Avenue; New York, NY 10027; (212) 749-3656; Fax: (212) 678-1094;
*Holt International Children's Services; 340 Scotch Road, 2nd Floor; Trenton, NJ 08628; (609) 882-4972; World Wide Web: http://www.holtintl.org; E-mail: info@holtintl.orgl *Homestudies and Adoption Placement Services (HAPS), Inc.;
668 American Legion Drive; Teaneck, NJ 07666; (201) 836-5554; Fax: (201) 836-0204; World Wide Web: http://www.haps.org; E-mail: marie@haps.org;
Jewish Child Care Association; 120 Wall Street, 12th Floor; New York, NY 10005-3904; (212) 425-3333; Fax: (212) 558-9993;
Jewish Family and Children's Service of Philadelphia Inc.; 10125 Verree Road, #200; Philadelphia, PA 19116; (215) 698-9950; E-mail: adoption@voicenet.com;
Jewish Family and Children's Services of Southern New Jersey; 1301 Springdale Road, Suite 150; Cherry Hill, NJ 08003-2729; (856) 424-1333; Fax: (856) 424-7384; E-mail: adoption@voicenet.com;
Jewish Family Services of Central New Jersey; 655 Westfield Avenue; Elizabeth, NJ 07208; (908) 352-8375;
Jewish Family Services of Metro West; 256 Columbia Turnpike, Suite 105; Florham Park, NJ 07932-0825; (973) 674-4210; Fax: (973) 765-0195;
Jewish Family Services of Monmouth County; 705 Summerfield Avenue; Asbury Park, NJ 07712; (732) 774-6886; Fax: (732) 774-8809;
Juvenile Justice Center of Philadelphia; 100 West Coulter Street; Philadelphia, PA 19144; (215) 849-2112; Fax: (215) 849-0393; World Wide Web: www.juvenilejustice.org; E-mail: rnchlas@hotmail.com;
LDS Social Services of New York; 22 IBM Road, Suite 205-B; Poughkeepsie, NY 12601; (914) 462-1288; Fax: (914) 462-1291;
Lutheran Social Ministries of New Jersey; 6 Terri Lane, Suite 300; Burlington, NJ 08016-4905; (609) 386-7171; Fax: (609) 386-7191; http://www.lsmnj.org/;
*New Beginnings Family and Children's Services, Inc.; 141 Willis Avenue; Mineola, NY 11501; (516) 747-2204; Fax: (516) 747-2505; World Wide Web: http://www.new-beginnings.org; E-mail: newbeginn@aol.com;

*NU-Roots and International Ties (NURIT, Inc.); 17 Blackhawk Court; Medford, NJ 08055; (609) 654-2052; Fax: (609) 654-2052; World Wide Web: http://www.geocities.com/NURITadoption; E-mail: Hnurit@aol.com;
*Reaching Out Thru International Adoption; 312 South Lincoln Avenue; Cherry Hill, NJ 08002; (856) 321-0777; Fax: (856) 321-0809; World Wide Web: http://www.rainbowkids.com/reachingout.htm; E-mail: reachoutnj@aol.com;
*Seedlings, Inc.; 375 Route 10 East; Whippany, NJ 07981; (973) 884-7488; Fax: (973) 884-8648; World Wide Web: http://www.seedlings-inc.org; E-mail: adoptions@seedlings-inc.org;
Small World Agency; New Jersey Branch Office; 257 West Broad Street; Palmyra, NJ 08065-1463; (609) 829-2769;
Spence-Chapin Services to Families and Children; Branch Office; 57 Union Place; Summit, NJ 07901; (908) 522-0043; Fax: (908) 598-1506; World Wide Web: http://www.spence-chapin.org;
Tabor Children's Services; 4700 Wissachickon Avenue, Building H; Philadelphia, PA 19144; (215) 842-4800; Fax: (215) 842-4809; E-mail: carlawilson@philadelphia.tabor.org;
The Gladney Center; 257 West Broad Street; Palmyra, NJ; 08065; (609) 829-2769;
The New York Foundling Hospital; 590 Avenue of the Americas; New York, NY 10011; (212) 727-6828; Fax: (212) 886-4098; World Wide Web: http://www.Nyfoundling.org;
United Family and Children's Society; 305 W. Seventh Street; Plainfield, NJ 07060; (908) 755-4848; Fax: (908) 755-3655;
*Voice for International Development and Adoption (VIDA); 354 Allen Street; Hudson, NY 12534; (518) 828-4527; Fax: (518) 828-0688; World Wide Web: http://members.aol.com/vidaadopt/vida.html; E-mail: vidaadopt@aol.com;
Welcome House Adoption Program; 520 Dublin Road, PO Box 181; Perkasie, PA 18944; (215) 249-0100; Fax: (215) 249-0125; World Wide Web: www.pearlsbuck.org; E-mail: mtomlinson@pearlsbuck.org;
*Welcome House Adoption Program of Pearl S. Buck International; 520 Dublin Road; Perksaie, PA 18944-3000; (215) 249-0100; Toll Free: (800) 220-2825; Fax: (215) 249-9657; World Wide Web: http://www.pearlsbuck.org; E-mail: info@pearl-s-buck.org;
Women's Christian Alliance; 1722 Cecil B. Moore Avenue; Philadelphia, PA 19121; (215) 236-9911; Fax: (215) 236-9808; http://www.wcafamily.org;
*World Child International; 9300 Colombia Boulevard; Silver Spring, MD 20910; (301) 588-3000; Fax: (301) 585-7879; World Wide Web: http://www.worldchild.org/; E-mail: info@worldchild.org;
Youth Consultation Services; 284 Broadway; Newark, NJ 07104; (973) 482-8411; Fax: (973) 482-5918

New Mexico

State Adoption Office: (505) 827-8456
Children, Youth and Families Department—Central Adoption Unit
PERA Building, Room 2258, P.O. Drawer 5160
Sante Fe, NM 87504 www.state.nm.us/cyfd/foster.htm

General Information. New Mexico permits both independent and agency adoption. Approximately 65% of New Mexico's infant adoptions are completed via independent adoption; 35% via agencies. Advertising is permitted. To file a Petition for Adoption within New Mexico the adoptive parents must be residents, or the child must be born there. If it is an agency adoption the Petition for Adoption can also be filed there if the agency having custody of the child is located in New Mexico. Normally, adoptions are finalized four months after the child's placement with the adoptive parents. The adoptive parents are not required to appear in court for the final hearing.

Independent Adoption. A preplacement home study of the adoptive parents is required before the child is placed in their home. The home study may be conducted by a licensed adoption agency or a certified social worker by the Children, Youth and Families Department. The fee varies but typical pre and post-placement services range from $1,500 to $2,500.

It is not required by law that the adoptive parents and birth mother meet in person and share identities, although it is done in some cases voluntarily. The adoptive parents are permitted to assist the birth mother with pregnancy-related expenses, including living expenses, although these expenses should be paid directly to the party supplying the related services and not directly to the birth mother. The child may be released directly from the hospital to the adoptive parents, although hospitals use various forms for the release.

The consent to adoption can be signed no sooner than 48 hours after the birth. It must be signed before a judge. It is irrevocable upon signing, but for proof of fraud or duress.

Agency Adoption. There is no difference regarding the process in which a birth mother signs her consent to adoption in an independent or agency adoption, although the consent is referred to as a *voluntary relinquishment* in an agency adoption. The information provided above regarding independent adoption (e.g. when it can be signed, before whom and the legal burden to seek to withdraw a signed consent) is identical regarding agency adoption.

Some agencies in New Mexico agree to do identified adoptions. Some agencies also agree to make immediate hospital "at risk" placements.

Adoption Attorneys

Harold O. Atencio   Tel (505) 839-9111
Atencio Law Firm   Fax (505) 839-0888
3809 Atrisco Drive NW, Suite B
Albuquerque, NM 87120

Mr. Atencio began practicing law in 1988 and is a graduate of the University of New Mexico School of Law. Approximately 75% of his practice consists of adoptions. He estimates he completes 30 adoptions annually. Of these, 45% are independent; 45% are agency; 10% are international. He is available to be retained in contested adoption cases. His clients locate their own birth mother.

Licensed Private Adoption Agencies (* Offers intercountry programs)

*A.M.O.R. Adoptions, Inc.; 3700 Coors Boulevard N.W., Suite F; Albuquerque, NM 87120; (505) 831-0888; Toll Free: (877) 712-2667; Fax: (505) 831-2800; World Wide Web: http://www.AMORADoptions.com; E-mail: info@AMORADoptions.com;
Adoption Assistance Agency; 2800 Eubank, NE; Alburquerque, NM 87122; (505) 821-7779; http://www.adoptionassistanceagency.org; E-mail: info@adopitonassistance.org;
Adoption Plus; 11811 Menaul NE, Suite 5; Albuquerque, NM 87112; (505) 262-0446; Fax: (505) 298-6653; E-mail: Adoptionsplus@concast.net;
Catholic Social Services, Inc.; 4985 Airport Road; Santa Fe, NM 87505-0443; (505) 424-9789;
Child Rite/AASK; 4801 Indian School Road, Suite 204; Albuquerque, NM 87106; (505) 797-4191; Taos: (505) 758-0343;
Choices Adoption and Counseling; 2811 Indian School Road, N.E.; Albuquerque, NM 87106; (505) 266-0456;
Christian Child Placement Services; 1356 NM 236; Portales, NM 88130; (505) 356-4232;

Families for Children; 6209 Hendrex NE; Alburquerque, NM 87110; (505) 881-4200;
Family Matters; 3301-R Coors NW, #286; Albuquerque, NM 87120; (505) 344-8811;
La Familia Placement Services; Suite 103, 707 Broadway NE; Alburquerque, NM 87102; (505) 766-9361; World Wide Web: http://www.la-familia-inc.org;
LDS Family Services; 3811 Atrisco Drive NW, Suite A; Albuquerque, NM 87120; (505) 836-5947;
LDS Social Services; 925 Cannery Court; Farmington, NM 87401; (505) 327-6123;
New Mexico Parent & Child Resources; 3500 Indian School NE; Albuquerque, NM 87106; (505) 268-4973;
*Rainbow House International; 19676 Highway 314; Belen, NM 87002; (505) 861-1234; Fax: (505) 864-8420; World Wide Web: http://www.rhi.org; E-mail: rainbow@rhi.org;

New York

State Adoption Office: (518) 474-9406; (800) 345-5437
Office of Children and Family Services—State Adoption Service
52 Washington Steet, Room 323 North
Rensselaer, NY 12144   www.afa.state.ny.us/adopt/adoption.htm

General Information. New York permits both independent and agency adoption. Approximately 70% of New York's infant adoptions are completed via independent adoption; 30% via agencies. Advertising is permitted. It is illegal for an intemediary, other than a licensed agency, to receive compensation for locating a birth mother for adoptive parents to create an adoptive match. To file a Petition for Adoption within New York either the adoptive parents, *or* the child being adopted, must reside there. If it is an agency adoption the Petition for Adoption may be filed in New York if the agency having custody of the child is located there. Normally, adoptions are finalized from three to ten months after the child's placement with the adoptive parents. The adoptive parents and the child are required to appear in court for the final hearing.

Independent Adoption. A preplacement home study of the adoptive parents is required before a child can be placed in their home. The home study is used to allow the adoptive parents to be "certified as qualified adoptive parents." If the adoptive parents have not been certified by the time the placement is to occur, a court may permit the adoptive parents to have physical custody of the child if they file a request for temporary guardianship within five days of having obtained custody. The home study may be conducted by a licensed agency, licensed social worker, state adoption office, or other person approved by the court. The fee varies.

It is not required by law that the adoptive parents and birth mother meet in person and share identities, although some elect to do so voluntarily. The adoptive parents are permitted to assist the birth mother with pregnancy-related medical, legal and living expenses, limited to two months pre-birth and one month post-birth. Assistance in excess of these periods require court approval. The child can be released from the hospital directly to the adoptive parents, although hospitals use different forms and have different policies.

The consent to adoption can be signed anytime after the birth. The consent must be witnessed by a judge or a notary public. Most consents are signed within several days of the birth. If the consent is signed before a judge, it is usually declared irrevocable upon signing, but for proof of fraud or duress. If the consent was witnessed by a notary public, the consent may be withdrawn for a period of 45 days from the time it is signed, if a court determines the child's best interests would be served by the child being removed from the adoptive parents.

Agency Adoption. The consent to adoption, called a *surrender* in an agency adoption, may be signed anytime after birth. If it is witnessed by a judge the surrender is irrevocable upon signing, but for proof of fraud or duress. The surrender may also be witnessed by a representative of the adoption agency, and one additional witness. If this non-judicial witnessing option is selected, the surrender may be withdrawn by proving the child's best interests would be served, but only until 30 days have elapsed from the time the surrender is signed, and the child must have been placed with the adoptive parents. Once 30 days have elapsed and the child is placed with the adoptive parents, the surrender is irrevocable and can only be withdrawn upon proof of fraud or duress.

Some agencies agree to do identified adoptions. Some agencies also agree to do immediate hospital "at risk" placements.

ADOPTING IN AMERICA

Adoption Attorneys

Robin A. Fleischner
11 Riverside Drive, Suite 14MW
New York, New York 10023

Tel (212) 362-6945
Fax (212) 875-1431
e-mail: adoptnjny@aol.com

Ms. Fleischner began practicing law in 1981 and is a graduate of the Benjamin N. Cardozo School of Law at Yeshiva University. She is also licensed to practice in New Jersey. Her practice is limited to adoptions. She estimates she has completed 500 adoptions in her career and presently completes 60 annually. Of these, 75% are independent; 25% are agency. She also has an office in New Jersey. She is a member of the Adoption Subcommittee of the New York State Bar Association. She is an adoptive parent.

Gregory A. Franklin
Ashcraft, Franklin & Young
95 Allens Creek Road; Bldg. 1, Suite 104
Rochester, New York 14618

Tel (585) 442-0540
Fax (585) 442-6889

e-mail: gfranklin@adoptionattorneys.org

Mr. Franklin began practicing law in 1984 and is a graduate of Fordham University School of Law. Approximately 90% of his practice consists of adoptions. He estimates he has completed over 400 adoptions in his career and presently completes 70 annually. Of these, 60% are independent; 10% are agency; 30% are intercountry. He is available to be retained in contested adoption cases. He is an adoptive parent. His website is www.adoption.com/franklin

Laurie B. Goldheim
55 Old Turnpike Road, Suite 406
Nanuet, NY 10954

Tel (845) 624-2727
Fax (845) 624-8400

Ms. Goldheim began practicing law in 1990 and is a graduate of Boston University School of Law. Her practice is limited to adoptions. She estimates she has completed over 500 adoptions in her career. Of these, 95% are independent; 5% are agency. She also has an office in New Jersey.

Michael S. Goldstein
62 Bowman Avenue
Rye Brook, New York 10573

Tel (914) 939-1111
Fax (914) 939-2369
e-mail: info@adoptgold.com

Mr. Goldstein began practicing law in 1982 and is a graduate of Fordham Law School. Approximately 95% of his practice consists of adoptions. He estimates he has completed 1,600 adoptions in his career and presently completes 100 annually. Of these, 85% are independent; 5% are agency; 15% are international. His clients locate their own birth mother. He is an adoptive parent.

Flory Herman   Tel (716) 691-1706
Law Office of Lisa M. Keating   Fax (716) 691-8320
260 Creekside Drive
Amherst, NY 14228

Ms. Herman began practicing law in 1988 and is a graduate of New York School of Law. Her practice is limited to adoptions. She estimates she completes 30 adoptions annually. Of these, 80% are independent; 10% are agency; and 10% are intercountry. She is an adoptive parent.

Cynthia Perla Meckler   Tel (716) 741-4164
8081 Floss Lane   Fax (716) 741-4164
Buffalo, NY 14051

Ms. Meckler began practicing law in 1980 and is a graduate of S.U.N.Y. at Buffalo. Her practice is limited to adoptions. She estimates she has completed 800 in her career. Of these, 70% are independent; 5% are agency; and 20% are intercountry. She is the chairperson of the Erie County Bar Association Adoption Committee.

Brendan O'Shea   Tel (518) 432-7511
Gleason, Dunn, Walsh & O'Shea   Fax (518) 432-5221
102 Hackett Blvd.   e-mail: boshea@gdwo.net
Albany, NY 12209

Mr. O'Shea began practicing law in 1980 and is a graduate of Albany Law School. Approximately 50% of his practice consists of adoptions. He estimates he has completed 800 adoptions in his career and presently completes 65 annually. Of these, 60% are independent; 20% are agency; and 20% are intercountry. He is a member of the New York State Bar Adoption Committee.

Denise Seidelman   Tel (914) 962-3001
1145 Baldwin Road   Fax (914) 962-1707
Yorktown Heights, NY 10598   e-mail: Rumseidlaw@aol.com

Ms. Seidelman began practicing law in 1979 and is a graduate of the Washington College of Law. Approximately 95% of her practice consists of adoptions. She

275

estimates she completes 50 adoptions annually. Of the adoptions she has completed, 50% are independent; 30% are agency. 20% are international.

Golda Zimmerman   Tel (315) 475-3322
711 E. Genesee Street, Suite 200   Fax (315) 475-7727
Syracuse, New York 13210   e-mail: gzimmerman@adoptionattorneys.org

Ms. Zimmerman began practicing law in 1980 and is a graduate of Syracuse University College of Law. Approximately 90% of her practice consists of adoptions. She estimates she completes more than 50 adoptions annually. Of the adoptions she has completed, 10% are independent; 90% are agency or international. She is a member of the New York State Bar Adoption Subcommittee and editor of *Adoption Law in New York*. She is an adoptive parent.

Licensed Private Adoption Agencies (* Offers intercountry programs)

Abbott House; 100 North Broadway; Irvington, NY 10533; (914) 591-3200, Ext: 224; World Wide Web: http://www.abbotthouse.net/;
Adoption and Counseling Services, Inc.; 1 Fayette Park; Syracuse, NY 13202; (315) 471-0109;
Adoption S.T.A.R., Inc.; 2001 Niagara Falls Blvd, Suite 5; West Amherst, NY 14228; (716) 691-3300; http://www.adoptionstar.com;
Adoption Services Associates; 5370 Prue Road; San Antonio, TX 78240; Toll Free: (800) 648-1807; http://www.adoptionservicesassociates.org;
*Adoption Services, Inc.; 28 Central Boulevard; Camp Hill, PA 17011; (717) 737-3960; http://www.adoptionservices.org/;
Advocates for Adoption, Inc.; 362 West 46th Street; New York, NY 10036; (212) 957-3938;
Angel Guardian Home; 6301 12th Avenue; Brooklyn, NY 11219; (718) 232-1500, Ext: 267;
ARISE Child and Family Services; 1065 James Street; Syracuse, NY 13203; (315) 477-4291;
Association to Benefit Children; 419 East 86 Street; New York, NY 10028; (212) 831-1322, Ext: 340; http://www.a-b-c.org; E-mail: info@a-b-c.org;
Astor Home for Children; PO Box 5005, 6339 Mill St; Rhinebeck, NY 12572; (914) 876-4081; World Wide Web: http://www.astorservices.org/;
Baker Victory Services; 790 Ridge Rd; Lackawanna, NY 14218; (716) 828-9510;
*Bethany Christian Services; Warwick Reformed Church, 16 Maple Avenue; Warwick, NY 10990; (914) 987-1453; http://www.bethany.org/warwick_ny/;
Brookwood Child Care; 25 Washington Street; Brooklyn, NY 11201; (718) 596-5555, Ext: 510; http://www.brookwoodchildcare.org;

Cardinal McCloskey School and Home; 2 Holland Avenue; White Plains, NY 10603; (914) 997-8000, Ext: 134;

Catholic Charities of Buffalo; 525 Washington Street; Buffalo, NY 14203; (716) 856-4494; Cortland: (607) 756-5992; Ogdensburg: (315) 393-2660; Oswego: (315) 343-9540; Plattsburgh: (518) 561-0470; Rome: (315) 337-8600; Syracuse: (315) 424-1871;

Catholic Family Center; 25 Franklin Street; Rochester, NY 14604; (716) 262-7134;

Catholic Guardian Society of New York; 1011 First Avenue; New York, NY 10022; (212) 371-1000;

Catholic Home Bureau for Dependent Children; 1011 First Avenue, 12th Floor; New York, NY 10022; (212) 371-1000; Fax: (212) 755-4233;

Catholic Social Services of Broome County; 232 Main Street; Binghamton, NY 13905; (607) 729-9166;

Catholic Social Services of Oneida and Madison Counties; 1408 Genesee Street; Utica, NY 13502; (315) 724-2158;

Child and Family Services of Erie; 844 Delaware Avenue; Buffalo, NY 14209-2008; (716) 882-0555, Ext: 106; Fax: (716) 882-1451;

Child Development Support Corporation; 352-358 Classon Avenue; Brooklyn, NY 11238; (718) 230-0056;

*Children At Heart Adoption Services, Inc.; 145 N. Main Street; Mechanicville, NY 12118; (518) 664-5988; http://www.childrenatheart.com;

*Children of the World; 27 Hillvale Road; Syosset, NY 11791-6916; (516) 935-1235; http://cwaany.org/; E-mail: cwaa@attglobal.net;

Children's Aid Society; Adoption and Foster Home Division; 150 E. 45th Street; New York, NY 10017; (212) 949-4961;

Children's Home of Poughkeepsie; 91 Fulton Street; Poughkeepsie, NY 12601; (914) 452-1420;

Children's Village; Echo Hills; Dobbs Ferry, NY 10522; (914) 693-0600, Ext: 1223; World Wide Web: http://www.childrensvillage.org;

Coalition for Hispanic Family Services; 315 Wyckoff Avenue, 4th Floor; Brooklyn, NY 11237; (718) 497-6090; E-mail: chfs_main@netzero.net;

Community Maternity Services; 27 N Main Avenue; Albany, NY 12203; (518) 482-8836; Fax: (518) 482-5805; World Wide Web: http://www.cccms.com;

Downey Side Families for Youth; PO Box 2139, 371 Seventh Avenue; New York, NY 10116-2139; (212) 714-2200; http://www.downeyside.org;

Dunbar Assoc., Inc.; 1453 S. State St; Syracuse, NY 13205; (315) 476-4269;

Edwin Gould Services for Children; 41 East 11th Street; New York, NY 10003; (212) 598-0051, Ext: 279;

Episcopal Mission Society; 305 Seventh Avenue, 3rd Floor; New York, NY 10001-6008; (212) 675-1000;

Family and Children's Services of Broome County; 257 Main Street; Binghamton, NY 13905; (607) 729-6206;
Ithaca: (607) 273-7494;
Schenectady: (518) 393-1369;
Family Connections; 20 Hyatt Street; Cortland, NY 13045; (607) 756-6574;
Family Service of Utica; 401 Columbia Street, Suite 201; Utica, NY 13502; (315) 735-2236; Westchester: (914) 948-8004; http://www.fsw.org;
Family Support Systems Unlimited; 2530 Grand Concourse; Bronx, NY 10458; (718) 220-5400, Ext: 403;
*Family Tree; 2 Crestmont Drive; Clifton Park, NY 12065; (518) 371-1336;
Forestdale, Inc.; 67-35 112th Street; Forest Hills, NY 11375; (718) 263-0740;
Gateway-Longview; 605 Niagara Street; Buffalo, NY 14201; (716) 882-8468, Ext: 3884;
Graham-Windham Child Care; 33 Irving Place; New York, NY 10003; (212) 529-6445, Ext: 386; Fax: (212) 614-9811;
Green Chimneys; Box 719, Doansburg Road; Brewster, NY 10509-0719; (914) 279-2996, Ext: 149;
Hale House Center, Inc.; 155 West 122nd Street; New York, NY 10027;
*Happy Families International Center, Inc.; 3 Stone Street; Cold Spring, NY 10516; (914) 265-9272;
Harlem-Dowling Children Services; 2090 7th Avenue; New York, NY 10027; (212) 749-3656; Fax: (212) 678-1094; Heartshare Human Services; 191 Joralemon Street; Brooklyn, NY 11201; (718) 422-4219; World Wide Web: http://www.heartshare.com;
Hillside Children's Center; 1337 East Main Street; Rochester, NY 14609; (716) 654-4528;
Ibero American Action League Inc.; 817 East Main Street; Rochester, NY 14605; (716) 256-8900;
Jewish Board of Family and Children Services; 120 W 57th Street; New York, NY 10019; (212) 582-9100; World Wide Web: http://www.jbfcs.org;
Jewish Child Care Association; 120 Wall Street, 12th Floor; New York, NY 10005-3904; (212) 425-3333; Fax: (212) 558-9993;
Jewish Family Services of Erie County; 70 Barker Street; Buffalo, NY 14209; (716) 883-1914; World Wide Web: http://www.jfsbuffalo.org; Rochester: (716) 461-0110; World Wide Web: http://www.jfsrochester.org;
*Karing Angels International Adoptions, Inc.; 302 Virginia Avenue; Oceanside, NY 11572-5433; (516) 764-9563; http://www.KaringAngelsIntl.org;
Lakeside Family and Children's Services; 185 Montague Street; Brooklyn, NY 11201; (718) 237-9700; World Wide Web: http://www.lakesidefamily.org;
LDS Social Services of New York; 22 IBM Road, Suite 205-B; Poughkeepsie, NY 12601; (914) 462-1288; Fax: (914) 462-1291;

Leake and Watts Children's Home; 463 Hawthorne Avenue; Yonkers, NY 10705; (914) 375-8700; World Wide Web: http://www.leakeandwatts.org;

Little Flower Children's Services; 186 Joralemon Street; Brooklyn, NY 11201; (718) 875-3500, Ext: 367; http://www.littleflowerny.org;

Lutheran Social Services, Inc.; 83 Christopher Street; New York, NY 10014; (212) 784-8904;

McMahon Services for Children; 305 Seventh Avenue; New York, NY 10001; (212) 243-7070, Ext: 259;

Miracle Makers, Inc.; 510 Gates Avenue; Brooklyn, NY 11216; (718) 483-3000;

New Alternatives for Children; 37 W. 26th Street; New York, NY 10010; (212) 696-1550;

*New Beginnings Family and Children's Services, Inc.; 141 Willis Avenue; Mineola, NY 11501; (516) 747-2204; http://www.new-beginnings.org;

New Hope Family Services; 3519 James Street; Syracuse, NY 13206; (315) 437-8300;

*New Life Adoption Agency; 711 East Genesee Street, Suite 210; Syracuse, NY 13210; (315) 422-7300; http://www.newlifeadoption.org;

Ohel Children's Home and Family Services; 4510 16th Avenue, 4th Floor; Brooklyn, NY 11204; (718) 851-6300;

*Parsons Child and Family Center; 60 Academy Road; Albany, NY 12208; (518) 426-2600; Fax: (518) 447-5234;

Pius XII Youth/Family Services; 188 W. 230 Street; Bronx, NY 10463; (718) 562-7855;

Salvation Army; Hearts and Homes; 677 South Salina Street; Syracuse, NY 13202; (315) 479-1324;

Salvation Army Foster Home; 132 West 14th Street; New York, NY 10011; (212) 807-6100, Ext: 561;

Seamen's Society for Children and Families; 25 Hyatt Street, 5th Floor; Staten Island, NY 10301; (718) 447-7740, Ext: 302; 0250ww@dfa.state.ny.us;

Sheltering Arms Children's Services; 122 East 29th Street; New York, NY 10016; (212) 679-4242, Ext: 300;

*Spence-Chapin Services to Families and Children; 6 East 94th Street; New York, NY 10128; (212) 369-0300; http://www.spence-chapin.org;

St. Augustine Center; 1600 Filmore Ave; Buffalo, NY 14211; (716) 897-4110;

St. Cabrini; Rt. 9 W; West Park, NY 12493; (914) 384-6500;

St. Christopher Ottilie; 175 Seacliff Avenue; Glenn Cove, NY 11542; (516) 759-1844; Jamaica: (718) 526-7533; http://www.stchristopher-ottilie.org; Brentwood: (516) 273-2733; Brooklyn: (718) 935-9466;

St. Christopher's Inc.; Office of Placement and Permanency; 881 Gerard Avenue; Bronx, NY 10452; (718) 537-5301, Ext: 120;

St. Dominics; 343 E. 137th Street; Bronx, NY 10454; (718) 993-5765;

St. Joseph's Children's Services; 540 Atlantic Avenue; Brooklyn, NY 11217-1982; (718) 858-8700;
St. Mary's Child and Family Services; 525 Convent Road; Syosset, NY 11791; (516) 921-0808;
St. Vincent's Services; 66 Boerum Place, P.O. Box 174; Brooklyn, NY 11202; (718) 522-3700, Ext: 251;
Talbot-Perkins Children Services; 116 West 32nd Street, 12th Floor; New York, NY 10001; (212) 736-2510, Ext: 291;
The ABSW Child Adoption, Counseling and Referral Service; 1969 Madison Avenue; New York, NY 10035; (212) 831-5181;
The New York Foundling Hospital; 590 Avenue of the Americas; New York, NY 10011; (212) 727-6828; http://www.Nyfoundling.org;
Urban League of Rochester, Minority Adoption Program; 265 North Clinton Avenue; Rochester, NY 14605; (716) 325-6530;
*Voice for International Development and Adoption (VIDA); 354 Allen Street; Hudson, NY 12534; (518) 828-4527;
http://members.aol.com/vidaadopt/vida.html; E-mail: vidaadopt@aol.com;
You Gotta Believe; 1220 Neptune Ave.; Brooklyn, NY 11224; (718) 372-3003;

North Carolina

State Adoption Office: (919) 733-5622
Department of Health and Human Services
2408 Mail Service Center
Raleigh, North Carolina 27699   www.dhhs.state.nc.us/dss/adopt

General Information. North Carolina permits both independent and agency adoption. Approximately 80 % of North Carolina's infant adoptions are completed via independent adoption; 20 % via agencies. Advertising is permitted only by licensed adoption agencies or adoptive parents with completed home studies. To file a Petition for Adoption the adoptive parents must reside there, usually for at least six months. Normally, adoptions are finalized approximately six months after the child's placement with the adoptive parents. The adoptive parents and child to be adopted are usually not required to appear in court for the final hearing.

Independent Adoption. A preplacement home study ("preplacement assessment") is required of the adoptive parents before a child is placed in their home. The home study may be conducted by a licensed adoption agency, or in some areas, the county department of social services. The fee varies.

It is required that the adoptive parents and birth mother share identities. Virtually all will also voluntarily meet in person. The adoptive parents are allowed to assist the birth mother with pregnancy-related medical and legal expenses. Assistance with living expenses is normally permitted for up to six weeks after birth. The child may be released from the hospital directly to the adoptive parents.

The consent to adoption may be signed anytime after the birth by the birth mother. (The birth father can usually sign before birth.) It must be witnessed by a notary or the clerk of the Superior Court. The birth mother has the automatic right to withdraw her consent for a period of 7 days after signing. If the placement occurs before the home study is delivered to the birth mother, she has an additional five business days. Once these time periods have elapsed the consent is irrevocable, but upon proof of fraud or duress.

Agency Adoption. There is no difference regarding the process in which a birth mother signs her consent to adoption in an independent or agency adoption. The information provided above regarding independent adoption (e.g. when it can be signed, before whom, and the legal burden to seek to withdraw a signed consent) is identical regarding agency adoption.

Few agencies within North Carolina agree to do identified adoptions. Some will agree to make immediate hospital "at risk" placements.

Adoption Attorneys

Bobby Dean Mills   Tel (919) 821-1860
Herring, McBennett, Mills & Finkelstein   Fax (919) 821-1816
2 Hannover Square, Suite 1677
Raleigh, NC 27602

Mr. Mills began practicing law in 1985 and is a graduate of Wake Forest School of Law. Approximately 50% of his practice consists of adoptions. Of these, 50% are independent; 50% are agency. Most of his clients locate their own birth mother.

ADOPTING IN AMERICA

W. David Thurman   Tel (704) 377-4164
Thurman, Wilson & Boutwell   Fax (704) 377-5503
301 S. McDowell Street, Suite 608
Charlotte, North Carolina 28204

Mr. Thurman began practicing law in 1983 and is a graduate of the University of North Carolina School of Law. Approximately 50% of his practice consists of adoptions. He estimates he has completed more than 200 adoptions in his career and presently completes 75 annually. Of these, 50% are independent; 40% are agency; and 10% are intercountry. His office accepts contested litigation cases.

Licensed Private Adoption Agencies (* Offers intercountry programs)

A Child's Hope; Two Hannover Square, Suite 1860; Raleigh, NC 27601; (919) 839-8800;
A Way for Children; 1811 Sardis Road; Charlotte, NC ; (704) 846-9824;
Adoption Options; 118 S. Colonial Avenue, Suite 300; Charlotte, NC 28207; (702) 344-8003; E-mail: Sraburn@aol.com;
AGAPE of N.C., Inc.; 302 College Road; Greensboro, NC 27410; (336) 855-7107; Toll Free: (800) 330-9449;
Amazing Grace Adoptions; 1215 Jones Franklin Road, Suite 205; Raleigh, NC 27606; (919) 858-8998; E-mail: Agadopt@bellsouth.net;
Another Choice for Black Children; 3028 Beatties Ford Road; Charlotte, NC 28216; (704) 394-1124; Toll Free: (800) 774-3534;
*Bethany Christian Services, Inc.; 25 Reed Street, P.O. Box 15569; Asheville, NC 28813-0569; (828) 274-7146; http://www.bethany.org/ncarolina;
Caring for Children, Inc.; 50 Reddick Road, P.O. Box 19113; Asheville, NC 28815; (828) 298-0186; Fax: (828) 236-2877;
*Carolina Adoption Services, Inc.; 120 West Smith Street; Greensboro, NC 27401-2028; (336) 275-9660; http://carolinaadoption.org;
Catholic Social Ministries of the Diocese of Raleigh, Inc.; 226 Hillsborough Street; Raleigh, NC 27603-1724; http://www.raldioc.org/csm/;
*Catholic Social Services of the Diocese of Charlotte, Inc.; 1123 South Church Street; Charlotte, NC 28203-4003; (704) 370-6155;
Children's Home Society of North Carolina, Inc.; 604 Meadow Street, P.O. Box 14608; Greensboro, NC 27415; (336) 274-1538;
*Christian Adoption Services; 624 Matthews-Mint Hill Road, Suite 134; Matthews, NC 28105; (704) 847-0038; http://www.christianadopt.org;
*Christian World Adoption; 303 7th Avenue; Hendersonville, NC 28792; (828) 685-3225; http://www.cwa.org; E-mail: cwa@cwa.org;

282

Faith Works Unlimited, Inc.; P.O. Box 14847; Raleigh, NC 27620; (919) 833-5220;

Family Services, Inc.; 610 Coliseum Drive; Winston-Salem, NC 27106-5393; (336) 722-8173;

*Frank Adoption Center; 2840 Plaza Place, Suite 325; Raleigh, NC 27612; (919) 510-9135; http://www.frankadopt.org; E-mail: info@frankadopt.org;

*Gladney Center For Adoption; 235 Commerce Street; Greenville, NC 27858; (252) 355-6267; World Wide Web: http://www.gladney.org;

Independent Adoption Center; 3725 National Drive, Suite 219; Raleigh, NC 27612; (919) 789-0707; http://www.adoptionhelp.org;

LDS Social Services; 5624 Executive Center Drive, Suite 109; Charlotte, NC 28212-8832; (704) 535-2436;

Lutheran Family Services in the Carolinas, Inc.; 112 Cox Avenue, P.O. Box 12287; Raleigh, NC 27605; (919) 832-2620;

*Mandala Adoption Services; 6601 Turkey Farm Road; Chapel Hill, NC 27514; (919) 942-5500; Fax: (919) 942-0248;

Methodist Home for Children; 1300 St. Mary's Street, P.O. Box 10917; Raleigh, NC 27605-0917; (919) 828-0345;

Nathanson Adoption Services, Inc.; 6060 J.A. Jones Drive, Suite 504; Charlotte, NC 28287; (704) 553-9506; http://www.NathansonAdopt.com;

Nazareth Children's Home; Box 1438; Rockwell, NC 28138; (704) 279-5556;

New Life Christian Adoptions; 500 Benson Road, Suite 202; Garner, NC 27529; (919) 779-1004;

Saint Mary International Adoptions, Inc.; 528 East Boulevard, Suite 105; Charlotte, NC 28203; (704) 375-6531; Fax: (704) 348-2320;

The ADOPTIONS; 118 N. College Ave. #2; Newton, NC; (828) 466-9848;

*The Datz Foundation; 2 Hanover Square, Suite 1860; Raleigh, NC 27601; (919) 839-8800; World Wide Web: http://www.datzfound.com;

Yahweh Center, Inc.; Box 10399; Wilmington, NC 28404; (910) 675-3533;

North Dakota

State Adoption Office: (701) 328-4805
Department of Human Services—Children and Family Services
600 East Boulevard Avenue
Bismark, North Dakota 58505   www.state.nd.us/humanservices

General Information. North Dakota permits only agency adoption. Advertising may be permitted. To file a Petition for Adoption within

North Dakota the adoptive parents must reside there. Normally, adoptions are finalized approximately seven months from the child's placement with the adoptive parents. Adoptive parents are required to appear in court for the final hearing.

Agency Adoption. A preplacement home study of the adoptive parents is required before a child can be placed in their home. The home study may be conducted by a licensed adoption agency. The fee typically varies from $7,000 to $8,000 for pre and post-placement services.

It is not required by law that the adoptive parents and birth mother meet in person and share identities, although some elect to do. However, if the adoption is designated an "identified adoption" full identities are shared. The adoptive parents are permitted to assist the birth mother with pregnancy-related medical, legal and living expenses. The child may be released directly to the adoptive parents from the hospital if they are licensed as foster parents. Otherwise, a court order is required if the placement occurs prior to the birth mother's termination of parental rights. The latter option is more common in identified adoptions.

The birth mother shows her assent to the adoption by filing a *Petition for Relinquishment* with the court. If she is under the age of 18, a guardian at litem must be appointed to be sure she understands the proceedings. Her signature must be witnessed by a notary or a representative of a licensed adoption agency. Although the Petition for Relinquishment can be signed and filed before the child's birth, the Petition will not be heard until at least 48 hours after the birth, or the signing of the Petition, whichever occurs later. Once the court has granted the birth mother's Petition for Relinquishment, the child cannot be reclaimed by the birth mother, unless proved to the court within 30 days that fraud or duress was used to obtain her consent.

Adoption Attorneys

There are no biographies available for attorneys in North Dakota.

Licensed Private Adoption Agencies

AASK (Adults Adopting Special Kids - a ND Collaborative for Special Needs Adoption); 1325 South 11th Street, Box 389; Fargo, ND 58103; Toll Free: (800) 551-6054;

Catholic Family Service; 1809 S Broadway, Suite W; Minot, ND 58703; (701) 852-2854; World Wide Web: http://www.cfsnd.org; Fargo: (701) 235-4457; Fax: (701) 239-8266;
Christian Family Life Services; 203 South 8th Street; Fargo, ND 58103; (701) 237-4473; Fax: (701) 280-9062;
LDS Social Services; P.O. Box 3100; Bismarck, ND 58502-3100; (763) 560-0900;
The Adoption Option: A collaborative of Lutheran Social Services of North Dakota and The Village Family Service Center; 1201 25th Street South, PO Box 9859; Fargo, ND 58106-9859; (701) 235-6433; Fax: (701) 235-9693;

Ohio

State Adoption Office: (614) 466-9274
Bureau of Family Services—Office of Family and Child Services
65 East State Street, 5th floor
Columbus, Ohio 43215   www.state.oh.us/odjfs

General Information. Ohio permits both independent and agency adoption. Approximately 70% of Ohio's infant adoptions are completed via independent adoptions; 30% via agencies. Advertising is not permitted. To file a Petition for Adoption within Ohio either the adoptive parents must reside there *or* the child must be born there. If it is an agency adoption the Petition for Adoption may also be filed in Ohio if the agency having custody of the child is located there. Normally, independent adoptions are finalized approximately six months after the child's placement with the adoptive parents; agency adoptions normally one year. The adoptive parents are required to appear in court for the final hearing.

    Ohio has a putative father registry. If the putative father fails to register within 30 days of the birth, the putative father has no right to object to the adoptive placement.

Independent Adoption. A preplacement home study is required before a child can be placed in the adoptive parents' home. Depending upon the policy of the county in which the Petition for Adoption is filed, the home study may be conducted by the state adoption office, a private licensed agency or a person approved by the court. The fee varies.

    It is not required by law that the adoptive parents and birth mother meet in person and share identities, although some elect to do so voluntarily. The adoptive parents are permitted to assist the birth mother with pregnancy-related medical and legal expenses, although assistance with living costs is generally not permitted. The child may be released directly from the hospital to the adoptive parents, although a court order is required. If a court hearing cannot be promptly scheduled, the child is usually placed in a foster home temporarily.

The consent to adoption can be signed no sooner than 72 hours after the birth, or the completion of the social work assessment, whichever occurs later. The birth mother must personally appear in court and request placement of the child with the adoptive parents. Once the placement is approved by the court, the child is placed in the custody of the adoptive parents and they may file their *Petition for Adoption*. Courts in different counties in Ohio differ. Some enter an *Interlocutory Order of Adoption* after the child has been with the adoptive parents for 30 days. This Interlocutory Order then becomes final about six months after the placement. Other counties do not enter an Interlocutory Order and wait about six months after the placement and enter a *Final Decree of Adoption*. The consent of the birth mother becomes irrevocable upon the entry of either the Interlocutory Order, or Final Decree, whichever occurs first. Prior to the granting of either order, the birth mother can withdraw her consent based upon proving the child's best interests would be served.

Agency Adoption. The birth mother executes a *surrender*, giving custody of the child to the adoption agency. The surrender can be signed no sooner than 72 hours after birth or the completion of the social work asessment, whichever occurs later. It is irrevocable upon signing. If the child is under the age of six months, the birth mother is not required to appear in court.

Some agencies in Ohio agree to do identified adoptions. Some agencies also agree to do immediate hospital "at risk" placements.

Adoption Attorneys

Jerry M. Johnson   Tel (419) 222-1040
Hunt & Johnson   Fax (419) 227-1826
400 W. North Street
Lima, Ohio 45801

Mr. Johnson began practicing law in 1975 and is a graduate of Ohio Northern University. Approximately 30% of his practice consists of adoptions. He estimates he has completed 500 adoptions in his career and presently completes 26. Of these, 60% are independent; 40% are agency. Of the adoptions he has completed, he reports 50% of his clients locate a birth mother through his office; 50% locate their own birth mother. His office accepts contested litigation cases.

Michael R. Voorhees   Tel (513) 985-2500
9521 Montgomery Road   Fax (513) 985-2503
Cincinnati, OH 45242

Mr. Voorhees began practicing law in 1987 and is a graduate of Chase Law School. Approximately 90% of his practice consists of adoptions. He estimates he completes 65 adoptions annually. Of these, 60% are independent; 30% are agency; 10% are international. Of the adoptions he has completed, he reports 20% of his clients locate a birth mother through his office; 80% locate their own birth mother. His office accepts contested litigation cases.

Licensed Private Adoption Agencies (* Offers intercountry programs)

A Child's Waiting Foster Care and Adoption Program; 710 Salisbury Way; Copley, OH 44321; (330) 665-1811; Fax: (330) 668-1889;
A Place to Call Home, Inc; 36 Central Station Place; Johnstown, OH 43031; (740) 967-2167; Fax: (740) 967-0785;
A.C.T.I.O.N.; 6000 Philadelphia Drive; Dayton, OH 45415; (937) 277-6101, Ext: 1; Fax: (937) 277-2962;
Adopt America Network; AASK Midwest; 1025 North Reynolds Road; Toledo, OH 43615-4753; (419) 534-3350; http://www.adoptamericanetwork.org; Shippensburg: (717) 532-9005;
Adoption at Adoption Circle; 2500 East Main Street, Suite 103; Columbus, OH 43209; (614) 237-7222; http://www.adoptioncircle.org;
Adoption by Gentle Care; 17 E Brickel Street; Columbus, OH 43215-1501; (614) 469-0007; http://www.adoptgentlecare.com;
Adoption Connection; 11223 Cornell Park Drive, Suite 201; Cincinnati, OH 45242; (513) 489-1616; http://www.adoptioncincinnati.org;
Adoption Specialists, Inc.; 3373 East Scarborough; Cleveland Heights, OH 44118; (216) 932-2880, Ext: 880; http://www.adoption-specialists.com;
Adriel School, Inc; 414 North Detroit Street; West Liberty, OH 43357; (937) 465-0010; Fax: (937) 465-8690;
Agape for Youth, Inc.; 8067 McEwen; Dayton, OH 45458; (937) 439-4406; Fax: (937) 439-2908;
*American International Adoption Agency; 7045 County Line Road; Williamsfield, OH 44093; (330) 876-5656; http://aiaagency.com/first.htm;

ADOPTING IN AMERICA

Applewood Centers, Inc.; 2525 East 22nd Street; Cleveland, OH 44115; (216) 741-2241; Fax: (216) 459-9821; http://www.applewoodcenters.org;
Baptist Children's Home and Family Ministries, Inc.; 1934 S. Limestone Street; Springfield, OH 45505; (937) 322-0006; Fax: (937) 322-0049;
Beacon Agency; 1836 Euclid Avenue, Suite 500; Cleveland, OH 44115; (216) 574-0300; Fax: (216) 274-0301;
Beech Acres; 6881 Beechmont Avenue; Cincinnati, OH 45230; (513) 231-6630; Fax: (513) 231-6837;
Berea Children's Home and Family Services; 202 East Bagley Road; Berea, OH 44017; (440) 234-2006; http://www.bchfs.org;
*Building Blocks Adoption Service, Inc.; P.O. Box 1028; Medina, OH 44258; (330) 725-5521; http://www.bbas.org; E-mail: denise@bbas.org;
Caring Hearts Adoption Agency Inc.; 771 Martin Street, Suite 2; Greenville, OH 45331; (937) 316-6168; http://www.caringheartsadoption.org;
Catholic Charities Diocese of Toledo; 1933 Spielbusch Avenue, PO Box 985; Toledo, OH 43624; (419) 244-6711; http://www.catholiccharitiesnwo.org;
Catholic Charities Family Center of Elyria; 628 Poplar Street; Elyria, OH 44115; (440) 366-1106; World Wide Web: http://www.clevelandcatholiccharities.org/;
Catholic Community Services of Warren; 1175 Laird Avenue; NE, 3rd Floor; Warren, OH 44483; (216) 393-4254; Fax: (216) 393-4050;
Catholic Service League, Inc. of Ashtabula County; 4200 Park Avenue, 3rd Floor; Ashtabula, OH 44004; (216) 992-2121; Fax: (216) 992-5974;
Catholic Social Service of Cuyahoga County; 7800 Detroit Avenue; Cleveland, OH 44102-2814; (216) 631-3499; Lake County: (216) 946-7264; Southwest Ohio: (513) 241-7745; Miami Valley: (513) 223-7217; Fax: (513) 222-6750;
Catholic Social Services, Inc.; 197 East Gay Street, 2nd Floor; Columbus, OH 43215-3229; (614) 221-5891; Fax: (614) 228-1125;
Children's Home of Cincinnati; 1811 Losantiville Avenue, Suite 250; Cincinnati, OH 45237; (513) 272-2800; Fax: (513) 272-2807;
Christian Children's Home of Ohio; 2685 Armstrong Road; Wooster, OH 44691; (330) 345-7949; Toll Free: (800) 643-9073; Fax: (330) 345-5218;
Cleveland Christian Home, Inc.; 1700 Denison Avenue, #203; Cleveland, OH 44109; (216) 416-4266; Fax: (216) 416-0088;
Crittenton Family Services, Inc.; 1414 East Broad Street; Columbus, OH 43215; (614) 265-9124; Fax: (614) 265-9125;
Diversion; 2215 North Main Street; Findlay, OH 45840; (419) 422-4770; Toll Free: (800) 824-3007; Fax: (419) 422-8117; E-mail: tjsas@bright.net;
*European Adoption Consultants; 9800 Boston Road; North Royalton, OH 44133; (440) 237-3554; http://www.eaci.com; E-mail: EACAdopt@aol.com;
*Family Adoption Consultants; 8536 Crow Drive, Macedonia Professional Building #230; Macedonia, OH 44056; (330) 468-0673; www.facadopt.org;

288

Family Services Association; 212 East Exchange Street; Akron, OH 44304; (330) 376-9494; Fax: (330) 376-4525;

Focus on Youth, Inc; 2718 East Kemper Road; Cincinnati, OH 45241; (513) 771-4710; Fax: (513) 771-4768;

Harbor House Adoptions; PO Box 357; Celina, OH 45822; (419) 586-9029; Fax: (419) 586-8961; World Wide Web: http://www.harborhouse.org;

Jewish Family Services of Toledo; 6525 Sylvania Avenue; Sylvania, OH 43560; (419) 885-2561; Fax: (419) 885-7427;

LDS Social Services; 4431 Marketing Place; Groveport, OH 43125; (614) 836-2466; Fax: (614) 836-1865;

Lighthouse Youth Services, Inc.; 1501 Madison Road; Cincinnati, OH 45206; (513) 221-3350; Fax: (513) 221-3665; World Wide Web: http://www.lys.org;

Lutheran Social Services of Columbus; 750 East Broad Street; Columbus, OH 43205; (614) 228-5200; Findlay: (419) 422-7917; Fremont: (419) 334-3431;

*Lutheran Social Services of Mid-America; 3131 S Dixie Drive, Suite 300; Dayton, OH 45439; (937) 643-0020; http://www.lssma.org/adoption; Cincinnati: (513) 326-5430; Northwest Ohio: (419) 243-9178; Perrysburg: (419) 872-9111; Miami Valley: (937) 325-3441; Mathias Care; 1191 Galbraith Road; Cincinnati, OH 45231; (513) 522-7390;

Mid-Western Children's Home; 4581 Long Spurling, PO Box 48; Pleasant Plain, OH 45162; (513) 877-2141; Fax: (513) 877-2145;

*New Hope Adoption International; 101 West Sandusky Street; Suite 311; Findlay, OH 45840; (419) 423-0760; http://www.bright.net/ ~ newhope/;

Northeast Ohio Adoption Services; 5000 East Market Street, Suite 26; Warren, OH 44484; (330) 856-5582; Toll Free: (800) 686-4277; Fax: (330) 856-5586;

Oklahoma Home Study; 1820 Threestars Road; Edmond, OK 73034; (405) 341-7959;

Options for Families and Youth; 5131 West 140th Street; Brook Park, OH 44142; (216) 267-7070; Fax: (216) 267-7075; E-mail: ofymrush@aol.com;

Private Adoption Services, Inc.; 3411 Michigan Avenue; Cincinnati, OH 45208; (513) 871-5777; Fax: (513) 871-8582;

Spaulding Adoption Program Beech Brook; 3737 Lander Road; Pepper Pike, OH 44124; (216) 831-0638;

Specialized Alternatives for Families and Youth; 10100 Elida Road; Delphos, OH 45833; (419) 695-8010; Toll Free: (800) 532-7239; Fax: (419) 695-0004;

St. Aloysius Orphanage; 4721 Reading Road; Cincinnati, OH 45237; (513) 242-7600; Fax: (513) 242-2845;

The Adoption Center, Inc.; 12151 Ellsworth Road; North Jackson, OH 44451; (330) 547-8255; Fax: (330) 547-3327;

The Twelve Inc.; 619 Tremont Avenue SW; Massillon, OH 44647; (330) 837-3555; Fax: (330) 837-0513;

United Methodis Children's Home; 1033 High Street; Worthington, OH 43085-4054; (614) 885-5020; Fax: (614) 885-4058;
Westark Family Services, Inc; 325 Third Street SE; Massillon, OH 46646; (216) 832-5043; Fax: (216) 830-2540;
Youth Engaged for Success; 5300 Salem Bend Drive; Trotwood, OH 45426; (937) 837-4200; Fax: (937) 837-4700;
Youth Services Network; 3817 Wilimington Pike; Kettering, OH 45429; Toll Free: (800) 686-8114; Fax: (937) 294-4440;

Oklahoma

State Adoption Office: (405) 521-2475
Department of Human Services—Division of Children & Family Services
P.O. Box 25352
Oklahoma City, Oklahoma 73125   www.okdhs.org/adopt

General Information. Oklahoma permits both independent and agency adoption. Approximately 60% of Oklahoma's infant adoptions are completed via independent adoption; 40% via agencies. Advertising is permitted. To file a Petition for Adoption in Oklahoma either the adoptive parents must reside there, *or* the child to be adopted must show significant contacts with the state, usually by having resided there at least six months. Normally, adoptions are finalized approximately seven months after the placement of the child with the adoptive parents. The adoptive parents and the child are required to appear in court for the final hearing.

Independent Adoption. A preplacement home study of the adoptive parents is required before a child can be placed in their home. It may be conducted by a licensed adoption agency or a person approved by the court. The fee for pre and post-placement home study services is $750 to $900.

It is not required by law that the adoptive parents and birth mother meet in person and share identities, although in a small number of cases it is done voluntarily. The adoptive parents are permitted to assist the birth mother with pregnancy-related expenses, although living assistance may not be provided directly to the birth mother. Prior court approval is required for any assistance exceeding $500. The child may be released directly from the hospital to the adoptive parents, although hospital policies differ. Some hospitals accept special release forms, while others require a court order.

The consent to adoption can be signed anytime after the birth by the birth mother. (A non-marital father may sign his consent before the birth witnessed by a notary public.) The birth mother's consent must be witnessed by a judge. If the birth mother is under the age of 16 the consent of one of the birth mother's parents, or her guardian, is also required. Most consents are signed within ten days of the birth. The consent to adoption is irrevocable immediately upon signing. It may only be withdrawn upon proof of fraud or duress, or the adoptive parents' failure to file their Petition for Adoption within nine months.

Agency Adoption. There is no difference regarding the process in which a birth mother signs her consent to adoption in an independent or agency adoption. The information provided above regarding independent adoption (e.g. when the consent can be signed, before whom, legal burden to seek to withdraw a signed consent) is identical regarding agency adoption.

Some agencies in Oklahoma agree to do identified adoptions. Agencies rarely agree to do immediate hospital "at risk" placements with the adoptive parents before the consents are irrevocable.

Adoption Attorneys

John M. O'Connor   Tel (918) 587-0101
Newton, O'Connor, Turner & Ketchum   Fax (918) 587-0102
15 West Sixth Street, Suite 2700   e-mail: joconnor@newtonoconnor.com
Tulsa, OK 74119

Mr. O'Connor began practicing law in 1980 and is a graduate of the University of Tulsa School of Law. Approximately 35% of his practice consists of adoptions. He estimates he has completed more than 100 adoptions and presently completes more than 25 annually. Of these, 83% are independent; 15% are agency; 2% are international. Of the adoptions he has completed, 10% of his clients locate a birth mother through his office; 90% locate their own birth mother. His office is available to be retained in contested cases. His website is www.newtonoconnor.com.

ADOPTING IN AMERICA

Licensed Private Adoption Agencies (* Offers intercountry programs)

Adoption Affiliates; 6136 E. 32nd Place; Tulsa, OK 74135; (918) 664-2275; Adoption Center of Northeastern Oklahoma; 6202 South Lewis, Suite Q; Tulsa, OK 74136; (918) 748-9200; Fax: (918) 748-0369;

Adoption Choices; 1616 East 19th Street, Suite 101 Edmond; Edmond, OK 73120; (405) 715-1991; http://www.adoptionchoices.org;

*Adoption Pathways; 1616 East Bryant; Edmond, OK 73013; (405) 715-1991;

Baptist Children's Home; 16301 South Western Avenue; Oklahoma City, OK 73170; (405) 691-7781;

Bethany Adoption Service; 3940 North College; Bethany, OK 73008; (405) 789-5423; Fax: (405) 787-6913; World Wide Web: http://www.bethany.org;

*Bless This Child, Inc.; Route 4, Box 1005; Checotah, OK 74426; (918) 473-7045; http://www.blessthischild.com; E-mail: blessthischild@ipa.net;

Catholic Social Services; P.O. Box 6429, 739 North Denver Avenue; Tulsa, OK 74106; (918) 585-8167;

Chosen Child Adoption Agency; P.O. Box 55424; Tulsa, OK 74155-5424; (918) 298-0082; Fax: (218) 749-8784;

*Christian Homes; 802 North 10th Street; Duncan, OK 73533; (405) 252-5131; http://www.christianhomes.com; E-mail: attention@christianhomes.com;

Christian Services of Oklahoma; 2221 East Memorial Road; Oklahoma, OK 73136; (405) 478-3362;

Cradle of Lawton; 902 N.W. Kingswood Road; Lawton, OK 73505; (580) 536-2478; E-mail: jan.howenstine@juno.com;

Crisis Pregnancy Outreach; 11323 S. Vine St; Jenks, OK 74037; (918) 296-3377;

Deaconess Home Pregnancy and Adoption Services; 5300 North Meridian Avenue, Suite 9; Oklahoma City, OK 73112; (405) 949-4200;

*Dillon International, Inc.; 3227 East 31st Street, Suite 200; Tulsa, OK 74105; (918) 749-4600; http://www.dillonadopt.com/;

Eagle Ridge; 601 NE 63rd; Oklahoma City, OK 73105; (405) 840-1359;

Foundations for Families, Inc.; 6202 South Lewis, #C; Tulsa, OK 74106; (918) 592-0539;

Foundations for Families, Inc.; 6202 South Lewis, #C; Tulsa, OK 74136; (918) 748-9177;

Fresh Start; 2115 North Boston Place; Tulsa, OK 74106; (918) 592-0539;

*Gladney Center for Adoption; 6300 John Ryan Drive; Fort Worth, TX 76132-4122; (817) 922-6088; http://www.gladney.org; E-mail: info@gladney.org;

Heritage Family Services; 5200 S. Yale #300; Tulsa, OK 74135; (918) 491-6767; Fax: (918) 491-6717; World Wide Web: http://www.heritagefamilyservices.org;

LDS Social Services of Oklahoma; 4500 S. Garnett, Suite 425; Tulsa, OK 74146; (918) 665-3090;

Lutheran Social Services; 3000 United Founders Boulevard, Suite 141; Oklahoma City, OK 73112-4279; (405) 848-1733; Natasha's Story, Inc.; 1554 S. Yorktown Place; Tulsa, OK 74104; (918) 747-3617;

Oklahoma Home Study; 1820 Threestars Rd; Edmond, OK 73034; (405) 341 7959;

*Pathways International, Inc.; 1616 East 19th, Suite 101B; Edmond, OK 73013; (405) 216-0909;

SAFY of America; 1209 Sovereign Row; Oklahoma City, OK 73108; (405) 942-5570; World Wide Web: http://www.safy.org;

*Small Miracles International; 1148 South Douglas Blvd; Midwest City, OK 73130; (405) 732-7295;

The Elizaveta Foundation; 6517 South Barnes Avenue; Oklahoma City, OK 73159; (405) 681-2722;

Women Care; P.O. Box 188; Edmond, OK 73083-0188; (405) 330-4700;

Oregon

State Adoption Office: (503) 945-5677
Department of Human Services
500 Summer Street NE, 2nd floor
Salem, Oregon 97310   www.scf.hr.state.or.us/adoption/index.htm

General Information. Oregon permits both independent and agency adoption. Approximately 70 % of Oregon's infant adoptions are completed via independent adoption; 30 % via agencies. Advertising is permitted if the adoptive parents have a completed home study and they have obtained a Certificate of Approval upon the home study by an Oregon agency. To file a Petition for Adoption within Oregon either the adoptive parents, the child to be adopted, *or* the birth parent whose consent to the adoption is required must reside there, usually for at least six months prior to filing the Petition for Adoption. Normally, adoptions are finalized approximately four to seven months after the child's placement with the adoptive parents. The adoptive parents and the child are usually not required to appear in court at the final hearing.

Independent Adoption. A preplacement home study of the adoptive parents by a licensed adoption agency is required. The fee for the pre and post-placement home study is approximately $1,500.

It is not required by law that the adoptive parents and birth mother meet in person and share identities, although some do so voluntarily. The adoptive parents are permitted to assist the birth mother with pregnancy-related expenses. The child may be placed with the adoptive parents directly from the hospital, although each hospital's forms and policies vary.

The consent to adoption can be signed anytime after the birth. It must be witnessed by a notary. Most consents are signed within days of the birth, sometimes in the hospital. The birth mother has the right to seek to withdraw her consent until the adoption is final. However, if the birth mother also signs a *Certificate of Irrevocability* (which is commonly done) after having been provided advice from an independent attorney, the consent is irrevocable, except upon proof of fraud or duress, provided that all the following conditions are met: the child is physically placed with the adoptive parents, the Petition for Adoption and homestudy have been filed with the court, the child's medical history has been obtained, and the judge signs an order naming a temporary guardian for the child.

Agency Adoption. The consent to adoption may be signed any time after birth. It may be witnessed by a notary or a representative of the adoption agency. Once the consent has been signed, and the child has been placed with the adoptive parents, the consent is irrevocable if the birth mother also signed a *Certificate of Irrevocability*, but for fraud or duress.

Some agencies in Oregon agree to do identified adoptions. Some also agree to do immediate hospital "at risk" placements, where the child is placed with the adoptive parents before the consents are irrevocable.

Adoption Attorneys

Catherine M. Dexter Tel (503) 582-9010
Dexter & Moffett Fax (503) 582-9940
25260 SW Parkway Avenue, Suite C
Wilsonville, OR 97070 e-mail: cdexter@oregonadopt.com

Ms. Dexter began practicing law in 1982 and is a graduate of the Northwestern School of Law at Lewis & Clark College. Her practice is limited to adoptions. She estimates she completes 70 adoptions annually. Of these, 60% are independent; 30% are agency; 10% are international. Of the adoptions she has completed, she reports 50% of her clients locate their birth mother through her office; 50% locate their own birth mother. She is available to be retained in contested cases. Her website is www.oregonadopt.com.

John R. Hassen   Tel (541) 779-8900
Hornecker, Cowling, Hawwen & Heysell   Fax (541) 773-2635
717 Murphy Road
Medford, OR 97504

Mr. Hassen began practicing law in 1965 and is a graduate of Stanford University School of Law. Approximately 15% of his practice consists of adoptions. He estimates he has completes 22 adoptions annually. Of these, 65% are independent; 34% are agency; and 1% is intercountry. Of the adoptions he has completed, he reports 1% of his clients locate a birth mother through his office; 99% locate their own birth mother. He is available to be retained in contested cases.

Susan Moffett   Tel (503) 582-9010
Dexter & Moffett   Fax (503) 582-9940
25260 SW Parkway Avenue, Suite C
Wilsonville, OR 97070   e-mail: smoffet@oregonadopt.com

Ms. Moffett began practicing law in 1987 and is a graduate of the Northwestern School of Law at Lewis & Clark College. Her practice is limited to adoptions. She estimates she completes more than 50 adoptions annually. Of these, 85% are independent; 10% are agency; 5% are international. Of the adoptions she has completed, she reports 50% of her clients locate their birth mother through her office; 50% locate their own birth mother. Her website is www.oregonadopt.com.

Laurence H. Spiegel   Tel (503) 635-7773
4040 S.W. Douglas Way   Fax (503) 635-1526
Lake Oswego, OR 97035   e-mail: LHSpiegel@msn.com

Mr. Speigel began practicing law in 1981 and is a graduate of Northwestern School of Law at Lewis & Clark College. Approximately 99% of his practice consists of adoptions. He estimates he has completed over 1,000 adoptions in his career and presently completes 70 annually. Of these, 30% are independent; 50% are agency; and 20% are intercountry. Of the adoptions he has completed, he reports 40% of his clients locate a birth mother through his office; 60% locate their own birth mother. He is an adoptive parent. His website is www.adoption-oregon.com

ADOPTING IN AMERICA

Licensed Private Adoption Agencies (* Offers intercountry programs)

Adventist Adoption and Family Services Program; 6040 SE Belmont Street; Portland, OR 97215; (503) 232-1211; http://www.tagnet.org/adventistadoption/;
*All God's Children International; 4114 NE Fremont, Suite 1; Portland, OR 97212; (503) 282-7652; http://www.allgodschildren.org; E-mail: agci@usa.net;
*Associated Services for International Adoption (ASIA); 5935 Willow Lane; Lake Oswego, OR 97035-5344; (503) 697-6863; http://www.asiadopt.org;
*Bethany Christian Services; 21125 NW West Union Road; Hillsboro, OR 97124-8543; (503) 533-2002; http://www.bethany.org;
*Cascade International Children's Services, Inc.; 133 SW 2nd; Troutdale, OR 97060; (503) 665-1589; http://www.cascadeadoptions.com;
Casey Family Program; 3910 S.E. Stark Street; Portland, OR 97214; (503) 239-9977; http://www.casey.org/; E-mail: hgilge@casey.org;
Catholic Charities, Inc.; Pregnancy Support & Open Adoption Services; 231 SE 12th Avenue; Portland, OR 97214-9813; (503) 231-4866; Fax: (503) 231-4327; World Wide Web: http://www.catholiccharitiesoregon.org;
Children's Choice; International Plaza Two, Suite 325; Philadelphia, PA 19113; (610) 521-6270; www.childrenschoice.org; E-mail: chichoice@aol.com;
*China Adoption Services; P.O. Box 19699; Portland, OR 97280; (503) 245-0976; Fax: (503) 246-2973; E-mail: info@chinadopt.org;
Columbia Adoption Services, Inc.; 1445 Rosemont Road; West Linn, OR 97068-2395; (503) 655-9470; Fax: (503) 557-8134; E-mail: cci@ipns.com;
*Dove Adoptions International, Inc.; 3735 S.E. Martins; Portland, OR 97202; (503) 774-7210; http://www.adoptions.net; E-mail: dove@adoptions.net;
Families Are Forever; 4114 N.E. Fremont Street; Portland, OR 97212; (503) 282-7652; Fax: (503) 282-2582; E-mail: agci@usa.net;
Give Us This Day, Inc.; 333 NE Russell Street, Suite 205; Portland, OR 97212-3763; (503) 282-1123; E-mail: Kmitchell@msn.com;
*Heritage Adoption Services; 10011 SE Division Street, Suite 314; Portland, OR 97266; (503) 233-1099; http://www.heritageadoption.org;
*Holt International Children's Services; PO Box 2880, 1195 City View; Eugene, OR 97402; (541) 687-2202; http://www.holtintl.org; E-mail: info@holtintl.org;
*Journeys of the Heart Adoption Services; P.O. Box 39; Hillsboro, OR 97123; (503) 681-3075; http://www.journeysoftheheart.net;
LDS Family Services; 7410 SW Beveland Road; Tigard, OR 97223-8658; (503) 581-7483; Fax: (503) 581-7484; E-mail: lloydcampbell@desertonlin;
Lutheran Community Services North West; 605 S.E. 39th Avenue; Portland, OR 97214; (503) 231-7480; http://www.lcsnw.org; E-mail: lss@Teleport.com;
Medina Children's Services; 123 16th Avenue; Seattle, WA 98122; (206) 260-1700; http://www.medinachild.org/; E-mail: info@medinachild.org;

New Hope Agency; 4370 NE Halsey St; Portland, OR 97213; (503) 282-6726; *New Hope Child and Family Agency; 2611 N.E. 125th Street, Suite 146; Seattle, WA 98125; (206) 363-1800; http://www.newhopekids.org; Northwest Adoptions and Family Services; PO Box 5724; Salem, OR 97304; (503) 581-6652; Fax: (503) 581-6652; E-mail: pinkerton@eathlink.net; Open Adoption & Family Services, Inc.; 5200 S.W. Macadam, Suite 250; Portland, OR 97201; (503) 226-4870; E-mail: adoptopen@aol.com; *Orphans Overseas; 14986 N.W. Cornell Road; Portland, OR 97229; (503) 297-2006; http://www.orphansoverseas.org; E-mail: info@orphansoverseas.org; *Plan Loving Adoptions Now (PLAN) Inc.; 203 East 3rd Street, (503) 472-8452; *The Boys and Girls Aid Society of Oregon; 018 SW Boundary Court; Portland, OR 97201; (503) 222-9661; http://boysandgirlsaid.org/; *Tree of Life Adoption Center; 9498 SW Barbur Blvd. # 304; Portland, OR 97219; (503) 244-7374; http://www.toladopt.org; E-mail: info@toladopt.org;

Pennsylvania

State Adoption Office: (717) 705-2412
Department of Public Welfare—Office of Children, Youth and Families
P.O. Box 2675
Harrisburg, Pennsylvania 17105

www.dpw.state.pa.us/ocyf/ocyfas.asp

General Information. Pennsylvania permits both independent and agency adoption. Approximately 50% of Pennsylvania's infant adoptions are completed via independent adoption; 50% via agencies. Advertising is permitted. To file a Petition for Adoption within Pennsylvania either the adoptive parents, *or* the birth parents, must reside there. If it is an agency adoption the Petition for Adoption can also be filed in Pennsylvania if the agency having custody of the child is located there. Normally, adoptions are finalized three months to one year after the child's placement with the adoptive parents. The adoptive parents and the child are required to appear in court for the final hearing.

Independent Adoption. A preplacement home study of the adoptive parents is required before a child can be placed in their home. The home study is conducted by a licensed adoption agency or licensed social worker. The fee varies.

It is not required by law that the adoptive parents and birth mother meet in person and share identities, although some do so voluntarily. The adoptive parents are permitted to assist the birth mother with pregnancy-related expenses medical, although living expenses are not permitted. The child may be released from the hospital directly to the adoptive parents, although hospital forms and policies differ.

The consent to adoption can be signed no sooner than 72 hours after the birth. It must be witnessed by two witnesses. The birth mother has the automatic right to withdraw her consent until the consent has been filed with the court, at which time the judge may approve the consent and issue an *Order Terminating Parental Rights*. This hearing could occur as soon as approximately 50 days after the birth, but is usually scheduled 90 days after birth. Once the court has issued the order terminating parental rights, the consents are basically irrevocable, but for fraud or duress.

Agency Adoption. There is no difference regarding the process in which a birth mother signs her consent to adoption in an independent or agency adoption. The information provided above regarding independent adoption (e.g. when the consent can be signed, before whom, legal burden to seek to withdraw a signed consent) is identical regarding agency adoption.

Many agencies in Pennsylvania agree to do identified adoptions. Immediate hospital "at risk" placements, where the child is placed with the adoptive parents before the consents to adoption are irrevocable, exist.

Adoption Attorneys

Denise M. Bierly   Tel (814) 237-6278
Delafield, McGee, Jones & Kauffman   Fax (814) 237-3660
300 S. Allen St., Suite 300
State College, PA 16801

Ms. Bierly began practicing law in 1990 and is a graduate of Dickinson School of Law. Approximately 80% of her practice consists of adoptions. She estimates she has completed more than 250 adoptions in her career and presently completes 36 annually. Of these, 40% are independent; 40% are agency; 20% are international. Of the adoptions she has completed, 50% of her clients locate their birth mother through her office; 50% locate their own birth mother. Her office is available to be retained in contested cases. She is an adoptive parent.

Harry L. Bricker, Jr.   Tel (717) 233-2555
407 N. Front Street   Fax (717) 233-8555
Harrisburg, PA 17101

Mr. Bricker is a graduate of Dickinson School of Law. Approximately 40%
of his practice consists of adoptions. He estimates he has completed 750 adoptions
in his career. He is a member of the Pennsylvania Academy of Adoption
Attorneys.

Barbara Binder Casey   Tel (610) 376-9742
527 Elm Street; P.O. Box 399   Fax (610) 376-9783
Reading, PA 19603   e-mail: bcasey@infantadoptions.com

Ms. Casey began practicing law in 1978 and is a graduate of the Unversity of
Pennsylvania School of Law. Her practice is limited to adoptions. She estimates
she has completed more than 350 adoptions in her career and presently completes
70 annually. Of these, 70% are independent; 20% are agency; 10% are
interational. Of the adoptions she has completed, she reports 80% of her clients
locate a birth mother through her office; 20% locate their own birth mother.

Steven G. Dubin   Tel (215) 322-4100
80 Second Street Pike, Suite 7   Fax (215) 322-7350
Southampton, PA 18966

Mr. Dubin began practicing law in 1979 and is a graduate of the Delaware School
of Law. Approximately 80% of his practice consists of adoptions. He estimates
he has completed more than 500 adoptions in his career and presently completes
40 annually. Of these, 90% are independent; 10% are agency. Of the adoptions
he has completed, 95% of his clients locate a birth mother through his office;
5% locate their own birth mother. His office is available to be retained in
contested cases. He is an adoptive parent.

Debra M. Fox   Tel (610) 896-9972
355 W. Lancaster Avenue   Fax (610) 642-4187
Haverford, PA 19041

Ms. Fox began practicing law in 1985 and is a graduate of Temple Law School.
Her practice is limited to adoptions. She estimates she completes 50 adoptions
annually. Of these, 35% are independent; 65% are agency.

ADOPTING IN AMERICA

Mary Ann Petrillo   Tel (724) 861-8333
Victorian Commons, 412 Main Street
Irwin, PA 15642

Ms. Petrillo began practicing law in 1983 and is a graduate of the University of Pittsburgh School of Law. Approximately 70% of her practice consists of adoptions. She estimates she completes 80 adoptions annually. Of these, 40% are independent; 40% are agency; 20% are international. Of the adoptions she has completed, he reports 30% of her clients find a birth mother through her office; 70% find their own birth mother. Her office is available to be retained in contested cases. She is an adoptive parent.

Licensed Private Adoption Agencies (* Offers intercountry programs)

A Brave Choice; 1011 Cedargrove Road; Wynnewood, PA 19096; (610) 642-7182;
A Second Chance; 1964 Hawthorne Lane; Hatfield, PA 19440; (215) 412-2966;
AAA Transitions Adoption Agency; 355 West Lancaster Avenue; Haverford, PA 19041; (610) 642-4155;
Adelphoi Village; 1003 Village Way; Latrobe, PA 15650; (724) 520-1111; World Wide Web: http://www.hso.blairco.org/Adelphoi.html;
*Adopt-A-Child; 6315 Forbes Avenue, Suite L-111; Pittsburgh, PA 15217; (412) 421-1911; http://www.adopt-a-child.org/; E-mail: info@adopt-a-child.org;
Adoption ARC, Inc.; 4701 Pine Street, J-7; Philadelphia, PA 19143; (215) 844-1082; http://www.adoptionarc.com; E-mail: taralaw@aol.com;
Adoption by Choice; 2503 W. 15th St, Suite 4; Erie, PA 16509; (814) 836-9887;
Adoption Horizons; 899 Petersburg Road; Carlisle, PA 17103; (717) 249-8850;
*Adoption Services of the Lutheran Home at Topton; Diakon Lutheran Social Ministries; One South Home Avenue; Topton, PA 19562-1317; (610) 682-1504; http://www.diakon.org; E-mail: roachk@lsn.org;
*Adoption Services, Inc.; 28 Central Boulevard; Camp Hill, PA 17011; (717) 737-3960; http://www.adoptionservices.org/;
Adoption Unlimited; 2148 Embassy Drive; Lancaster, PA 17603; (717) 431-2021; http://www.adoptionunlimited.org; E-mail: adoptionunlimited.org;
*Adoptions From The Heart; 800 Main Street, Suite 101; Hellertown, PA 18055; World Wide Web: http://www.adoptionsfromtheheart.org;
*Adoptions From The Heart; 1525 Oregon Pike, Suite 401-402; Lancaster, PA 17601; (717) 399-7766; http://www.adoptionsfromtheheart.org/; Wynnewood: (610) 642-7200; Greensburg: (724) 853-6533;
*Adoptions International Inc.; 601 S. 10th Street; Philadelphia, PA 19147; (215) 627-6313; http://www.rainbowkids.com/adoptionsinternational72.html;

American Friends of Children; 619 Gawain Road; Plymouth Meeting, PA 19464; (610) 828-8166;

Asian Angels; 124 Chestnut Street #2; Philadelphia, PA 19106; (215) 733-0494;

*Asociacion Puertorriquenos en Marcha; 2147 North Sixth St.;
Philadelphia, PA 19122; (215) 235-6788; http://www.apm-phila.org;

Bennett and Simpson Enrichment Services Adoption; 4300 Monument Road; Philadelphia, PA 19131; (215) 877-1925;

Best Nest; 325 Market Street; Williamsport, PA 17701; (570) 321-1969; Philadelphia: (215) 546-8060;

Bethanna; 1030 Second Street Pike; Southampton, PA 18966; (215) 849-8815;

*Bethany Christian Services; 550 Pinetown Road, Suite 100; Fort Washington, PA 19034-2606; (215) 628-0202; http://www.bethany.org; Fort Washington: (302) 732-2890; Lancaster: (717) 399-3213; Pittsburgh: (412) 734-2662;

Catholic Charities Counseling and Adoption Services; 90 Beaver Drive, Suite 111B; Dubois, PA 15801-2424; (814) 371-4717;

Catholic Charities Diocese of Erie; 329 West Tenth Street; Erie, PA 16502; (814)456-2091;Greensburg:(724)837-1840;www.dioceseofgreensburg.org; Harrisburg: (717) 238-5944; Pittsburgh: (412) 456-6960; www.ccpgh.org;

Catholic Social Agency; 2147 Perkiomen Avenue; Reading, PA 19606; (610) 370-3378;

Catholic Social Agency; 530 Union Blvd; Allentown, PA 17109; (610) 435-1541; Fax: (610) 435-4367; E-mail: csa@fast.net;

Catholic Social Services; 411 Main Street; Stroudsburg, PA 18360; (570) 476-6460; Hazleton: (570) 455-1521; Tunkhannock: (570) 835-1101;

Catholic Social Services Diocese of Philadelphia; 4th Floor; 222 North 17th Street; Philadelphia, PA 19103; (215) 854-7050;

Catholic Social Services of Luzerne County; 33 E. Northhampton Street; Wilkes-Barre, PA 18701-2406; (570) 822-7118; Williamsport: (570) 322-4220;

Catholic Social Services of the Archdiocese of Philadelphia; 222 N. 17th Street; Philadelphia, PA 19103; (215) 587-3900;

Catholic Social Services of the Diocese of Altoona-Johnstown; P.O. Box 1349, 1300 Twelfth Avenue; Altoona, PA 16603; (814) 944-9388;

Catholic Social Services of the Diocese of Scranton; 400 Wyoming Avenue; Scranton, PA 18503; (570) 346-8936;

*Child and Home Study Associates; 1029 Providence Road; Media, PA 19063; (610) 565-1544; Fax: (610) 565-1567;

Children's Aid Home Programs of Somerset County; 574 E. Main Street; Somerset, PA 15501; (814) 443-1637; http://www.cahprogram.org;

Children's Aid Society in Clearfield County; 1008 South Second Street; Clearfield, PA 16830; (814) 765-2685; http://www.childaid.org; Chambersburg: (717) 263-4159; Mercer: (724) 662-4730;

301

Children's Choice; 2909 North Front Street; Harrisburg, PA 17110; (717) 230-9980; Philadelphia: (610) 521-6270; http://www.childrenschoice.org;

Children's Home of York; 77 Shoehouse Road; York, PA 17406; (717) 755-1033; http://www.choyork.org; E-mail: choy@blazenet.net;

Children's Services, Inc.; 1315 Walnut Street, 3rd Floor; Philadelphia, PA 19107-4769; (215) 546-3503; Fax: (215) 546-7977;

Church of the Brethren Youth Services; 1417 Oregon Road; Leola, PA 17540; (717) 656-6580;

*Common Sense Adoption Services; 5021 E. Trindle Road; Mechanicsburg, PA 17050; (717) 766-6449; http://www.csas-swan.org;

Community Adoption Services of Heavenly Vision Ministries; 6513 Meadow Street; Pittsburgh, PA 15206; (412) 661-4774;

Concern; 1 W. Main Street; Fleetwood, PA 19522; (610) 944-0445; Fax: (610) 944-1195; www.concern4kids.org; E-mail: concerngbo@fast.net;

Council of Spanish Speaking Organization, Inc.; 705-09 North Franklin Street; Philadelphia, PA 19123; (215) 627-3100; http://www.elconcilio.net;

Covenant Family Resources; 743 Roy Road; King of Prussia, PA 19406; (610) 354-0555;

Delta Community Supports; 2210 Mt. Carmel Avenue, Suite 105; Glenside, PA 19038; (215) 887-6300;

Diversified Family Services; 3679 East State Street; Hermitage, PA 16148; (724) 346-2123;

Every Child, Inc.; East Liberty Station, Suite 300, 6401 Penn Avenue; Pittsburgh, PA 15206; (412) 665-0600;

Families Caring for Children; 96 Front Street; Nanticoke, PA 18634; (570) 735-9028;

Families United Network; PO Box 144, Brinton Avenue; Trafford, PA 15085; (412) 373-2355;

*Family Adoption Center; 960 Penn Avenue, Suite 600; Pittsburgh, PA 15222; (412) 288-2130; http://www.fhcinc.org; E-mail: adoption@fhcinc.org;

*Family Service; 630 Janet Avenue; Lancaster, PA 17601; (717) 397-5241;

Family Services and Children's Aid Society of Venango County; 716 E. Second Street; Oil City, PA 16301; (814) 677-4005;

Family Services of Western Pennsylvania; 3230 William Pitt Way; Pittsburgh, PA 15238; (412) 820-2050; http://www.fswp.org; E-mail: fswp@fswp.org;

Friends Association for the Care and Protection of Children; P.O. Box 439, 206 North Church Street; West Chester, PA 19381; (610) 431-3598; Fax: (610) 431-9768; World Wide Web: http://www.angelfire.com/pa/friendsassoc/;

Friendship House; 1561 Medical Drive; Pottstown, PA 19464; (610) 327-2200;

Genesis of Pittsburgh; P.O. Box 41017; Pittsburgh, PA 15202; (412) 766-2693; World Wide Web: http://trfn.clpgh.org/genesis;

Heart to Heart Adoption Services, Inc.; Fox Lure Building, 504; Benner Pike; Bellefonte, PA 16823; (814) 355-4310; www.heartadoptions.com;

ILB Adoption Agency; 734 Melbourne St; Pittsburgh, PA 15217; (412) 521-2413;

Institute for Human Resources & Services; Pierce Office Center, Suite 301; Kingston, PA 18704; (570) 288-9386; E-mail: insthumers@aol.com;

*International Assistance Group; 531 Fifth Street; Oakmont, PA 15139; (412) 828-5800; http://www.iagadoptions.org; E-mail: info@iagadoptions.org;

*International Families Adoption Agency; 518 S. 12th St; Philadelphia, PA 19147; (215) 735-7171; http://www.4adoption.com;

Jewish Family and Children's Service; 5743 Barlett Street; Pittsburgh, PA 15217; (412) 428-7200;

Jewish Family and Children's Service of Philadelphia Inc.; 10125 Verree Road, #200; Philadelphia, PA 19116; (215) 698-9950; Fax: (215) 698-2148;

Jewish Family Services; 3333 North Front Street; Harrisburg, PA 17110; (717) 233-1681; Fax: (717) 234-8258; E-mail: ellenrabin@aol.com;

Juvenile Justice Center of Philadelphia; 100 West Coulter Street; Philadelphia, PA 19144; (215) 849-2112; www.juvenilejustice.org;

KidsPeace National Centers for Kids in Crisis; KidsPeace Hospital; 5300 KidsPeace Drive; Orefield, PA 18069; admissions@kidspeace.org;

*La Vida Adoption Agency; 150 South Warner Road, Suite 144; King of Prussia, PA 19406; (610) 688-8008; http://www.lavida.org/; E-mail: info@lavida.org;

*La Vida International; 150 S. Warner Rd., Ste.144; King of Prussia, PA 19406; (610) 688-8008; Fax: (610) 688-8028; World Wide Web: http://www.lavida.org;

LDS Social Services; 46 School Street; Greentree, PA 15205; (412) 921-8303;

*Little Emperor Adoption Services; 202 Berkshire Lane; Royersford, PA 19468; (610) 409-9711; http://www.littleemperor.com;

Living Hope Adoption Agency; P.O. Box 439; Telford, PA 18969; (215) 672-7471; http://www.livinghopeadoption.org;

*Love the Children; 221 West Broad Street; Quakertown, PA 18951; (215) 536-4181; http://www.lovethechildren.com; E-mail: cecelia@lovethechildren.com;

Lutheran Children & Family Services-East Pennsylvania; 1256 Easton Road; Roslyn, PA; (215) 881-6800; Fax: (215) 884-3110; E-mail: richg@lcfsinpa.org;

Lutheran Service Society of Western Pennsylvania; 1011 Old Salem Road, Suite 107; Greensburg, PA 15601; (724) 837-9385; www.lsswpa.org;

Madison Adoption Associates; 2414 Blueball Avenue; Boothwyn, PA 19061; (610) 459-4970; World Wide Web: http://www.madisonadoption.org/;

New Beginnings Family and Children's Services; 8 Pennsylvania Avenue; Matamoras, PA 18336; (570) 491-2366; http://www.new-beginnings.org;

New Foundations; 6801-17 North 16th Street; Philadelphia, PA 19126; (215) 424-1144;

Northeast Treatment Center; 493 North 5th Street, Suite A; Philadelphia, PA 19123; (215) 574-9500;

One Another Adoption Program; 50 Market Street; Hellam, PA 17406; (717) 600-2059;

Open Door Children and Youth Services; 606 Court Street, Suite 404; Reading, PA 19601; (610) 372-2200; World Wide Web: http://www.opendoorcys.com;

PAACT; 703 N. Market Street; Liverpool, PA 17045; (717) 444-3629;

Perl, Inc.; 434 West Carpenter Lane; Philadelphia, PA 19119; (215) 849-8072;

Pinebrook Services for Children & Youth; 402 North Fulton Street; Allentown, PA 18102-2002; (610) 432-3919; http://www.pinebrookservices.org;

*Plan-It For Kids, PC; 501 Main Street, Suite 101; Berlin, PA 15530; (814) 267-3182; http://www.plan-itforkids.org; E-mail: carol@plan-itforkids.org;

Presbyterian Children's Village; 452 South Roberts Road; Rosemont, PA 19010; (610) 525-5400; http://www.pcv.org; E-mail: village@pcv.org;

Project STAR of Permanency Planning Advocates of Western Pennsylvania; 6301 Northumberland Street; Pittsburgh, PA 15217; (412) 521-9000;

Rainbow Project; 120 Charles Street; Pittsburgh, PA 15238; (412) 782-4457;

REJOICE; 1800 State Street; Harrisburg, PA 17101; (717) 221-0722;

Spectrum Family Network Adoption Services; 415 Gettysburg Street; Pittsburgh, PA 15206; (412) 362-3600;

St. Joseph's Center; 2010 Adams Avenue; Scranton, PA 18509; (570) 963-1261; www.stjosephscenter.org; E-mail: wecare@stjosephscenter.org;

Tabor Children's Services; 601 New Britain Road; Doylestown, PA 18901-4248; (215) 348-4071; World Wide Web: http://www.tabor.org;

Tabor Children's Services; 4700 Wissachickon Avenue, Building H; Philadelphia, PA 19144; (215) 842-4800; carlawilson@philadelphia.tabor.org;

The Adoption Connection; 709 Third Avenue; New Brighton, PA 15066; (724) 846-2615;

The Bair Foundation; 241 High Street; New Wilmington, PA 16142; (724) 946-8711; http://www.the-plaza.com/bair/; E-mail: info@bair.org;

The Children's Home of Pittsburgh; 5618 Kentucky Ave; Pittsburgh, PA 15232; (412) 441-4884; Fax: (412) 441-0167;

The Children's Home Society of New Jersey; 771 North Pennsylvania Avenue; Morrisville, PA 19067; (215) 736-8550; http://www.chsofnj.org;

The Eckels Adoption Agency; 994 Vallamont Drive; Williamsport, PA 17701; (570) 323-2520; Fax: (570) 323-2520;

The Social Work Agency; 1158 York Rd; Warminster, PA 18974; (218) 343-8500;

Three Rivers Adoption Council/Black Adoption Services; 307 4th Avenue, Suite 710; Pittsburgh, PA 15222; (412) 471-8722; Three Rivers American Indian Center; 120 Charles Street; Pittsburgh, PA 15328; (412) 782-4457;

Tressler Lutheran Services; 836 South Geoirge Street; York, PA 17403; (717) 845-9113; Fax: (717) 852-8439;

Try-Again Homes; 365 Jefferson Ave; Washington, PA 15301; (724) 225-0510;

Welcome House Adoption Program; 520 Dublin Road, PO Box 181; Perkasie, PA 18944; (215) 249-0100; www.pearlsbuck.org;

*Welcome House Adoption Program of Pearl S. Buck International; 520 Dublin Road; Perksaie, PA 18944-3000; (215) 249-0100; http://www.pearlsbuck.org;

Women's Christian Alliance; 1722 Cecil B. Moore Avenue; Philadelphia, PA 19121; (215) 236-9911; http://www.wcafamily.org;

World Links; 1418 Main Street; Blakely, PA 18452; (570) 344-8890;

Rhode Island

State Adoption Office: (401) 254-7010
Department of Children, Youth and Families
530 Wood Street
Bristol, RI 02805   www.adoptionri.org

General Information. Rhode Island permits both independent and agency adoption. Advertising is not permitted. To file a Petition for Adoption within Rhode Island the adoptive parents must reside there. If it is an agency adoption the Petition for Adoption can also be filed there if the agency having custody of the child is located there. Normally, adoptions are finalized approximately six to eight months after the child's placement with the adoptive parents. The adoptive parents and the child are usually required to appear in court for the final hearing, although the court may waive this requirement.

Independent Adoption. A preplacement home study of the adoptive parents is not required before a child is placed in their home. The postplacement home study may be conducted by the state adoption office. There is no fee.

It is not required by law that the adoptive parents and birth mother meet in person and share identities, although some elect to do so voluntarily. There are no specific laws governing whether the adoptive parents are permitted to assist the birth mother with pregnancy-related expenses, including living assistance, so most practitioners view it as permitted. The child may be released directly from the hospital to the adoptive parents, although this is usually done by discharging the baby to the birth mother or a relative, who in turn places the child with the adoptive parents. If the birth mother does not wish to be discharged with the baby, most hospitals will require a court order authorizing release of the child directly to the adoptive parents.

The consent to adoption can be signed any time after the birth. It has no enforceability, however, until the birth mother affirms her desire to consent to the adoption before a judge in a *Placement Hearing*. This hearing usually occurs about three months after the child's placement with the adoptive parents. Once the court approves the consent at this hearing, state law provides that the consent is irrevocable and can only be withdrawn upon proof of fraud or duress. Once the adoption is finalized by the court (usually six to eight months after the child's placement with the adoptive parents), however, the consent is irrevocable.

Agency Adoption. The adoption agency can file a Petition to Terminate Parental Rights no sooner that the fifteenth day after the birth, with the birth mother's agreement that her rights be voluntarily terminated. Once the court has issued its order terminating her parental rights she has lost the automatic right to stop the adoption. There are no state laws governing a request to withdraw consent, but case law indicates it can only be done upon proof of fraud or duress.

Some agencies in Rhode Island agree to do identified adoptions. Agencies rarely agree to make immediate hospital "at risk" placements.

Adoption Attorneys

There are no attorney biographies available for attorneys in Rhode Island.

Licensed Private Adoption Agencies (* Offers intercountry programs)

A Red Thread Adoption Services; 333 Westminister Street; Providence, RI 02903; Toll Free: (888) 871-9699; E-mail: redthreadadopt@aol.com;
Adoption Network, Ltd.; P.O. Box 195; Wakefield, RI 02880-0195; Toll Free: (800) 285-0450; http://www.adoptionnetworklimited.com;
*Alliance for Children; 500 Prospect Street; Pawtucket, RI 02860; (401) 725-9555; World Wide Web: http://www.allforchildren.org;
*American-International Children's Alliance, Inc.; 1445 Wampanoag Trail, Suite 101; East Providence, RI 02915; http://www.adopting.com/aica;

*Bethany Christian Services; PO Box 8939, 706 Warwick Ave; Warwick, RI 02888; (401) 467-1395; www.bethany.org; Lancaster: (717) 399-3213;
Catholic Social Services; Reaching Out Adoption & Foster Care; 311 Hooper Street; Tiverton, RI 02878; (401) 624-0970;
Children's Friend & Service; 153 Summer Street; Providence, RI 02903; (401) 331-2900; World Wide Web: http://www.cfsri.org;
Communities for People; 221 Waterman Street; Providence, RI 02906; (401) 273-7103;
*Friends in Adoption; P.O. Box 1194; Newport, RI 02840-0012; (401) 831-1120; http://www.friendsinadoption.org; E-mail: fia@vermontel.com;
*Gift of Life Adoption Services, Inc; 1051-1053 Park Ave; Cranston, RI 02910; (401) 943-6484; http://www.giftoflife.cc;
International Adoptions; 726 Front Street; Woonsocket, RI 02895; (401) 767-2300;
Jewish Family Services/ Adoption Options; 229 Waterman Avenue; Providence, RI 02906; (401) 331-5437; E-mail: jfs@intap.net;
Links to Adoption; 21 Carlton Avenue; East Providence, RI 02916; (401) 434-1353;
*Little Treasures Adoption Services; P.O. Box 20555; Cranston, RI 02920; (401) 828-7747; http://www.littletreasuresadopt.org;
*Lutheran Social Services of New England; Rhode Island Adoption Program; 116 Rolfe Street; Cranston, RI 02910; (401) 785-0015; www.adoptlss.org/;
Urban League of Rhode Island, Inc.; Minority Recruitment and Child Placement Program; 246 Prairie Ave; Providence, RI 02905; (401) 351-5000;
*Wide Horizons for Children; 245 Waterman Street, Suite 504; Providence, RI 02906; (401) 421-4752; http://www.whfc.org; E-mail: info@whfc.org;

South Carolina

State Adoption Office:*   (803) 898-7707
Department of Social Services—Division of Family Services
P.O. Box 1520
Columbia, South Carolina 29202   www.state.sc.us/dss/adoption

General Information. South Carolina permits both independent and agency adoption. Approximately 70% of South Carolina's infant adoptions are completed via independent adoption; 30% via agencies. Advertising is permitted. To file a Petition for Adoption within South Carolina either the adoptive parents, *or* the child to be adopted, must reside there. Most judges, however, require that "special circumstances" exist to allow non-residents to file there Petition for Adoption there. If it is an agency adoption the Petition for Adoption can also be filed in South Carolina if the agency having custody of the child is located there. Normally, adoptions are finalized three to six months after the child's placement with the adoptive parents. The adoptive parents and the child are required to appear in court for the final hearing.

Independent Adoption. A preplacement home study of the adoptive parents is required before a child can be placed in their home. The home study is conducted by a licensed adoption agency or social worker approved by the State Department of Social Services to conduct home studies. The fee is approximately $550.

It is not required by law that the adoptive parents and the birth mother meet in person and share identities, although a small number elect to do so voluntarily. The adoptive parents are permitted to assist the birth mother with pregnancy-related medical and living expenses. The child may be released from the hospital directly to the adoptive parents, although hospital forms and policies differ.

The consent to adoption can be signed anytime after the birth. It may be witnessed by a judge, an attorney not representing the adoptive parents, or a certified adoption worker. Consents are usually signed one to two days after the birth. Once signed, the consent is irrevocable, except upon proof of fraud or duress, and that the child's best interests would be served by being removed from the adoptive parents.

Agency Adoption. There is no difference regarding the process in which a birth mother signs her consent to adoption in an independent or agency adoption. The information provided above regarding independent adoption (e.g. when the consent can be signed, before whom, legal burden to seek to withdraw a signed consent) is identical regarding agency adoption.

Few agencies in South Carolina agree to do identified adoptions. Some also agree to make immediate hospital "at risk" placements, where the child is placed with the adoptive parents before the consents to adoption are irrevocable.

Adoption Attorneys

Stephen Yacobi   Tel (864) 242-3271
408 North Church Street   Fax (864) 233-3750
Greenville, SC 29601

Mr. Yacobi is a graduate of University of South Carolina School of Law. Approximately 50% of his practice consists of adoptions. He estimates he has completes 60 adoptions annually. Of these, 80& are independent; 10% are agency; 10% are international. His office is available to be retained in contested cases.

Licensed Private Adoption Agencies (* Offers intercountry programs)

*A Chosen Child Adoption Services; 415 King Charles Circle; Summerville, SC 29485; (843) 851-4004; http://www.ACCAdoptionServices.com;
Adoption Center of South Carolina; PO Box 5961; Columbia, SC 29250; (803) 771-2272;
*Bethany Christian Services; 2141 B Hoffmeyer Road; Florence, SC 29501-4077; (843) 629-1177; http://www.bethany.org; Myrtle Beach: (843) 839-5433; Greenville: (864) 235-2273; Columbia: (803) 779-0541;
Carolina Hope Christian Adoption Agency; 300 Yorkshire Drive; Greenville, SC 29615; (864) 268-0570; http://www.carolinahopeadoption.org;
Catholic Charities of Charleston; 1662 Ingram Road; Charleston, SC 29407; (843) 769-4466; World Wide Web: http://www.catholiccharities.org;
Child of the Heart; 741 Johnnie Dodds Boulevard, Suite 207; Mt. Pleasant, SC 29407; (843) 881-2973; Fax: (843) 971-7901;
Children First; P.O. Box 11907; Columbia, SC 29211; (803) 771-0534;
Children Unlimited, Inc.; The Attachment Center of South Carolina; 1825 Gadsden Street; Columbia, SC 29211; (803) 799-8311; Toll Free: (800) 822-0877; http://www.children-unlimited.org/;
*Christian Family Services; 2166 Gold Hill Road, #A; Fort Mill, SC 29708-9351; (803) 548-6030;
Christian Family Services Inc.; 2166-A Gold Hill Road; Ft. Mill, SC 29708-9351; (843) 548-6030;
*Christian World Adoption, Inc.; 111 Ashley Avenue; Charleston, SC 29401; (843) 722-6343; http://www.cwa.org/; E-mail: cwa@cwa.org;
Epworth Children's Home; P.O. Box 50466, 2900 Millwood Avenue; Columbia, SC 29250; (803) 256-7394; http://www.epworthchildrenshome.org;
LDS Social Services; 5624 Executive Center Drive, Suite 109; Charlotte, NC 28212-8832; (704) 535-2436;

Reid House; P.O. Box 22132, 169 St. Phillip Street; Charleston, SC 29413; (843) 723-7138; http://www.reid-house.com; E-mail: ariley@reid-house.com; Southeastern Children's Home, Inc.; 155 Children's Home; Duncan, SC 29334; (864) 439-0259;

South Dakota

State Adoption Office: (605) 773-3227
Department of Social Services—Child Protection Services
700 Governors Drive
Pierre, SD 57501   www.state.sd.us/social/cps/adoption/index/htm

General Information. South Dakota permits both independent and agency adoption. Approximately 40% of South Dakota's infant adoptions are completed via independent adoption; 60% via agencies. Advertising is permitted. To file a Petition for Adoption within South Dakota the adoptive parents must reside there. Normally, adoptions are finalized approximately six months after the child's placement with the adoptive parents. The adoptive parents and the child are required to appear in court for the final hearing.

Independent Adoption. A preplacement home study of the adoptive parents is required before a child can be placed in their home. The home study may be conducted by a licensed adoption agency or a certified social worker with a *private independent practitioner certificate.* The fees for pre and post-placement home study services typically varies from $800 to $1,200.

It is not required by law that the adoptive parents and birth mother meet in person and share identities, although some do so voluntarily. The adoptive parents are permitted to assist the birth mother with pregnancy-related expenses, including living expenses, but prior court approval is required. The child may be released to the adoptive parents directly from the hospital, although most hos-pitals will discharge the baby with the birth mother, who then places the child with the adoptive parents outside the hospital.

The consent to adoption is made by the birth mother filing a *Petition for Voluntarily Termination of Parental Rights,* which cannot be filed prior to the fifth day after birth. The court's hearing on the petition can often occur immediately upon filing, provided the birth mother has had at least 15 hours of prior adoption counseling. The birth mother must appear in court for the court to grant the order that her parental rights be voluntarily terminated. Once the court has made the order, the consent is irrevocable, although the birth mother has a 30 day period in which she may withdraw her consent upon proof of fraud or duress.

Agency Adoption. There is no difference regarding the process in which a birth mother signs her consent to adoption in an independent or agency adoption. The information provided above regarding independent adoption (e.g. when the consent can be signed, before whom, legal burden to seek to withdraw a signed consent) is identical regarding agency adoption.

Some agencies in North Dakota agree to do identified adoptions. Some agencies also agree to make immediate hospital "at risk" placements, where the child is placed with the adoptive parents before the consents to adoption are irrevocable.

Adoption Attorneys

John R. Hughes	Tel (605) 339-3939
Hughes Law Offices	Fax (605) 339-3940
431 N. Phillips Ave., Suite 330	
Sioux Falls, SD 57014	

Mr. Hughes began practicing law in 1982 and is a graduate of the University of Nebraska College of Law. Approximately 25% of his practice consists of adoptions. He estimates he has completes 20 adoptions annually. Of these, 70& are independent; 20% are agency; 10% are international. His office is available to be retained in contested cases. Of the adoptions he has handled, he reports 40% of his clients locate a birth mother through his office; 60% find their own birth mother. His website is www.adoptionhelp.net.

Licensed Private Adoption Agencies (* Offers intercountry programs)

Bethany Christian Services; 2525 West Main Street, #309; Rapid City, SD 57702; (605) 343-7196; Sioux Falls: (605) 336-6999; http://www.bethany.org; Catholic Family Services; Catholic Diocese of Sioux Falls; 523 N. Duluth Ave.; Sioux Falls, SD 57104-2714; (605) 334-9861; Fax: (605) 988-3746; World Wide Web: http://www.diocese-of-sioux-falls.org;

311

Catholic Social Services; 918 Fifth Street; Rapid City, SD 57701-3798; (605) 348-6086;
Child Protection Program; Sisseton Wahpeton Dakota Nation; P.O. Box 509; Agency Village, SD 57262-9802; (605) 698-3992;
Children's Home Society; P.O. Box 1749; Sioux Falls, SD 57101-1749; (605) 334-3431;
LDS Social Services; 2525 West Main Street, #310; Rapid City, SD 57702-2443; (605) 342-3500;
Lutheran Social Services; 705 East 41st Street, Suite 200; Sioux Falls, SD 57105-6048; (605) 357-0100; Toll Free: (800) 568-2401; Fax: (605) 357-0140;
*New Horizons Adoption Agency; 27213 473rd Avenue; Sioux Falls, SD 57106; (605) 332-0310; World Wide Web: http://www.nhadoptionagency.com;
South Dakota Department of Social Services; PO Box 310, 116 East 11th Street; Mitchell, SD 57301-0310; (605) 995-8000; Fax: (605) 996-0681; World Wide Web: http://www.state.sd.us/social/dss/offices/addresses.htm;
Yankton Sioux Tribal Social Services; P.O. Box 248; Marty, SD 57361-0248; (605) 384-3804;

Tennessee

State Adoption Office:*   (615) 532-5637
Department of Children's Services
Cordell Hall Bldg.
436 6th Avenue North
Nashville, TN 37243   www.state.tn.us/youth/adoption/

General Information. Tennessee permits both independent and agency adoption. Approximately 60% of Tennessee's infant adoptions are completed via independent adoption; 40% via agencies. Advertising is permitted. To file a Petition for Adoption within Tennessee the adoptive parents must be residents for at least six months prior to filing the Petition for Adoption. Normally, adoptions are finalized six months after the child's placement with the adoptive parents. The adoptive parents are required to appear in court at the final hearing.

Independent Adoption. A preplacement home study of the adoptive parents is required before a child is placed in their home. The postplacement home study may be conducted by a licensed adoption agency. The fee varies but usually does not exceed $1,200.

It is not required by law that the adoptive parents and the birth mother meet in person and share identities, although it is voluntarily done in most adoptions. The adoptive parents are permitted to assist the birth mother with pregnancy-related expenses, although living expenses may not be provided beyond 45 days after the birth. The child may be released directly from the hospital to the adoptive parents, although hospital policies differ. Some hospitals simply require a written release, while others require a copy of the birth mother's consent to the adoption.

The consent to adoption, called a *surrender,* cannot be signed before the fourth day after the birth, unless a court waives this period. It must be witnessed by a judge. Once signed, the birth mother has the automatic right to withdraw the consent for a period of 10 days. Once the 10 day period has elapsed the consent is irrevocable, but for fraud or duress.

Agency Adoption. There is no difference regarding the process in which a birth mother signs her consent to adoption in an independent or agency adoption. The information provided above regarding independent adoption (e.g. when the consent can be signed, before whom, legal burden to seek to withdraw a signed consent) is identical regarding agency adoption.

Some agencies in Tennessee agree to do identified adoptions. Some agencies also agree to make immediate hospital "at risk" placements, allowing the child to be placed with the adoptive parents before the consents to adoption are final.

Adoption Attorneys

Dawn Coppock   Tel (865) 933-8173
P.O. Box 388   Fax (865) 933-3272
Strawberry Plains, Tennessee 37871

Ms. Coppock began practicing law in 1987 and is a graduate of Wythe School of Law at the College of William & Mary. Approximately 99% of her practice consists of adoptions. She has completed more than 500 adoptions in her career and presently completes more than 100 annually. Of these, the majority are agency adoptions, but she also does some independent and international adoptions. Of the adoptions she has handled she reports 10% of her clients locate a birth mother through her office; 90% locate their own birth mother. She is available to be retained in contested cases.

Michael S. Jennings	Tel (423) 892-2006
Sample, Jennings, Ray & Gibbons	Fax (423) 892-1919
130 Jordan Drive	
Chattanooga, TN 37421	

Mr. Jennings began practicing law in 1984 and is a graduate of the University of Georgia School of Law. Approximately 60% of his practice consists of adoptions. He estimates he has completed several hundred adoptions in his career and presently completes 175 annually. Of these, 55% are independent; 30% are agency; 15% are international. Of the adoptions he has completed, he reports 5% of his clients locate a birth mother through his office; 95% locate their own birth mother.

Private Licensed Adoption Agencies (* Offers intercountry programs)

A Child's Dream; 1346 Quai Valley Trail; Apison, TN 37302-9533; (423) 236-4509;

Adoption Advantage, Inc.; 1661 International Drive, Suite 400; Memphis, TN 38120; (901) 758-2997;

Adoption Consultants In Tennessee, Inc.; 8921 Shallowford Road; Knoxville, TN 37923; (865) 769-9441; E-mail: actadopt@mindspring.ocm;

Adoption Counseling Services; 2185 Wickersham Lane; Germantown, TN 38139; (901) 753-9089;

Adoption Home Studies and Social Services; 909 Oak Street; Chattanoooga, TN 37403; (423) 756-3134; Fax: (423) 756-2530;

Adoption Place, Inc.; 505 Oak Forest Circle; Antioch, TN; (615) 365-7020;

Adoption Resource Services, Inc.; 218 South Third Street, #2; Elkhard, IN 46516; (800) 288-2499; Fax: (574) 293-2210; E-mail: rcmarco@yahoo.com;

AGAPE Child and Family Services, Inc.,; 111 Racine Street; Memphis, TN 38111; (901) 323-3600; Fax: (901) 272-7488;

Associated Catholic Charities of the Diocese of Memphis; St. Peter's Home; 3060 Baskin Street; Memphis, TN 38127-7799; (901) 354-6300; Fax: (901) 354-6343; World Wide Web: http://www.cathchar.org;

Association for Guidance, Aid, Placement and Empathy (AGAPE); 4555 Trousdale Drive; Nashville, TN 37204-4513; (615) 781-3000; E-mail: jrister@agapenashville.org;

*Bethany Christian Services; 400 South Germantown Road; Chattanooga, TN 37411-5025; (423) 622-7360; http://www.bethany.org/chattanooga/;

Catholic Charities of Tennessee, Inc.,; 30 White Bridge Road; Nashville, TN 37205; (615) 352-3087; http://www.midtnads.com/choices.shtml;

Child and Family Services of Knox County; 901 East Summit Hill Drive; Knoxville, TN 37915; (865) 524-7483; http://www.child-family.org;

Child & Family Services, Inc; 201 N. Royal St; Jackson, TN; (615) 422-1107;

Children's Hope International; 7003 Chadwick Drive, Suite 350; Brentwood, TN 37027; (615) 309-8109; http://www.childrensHopeInt.org;

Christian Children's Homes of Tennessee; 2600 State Line Road, P.O. Box 285; Elizabethton, TN 37644; (423) 542-4245; Fax: (423) 542-4369;

Exceptional Needs Care Management Agency, Inc.; 2755 Colony Park, Suite 7; Memphis, TN 38118; (901) 360-0194; Fax: (901) 947-9707;

Family and Children's Services of Chattanooga, Inc.; 1800 McCallie Avenue; Chattanooga, TN 37403; (423) 755-2800; http://www.fcschatt.org;

Family and Children's Services-Center for Adoption; 1210 Foster Avenue; Nashville, TN 37243; (615) 253-3289; Toll Free: (800) 807-3228;

Frontier Health/Traces; 2001 Stonebrook Place; Kingsport, TN 37660; (424) 224-1067; Fax: (423) 224-1095;

*Global Village International Adoptions; 615 Tides Ridge Court; Murfreesboro, TN 37128; (615) 848-5278; http://www.globalvillageadopt.org;

Greater Chattanooga Christian Services and Children's Home; 744 McCallie Avenue, Suite 329; Chattanooga, TN 37403; (423) 756-0281;

*Guardian Angel International Adoptions; 408 Douglass Drive; Lawrenceburg, TN 38464; (931) 766-5277; Fax: (931) 766-1503;

Happy Haven Homes, Inc.; 2311 Wakefield Drive; Cookeville, TN 38501; (931) 526-2052; Fax: (931) 372-8837;

Harmony Adoptions of Tennessee, Inc.; 311 High Street; Maryville, TN 37804; (865) 892-5225;

*Heaven Sent Children, Inc.; P.O. Box 2514; Murfreesboro, TN 37130; (615) 898-0803; Fax: (615) 898-1990;

*Holston United Methodist Home for Children, Inc.; 404 Holston Drive, PO Box 188; Greeneville, TN 37744; (423) 638-4171; www.usit.net/children;

International Assistance and Adoption Project; 1210-G Taft Highway; Signal Moutain, TN 37377; (423) 886-6986; Fax: (423) 886-7680;

Jewish Family Services, Inc.; 6560 Poplar Avenue; Memphis, TN 38138; (901) 767-8511; Fax: (901) 763-2348;

Karan E. Goins, LCSW, P.C.; Dba Crossroads Counseling Center; 620 West 5th Street; Morristown, TN 37814; (423) 581-5342; Fax: (423) 581-8650;

Knoxville Family Service Center; 9915 D Kingston Pike; Knoxville, TN 37992; (865) 691-9963; Fax: (865) 691-6541;

Life Choices, Inc.; 813 Timbercreek Drive, PO Box 806; Cordova, TN 38018; (901) 323-5433; Fax: (901) 388-1225;

Madison Children's Home; PO Box 419, 616 North Dupont Avenue; Madison, TN 37116-0419; (615) 860-4461; Fax: (615) 860-6817;
Memphis Family Service Center; 2969 South Mendenhall; Memphis, TN 38115; (901) 636-1189; Fax: (901) 363-1180;
Mercy Ministries of America; 15328 Old Hickory Boulevard, P.O. Box 111060; Nashville, TN 37222-1060; (615) 831-6987; Fax: (615) 315-9749;
Mid-Cumberland Children's Services, Inc.; 106 N. Mountain Street; Smithville, TN 37166; (615) 597-7134;
Mid-South Christian Services; 1044 Brookfield Road, Suite 102; Memphis, TN 38119; (901) 818-9996; Fax: (901) 761-9350;
Northeast Region Adoption; PO Box 2120, 213 West Maple Street; Johnson City, TN 37601; (423) 434-6921; Fax: (423) 434-6962;
Omni Visions; 101 Lea Avenue; Nashville, TN 37210; (615) 726-3603;
Porter-Leath Children's Center; 868 North Manassas Street; Memphis, TN 38107-2516; (901) 577-2500; http://www.porter-leath.org;
*Small World Adoption Programs; 401 Bonnaspring Drive; Hermitage, TN 37076; (615) 883-4372; http://www.swa.net; E-mail: tom@swa.net;
Smoky Mountain Children's Home; P.O. Box 4391, 449 McCarn Circle; Sevierville, TN 37864-4391; (865) 453-4644; Fax: (865) 453-8812;
Tennessee Baptist Children's Homes, Inc.; PO Box 2206; Brentwood, TN 37024; (615) 376-3140; www.tbch4kids.org; E-mail: office@tbch4kids.org;
Tennessee Children's Home; 1115 Ranch Road; Ashland City, TN 37015; (615) 307-3205; Fax: (615) 307-2300;
*Williams International Adoptions, Inc.; 5100 Stage Road, Suite A; Memphis, TN 38134; (901) 373-6003; http://www.williamsinternational.org;
Zambo Counseling and Consulting Services; 20796 East Main Street; Huntingdon, TN 38344; (731) 986-2001; Fax: (901) 986-4889;

Texas

State Adoption Office: (512) 438-3412
Texas Department of Protective and Regulative Services
P.O. Box 149030
Austin, Texas 78717

General Information. Texas permits both independent and agency adoption. Approximately 40 % of Texas' infant adoptions are completed via independent adoption; 60 % via agencies. Advertising is permitted only by licensed adoption agencies. To file a Petition for Adoption within Texas either the adoptive parents must reside there, *or* the child to be adopted must have been born there or reside there. If it is an agency adoption the Petition for Adoption can also be filed in Texas if the adoption agency having custody of the child is located there. Normally, adoptions are finalized approximately six months after the birth or the placement of the child with the adoptive parents. The adoptive parents are required to appear in court for the final hearing, although the court may waive this requirement.

Independent Adoption. A preplacement home study (called an *adoption home screening*) of the adoptive parents is required before a child can be placed in their home. The home study may be conducted by a licensed adoption agency or licensed social worker approved by the court. The fee for pre and post-placement home studies is typically under $1,000.

It is not required by law that the adoptive parents and birth mother meet in person but it is required that they share identities. The adoptive parents are permitted to assist the birth mother with pregnancy-related medical and legal expenses. Non-medical expenses may be provided to her only through a licensed adoption agency. The child can be released directly from the hospital to the adoptive parents with a state-mandated form.

The consent to adoption, called a *relinquishment*, can be signed no sooner than 48 hours after the birth. It must be witnessed by a notary and two witnesses. Most consents are signed within several days of the birth. The relinquishment is irrevocable once it is signed. However, if the adoptive parents do not promptly file the relinquishment with the court and obtain a court order terminating parental rights, the surrender may be withdrawn if the birth mother wishes. Usually this period in which the court order must be obtained is 60 days, unless the relinquishment specifies a shorter period. Also, if fraud or duress are proved, the relinquishment may be withdrawn.

Agency Adoption. There is little difference regarding the process in which a birth mother signs her consent to adoption in an independent or agency adoption (e.g. when the surrender is signed, etc.). However, a birth mother's relinquishment in an agency adoption is irrevocable upon signing. There is no 60 day period after which she has the right to seek to withdraw her relinquishmentA preplacement home study is

317

required before a child is placed with the adoptive parents. The consent, called a *relinquishment* in an agency adoption, may be signed no sooner than 48 hours after the birth. Once the relinquishment is signed it is irrevocable, except upon proof of fraud or duress.

Some agencies in Texas agree to do identified adoptions. Some agencies also agree to make immediate hospital "at risk" placements, allowing the child to be placed before the consents to adoption are final.

Adoption Attorneys

Vika Andrel   Tel (512) 448-4605
3908 Manchaca Road   Fax (512) 448-1905
Austin, TX 78704

Ms. Andrel began practicing law in 1985 and is a graduate of the University of Texas School of Law. Her practice is limited to adoptions. She estimates she completes 20 adoptions annually. Of these, 70% are independent; 25% are agency; 5% are international. Of the adoptions she has handled, she reports 70% of her clients locate a birth mother through her office; 30% locate their own birth mother.

David C. Cole   Tel (214) 363-5117
8330 Meadow Road, Suite 218   Fax (214) 750-1970
Dallas, TX 75231

Mr. Cole began practicing law in 1987 and is a graduate of Pepperdine University School of Law. Approximately 90% of his practice is dedicated to adoptions. He estimates he had completed more than 500 adoptions in his career and presently completes 150 annually. Of these, 35% are independent; 65% are agency. Of the adoptions he has handled, he reports 10% of her clients locate a birth mother through her office; 90% locate their own birth mother. His office is available to be retained in contested cases.

Steven Watkins   Tel (903) 454-6688
Watkins & Perkins   Fax (903) 454-1772
5602 Wesley Street; P.O. Box 876
Greenville, TX 75403

Mr. Watkins began practicing law in 1980 and is a graduate of Texas Tech University School of Law. Of the adoptions he has handled, he reports 80%

are independent; 20% are agency. He reports his cliens all find their own birth mother. His office is available to be retained in contested cases.

Licensed Private Adoption Agencies (* Offers intercountry programs)

*A Cradle of Hope; 311 North Market Street, Suite 300; Dallas, TX 75202; (214) 747-4500;
AAA-Alamo Adoption Agency; P.O. Box 781; Adkins, TX 78101-0781; (210) 967-5337;
ABC Adoption Agency, Inc.; 417 San Pedro Avenue; San Antonio, TX 78212; (210) 227-7820; Fax: (210) 227-7820; Abrazo Adoption Associates; 10010 San Pedro; San Antonio, TX 78216; (210) 342-5683; http://www.abrazo.org;
Adoption Access; 8330 Meadow Road, Suite 222; Dallas, TX 75231; (214) 750-4847; World Wide Web: http://adoptionaccess.com;
Adoption Advisory, Inc.; 3607 Fairmount; Dallas, TX 75219; (214) 520-0004; World Wide Web: http://www.adoptadvisory.com;
Adoption Advocates, Inc.; 328 West Mistletoe Avenue; San Antonio, TX 78212; (210) 734-4470; http://www.netxpress.com/adoptionadvocates/;
Adoption Affiliates, Inc.; 215 W. Olmos Drive; San Antonio, TX 78212; (210) 824-9939;
Adoption Angels, Inc.; 118 Broadway, Suite 517; San Antonio, TX 78205; (210) 227-2229; http://www.adoptionangels.com;
Adoption As An Option; 12611 Kingsride Lane; Houston, TX 77024; (713) 468-1053;
Adoption Family Service; 5402 Arapaho; Dallas, TX 75240; (972) 437-9950;
Adoption Information and Counseling; 2020 Southwest Freeway, Suite 326; Houston, TX 77098; (713) 529-5125; http://www.adoptquest.com;
*Adoption Resource Consultants; P.O. Box 1224; Richardson, TX 75083; (972) 517-4119; Fax: (972) 423-1297;
Adoption Services Associates; 5370 Prue Road; San Antonio, TX 78240; Toll Free: (800) 648-1807; http://www.adoptionservicesassociates.org;
*Adoption Services Worldwide, Inc.; 7300 Blanco Road, Suite 206; San Antonio, TX 78216; (210) 342-0444; http://www.babyasw.com;
Adoption Services, Inc.; 3500 Overton Park West; Fort Worth, TX 76109; (817) 921-0718;
Adoption-A Gift of Love; P.O. Box 50384; Denton, TX 76206; (817) 387-9311;
*Adoptions International, Inc.; 6510 Abrams Road, Suite 600; Dallas, TX 75231; (214) 342-8388; http://www.adoptmeinternational.org;
All-Church Home for Children; 1424 Summit Avenue; Fort Worth, TX 76102; (817) 335-4041; Fax: (817) 335-4043; http://www.allchurchhome.org;

Andrel Adoptions; 3908 Manchaca; Austin, TX 78704; (512) 448-4605;
Angel Adoptions of the Heart; 2715 Bissonet #221; Houston, TX 77005; (713) 523-2273;
Atlantis Foundation; 2800 NASA Road One, Suite 1406; Seabrook, TX 77586; (281) 326-1201;
*Bethany Christian Services of North Texas; 10310 N Central Expressway, Building III, Suite 360; Dallas, TX 75231-8627; (214) 373-8797; Toll Free: (800) 650-6226; Fax: (214) 373-4797; http://www.bethany.org;
*Buckner Adoption and Maternity Services Inc.; 4830 Samuell Boulevard; Dallas, TX 75228; (214) 381-1552; http://www.buckner.org;
Catholic Counseling Services; P.O. Box 190507; Dallas, TX 75219-0507; (214) 526-2772; World Wide Web: http://www.catholiccharitiesdal.org;
Catholic Family Service; P.O. Box 15127; Amarillo, TX 79105; (806) 376-4571; Fax: (806) 345-7947; http://www.catholicfamilyservice.org;
Catholic Social Services of Laredo; P.O. Box 3305; Laredo, TX 78044; (210) 722-2443;
Child Placement Center; 2212 Sunny Lane; Killeen, TX 76541; (254) 690-5959; World Wide Web: http://www.childplacementcenter.com;
Children and Family Institute; 5787 S. Hampton Road, Suite 360; Dallas, TX 75232; (214) 337-9979; http://www.cfiadopt.org;
Children's Home of Lubbock; P.O. Box 2824; Lubbock, TX 79408; (806) 762-0481; http://www.childshome.org; E-mail: info@childshome.org;
Chosen Heritage - Christian Adoptions; 121 N.E. Loop 820; Hurst, TX 76053; (817) 589-7899;
*Christian Homes; P.O. Box 270; Abilene, TX 79604; (915) 677-2205; Toll Free: (800) 592-4725; http://www.christianhomes.com;
Christian Services of the Southwest; 6320 LBJ Freeway, Suite 122; Dallas, TX 75240; (972) 960-9981; http://www.christianservices-sw.org;
Counsel for Adoption Resources; 1201 South W.S. Young Drive, Suite F; Killeen, TX 76541; (254) 690-2223;
Cradle of Life Agency; 245 N. 4th St; Beaumont, TX 77701; (409) 832-3000;
DePelchin Children's Center; 100 Sandman Street; Houston, TX 77007; (713) 730-2335; Toll Free: (888) 730-2335; http://www.depelchin.org;
El Paso Adoption Services; 905 Noble; El Paso, TX 79902; (915) 542-1086; Fax: (915) 544-7080;
El Paso Center for Children; 3700 Altura Boulevard; El Paso, TX 79930; (915) 565-8361;
*Gladney Center for Adoption; 6300 John Ryan Drive; Fort Worth, TX 76132-4122; (817) 922-6088; http://www.gladney.org; E-mail: info@gladney.org;
*Great Wall China Adoption; 248 Addie Roy Road, A102; Austin, TX 78746; (512) 323-9595; http://www.gwcadopt.org; E-mail: info@gwcadopt.org;

Homes of Saint Mark; 3000 Richmond Avenue, Suite 570; Houston, TX 77098; (713) 522-2800; Fax: (713) 522-3769;

*Hope Cottage Pregnancy and Adoption Center; 4209 McKinney Avenue; Dallas, TX 75205; (214) 526-8721; http://www.hopecottage.org;

*Hope Cottage, Inc. Circle of Hope; 4209 McKinney Avenue; Dallas, TX 75205; (214) 526-8721;

Hope for Tomorrow; 1305 Early Blvd; Early, TX 76802; (915) 646-4673;

*Hope International; 311 N. Market Street, Suite 300; Dallas, TX 75202; (214) 672-9399; http://www.hopeadoption.com;

Inheritance Adoptions; P.O. Box 2563; Wichita Falls, TX 76307; (817) 322-3678; World Wide Web: http://www.inheritanceadoptions.org;

J&B Kids, Inc. Placing Agency; Route 1, Box 173 F; Yorktown, TX 78164; (512) 564-2964;

LDS Social Services-Texas; 1100 W. Jackson Road; Carrollton, TX 75006; (972) 242-2182;

Lena Pope Home, Inc.; 3131 Sanguinet Street; Fort Worth, TX 76107; (817) 731-8681; Fax: (817) 731-9858; http://www.lenapopehome.org;

*LIMIAR; 111 Broken Bough; San Antonio, TX 78231; (210) 479-0300; Fax: (210) 479-3772; World Wide Web: http://www.limiar.org;

*Los Ninos International Adoption Center; 2408 Timberloch Place, Suite D1; The Woodlands, TX 77380; (281) 363-2892; Fax: (281) 297-4191; World Wide Web: http://www.losninos.org; E-mail: jerichsen@LosNinos.org;

Loving Alternatives; P.O. Box 131466; Tyler, TX 75713; (903) 581-7720;

*Lutheran Social Services of the South, Inc.; 8305 Cross Park Drive, PO Box 140767; Austin, TX 78714; (512) 459-1000; http://www.lsss.org;

Marywood Children and Family Services; 510 W. 26th St; Austin, TX 78705; (512) 472-9251; http://www.marywood.org; E-mail: marywood@eden.com;

Methodist Children's Home; 1111 Herring Avenue; Waco, TX 76708; (254) 750-1260; World Wide Web: http://www.methodistchildrenshome.org/;

New Life Children's Services; 19911 State Hwy 249; Houston, TX 77070; (713) 955-1001; http://www.newlifeadopt.com;

PAC Child Placing Agency; 4655 S.FM 1258; Amarillo, TX 79118-7219; (806) 335-9138;

Read Adoption Agency, Inc.; 1011 North Mesa; El Paso, TX 79902; (915) 533-3697;

Smithlawn Maternity Home and Adoption Agency; P.O. Box 6451; Lubbock, TX 79493; (806) 745-2574;

Spaulding for Children; 8552 Katy Freeway, Suite 300; Houston, TX 77024; (713) 681-6991; http://www.spauldingforchildren.org;

Texas Baptist Children's Home; P.O. Box 7; Round Rock, TX 78664; (512) 388-8256; http://www.tbch.org; E-mail: info@tbch.org;

The Adoption Alliance; 7303 Blanco Road; San Antonio, TX 78216; (210) 349-3991;
Unity Children's Home; 12027 Blue Mountain; Houston, TX 77067; (713) 537-6148;

Utah

State Adoption Office: (801) 538-4078
Department of Human Services—Division of Family Services
120 North 200 West; P.O. Box 45500
Salt Lake City, UT 00008 www.hsdcfs.state.ut.us

General Information. Utah permits both independent and agency adoption. Approximately 30% of Utah's infant adoptions are completed via independent adoptions; 70% via agencies. Advertising is permitted. To file a Petition for Adoption within Utah the adoptive parents must reside there or the child must have been conceived and born there. Normally, adoptions are finalized six months after the child's placement with the adoptive parents. The adoptive parents and the child are required to appear in court for the final hearing.

Independent Adoption. A preplacement home study of the adoptive parents is required before a child can be placed in their home. The home study is conducted by a licensed adoption agency or licensed social worker. The fee for pre and post-placement home study services is typically $700.

It is not required by law that the adoptive parents and birth mother meet in person and share identities, but it is usually done voluntarily. The adoptive parents are permitted to assist the birth mother with pregnancy-related medical, legal and living expenses. The child may be released directly from the hospital to the adoptive parents, usually via a release form prepared by the adoptive parents' attorney.

The consent to adoption can be signed no sooner than 24 hours after the birth. It must be witnessed by a judge or a public officer appointed by the court. Most consents are signed within three days of the birth. Once signed, the consent to adoption is irrevocable, but for proof of fraud or duress.

Agency Adoption. There is no difference regarding the process in which a birth mother signs her consent to adoption in an independent or agency adoption, although the consent may usually be witnessed by a notary and agency representative. The information provided above regarding independent adoption (e.g. when the consent can be signed and the legal burden to withdraw the consent) is identical regarding agency adoption.

Some agencies in Utah agree to do identified adoptions. Virtually no agencies will agree to make immediate hospital "at risk" placements, allowing the child to be placed with the adoptive parents before the consents to adoption are final.

Adoption Attorneys

Larry S. Jenkins   Tel (801) 366-6060
Wood Crapo LLC   Fax (801) 366-6061
60 East South Temply Street, Suite 500
Salt Lake City, UT 84111

Mr. Jenkins began practicing law in 1986 and is a graduate of Brigham Young University School of Law. Approximately 75% of his practice consists of adoptions. He estimates he completes more than 100 adoptions annually. Of these, 25% are independent; 75% are agency. Of the adoptions he has handled, he reports 10% of his clients locate a birth mother through his office; 90% locate their own birth mother. His office is available to be retained in contested cases.

Licensed Private Adoption Agencies (* Offers intercountry programs)

A Cherished Child Adoption Agency; 2120 Willow Park Lane; Sandy, UT 84093; (801) 947-5900;
Adopt an Angel; 254 West 400 South, Suite 320; Salt Lake City, UT 84101; (801) 537-1622; Fax: (801) 359-6873;
Adoption Center of Choice, Inc.; 241 West, 520 North; Orem, UT 84057; (801) 224-2440; Fax: (801) 224-1899;
Catholic Community Services; 2570 West 1700 South; Salt Lake City, UT 84104; (801) 977-9119; Fax: (801) 977-8227;
Children of Peace; 715 East, 3900 South, Suite 203; Salt Lake City, UT 84107-2182; (801) 263-2111; Fax: (801) 262-2259;
*Children's Aid Society of Utah; 652 26th Street; Ogden, UT 84401; (801) 393-8671;

*Children's House International; 1236 North 150 West; American Fork, UT 84003; (801) 756-0587; http://www.adopting.com/chi; E-mail: chi4@aol.com;
Children's Service Society; 124 South, 400 East, Suite 400; Salt Lake City, UT 84111; (801) 355-7444; Toll Free: (800) 839-7444;
Families for Children; P.O. Box 521192; Salt Lake City, UT 84152-1192; (801) 467-3413;
Family and Adoption Counseling Center; 211 East Highland Avenue; Sandy, UT 84070; (801) 568-1771; Fax: (801) 568-1991;
Heart to Heart, Inc.; P.O. Box 57573; Murray, UT 84157; (801) 270-8017;
LDS Family Services; 625 East, 8400 South; Sandy, UT 84700; (801) 566-2556; Farmington: (801) 451-0475; Logan: (435) 752-5302; Ogden: (801) 621-6510; Price: (435) 637-2991; Richfield: (435) 896-6446; Salt Lake City: (801) 240-6500; Kearns: (801) 969-4181; St. George: (435) 673-6446; Pleasant Grove: (801) 796-9509; Provo: (801) 378-7620; Cedar City: (435) 586-4479; Premier Adoption Agency; 952 S. Freedom Blvd. #26; Provo, UT 84601; (801) 808-9738;
*West Sands Adoption and Counseling; 461 East 2780 North; Provo, UT 84604; (801) 377-4379;

Vermont

State Adoption Office: (802) 241-2142
Department of Social and Rehabilitation—Social Services Division
103 South Main Street
Waterbury, VT 05671
www.state.vt.us/srs/adoption/adoptioninfo.html

General Information. Vermont permits both independent and agency adoption. Approximately 40% of Vermont's infant adoptions are completed via independent adoption; 60% via agencies. Advertising is permitted. To file a Petition for Adoption within Vermont the adoptive parents must be residents. If it is an agency adoption the Petition for Adoption may also be filed in Vermont if the agency having custody of the child is located there, even when the adoptive parents live out of state. (At the time of this book's publication, legislation was pending to stop non-resident adoptions, but it is not yet known if it will become law.) Normally, adoptions are finalized approximately seven months after the child's placement. The adoptive parents are required to appear in court for the final hearing.

Independent Adoption. A preplacement home study of the adoptive parents is required before a child is placed in their home. The postplacement home study may be conducted by a licensed adoption agency. The fee for the pre and post-placement home study varies but is usually $1,200.

It is not required that the adoptive parents and the birth mother meet in person and share identities, although it is usually done voluntarily. The adoptive parents are permitted to assist the birth mother with pregnancy-related expenses, including living costs. The child may be released directly to the adoptive parents from the hospital, although each hospital may employ a different release form.

The consent to adoption can be signed no sooner than 36 hours after the birth. It must be witnessed by a judge. Most consents are signed within days of the birth. Once signed, the birth mother has the automatic right to withdraw the consent for 21 days. After the 21 day period has expired, the consent is irrevocable except upon proof of fraud or duress.

Agency Adoption. There is no difference regarding the process in which a birth mother signs her consent to adoption in an independent or agency adoption. The information provided above regarding independent adoption (e.g. when the consent can be signed, before whom and the legal burden to withdraw the consent) is identical regarding agency adoption.

Some agencies in Vermont agree to do identified adoptions. Some agencies also agree to make immediate hospital "at risk" placements, allowing the child to be placed with the adoptive parents before the consents to adoption are final.

Adoption Attorneys

Kurt Hughes   Tel (802) 864-9811
Murdock & Hughes   Fax (802) 864-4136
P.O. Box 363
Burlington, VT 05402

Mr. Hughes began practicing law in 1985 and is a graduate of Vermont Law School. Approximately 35% of his practice consists of adoptions. He estimates he completes 25 adoptions annually. Of these, 45% are independent; 45% are agency; 10% are international. His clients locate their own birth mother. His office is available in contested cases.

Licensed Private Adoption Agencies (* Offers intercountry programs)

*Acorn Adoption Inc.; 278 Pearl Street; Burlington, VT 05401-8558; (802) 865-3898; World Wide Web: http://www.acornadoption.org;
*Adoption Advocates; 521 Webster Rd.; Shelburne, VT 05482-6513; (802) 985-8289;
*Angels' Haven Outreach; PO Box 53; Monkton, VT 05469; (802) 453-5450; World Wide Web: http://www.angels-haven.com;
*Bethany Christian Services; 1538 Turnpike Street; North Andover, MA 01845-6221; (978) 794-9800; http://www.bethany.org;
Casey Family Services; 160 Palmer Court; White River Junction, VT 05001-3323;(802)649-1400;http://www.caseyfamilyservices.org;Waterbury:(802) 244-1408; http://www.caseyfamilyservices.org;
*Friends in Adoption; The Maltex Building, 431 Pine Street, #7; Burlington, VT 05401-4726; (802) 865-9886; http://www.friendsinadoption.org; Middletown Springs: (802) 235-2373;
Lund Family Center; 76 Glen Road, P.O. Box 4009; Burlington, VT 05406-4009; (802) 864-7467; http://www.lundfamilycenter.org;
*Maine Adoption Placement Service (MAPS);400 Commonwealth Avenue; Boston, MA 02115; (617) 267-2222; http://www.mapsadopt.org/;
Vermont Catholic Charities; 24 1/2 Center Street; Rutland, VT 05701; (802) 773-3379; World Wide Web: http://www.vermontcatholic.org/vcc/vcc.html;
Vermont Catholic Charities; 351 North Avenue; Burlington, VT 05401-2921; (802) 658-6110, Ext: 312; http://www.vermontcatholic.org/vcc/vcc.html;
*Vermont Children's Aid Society; 32 Pleasant Street; Woodstock, VT 05091; (802) 457-3084; http://www.vtcas.org/; Bennington: (802) 422-7901; Winooski: (802) 655-0006; E-mail: mainadmn@vtcas.org;
*Wide Horizons For Children; PO Box 53; Monkton, VT 05469; (802) 453-2581; World Wide Web: http://www.whfc.org/; E-mail: info@whfc.org;

Virginia

State Adoption Office: (804) 692-1290
Department of Social Services, Adoptions Unit
730 E. Broad Street
Richmond, VA 21219   www.dss.state.uv.us/family/adoption.html

General.   Virginia allows both independent and agency adoption. Approximately 75 % of Virginia's newborn adoptions are completed via independent adoption, 25 % via agencies. Advertising is permitted. To file a Petition for Adoption within Virginia the adoptive parents must reside there. If it is an agency adoption the Petition for Adoption can also be filed in Virginia if the agency having custody of the child is located there. Normally, adoptions are finalized seven to nine months after the child's placement with the adoptive parents in independent adoption, and eleven months in agency adoptions. The adoptive parents and the child are generally not required to attend a final hearing in which the adoption is finalized, as typically the order granting the adoption is signed by the judge simply upon receipt of the social worker's report, without any hearing.

Independent Adoption. A preplacement home study of the adoptive parents is not mandatory before a child can be placed in the adoptive parents' home, although the birth mother's consent will not be accepted by the court until a home study has been completed. The home study may be conducted by the state adoption office or a licensed adoption agency. The fee varies but is usually a sliding scale based upon income.

It is required by law that the adoptive parents and birth mother meet in person and share identities. The adoptive parents are permitted to assist the birth mother with pregnancy-related medical, counseling and legal expenses. Living costs may also be provided, but requires written confirmation from her physician that she is physically unable to work. The child can be released directly from the hospital to the adoptive parents, although each hospital may employ a different release form.

The consent to adoption may be signed no sooner than ten days after the birth. It must be witnessed by a judge. The courts give preference to adoption matters and try to schedule the signing of adoption consents within ten days of the filing of the petition. Putative fathers may sign their consent anytime after birth before a notary. Once the consent is signed, the birth parent has the automatic right to withdraw thier consent for a period of 15 days. After the 15 day period has elapsed the consent is irrevocable, except upon proof of fraud or duress.

Agency Adoption. The consent to adoption, called an *entrustment agreement* in an agency adoption, can be signed anytime after birth. It may be witnessed by a notary. As in independent adoption, the *entrustment* becomes irrevocable 15 days after execution, upon the child reaching

25 days of age, or when the child is placed with the adoptive parents, whichever is later.

Some agencies will make immediate "at risk" placements.

Adoption Attorneys

Jennifer A. Brust   Tel (703) 525-4000
Bean, Kinney & Korman   Fax (703) 525-2207
2000 N. 14th Street, Suite 100
Arlington, VA 22201

Ms. Brust began practicing law in 1989 and is a graduate of George Mason University School of Law. Approximately 30% of her practice consists of adoptions. She estimates he completes more than 25 adoptions annually. Of these, 75% are independent; 25% are international. Of the adoptions she has handled, she reports 5% of her clients locate a birth mother through her office; 95% locate their own birth mother. Her office is available to be retained in contested cases.

Mark Eckman   Tel (703) 242-8800
311 Maple Avenue West   Fax (703) 242-8804
Vienna, VA 22180

Mr. Eckman began practicing law in 1984 and is a graduate of Catholic University School of Law. Approximately 80% of his practice consists of adoptions. He estimates he completes 50 adoptions annually. Of these, 60% are independent; 20% are agency; 20% are international. His office accepts contested litigation cases. He is an adoptive parent.

Mark T. McDermott   Wash D.C. office: Tel (202) 331-1955
Joseph, Gajarsa, McDermott & Reiner   Fax (202) 293-2309
8045 Leesburg Pike, Suite 750
Vienna, VA 22182

Mr. McDermott began practicing law in 1974 and is a graduate of Indiana University School of Law. He is also licensed to practice law in California, the District of Columbia, Indiana and Maryland. Approximately 70% of his practice consists of adoptions. He estimates he has completed 1,200 adoptions in his career and presently completes 100 annually. Of these, 80% are independent adoptions; 20% agency. His clients locate their own birth mother. His office also accepts contested adoption litigation cases. He is an adoptive parent and is a past president of the American Academy of Adoption Attorneys.

Thomas G. Nolan   Tel (434) 977-8590
Richmond & Fishburne   Fax (434) 296-9861
214 East High Street
Charlottesville, VA 22902

Mr. Nolan began practicing law in 1984 and is a graduate of the University of Virginia College of Law. Approximately 10% of his practice consists of adoptions. He estimates he completes 20 adoptions annually. Of these, 75% are independent; 5% are agency; 20% are intercountry. His office accepts contested litigation cases. His clients find their own birth mother. He is an adoptive parent.

Stanton Phillips   Tel (703) 891-2400
1921 Gallows Road, Suite 110   Fax (703) 891-2404
Vienna (Tyson Corner), VA 22182   e-mail: phillips@babylaw.us

Mr. Phillips began practicing law in 1980 and is a graduate of George Mason University College of Law. He is also licensed to practice law in the District of Columbia. His practice is limited to adoptions. He estimates he has completed more than 2,000 adoptions in his career and presently completes 150 annually. Of these, 60% are independent; 20% are agency; 10% are intercountry. His office accepts contested litigation cases. He also practices in the District of Columbia.

Colleen M. Quinn   Tel (804) 343-4375
Cantor Arkema PC   Fax (804) 644-9205
823 E. Main Street   e-mail: cquinn@cantorarkema.com
Richmond, VA 23239

Ms. Quinn began practicing law in 1988 and is a graduate of the University of Virginia College of Law. Approximately 35% of her practice consists of adoptions. She estimates she completes more than 25 adoptions annually. Of these, 75% are independent; 15% are agency; 10% are intercountry. Of the adoptions she has handled, she reports 5% of her clients locate a birth mother through her office; 95% find their own birth mother. Her office accepts contested litigation cases. Her website is www.cantorarkema.com

Licensed Private Adoption Agencies (* Offers intercountry programs)

*ABC Adoption Services, Inc.; 4725 Garst Mill Road; Roanoke, VA 24018; (540) 989-2845;

ADOPTING IN AMERICA

*Adoption Center of Washington; 100 Daingerfield Road, Suite 101; Alexandria, VA 22314; (703) 549-7774; Toll Free: (800) 452-3878; Fax: (703) 549-7778; World Wide Web: http://www.adoptioncenter.com; Adoption Home Studies and Placement Services Inc.; TIA Adoption Connections; 207 Park Avenue, B-4; Falls Church, VA 22046; (703) 536-8523; *Adoption Service Information Agency, Inc. (ASIA); 1305 North Jackson Street; Arlington, VA 22201; (703) 312-0263; http://www.asia-adopt.org; *Adoptions From the Heart, Inc.; 625 Water Oak Court; Chesapeake, VA 23322; (757) 546-3874; World Wide Web: http://www.adoptionsfromtheheart.org; *America World Adoption Association; 6723 Whittier Avenue, Suite 406; McLean, VA 22101; (703) 356-8447; http://www.america-world.org; *America-China Adoption Association; 6723 Whittier Avenue, Suite 406; McLean, VA 22101; (703) 356-8447; http://www.america-china.org; *Barker Foundation, The; 2955 Monticello Drive; Falls Church, VA 22042; (703) 536-1827; http://www.barkerfoundation.org; *Beam of Hope; 13801 Village Mill Drive; Midlothian, VA 23114; (804) 594-3737; http://www.beamofhope.org; E-mail: Beamofhope2@aol.com; *Bethany Christian Services, Inc.; 10378-B Democracy Lane; Fairfax, VA 22030-2522; (703) 385-5440; http://www.bethany.org; Charlottesville: (804) 979-9631; Fairfax: (540) 373-5165; Virginia Beach: (757) 499-9367; Catholic Charities of Hampton Roads, Inc.; 12829-A Jefferson Ave; Newport News, VA 23608; (757) 875-0060; http://sites.communitylink.org/cath/; Catholic Charities of Hampton Roads, Inc.; 4855 Princess Anne Road; Virginia Beach, VA 23462-4446; (757) 467-7707; http://sites.communitylink.org/cath/; Catholic Charities of Hampton Roads, Inc.; 3757 Poplar Hill Road, Suite A; Chesapeake, VA 23321; (757) 484-0703; World Wide Web: http://sites.communitylink.org/cath/; Norfolk: (757) 625-2568; Catholic Charities of the Diocese of Arlington, Inc.; 1011 Berryville Avenue, Suite 1; Winchester, VA 22601; (540) 667-7940; Arlington: (703) 841-3830; Fredericksburg: (540) 371-1124; Children's Home Society of Virginia, Inc.; 4200 Fitzhugh Avenue; Richmond, VA 23230; (804) 353-0191; World Wide Web: http://www.chsva.org/; Children's Home Society of Virginia, Inc.; 1620 Fifth Street, S.W.; Roanoke, VA 24016; (540) 344-9281; World Wide Web: http://www.chsva.org/; Children's Services of Virginia, Inc.; Manassas Branch Office; 7547 Presidential Lane; Manassas, VA 20109; (703) 331-0075; Winchester: (540) 667-0116; http://www.childrensservicesofva.com/; Harrisonburg: (540) 801-0900; Commonwealth Catholic Charities; Staunton; St. Francis of Assisi Catholic Church, 121 North Augusta; Staunton, VA 24401; www.cccofvirginia.org; Richmond: (804) 285-5900; Roanoke: (540) 344-0411; Norton: (540) 679-1195; Charlottesville: (804) 974-6880; Alexandria: (703) 256-4530;

330

*Datz Foundation; 311 Maple Avenue West, Suite E; Vienna, VA 22180; (703) 242-8800; http://www.datzfound.com; E-mail: markeckman@hotmail.com;
Families United Through Adoption; 102 Lide Place; Charlottesville, VA 22902; (804) 923-8253;
Family Life Services; 1971 University Blvd., Building 61-B; Lynchburg, VA 24502; (804) 582-2969;
Holston United Methodist Home for Children; 115 East Main Street; Abingdon, VA 24210; (276) 628-1023; E-mail: fsc-abingdon@holstonhome.org;
Holy Cross Child Placement Agency Inc.; 400 South Washington Street; Alexandria, VA 22314; (703) 356-8824;
Jewish Family Service of Tidewater, Inc.; 7300 Newport Avenue; Norfolk, VA 23505; (757) 489-3111; http://www.jfshamptonroads.org; Virginia Beach: (757) 473-2695; Newport News: (757) 489-3111;
Jewish Family Services, Inc.; 6718 Patterson Avenue; Richmond, VA 23226; (804) 282-5644; World Wide Web: http://www.jfsrichmond.org;
LDS Social Services of Virginia, Inc.; 8110 Virginia Pine Court; Richmond, VA 23237; (804) 743-0727;
*Loving Families, Inc.; 101 South Whiting Street, Suite 212; Alexandria, VA 22304; (703) 370-7140; http://www.alovingfamily.org;
Lutheran Family Services, Inc.; 2609 McVitty Road SW, PO Box 21609; Roanoke, VA 24018-0574; (540) 774-7100;
*Lutheran Social Services of the National Captial Area; 9506-A Lee Highway; Fairfax, VA 22031; (703) 273-0303; World Wide Web: http://www.lssnca.org;
People Places; 1215 N. Augusta Street; Staunton, VA 24401; (540) 885-8841;
Rainbow Christian Services; 6004 Artemus Road; Gainesville, VA 20156; (703) 754-8516; http://www.manassaschurch.org/rainbow/;
Shore Adoption Services, Inc.; 113 Holly Crescent, Suite 102; Virginia Beach, VA 23451; (757) 422-6361; http://www.shoreadoptionservices.org;
United Methodist Family Services of Virginia; 6335 Little River Turnpike; Alexandria, VA 22312; (703) 941-9008; http://www.umfs.org;
United Methodist Family Services of Virginia; 715 Baker Road, Suite 201; Virginia Beach, VA 23462; (757) 490-9791; http://www.umfs.org; Fredericksburg: (540) 898-1773; Harrisonburg: (540) 438-1577; E-mail: harrburg@umfs.org; Richmond: (804) 353-4461;
Virginia Baptist Children's Home and Family Services; 860 North Mt. Vernon Lane; Salem, VA 24153; (540) 389-5468; http://www.vbchfs.org; Richmond: (804) 231-4466;
Welcome House; 520 Dublin Road, PO Box 181; Perkasie, PA 18944; (215) 249-0100; www.pearlsbuck.org; E-mail: mtomlinson@pearlsbuck.org;
*Welcome House of the Pearl S. Buck Foundation Inc.; 9412 Michelle Place; Richmond, VA 23229; (804) 740-7311; http://www.pearl-s-buck.org;

Washington

State Adoption Office: (360) 902-7968
Department of Social and Health Services
P.O. Box 45713
Olympia, WA 98504   www.wa.gov/dshs/ca/ca3ou.html

General Information. Washington permits both independent and agency adoption. Approximately 70% of Washington's infant adoptions are completed via independent adoption; 30% via agencies. Advertising is permitted, but only when placed by adoption agencies, attorneys licensed by the State of Washington, or adoptive parents with an approved Washington home study. To file a Petition for Adoption in Washington either the adoptive parents, the child, *or* the birth mother must reside there. Normally, adoptions are finalized two to three months after the placement of the child with the adoptive parents. The adoptive parents are usually required to appear in court for the final hearing, although the court may waive this requirement.

Independent Adoption. A preplacement home study of the adoptive parents is required before a child may be placed in their home. The home study may be conducted by the state adoption office, a licensed adoption agency, or licensed social worker or other person approved by the court. The fee varies but is usually $300 to $2,000.

It is not required by law that the adoptive parents and the birth mother meet in person and share identities, although most do so voluntarily. The adoptive parents are permitted to assist the birth mother with pregnancy-related expenses with court approval. The child can be released directly from the hospital to the adoptive parents. Some hospitals only require a hospital release form but most others require a court order.

The consent to adoption may be signed *before or after* the birth. It must be witnessed by a witness selected by the birth parent. Birth parents under the age of 18 must have a guardian ad litem appointed to make sure they understand the proceedings. The consent to adoption becomes effective only after it has been filed and approved by the court, at which point the court terminates the parental rights of the parent. This can occur no sooner than 48 hours after birth, or the signing of the consent, whichever occurs later. Before the court has approved the consent, the birth mother has the automatic right to withdraw her consent without any legal burden. After the court has approved the consent, the consent is irrevocable, except upon proof of fraud, duress or mental incompetency.

Agency Adoption. There is no difference regarding the process in which a birth mother signs her consent to adoption in an independent or agency adoption. The information provided above regarding independent adoption (e.g. when the consent can be signed, before whom and the legal burden to withdraw the consent) is identical regarding agency adoption.

Some agencies in Washington agree to do identified adoptions. Some agencies also agree to make immediate hospital "at risk" placements, allowing the child to be placed with the adoptive parents before the consents to adoption are final.

Adoption Attorneys

Rita L. Bender	Tel (206) 623-6501
Skellenger Bender P.S.	Fax (206) 447-1973
1301 Fifth Avenue, Suite 3401	e-mail: rbender@skellengerbender.com
Seattle, Washington 98101	

Ms. Bender began practicing law in 1968 and is a graduate of Rutgers Law School. Approximately 50% of her practice consists of adoptions. She estimates she has completed more than 600 adoptions in her career and presently completes 57 adoptions annually. Of these, 85% are independent; 10% are agency; and 5% are intercountry. Of the adoptions she has handled, she reports 30% of her clients locate a birth mother through her office; 70% locate their own birth mother. Her office accepts contested litigation cases. She is an adoptive parent. Her website is www.skellengerbender.com.

J. Eric Gustafson	Tel (509) 248-7220
Lyon, Weigand & Gustafson	Fax (509) 575-1883
222 N. 3rd Street	e-mail: egustafson@lyon-law.com
Yakima, WA 98901	

Mr. Gustafson began practicing law in 1973 and is a graduate of Lewis & Clark College of Law at Portland, Oregon. Approximately 55% of his practice consists of adoptions. He estimates he completes more than 50 adoptions annually. Of these, 90% are independent; 5% are agency; and 5% are intercountry. Of the adoptions he has handled, he reports 95% of his clients locate a birth mother through his office; 5% locate their own birth mother. His office is available to be retained in contested cases. He is an adoptive parent. His website is www.NorthwestAdoptions.com

Michele Gentry Hinz   Tel (253) 735-0928
33035 52nd Avenue S.
Auburn, WA 98001

Ms. Hinz began practicing law in 1978 and is a graduate of the University of Washington School of Law. Approximately 90% of her practice consists of adoptions. She estimates she completes 10 adoptions annually. Of these, 85% are independent; 15% are agency. Of the adoptions she has handled, she reports 10% of his clients locate a birth mother through her office; 90% locate their own birth mother.

Margaret Holm   Tel (360) 943-6933
2011 State Avenue N.E.
Olympia, WA 98506

Ms. Holm began practicing law in 1983 and is a graduate of Seattle University School of Law. Approximately 45% of her practice consists of adoptions. She estimates she completes 55 adoptions annually. Of these, 80% are independent; 15% are agency; 5% are international. Of the adoptions she has handled, she reports 40% of her clients locate a birth mother through his office; 60% locate their own birth mother. Her office is available to be retained in contested cases.

Albert G. Lirhus   Tel (206) 728-5858
Dubuar, Lirhus & Engel   Fax (206) 728-5863
720 Olive Way, Suite 625   e-mail: lirhus@dle-law.com
Seattle, Washington 98101

Mr. Lirhus began practicing law in 1973 and is a graduate of the University of Washington School of Law. Approximately 95% of his practice consists of adoptions. He estimates he has completed 2,000 adoptions in his career and presently completes 250 annually. Of these, 35% are independent; 50% agency; and 15% intercountry. Of the adoptions he has handled, he reports 20% of his clients locate a birth mother through his office; 80% locate their own birth mother. His office is available to be retained in contested cases. His website is www. dle-law.com.

Joyce E. Robeson   Tel (253) 572-5104
2511 S. Hood Street   Fax (253) 383-1842
Tacoma, WA 98402

Ms. Robeson began practicing law in 1988 and is a graduate of the University of Puget Sound School of Law. Approximately 90% of her practice consists of adoptions. She estimates she has completed more than 300 adoptions in her career and presently completes 75 annually. Of these, 50% are independent; 50% are agency. Of the adoptions she has completed, she reports 20% of her clients locate abirth mother through heroffice; 80% locate their own birth mother. Her office is available to be retained in contested cases. She is an adoptive parent.

Raegen N. Rasnic   Tel (206) 623-6501
Skellenger Bender P.S.   Fax (206) 447-1973
1301 Fifth Avenue, Suite 3401
Seattle, Washington 98101

Ms. Rasnic began practicing law in 1995 and is a graduate of the University of California - The Hastings College of Law. Approximately 40% of her practice consists of adoptions. She estimates she completes 55 adoptions annually. Of these, 85% are independent; 10% are agency; and 5% are intercountry. Of the adoptions she has handled, she reports 30% of her clients locate a birth mother through her office; 70% locate their own birth mother. Her office accepts contested litigation cases.

Licensed Private Adoption Agencies (* Offers intercountry programs)

*Adoption Advocates International; 401 East Front Street; Port Angeles, WA 98362; (360) 452-4777; http://www.adoptionadvocates.org;
*Americans Adopting Orphans; 12345 Lake City Way NE, #2001; Seattle, WA 98125; (206) 524-5437; http://www.orphans.com/; E-mail: aao@orphans.com;
Catholic Children and Family Services of Walla Walla; Drumheller Building, #418; Walla Walla, WA 99362; (509) 525-0572; http://www.ccfs-walla2.org;
Catholic Children's Services of Northwest Washington; 1133 Railroad Ave, Suite 100; Bellingham, WA 98226; (360) 733-5800;
Catholic Community Services; 100 23rd Avenue South; Seattle, WA 98144; (206) 323-1950;
Catholic Family and Child Service; 1023 Riverside Ave; Spokane, WA 99201; (509) 358-4260; Wenatchee: (509) 663-3182; Yakima: (509) 965-7108; Richland: (509) 946-4645;

*Children of the Nations International Adoptions, Inc.; P.O. Box 3970; Silverdale, WA 98383; (360) 598-5437; http://www.cotni.org; Silverdale: (360) 598-5437;

Children's Home Society of Washington; Regional Headquarters; 3300 NE 65th Street, Box 15190; Seattle, WA 98115-0190; (206) 695-3200; World Wide Web: http://www.chs-wa.org/; E-mail: chswa@chs-wa.org;

*Children's House International; P.O. Box 1829; Ferndale, WA 98248; (360) 380-5370; http://www.childrenshouseinternational.com;

*Faith International Adoptions; 535 E Dock Street, Suite 103; Tacoma, WA 98402; (253) 383-1928; http://vanity.qwestdex.com/faithadopt/Page1.html;

*International Children's Care; 2711 NE 134th Street; Vancouver, WA 98682; (360) 573-0429; http://www.forhiskids.org; E-mail: robyn@ForHisKids.org;

Lutheran Community Services North West; Symons Building, Suite 200; Spokane, WA 99204; (509) 747-8224; http://www.lcsnw.org; Seattle: (206) 694-5700; E-mail: lssnw@aol.com;

Lutheran Social Services of Washington, Southeast Area; 3321 Kennewick Ave; Kennewick, WA 99336; (509) 735-6446;

Medina Children's Services; 123 16th Avenue; Seattle, WA 98122; (206) 260-1700; http://www.medinachild.org/; E-mail: info@medinachild.org;

*New Hope Child and Family Agency; 2611 N.E. 125th Street, Suite 146; Seattle, WA 98125; (206) 363-1800; http://www.newhopekids.org;

*World Association for Children and Parents (WACAP); PO Box 88948; Seattle, WA 98138; (206) 575-4550; http://www.wacap.org; E-mail: wacap@wacap.org;

West Virginia

State Adoption Office: (304) 558-2891
Office of Social Services - Adoption Resource Network
350 Capitol Street, Room 691
Charleston, WV 25301

General Information. West Virginia allows both independent and agency adoption. Approximately 50% of West Virginia's infant adoptions are completed via independent adoption; 50% via agencies. Advertising is permitted. To file a Petition for Adoption within West Virginia the adoptive parents must reside there. Normally, adoptions are finalized six to nine months after the child's placement with the adoptive parents. The adoptive parents and the child are usually required to attend the court hearing in which the adoption is finalized.

Independent Adoption. A preplacement home study of the adoptive parents is not required. The postplacement home study may be conducted by a licensed adoption agency or a person approved by the court. The fee varies but is typically $1,300.

It is not required by law that the adoptive parents and the birth mother meet in person and share identities, although this is sometimes done voluntarily. The adoptive parents are permitted to assist the birth mother with pregnancy-related expenses. The child can be released directly from the hospital to the adoptive parents, although hospital forms and policies vary. Some hospitals will only release the child to an attorney. and will not permit adoptive parents in the hospital.

The consent to adoption may be signed no sooner than 72 hours after the birth. It must be witnessed by a notary. If the birth mother is under the age of 18, the consent must be witnessed by a judge. If the consent is an *Irrevocable Consent*, the consent is irrevocable effective immediately. It can only be withdrawn upon proof of fraud or duress. Birth parents are alernatively permitted to sign a *Conditional Consent*, however, in which they may give themselves the right to stop the adoption within the conditions set forth in the consent (such as a number of days to reconsider, or if the birth father were to object).

Agency Adoption. There is no difference regarding the process in which a birth mother signs her consent to adoption, called a *relinquishment,* in an independent or agency adoption. The information provided above regarding independent adoption (e.g. when the consent can be signed, before whom and the legal burden to withdraw the consent) is identical regarding agency adoption.

Some agencies in West Virginia agree to do identified adoptions. Some agencies also agree to make immediate hospital "at risk" placements, allowing the child to be placed with the adoptive parents before the consents to adoption are final.

Adoption Attorneys

There are no biographies available for adoption attorneys in West Virginia.

Licensed Private Adoption Agencies (* Offers intercountry programs)

*Adoption Services, Inc.; 28 Central Boulevard; Camp Hill, PA 17011; (717) 737-3960; Fax: (717) 731-0517; http://www.adoptionservices.org/;
*Adoptions From The Heart; 7014 Grand Central Station; Morgantown, WV 26505; (304) 291-5211; http://www.adoptionsfromtheheart.org;
*Burlington United Methodist Family Services; P.O. Box 370; Scott Depot, WV 25560-0370; (304) 757-9127; http://www.bumfs.org;
*Burlington United Methodist Family Services; Route 3, Box 3122; Keyser, WV 26726; (304) 788-2342; http://www.bumfs.org; Grafton: (304) 265-1575;
Childplace, Inc.; 5101 Chesterfield Avenue SE; Charleston, WV 25304; (304) 757-0763; http://www.childplace.org; Jeffersonville, IN: (812) 282-8248;
Children's Home Society of West Virginia; P.O.Box 5533, 316 Oakvale Road; Princeton, WV 24740; (304) 425-8438; http://www.childhswv.org;
LDS Social Svcs; 4431 Marketing Pl; Groveport, OH 43125; (614) 836-2466;

Wisconsin

State Adoption Office: (608) 266-3595
Department of Health and Family Services - Child and Family Services
P.O. Box 8916
Madison, WI 53708
www.dhfs.state.wi.us/children/adoption/index.htm

General Information. Wisconsin permits both independent and agency adoption. Approximately 60% of Wisconsin's infant adoptions are completed via independent adoption; 40% via agencies. Advertising is permitted if the adoptive parents have a favorable home study. To file a Petition for Adoption within Wisconsin the adoptive parents must be residents. Normally, adoptions are finalized approximately six months after the child's placement with the adoptive parents. The adoptive parents are required to appear in court for the final hearing.

Independent Adoption. A preplacement home study of the adoptive parents is required before a child is placed in their home. The home study may be conducted by a licensed adoption agency. The fee varies.

It is not required by law that the adoptive parents and the birth mother meet in person and share identities, although it is often done voluntarily. The adoptive parents are permitted to assist the birth mother with necessary pregnancy-related medical, living and legal expenses. However, assistance with living expenses cannot exceet $1,000. The child may be released directly from the hospital only into a licensed foster home. This can be the home of the adoptive parents, if they have a foster home license. If so, the child is placed with them in a "legal risk placement."

The consent to adoption is made by means of a *Petition for Voluntary Termination of Parental Rights*, which is filed with the court anytime after the birth. The birth mother then appears in court to consent to the termination of her parental rights, which usually occurs two to four weeks after the birth or placement with the adoptive parents. The adoptive parents normally attend this hearing as well, and should have had their initial home study previously filed with the court. The court then signs a *Termination of Parental Rights Order*. Before the court's order terminating parental rights, the birth mother has the automatic right to withdraw her consent. After the court's order, the consent is irrevocable, although there is a 30 day period in which an appeal can be filed to withdraw the consent based upon fraud, duress or court error.

Agency Adoption. There is no difference regarding the process in which a birth mother signs her consent to adoption in an independent or agency adoption. The information provided above regarding independent adoption (e.g. when the consent can be signed, before whom and the legal burden to withdraw the consent) is identical regarding agency adoption.

Some agencies in Wisconsin agree to do identified adoptions. Many agencies will agree to make immediate hospital "at risk" placements.

Adoption Attorneys

Carol Gapen   Tel (608) 821-8200
Law Center for Children and Families   Fax (608) 821-8201
434 S. Yellowstone Drive
Madison, WI 53719

Ms. Gapen began practicing law in 1988 and is a graduate of the University of Wisconson School of Law. Approximately 80% of her practice consists

ADOPTING IN AMERICA

of adoptions. She estimates she completes 50 adoptions annually. Of these, 45% are independent; 50% are agency; 5% are international. Her office is available to be retained in contested cases.

Stephen W. Hayes   Tel (262) 798-8220
The Schroeder Group   Fax (262) 798-8232
20800 Swenson Drive, Suite 475
Waukesha, WI 53186

Mr. Hayes began practicing law in 1969 and is a graduate of the University of Illinois School of Law. Approximately 60% of his practice consists of adoptions. He estimates he has completed over 2,500 adoptins in his career and presently completes 100 adoptions annually. Of these, 45% are independent; 45% are agency; 10% are international. His clients all locat their own birth mother. His office is available to be retained in contested cases.

Victoria J. Schroeder   Tel (262) 646-2054
2574 Sun Valley Drive, Suite 200   Fax (262) 646-2075
Delafield, WI 53018

Ms. Schroeder began practicing law in 1980 and is a graduate of the University of Wisconson School of Law. Approximately 90% of her practice consists of adoptions. She estimates she has completed over 600 adoptions in her career and presently completes 50 annually. Of these, 33% are independent; 65% are agency; 2% are international. All of her clients locate their own birth mother. Her office is available to be retained in contested cases.

Licensed Private Adoption Agencies (* Offers intercountry programs)

*Adoption Advocates, Inc.; 2601 Crossroads Drive, Suite 173; Madison, WI 53704; (608) 246-2844;
*Adoption Choice; 924 East Juneau Avenue, #813; Milwaukee, WI 53202-2748; (414) 276-3262; http://www.adoption.com/adoptionchoice;
*Adoption Services Inc.; 911 North Lynndale Drive, Suite 2-C; Appleton, WI 54914; (920) 735-6750;
*Bethany Christian Services; 2312 North Grandview Boulevard, Suite 207; Waukesha, WI 53188-1606; (414) 547-6557; http://www.bethany.org;
Catholic Charities, Inc.; 128 South 6th Street, PO Box 266; LaCrosse, WI 54602-0266; (608) 782-0704; http://www.catholiccharitieslax.org/;;
Catholic Charities/ Diocese of Milwaukee; 2021 North 60th Street; Milwaukee, WI 53208; (414) 771-2881; Fax: (414) 771-1674; http://www.archmil.org;

Catholic Social Services - Green Bay; P.O. Box 23825; Green Bay, WI 54305-3825; (920) 437-6541; World Wide Web: http://www.gbdioc.org;
*Children's Home Society of Minnesota; 1605 Eustis Street; St. Paul, MN 55108-1219; (651) 646-7771; http://www.chsm.com; E-mail: info@chsm.com;
Children's Service Society of Wisconsin; 1212 S. 70th Street; Milwaukee, WI 53214; (414) 453-1400;
Community Adoption Center; 3701 Kadow Street; Manitowoc, WI 54220; (920) 682-9211; Fax: (920) 682-8611;
Crossroads Adoption Services; 911 Fourth Street, Suite B5; Hudson, WI 54016; (715) 386-5550; http://www.crossroadsadoption.com;
Evangelical Child and Family Agency, District Office; 1617 S. 124th Street; New Berlin, WI 53151-1803; (414) 789-1881;
*HOPE Adoption & Family Services International, Inc.; 5850 Omaha Avenue North; Oak Park Heights, MN 55082; (651) 439-2446; Fax: (651) 439-2071; World Wide Web: http://www.hopeadoptionservices.org;
LDS Social Svcs; 1711 University Ave; Madison, WI 53705; (608) 238-5377;
Lutheran Counseling and Family Services; 3800 N. Mayfair Road, PO Box 13367; Wauwatosa, WI 53222; (414) 536-8333;
*Lutheran Social Services of Wisconsin & Upper Michigan, Inc.; 647 W. Virgina Street, Suite 300; Milwaukee, WI 53204; (800) 488-5181; Fax: (414) 325-3208; http://www.lsswis.org; Mlwaukee: (414) 281-4400;
Pauquette Children's Services, Inc.; 315 W. Conant Street, PO Box 162; Portage, WI 53901-0162; (608) 742-8004; Fax: (608) 742-7937;
*Special Children, Inc.; 15285 Watertown Plank Road, Stop 3; Elm Grove, WI 53122-2339; (414) 821-2125; Fax: (414) 821-2157;
*Van Dyke, Inc.; 1224 Weeden Creek Road, Suite 4; Sheboygan, WI 53081-7850; (920) 452-5358; http://www.execpc.com/romanian_adoption_assistance/;

Wyoming

State Adoption Office: (307) 777-3570
Department of Family Services
Hathaway Building, Third Floor, Room 376
2300 Capitol Avenue
Cheyenne, WY 82002
                        www.dfsweb.state.wy.us/CHILDSUC/TOCI.HTM

General Information. Wyoming permits both independent and agency adoption. Advertising is permitted. To file a Petition for Adoption within Wyoming the adoptive parents must be residents. Normally, adoptions are finalized approximately six months after the child's placement. The adoptive parents are required to appear in court for at least one court hearing, either the initial court appearance for an *interlocutory decree*, or the final hearing to grant the adoption.

Independent Adoption. A preplacement home study of the adoptive parents is not required before a child is placed in their home. The home study may be conducted by a licensed adoption agency or licensed social worker. The fee for the post-placement home study is typically $350-$550.

It is not required that the adoptive parents and the birth mother meet in person and share identities, although it is often done voluntarily. Wyoming law has no provisions for or against the adoptive parents being permitted to assist the birth mother with pregnancy-related expenses. Typically, adoptive parents obtain court approval and can provide pregnancy-related medical, living and legal assistance if needed. Normally, the child may be released directly to the adoptive parents from the hospital, although some adoptive parents prefer that the child be released to an intermediary, often an attorney, to maintain confidentiality.

The consent to adoption may be signed anytime after the birth. It must be witnessed by a notary, representative of a licensed adoption agency or a judge. Once signed, the consent is irrevocable except upon proof of fraud or duress.

Agency Adoption. There is no difference regarding the process in which a birth mother signs her consent to adoption in an independent or agency adoption. The information provided above regarding independent adoption (e.g. when the consent can be signed, before whom and the legal burden to withdraw the consent) is identical regarding agency adoption.

Some agencies in Wyoming agree to do identified adoptions. Some agencies also agree to make immediate hospital "at risk" placements, allowing the child to be placed with the adoptive parents before the consents to adoption are final.

Adoption Attorneys

Peter J. Feeney   Tel (307) 266-4422
100 West B Street, Suite 100   Fax (307) 235-4648
P.O. Box 436
Casper, WY 82602

Mr. Feeney began practicing law in 1974 and is a graduate of the University of Wyoming School of Law. Approximately 20% of his practice consists of adoptions. He estimates he has completed more than 1,000 adoptions in his career and presently completes 30 annually. Of these, 50% are independent; 45% are agency; 5% are international. All of his clients locate their own birth mother. His office is available to be be retained in contested cases.

Licensed Private Adoption Agencies (* Offers intercountry programs)

*A.D.O.P.P.T., Inc.; Gillette, WY 82716; (307) 687-7147;
Casey Family Program; 130 Hobbs Avenue; Cheyenne, WY 82009; (307) 638-2564; Fax: (307) 632-5251; World Wide Web: http://www.casey.org;
Catholic Social Services of Wyoming; 2121 Capitol Avenue, P.O. Box 1026; Cheyenne, WY 82003; (307) 638-1530; Toll Free: (800) 788-4606; Fax: (307) 637-7936; http://www.dioceseofcheyenne.org/catholic_social_services.htm;
*Focus on Children; 405 Sage Street; Cokeville, WY 83114; (307) 279-3434; http://www.focus-on-children.com/; E-mail: thorns@allwest.net;
*Global Adoption Services, Inc.; 50 East Loucks, Suite 205; Sheridan, WY 82801; (307) 674-6606; Toll Free: (866) 237-9538; Fax: (307) 672-7605; http://www.globadoption.com; E-mail: Wyoming@adoptglobal.org;
LDS Family Services; 7609 Santa Marie Drive; Cheyenne, WY 82009; (307) 637-8929; Toll Free: (800) 537-2229; E-mail: jccarmenii@aol.com;
*Wyoming Children's Society; 716 Randall Avenue, P.O. Box 105; Cheyenne, WY 82003; (307) 632-7619; http://www.wyomingcs.org;
*Wyoming Parenting Society; PO Box 3774; Jackson, WY 83001; (307) 733-5680; E-mail: kingwill@blissnet.com;

ADOPTING IN AMERICA

Conclusion

The potential complexities of adoption discussed in the preceding chapters can be intimidating. However, imagining what can go wrong in an adoption is like a hypochondriac reading a book on medical illnesses. Usually, you go to the doctor and find that none of the thousands of possible illnesses apply to you, and all your worry was for nothing. You are sent home happy to know you are in good health.

Adoptions are no different. Generally, only a few, if any, of the potential complications that can arise will apply in a particular adoption. Hopefully, a visit to your adoption attorney or agency will give you peace of mind about your adoption, knowing your potential adoption is in "good health."

Success in adoption is not as difficult as people imagine. That's not to say it's easy, but the myths of impossibility of adopting a child—whether you hope to adopt a newborn child of your own ethnic group, an older child, or a child from another country—are greatly exaggerated. Without a doubt, however, you will never succeed at adoption unless you start the process. Success in adoption is waiting for you. Good luck!

APPENDIX A Helpful Organizations and
Publications

ADOPTION101.COM

Dubbed "The Adoption School," a free internet educational resource providing helpful articles on many areas of adoption, from "how to" aspects to discussing adoption with your child. Their internet bookstore offers many adoption titles and also offers pre-printed networking mailing labels. Their website is adoption101.com

ADOPTIVE FAMILIES OF AMERICA (AFA)
42 West 38th Street, Suite 901
New York, NY 10018   (646) 366-0830

A national adoption support organization. It publishes the excellent *Adoptive Families* magazine, which offers excellent articles regarding both pre and post adoption issues. Their website is www.adoptivefamilies.com

AMERICAN ACADEMY OF ADOPTION ATTORNEYS
P.O. Box 33053; Washington, D.C. 20033

National membership organization of adoption attorneys with special knowledge of, or interest in, adoption. Their website is www.adoptionattorneys.org

THE CAP BOOK
595 Blossom Road, Suite 306
Rochester, NY 14610   (888) 835-8802

Provides a photo-listing of hard-to-place children waiting for adoptive parents. Their website is www.capbook.org

NATIONAL ADOPTION INFORMATION CLEARINGHOUSE
370 L'Enfant Promenade
Washington, D.C. 20201

An excellent government site regarding adoption. Their very helpful website is http://naic.acf.hhs.gov

APPENDIX A Helpful Organizations and Publications

NORTH AMERICAN COUNCIL ON ADOPTABLE
CHILDREN (NACAC)
970 Raymond Avenue
St. Paul, MN 55104   (651) 644-3036

Promotes the adoption of special-needs children. They publish
The Roundtable, a helpful magazine focusing on special-needs
adoption issues. Their website is www.nacac.org

RESOLVE, INC.
1310 Broadway
Somerville, MA 02144   (617) 623-0744

A widely recognized and highly respected national infertility
organization assisting individuals with infertility issues,
including adoption. Membership includes an excellent
magazine. Regional chapters are located throughout the United
States, many of which frequently offer helpful seminars on
adoption. Their website is www.resolve.org

APPENDIX B Sample Photo-Resume Letter

Hi!

We are Mark and Angela
Brenner. We have been
happily married for more
than six years, but our doctor has told us we will never
be able to conceive children.
We are now turning to adoption to make our dreams of
having a family come true.

We live in San Diego, California. We are near the beach, and the
mountains are only a few hours away for snow skiing in the winter. We
recently bought our first home and we enjoy fixing up our *dream house*.
Mark loves to spend his weekends building things in the backyard
playing handyman. Together, we enjoy going to baseball games, the
movies, and jogging on the beach. Mark is a high school teacher and
is great with kids. I am a secretary. When we adopt I will stop working
and be a full-time mom. We believe the first few years of a baby's life
are very important so we want to be "homebodies."

We have worked hard to be ready to be parents and look forward to
sharing our love with a child. We hope you will consider us if you are
thinking about adoption. Please call us collect, night or day, at our home:
(619) 555-3145. We are willing and able to help with maternity and
medical expenses. To make sure we do everything right, we have retained
an attorney who specializes in adoption—Randy Hicks. If you prefer to
call him first to learn more about how adoption works his address and
phone number is below. He is very easy to talk to. We hope to hear from
you!

Sincerely,

Mark &
Angela

Our attorney is Randy Hicks
6690 Alessandro Blvd., Suite D
Riverside, California 92506
His telephone number is 1 (909) 789-6800

APPENDIX C Sample Cover Letter

Dear Friends and Colleagues:

We want very much to adopt a baby. We are sending you our photo-resume with the hope you may know of an expectant mother searching for the family that can offer all the love and security she wants for her baby. We hope you can help us find each other.

Our home state allows "open" adoption, allowing adoptive parents and birth parents to meet in person and share identities. This allows the baby's parents to be completely confident in their choice of us as adoptive parents. We are permitted by law to help with her pregnancy-related expenses, such as her doctor and hospital bills.

If you do not know of a woman who is facing an unplanned pregnancy at this time, please retain our resume letter or share it with a colleague or friend who may be able to help.

Please do not hesitate to call us collect at our home at (909) 555-1212 if we can answer any questions you may have, or if you know of anyone we should contact. Our adoption (attorney or agency) can be contacted as well at (555) 555-1234, should you have any questions about us, or the adoption process.

We sincerely thank you for your kind assistance and cooperation.

Sincerely,

Raul & Marie

Raul and Marie Herrera

Suggested Reading

The following books are considered "required reading" by the author in planning a successful adoption, as he believes an "adoption education" is critical to success in both starting a placement, and raising your child thereafter. Even books dealing with post-adoption issues (discussing adoption with your child, etc.) should be read pre-adoption. This is not only to prepare yourself for becoming an adoptive parent, but also to show others your dedication is obtaining the knowledge contained in such books (birth mothers considering selecting you as adoptive parents, agency caseworkers asked to approve you to adopt, etc.).

All the listed books can easily be found on the internet at: Amazon.com (offers discounted books but charges are high for shipping); barnesandnoble.com (offers discounted books but charges are high for shipping); adoption101.com (sells books at retail but provides free shipping and packaging).

✓ ***Dear Birthmother*** by Kathleen Silber & Phyllis Speedlin
Explains adoption from a birth mother's point of view, particularly the emotional issues surrounding placing a baby for adoption. Helps adoptive parents work with a birth mother.

✓ ***Adoption Without Fear*** by James Gritter
An emotional series of true stories showing what adoption means to adoptive parents, and how it effects them, as well as birth parents and adoptees. Helps adoptive parents by seeing others go through what they will soon be experiencing.

✓ ***Raising Adopted Children*** by Lois Melina
Excellent advice to adoptive parents regarding "what to say and when to say it" when discussing adoption with a child.

✓ ***Adoption Stories for Young Children*** by Randall B. Hicks
Ryan, a 5 year old boy, introduces us to his many friends who are adopted, just like him. Fun and sweet text with 22 full page photos kids enjoy and identify with.

✓ ***Tell Me Again About the Night I Was Born*** by Jaime Lee Curtis
A beautifully illustrated book for children by actress and adoptive mother, Jaime Lee Curtis.

Index

Index